T0203041

IFIP Advances in Information and Communication Technology

622

Editor-in-Chief

Kai Rannenberg, Goethe University Frankfurt, Germany

IFIP – The International Federation for Information Processing

IFIP was founded in 1960 under the auspices of UNESCO, following the first World Computer Congress held in Paris the previous year. A federation for societies working in information processing, IFIP's aim is two-fold: to support information processing in the countries of its members and to encourage technology transfer to developing nations. As its mission statement clearly states:

IFIP is the global non-profit federation of societies of ICT professionals that aims at achieving a worldwide professional and socially responsible development and application of information and communication technologies.

IFIP is a non-profit-making organization, run almost solely by 2500 volunteers. It operates through a number of technical committees and working groups, which organize events and publications. IFIP's events range from large international open conferences to working conferences and local seminars.

The flagship event is the IFIP World Computer Congress, at which both invited and contributed papers are presented. Contributed papers are rigorously refereed and the rejection rate is high.

As with the Congress, participation in the open conferences is open to all and papers may be invited or submitted. Again, submitted papers are stringently refereed.

The working conferences are structured differently. They are usually run by a working group and attendance is generally smaller and occasionally by invitation only. Their purpose is to create an atmosphere conducive to innovation and development. Refereeing is also rigorous and papers are subjected to extensive group discussion.

Publications arising from IFIP events vary. The papers presented at the IFIP World Computer Congress and at open conferences are published as conference proceedings, while the results of the working conferences are often published as collections of selected and edited papers.

IFIP distinguishes three types of institutional membership: Country Representative Members, Members at Large, and Associate Members. The type of organization that can apply for membership is a wide variety and includes national or international societies of individual computer scientists/ICT professionals, associations or federations of such societies, government institutions/government related organizations, national or international research institutes or consortia, universities, academies of sciences, companies, national or international associations or federations of companies.

More information about this series at http://www.springer.com/series/6102

Yuko Murayama · Dimiter Velev ·
Plamena Zlateva (Eds.)

Information Technology in Disaster Risk Reduction

5th IFIP WG 5.15 International Conference, ITDRR 2020
Sofia, Bulgaria, December 3–4, 2020
Revised Selected Papers

 Springer

Editors
Yuko Murayama
Tsuda University
Tokyo, Japan

Plamena Zlateva
Institute of Robotics
Bulgarian Academy of Sciences
Sofia, Bulgaria

Dimiter Velev
Science Research Centre for Disaster Risk
Reduction
University of National and World Economy
Sofia, Bulgaria

ISSN 1868-4238   ISSN 1868-422X (electronic)
IFIP Advances in Information and Communication Technology
ISBN 978-3-030-81471-7   ISBN 978-3-030-81469-4 (eBook)
https://doi.org/10.1007/978-3-030-81469-4

This Springer imprint is published by the registered company Springer Nature Switzerland AG
The registered company address is: Gewerbestrasse 11, 6330 Cham, Switzerland

Preface

The effects of disasters are very serious and it may take a very long time to recover from the destruction caused. Related damage can be severe and offering relief may lead to expenses in the billions of euros. There has been an increase in natural disasters that has occurred in the past years and it is expected that their frequency will continue in the coming years.

Due to the multidisciplinary nature of work in the field of disaster risk reduction, people from various backgrounds will be included in this field of research and activity. Their backgrounds are likely to include industry, diverse geographical and global settings, not-for-profit organizations, agriculture, marine life, welfare, risk management, safety engineering, and social networking services.

At present, at global and national levels, a wide range of scientific and applied research activity is conducted in the area of disaster risk reduction concerning individual types of disasters. Modern information and communication technologies (ICT) can facilitate significantly the decision-making processes from the point of view of disaster risk reduction.

Following the increasing number of disasters worldwide and the growing potential of both ICT and ICT expertise, at its General Assembly held during October 8–9, 2015, at the Daejeon Convention Center, Daejeon, Korea, IFIP established the Domain Committee on Information Technology in Disaster Risk Reduction (DCITDRR) under which the ITDRR 2016–2019 conferences were organized.

Since 2020, DCITDRR has been transformed into IFIP WG 5.15 – Information Technology in Disaster Risk Reduction with the following goals:

- To promote disaster risk reduction within the ICT community;
- To provide an additional opportunity for IFIP members to work with other specialized bodies such as the UN, UNISDR, ICSU, ITU, and ISCRAM;
- To coordinate the efforts of member societies as well as different Technical Committees and Working Groups of IFIP in the disaster-related field.

The disaster support offered by WG 5.15 is based on the following major pillars:

- Information acquisition and provision;
- Shelter information management for local governments;
- Disaster information systems;
- State-of-the-art ICT (such as the internet of things, mobile computing, big data, cloud computing, and artificial intelligence).

IFIP WG 5.15 on Information Technology in Disaster Risk Reduction organized the *Fifth IFIP Conference on Information Technology in Disaster Risk Reduction (ITDRR 2020)*, held during December 3–4, 2020, at the University of National and World Economy (UNWE), Sofia, Bulgaria, in close collaboration with the Science

Research Center for Disaster Risk Reduction at UNWE. Due to the COVID-19 pandemic, ITDRR 2020 was held virtually in online mode.

ITDRR 2020 provided an international forum for researchers and practitioners to present their latest R&D findings and innovations. The conference was focused on various ICT aspects and the challenges of disaster risk reduction. The main topics included areas such as natural-disasters, remote sensing, big data, cloud computing, Internet of Things, mobile computing, emergency management, disaster information processing, and disaster risk assessment and management.

ITDRR 2020 invited experts, researchers, academicians, and all others who were interested in disseminating their work to attend the conference. The conference established an academic environment that fostered the discussion and exchange of ideas among different levels of academic, research, business, and public communities.

The Program Committee received 52 paper submissions, out of which 24 research papers were finally accepted. The volume editors would like to express their special gratitude to the members of the Program Committee, and to the many reviewers of the papers, for their dedication in helping produce this volume.

June 2021

Yuko Murayama
Dimiter Velev
Plamena Zlateva

Organization

Honorable Chairs

Yuko Murayama   IFIP Vice President, Japan
Dimitar Dimitrov   University of National and World Economy, Bulgaria

Program Committee Co-chairs

Dimiter Velev   University of National and World Economy, Bulgaria
Plamena Zlateva   Institute of Robotics, Bulgarian Academy of Sciences,
     Bulgaria

Finance Chair

Eduard Dundler   IFIP Secretary, Austria

Publicity Chair

Jun Sasaki   Iwate Prefectural University, Japan

Steering Committee

Diane Whitehouse   IFIP TC9: ICT and Society Chair, UK
Erich Neuhold   IFIP TC5: Information Technology Application Chair,
     Austria
Jose G. Gonzalez   University of Agder, Norway
A Min Tjoa   IFIP Honoray Secretary, Austria
Igor Grebennik   Kharkiv National University of Radio Electronics,
     Ukraine

Program Committee

Andreas Karcher   Universität der Bundeswehr, Germany
Benny Benyamin Nasution   Politeknik Negeri Medan, Indonesia
Boris Delibasic   University of Belgrade, Serbia
Chrisantha Silva   Computer Society of Sri Lanka, Sri Lanka
Denis Trcek   University of Ljubljana, Slovenia
Gabriela Marín-Raventós   IFIP Councillor, Costa Rica
Gansen Zhao   South China Normal University, China
Hans J. Scholl   University of Washington, USA
Henrik Eriksson   Linköping University, Sweden
Hsin-Hung Wu   National Changhua University of Education, Taiwan

Igor Petuhov	Volga State University of Technology, Russia
Jaziar Radianti	University of Agder, Norway
Jian Cao	Shanghai Jiaotong University, China
Josune Hernantes	University of Navarra, Spain
Julie Dugdale	Grenoble Alps University, France
Jun-Seok Ioseph Hwang	Seoul National University, South Korea
Kai Ranenberg	IFIP Vice President, Germany
Kaninda Musumbu	Université Bordeaux, France
Kim Hee Dong	Hankuk University of Foreign Studies, South Korea
Kyungsoo Pyo	National Disaster Management Research Institute, South Korea
Leire Labaka	University of Navarra, Spain
Lyudmila Steshina	Volga State University of Technology, Russia
Marcos R. S. Borges	Universidade Federal do Rio de Janeiro, Brazil
Mariki Eloff	University of South Africa, South Africa
Mariyana Nikolova	NIGGG – BAS, Bulgaria
Michinori Hatayama	Kyoto University, Japan
Mihoko Sakurai	University of Agder, Norway
Mike Diver	Australian Computer Society, Australia
Monika Buscher	Lancaster University, UK
Murray Turoff	New Jersey Institute of Technology, USA
Norberto Patrignani	Politecnico di Torino, Italy
Naoto Matsumoto	Sakura Internet Research Center, Japan
Nariyoshi Yamai	Tokyo University of Agriculture and Technology, Japan
Nirit Bernstein	Institute of Soil, Water and Environmental Science, Israel
Olena Chaikovska	Kyiv National University of Culture and Arts, Ukraine
Orhan Altan	Istanbul Technical University, Turkey
Rainer Malaka	Bremen University, Germany
Remy Dupas	University of Bordeaux, France
Saji Baby	GEO International Environmental Consultation Co., Kuwait
Sergei Kavun	University of Banking of the National Bank of Ukraine, Ukraine
Sergei Ohrimenco	Laboratory of Information Security – AESM, Moldova
Shi Yizhe	Shenyang University of Chemical Technology, China
Shunsuke Fujieda	University of Tokyo, Japan
Starr Roxanne Hiltz	New Jersey Institute of Technology, USA
Stewart James Kowalski	Norwegian University of Science and Technology, Norway
Tadeusz Czachorski	Institute of Theoretical and Applied Informatics – PAS, Poland
Tao Bo	Earthquake Administration of Beijing Municipality, China
Tatsuya Yamazaki	Niigata University, Japan

Tetsuo Noda	Shimane University, Japan
Tullio Tanzi	Institut Mines-Telecom, France
Valentina Komyak	National University of Civil Defence of Ukraine, Ukraine
Victor Amadeo Bañuls Silvera	Universidad Pablo de Olavide, Spain
Wei-Sen Li	National Science and Technology Center for Disaster Reduction, Taiwan
Wolfgang Reinhardt	Universität der Bundeswehr, Germany
Youwei Sun	Earthquake Administration of Beijing Municipality, China
Yoshitaka Shibata	Iwate Prefectural University, Japan
Yutaka Kikuchi	Kochi University of Technology, Japan
Zong Xuejun	Shenyang University of Chemical Technology, China

Local Organizing Committee

Marin Galabov	University of National and World Economy, Bulgaria
Sonya Damyanova	University of Forestry, Bulgaria
Valentina Nikolova	University of Mining and Geology, Bulgaria
Kostadin Sheyretski	University of National and World Economy, Bulgaria
Vladimir Velev	Creativity and Harmony Society, Bulgaria

Contents

Web Portal to Support Remote Island for Sightseeing and Disaster Management

Kayoko Yamamoto[1]([⊠]) and Yuko Murayama[2]

[1] The University of Electro-Communications, Chofugaoka, Chofu, Tokyo, Japan
`kayoko.yamamoto@uec.ac.jp`
[2] Tsuda University, Tsuda-Machi, Kodaira, Tokyo, Japan
`murayama@tsuda.ac.jp`

Abstract. The present study designed, developed and operated a web portal to support remote island for sightseeing and disaster management. The web portal is developed adopting web-geographic information systems (Web-GIS), and connecting with external Social Networking Services (SNS) and the watch over system. The web portal is operated in Tashirojima Island that is a small island in Ishinomaki City, Miyagi Prefecture in the eastern part of Japan.

The web portal enables to visualize the necessary information concerning sightseeing on the digital maps of Web-GIS. Using Twitter, it is also possible for users to share a variety of information transmitted from an islander in real time. Additionally, using the watch over system, users can usually watch over islanders from the outside of Tashirojima Island. When natural disasters suddenly occur, users can notice the serious situations, and rescue teams to quickly rescue islanders, and support for recovery and reconstruction of Tashirojima Island.

The web portal has been operated since February 22 in 2019, and it has been continuously accessed from the inside and outside of Japan until now. Additionally, users access to the web portal using various types of information terminals. Therefore, the further use of each function can be expected by the continuous operation of the web portal.

Keywords: Web portal · Remote islands · Sightseeing · Disaster management · Web-geographic information systems (Web-GIS) · Social media · Watch over system

1 Introduction

According to the survey conducted by the Ministry of Land, Infrastructure, Transport and Tourism in 2019 [1], Japan is composed of 6,852 islands including Hokkaido, Honshu, Shikoku, Kyusyu and Okinawa islands. Excluding these large-scale islands, the numbers of remote islands, which are manned and unmanned, are respectively 416 and 6,432. The total area of remote islands is 5,323 km^2 that is 1.41% of Japanese national land. Approximately 380 thousand people, which is equivalent to 0.30% of total Japanese population, live in the manned remote islands. Nevertheless, the remote islands play

Y. Murayama et al. (Eds.): ITDRR 2020, IFIP AICT 622, pp. 1–13, 2021.
https://doi.org/10.1007/978-3-030-81469-4_1

an important role in the protection and increase of the profits for Japan and Japanese people in terms of its territory and exclusive economic zones, use of marine resources, succession of diverse cultures, conservation of nature environments, etc.

However, the populations of remote islands have been continually in the decrease since 1955. Additionally, in 2013, the aging rates (the percentage share of people aged 65 or older against the total population) of the whole Japan and underpopulation areas are respectively 22.7% and 33.0%, while that of remote islands is 35.0%. Thus, most remote islands have tremendously serious issues related to declining birth rate and aging population in particular. Though the main industry of the remote island is fishery, there has been lack of new blood and insufficient human resources to carry on such an occupation.

On the other hand, in recent years, more tourists visit remote islands. With the increase of the tourists visiting remote islands from the inside and outside of Japan, it is possible to promote the sustainable development and local revitalization in such islands. However, there are very few guidebooks and websites that introduce remote islands. Additionally, the islanders could hardly transmit sightseeing information concerning their islands by themselves. Therefore, it is difficult for tourists to obtain the information concerning the remote islands.

Furthermore, in addition to such issues related to declining birth rate and aging population, natural disasters such as typhoons, tsunami, heavy rain, strong wind and volcanic eruption frequently attack remote islands. Therefore, it is essential to watch over islander all the time from the outside of remote islands. As a countermeasure against such issues, Murayama et al. (2019, 2020) [2, 3] developed and operated a watch over system that will be particularly mentioned in Sect. 3. Against such a backdrop, in order to support a remote island for sightseeing and disaster management, the present study aims to develop a web portal using web-geographic information systems (Web-GIS), and connecting with external Social Networking Services (SNS) and the watch over system developed and operated by Murayama et al. (2019, 2020) [2, 3]. Additionally, in the present study, as mentioned in Sect. 5, Tashirojima Island in Ishinomaki City, Miyagi Prefecture in the eastern part of Japan was selected as the operation target area.

2   Related Work

The present study develops a unique system using Web-GIS and connecting with external SNS and the watch over system. Therefore, considering the characteristics of the system, the present study is related 2 study fields, namely, (1) studies concerning activity support system, and (2) studies concerning social media GIS. The following will introduce the major preceding studies of recent years in the above 2 study fields, and demonstrate the originality of the present study in comparison with the others.

In (1) studies concerning activity support system, Kurashima et al. (2011) [4] proposed a travel route recommendation method using the geotags of photo-sharing sites. Kurata (2012) [5] developed an automatic sightseeing route system using Web-GIS and genetic algorithms (GAs). Sasaki et al. (2013) [6] gathered the information concerning regional resources and developed a system that offers travel support for each user. Fujitsuka et al. (2014) [7] used the pattern-mining method, which lists and extracts the chronological movement of those visiting sightseeing spots, to develop an outing plan recommendation system. Ueda et al. (2015) [8] generated posterior information from the movement of users while sightseeing, and developed a sightseeing support system that shares such information as prior information with other users.

Fujita et al. (2016) [9] developed a navigation system to support sightseeing activities during normal times and evacuation in case of a disaster integrating augmented reality (AR), Web-GIS, social media (Twitter and SNS) and recommendation system. Zhou et al. (2016) [10] develop a sightseeing spot recommendation system integrating AR, Web-GIS, SNS and recommendation system. Mizushima et al. (2017) [11] proposed a service data model in design support system for sightseeing tours, based on tourists' 3 types requests (geographical, time and meaning information). Naitou et al. (2018) [12] developed a navigation system to support users to select their suitable city walking courses in response to their health conditions, needs and preferences adopting Web-GIS and Twitter. With Fujita et al. (2016) [9] as a reference, Yamamoto (2018) [13] developed a sightseeing navigation system, using two-dimensional and three-dimensional digital maps of Web-GIS and just targeting foreign tourists. Abe et al. (2019) [14] developed a tourism information system with language-barrier-free interfaces, mainly targeting foreign tourists. Murayama et al. (2019, 2020) [2, 3] developed and operated a watch over system using cameras of mobile phones. Sasaki et al. (2019) [15] developed a system to provide guidance and information concerning sightseeing spots integrating location-based AR and object-recognition AR and using pictograms.

In (2) studies concerning social media GIS, Yanagisawa et al. (2012) [16] and Naka-hara et al. (2012) [17] developed social media GIS to accumulate and share regional knowledge in local communities integrating Web-GIS, SNS and Wiki. Yamada et al. (2013) [18] developed a social media GIS for the information exchange between regions integrating Web-GIS, SNS and Twitter. Ikeda et al. (2014) [19] and Mizutani et al. (2018) [20] developed social recommendation media GIS to recommend sightseeing spots integrating social media GIS and recommendation system. Okuma et al. (2013) [21], Murakoshi et al. (2014) [22] and Yamamoto et al. (2015) [23] developed social media GIS to accumulate and utilize urban disaster information integrating Web-GIS, SNS and Twitter. Asukai et al. (2018) [24] developed a recommendation system for meeting places targeting groups integrating recommendation system as well as an accessibility database, and linking with external Web-GIS and SNS (Twitter and LINE).

Referring to the results of the preceding studies in the 2 fields as listed above, the present study demonstrates the first point of originality to support activities for both sightseeing and disaster management. Among the preceding studies, Fujita et al. (2016) [9] developed a navigation system to support sightseeing activities during normal times and evacuation in case of a disaster. Therefore, the present study develops a web portal to support a remote island for both sightseeing and disaster management with Fujita et al. (2016) [9] as a reference. The second point of originality is to target remote island and consider its specific conditions. As mentioned in Sect. 1, in Japan, approximately 380 thousand people live in the manned remote islands that have issues related to declining birth rate and aging population. Accordingly, it is necessary to support islanders from the outside of remote islands. The third point of originality is to develop a unique web portal to support islanders to transmit sightseeing information, and watch over them all the time from the outside of remote islands.

3 System Design

3.1 System Configuration

The web portal of the present study is developed by means of Web-GIS and the connection with external social media (Twitter) and the watch over system. Figure 1 shows the system design of the web portal. The web portal was based on the result of Naitou et al. (2018) [12] that developed a navigation system to support users to select their suitable city walking courses for Japanese urban areas. Regarding the watch over system, the cameras of mobile phones, which are installed in some points of remote island, are used.

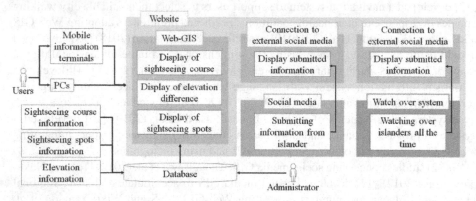

Fig. 1. System design

The web portal has the purpose to support remote island for sightseeing and disaster management. Specifically, it enables to visualize height, sightseeing spots and course on the digital maps, and accumulate the related information in the database of Web-GIS. Due to the connection of social media, it is possible for users to obtain the information submitted from an islander (one of main characters) using Twitter, and display her tweets on the screens of the web portal. Additionally, using the watch over system, as the moving images taken by the cameras of mobile phones are also displayed on the screens of the web portal, it is also possible to watch over islanders all the time from the outside of remote islands. Therefore, when natural disasters occur in remote islands, it is possible for rescue teams to quickly relieve islanders, and support for the recovery and reconstruction of their islands.

3.2 Target Information Terminals

Though the web portal is meant to be used from PCs or mobile information terminals, as there is no difference in functions on different information terminals, the same function can be used from any information terminal. PCs are assumed to be used indoors for gathering a variety of sightseeing information and watch over islanders from the outside of remote island. On the other hand, mobile information terminals are assumed to be used both indoors and outdoors to gather information concerning sightseeing spots, and watch over islanders from the inside and outside of remote island.

3.3   System Operation Environment

The web portal operates using the web server and the GIS server. For the web server, the Heroku, which is a Platform as a Service (PaaS) provided by the Salesforce Company, was used. On the other hand, for the GIS server, the ArcGIS Online was used. The web application developed with the web portal was implemented using PHP and JavaScript as main computer languages.

3.4   Design of Each System

3.4.1   Web-GIS

In order to display a variety of information referring to the location information on the digital maps, it is essential to adopt Web-GIS into the web portal. However, as there are a variety of Web-GIS types, it is necessary to select the most suitable type according to the purpose of developing the web portal. In terms of convenience, the system should be used without having to download any special softwares, which would be inconvenient for users, and it would be desirable if it could be used by accessing the website on any PCs or mobile information terminals connected to the Internet. Therefore, a series of the GIS provided by the Environmental Systems Research Institute, Inc. (ESRI) were selected to develop Web-GIS in the present study.

Additionally, as most of the roads are very narrow in remote islands, these are not included into the base map provided by the ESRI. Therefore, Open Street Map, which includes minor streets as well as main roads, was used as the base map of the system. Additionally, it is possible for everyone who registered the system of Open Street Map to edit it.

3.4.2   Connection to External SNS

As the web portal is connected to Twitter, users can obtain the information submitted from an islander using Twitter. Among various kinds of social media, Twitter, which is provided by the twitter Japan Inc., was selected as social media for the web portal. Using Twitter publish, which is also provided by the twitter Japan Inc., the widget to display the timeline of tweets was created, and the URL related to a specific Twitter account was developed to be embedded in the web portal.

3.4.3   Connection to the Watch Over System

As the web portal is also connected to the watch over system developed and operated by Murayama [2, 3], users can usually watch over islanders. According to Murayama et al. [2, 3] and Saito et al. (2012) [25], the watch over system was developed, and it was applied for the damaged areas by the East Japan Earthquake (2011). Additionally, according to Sato, 2017 [26], the system was also applied for the campus of Tusda University to watch over handicapped people.

4 System Development

4.1 System Frontend

4.1.1 Overview of System Frontend

The web portal will implement 5 unique functions for users, which will be mentioned below, in response to the purpose of the present study as mentioned in Sect. 1. In order to implement these unique functions, the web portal was developed by means of Web-GIS, and was also connected with external social media and the watch over system. The viewing function of the moving images submitted by the watch over system is for disaster management, while the other 4 functions are for sightseeing.

In addition to these unique functions, all of the information concerning Tashirojima Island was consolidated into the web portal, and users can obtain their necessary information from the system. Specifically, the web portal includes the traffic information guide, the original walking map created by a former postmaster in Tashirojima Island, and the unique photo book of cats. Furthermore, the web portal links to a famous cartoonist's blog entitled "Cats Information from Tashirojima Island". Referring to these, users can efficiently and easily obtain their necessary information before, during and after their sightseeing in Tashirojima Island while enjoying.

4.1.2 Display Function of Sightseeing Course

Selecting "Sightseeing course" in the menu bar on the homepage, users can go to the page for the display function of the sightseeing course to confirm its outline on the digital map of Web-GIS (Fig. 2). The sightseeing course is clearly displayed by an orange line. A pink marker shows a sightseeing spot, a blue marker shows a cat area where tourists can meet a lot of cats, and a green marker shows an accommodation. Users can obtain the present location information by GPS of their mobile information terminals, and go to the next destination while grasping their present locations. Additionally, users can easily scale the size of the digital maps of Web-GIS as they like.

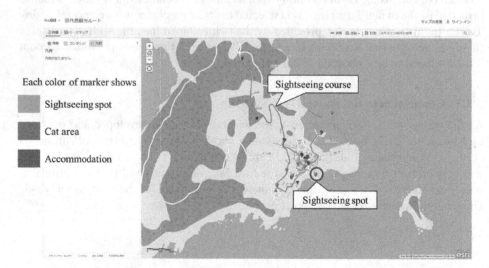

Fig. 2. Page for the display function of sightseeing course (Color figure online)

4.1.3   Display Function of the Elevation Difference of Sightseeing Course

After confirming the outline of selected sightseeing course, by clicking its line on the digital map, users can go to the page for the display function of the elevation difference of sightseeing course (Fig. 3) to confirm the elevation difference. In the graph shown in Fig. 3, the vertical axis indicates elevation [m], and the horizontal axis indicates the distance [km]. By moving the cursor in the graph, the location corresponding to the sightseeing course is displayed by a blue circle.

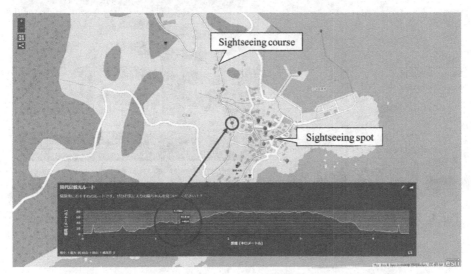

Fig. 3. Page for the display function of the elevation difference of sightseeing course (Color figure online)

4.1.4   Viewing Function of Sightseeing Spot Information

Selecting "Sightseeing spot" in the menu bar on the homepage, users can go to the page for the viewing function of the sightseeing spot information (location, explanation and image) on the digital map of Web-GIS (Fig. 4). The marker indicating the position of each sightseeing spot is displayed on the digital map. Specifically, as described in Sect. 4.1.2, a pink marker shows a sightseeing spot, a blue marker shows a cat area where tourists can meet a lot of cats, and a green marker shows an accommodation.

4.1.5   Viewing Function of the Information Submitted by Twitter

Selecting "Twitter of the Kuroneko-do" in the menu bar on the homepage, users can go to the page for the viewing function of the information submitted by Twitter (Fig. 5). The Kuroneko-do is managed by an islander who is a main character, and it is an information transmission source on the internet in addition to a tourist information center in Tashirojima Island. Users can usually view her tweets, and obtain a variety of information concerning the cats, beautiful landscapes and events in Tashirojima Island.

Additionally, users can also confirm the information concerning the weather report in northeastern Japan and the ferry service as a unique transportation means to Tashirojima Island. The ferry service is frequently suspended due to the bad weather especially in

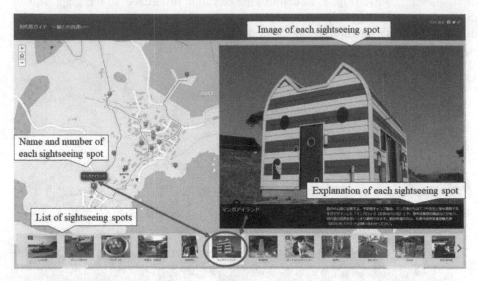

Fig. 4. Page for the viewing function of sightseeing spot information (Color figure online)

Fig. 5. Pages for the viewing function of the information submitted by twitter

winter. Therefore, the above information is extremely important and useful for users to visit Tashirojima Island. If situations are changed, the above information is immediately updated by the islander. Furthermore, when users who have Twitter accounts hope to obtain accurate information in detail, they can keep in touch with the above islander and her followers using Twitter.

4.1.6 Viewing Function of the Moving Images Submitted by the Watch over System

Selecting "Moving images" in the menu bar on the homepage, users can go to the page for the viewing function of the moving images submitted by the watch over system. Due to the function, users can usually watch over islanders. Additionally, when natural disasters occur in remote islands, rescue teams can quickly relieve islanders, and support for the recovery and reconstruction of their islands.

4.2 System Backend

4.2.1 Overview of System Backend

The following processes are implemented in the backend of the system, and have close connections with the functions for users in the frontend. Specifically, the first process is related to the display function of sightseeing course, the display function of the elevation difference of sightseeing course, and the viewing function of sightseeing spot information. The second process is related to the viewing function of the information submitted by Twitter.

4.2.2 Process to Display Information on the Digital Map of Web-GIS

Markers and lines respectively showing sightseeing spots and courses are included into the layers that connects to specific location information. Therefore, based on the location information, the layers are overlaid on the base map using GIS. Using GPS of users' mobile information terminals, the web portal automatically can obtain their present locations to display it on the digital map of Web-GIS. Additionally, using the line information accumulated in layer, the web portal can grasp the elevation difference of the sightseeing course, and display it in the graph.

4.2.3 Process to Obtain the Information Submitted by Twitter

Using the widget to display timeline, the web portal can automatically obtain all of the information submitted from the specific Twitter account of an islander who manages the Kuroneko-do introduced in Sect. 4.1.5.

4.3 System Interface

The interfaces are optimized according to the user's PC screens and mobile information terminal screens. The interface for PC screens has the layout with a menu bar allowing easy access to each function. As the menu bar is displayed on the right side of top page, the users who are new to the web portal can easily use it. Though the interface for mobile information terminal screens is basically the same as that of PC screens, by changing the layout and size of items according to the size of the screen, the operability of the web portal is made easy.

5 Operation

5.1 Operation Target Area

Among the remote islands in Japan, Tashirojima Island is selected as the target for the present study. It is a remote island in Ishinomaki City, Miyagi Prefecture in the northeastern part of Japan. The island is small, and the perimeter is approximately 11 km. Approximately 80 islanders live in the island, and most of them are elder fishermen.

The Great East Japan Earthquake caused serious damages to the main ports of Tashirojima Island. However, though most of the islanders were elder people, they cooperated with each other to succeeded in the recovery and reconstruction of the island just by their own efforts. Other natural disasters such as heavy rain and strong wind frequently attack the island, these sometimes causes the interruption of electric service and the suspension of ferry service. Therefore, it is expected that the web portal will work as a disaster information system in addition to sightseeing information system. Because the web portal can watch over islanders from the outside of Tashirojima Island all the time, and users can notice that natural disasters suddenly occur.

At present, Tashirojima Island is well-known to all over the world as a "cat island". The islanders usually take care of cats as a god of promising success in fishing. They established a shrine for cats called "Cat Shrine" in the center of the island, and the number of cats are more than that of the islanders. The islanders and cats live together in harmony. Many people who love cats visit the island from all over the world, and they frequently transmit the specific information concerning the island using social media. Additionally, most of them become the followers of an islander who manages the Kuroneko-do introduced in Sect. 4.1.5 on Twitter, and exchange the information with her after leaving the island.

However, there are very few guidebooks that introduce Tashirojima Island in detail. Additionally, in the island, as most of the tourists take a day trip, and they have to efficiently visit sightseeing spots including cat areas. Therefore, it is also expected that the web portal designed and developed in the present study can appropriately support the tourists who do not have a good sense of locality in the island.

5.2 Overview of Operation

The web portal has been operated since February 22 in 2019. Whether inside or outside the operation target area, the operation of the web portal was advertised using the website, Twitter and Facebook of the authors' lab as well as Twitter of the Kuroneko-do. The web portal has been continuously accessed until now, and users access to the web portal using various types of information terminals. 94.6% were from Japan, and 5.4% were from other countries such as the United State, Germany, China and Thailand. From these, it is evident that the web portal is well-known to not only Japanese but also foreigners. The web portal has approximately 4,600 users at the beginning of January in 2021.

6 Conclusion

The present study designed, developed and operated a web portal to support Tashirojima Island that is a remote island for sightseeing and disaster management. The web portal is developed adopting Web-GIS, and connecting with external SNS and the watch over system developed and operated by Murayama et al. [2, 3].

The web portal enables to visualize the information concerning sightseeing course, elevation difference of sightseeing course, and sightseeing spots on the digital maps of Web-GIS. Therefore, it is possible for users to efficiently obtain the necessary information concerning sightseeing. Using Twitter, it is also possible for users to share a variety of information transmitted from an islander who is a main character in real time. Additionally, using the watch over system, users can usually watch over islanders from the outside of Tashirojima Island. When natural disasters suddenly occur, users can immediately notice the tense critical situation, and rescue teams can quickly relieve islanders and support for the recovery and reconstruction of Tashirojima Island.

The web portal has been continuously accessed from the inside and outside of Japan until now, and users access to the web portal using various types of information terminals. Therefore, the further use of each function can be expected by the continuous operation of the web portal. However, it is necessary to conduct a web questionnaire survey to users in order to evaluate the web portal. Based on the evaluation result, it is also necessary to improve the web portal to raise the usability.

The future research is to expand and improve all of the functions, and to apply the web portal in other remote islands. Furthermore, referring to Saito et al. (2012) [25], Sato et al. (2017) [26] and Murayama et al. (2019) [2, 3], it is hopeful to particularly improve the viewing function of the moving images submitted by the watch over system. Because the function will support remote islands for disaster management, and it will be useful from the normal times to disaster outbreak times. Using the function, users can easily know the situation of Tashirojima Island whenever they like. Additionally, it is also expected that the function will play a role to watch over the elder islanders from the outside of the island during normal times.

At present, the coronavirus disease 2019 (COVIT-19) epidemic is expanding fast all over the world. Therefore, it is tremendously difficult for tourists to visit remote islands where most islander are elder people, and medical facility is not sufficiently arranged. Under these circumstances, it is possible that the viewing function of the moving images submitted by the watch over system will be effective to inform users of the changing situations of remote islands in real time.

Acknowledgment. In the design, development and operation of the web portal to support remote island for sightseeing and disaster management of the present study, enormous cooperation was received from the islanders in Tashirojima Island and users. We would like to take this opportunity to gratefully acknowledge them.

References

1. Ministry of Land, Infrastructure, Transport and Tourism: Present Situations and Development Related to the Remote Islands in Japan. https://www.mlit.go.jp/common/001290710.pdf. Accessed 16 Jul 2019
2. Murayama, Y., Yamamoto, K., Sasaki, J.: Recovery watcher: a disaster communication system for situation awareness and its use for barrier-free information provision. In: Murayama, Y., Velev, D., Zlateva, P. (eds.) ITDRR 2018. IAICT, vol. 550, pp. 1–11. Springer, Cham (2019). https://doi.org/10.1007/978-3-030-32169-7_1
3. Murayama, Y., Yamamoto, K.: Issues in the use of the recovery watcher for situation awareness in disaster and inclusive communications. In: Murayama, Y., Velev, D., Zlateva, P. (eds.) ITDRR 2019. IAICT, vol. 575, pp. 1–8. Springer, Cham (2020). https://doi.org/10.1007/978-3-030-48939-7_1
4. Kurashima, T., Iwata, T., Irie, G., Fujimura, K.: Travel route recommendation using geotags on photo sharing service. In: Proceedings of the 19th ACM International Conference on Information and Knowledge Management, Toronto, ON, Canada, pp. 55–60 (2011)
5. Kurata, Y.: Introducing a hot-start mechanism to a web-based tour planner CT-planner and increasing its coverage areas. In: Proceedings of the Geographic Information Systems Association of Japan, Hiroshima, Japan, p. 4 (2012)
6. Sasaki, J., Uetake, T., Horikawa, M., Sugawara, M.: Development of personal sightseeing support system during long-term stay. In: Proceedings of the 75th National Convention of IPSJ, Sendai, Miyagi, Japan, pp. 727–728 (2013)
7. Fujitsuka, T., Harada, T., Sato, T., Takadama, K.: Recommendation system for sightseeing plan using pattern mining to evaluate time series action. In: Proceedings of the Annual Conference on Society of Instrument and Control Engineering, Hangzhou, China, pp. 802–807 (2014)
8. Ueda, T., Ooka, Y., Kumano, K., Hiroyuki, T., Toshihiro, H., Masato, Y.: Sightseeing support system to support generation/sharing of sightseeing information. In: The Special Interest Group Technical Reports of IPSJ: Information System and Social environment (IS); Information Processing Society of Japan, Tokyo, Japan, pp. 1–7 (2015)
9. Fujita, S., Yamamoto, K.: Development of dynamic real-time navigation system. Int. J. Adv. Comput. Sci. Appl. 7(11), 116–130 (2016)
10. Zhou, J., Yamamoto, K.: Development of the system to support tourists' excursion behavior using augmented reality. Int. J. Adv. Comput. Sci. Appl. 7(7), 197–209 (2016)
11. Mizushima, T., Hirota, J., Oizumi, K., Aoyama, K.: Service data model in design support system for sightseeing tours. In: Sawatani, Y., Spohrer, J., Kwan, S., Takenaka, T. (eds.) ICServ 2015, pp. 55–64. Springer, Tokyo (2017). https://doi.org/10.1007/978-4-431-56074-6_7
12. Naitou, K., Yamamoto, K.: Walking support system with users' circumstances. In: Roka, R. (ed.) Advances in Human and Machine Navigation Systems, pp. 9–27. INTECH, London (2018)
13. Yamamoto, K.: Navigation system for foreign tourists in Japan. J. Environ. Sci. Eng. 10B(6), 521–541 (2018)
14. Abe, S., Yoshitsugu, N., Miki, D., Yamamoto, K.: An information retrieval system with language-barrier free interfaces. J. Inf. Syst. Soc. Jpn. 14, 57–64 (2019)
15. Sasaki, R., Yamamoto, K.: A sightseeing support system using augmented reality and pictograms within urban tourist areas in Japan. Int. J. Geo-Inf. 8(9), 381 (2019). https://doi.org/10.3390/ijgi8090381
16. Yanagisawa, T., Yamamoto, K.: Study on information sharing GIS to accumulate local knowledge in local communities. Theory Appl. GIS 20(1), 61–70 (2012)
17. Nakahara, H., Yanagisawa, T., Yamamoto, K.: Study on a Web-GIS to support the communication of regional knowledge in regional communities: focusing on regional residents' experiential knowledge. Socio-Informatics 1(2), 77–92 (2012)

18. Yamada, S., Yamamoto, K.: development of social media GIS for information exchange between regions. Int. J. Adv. Comput. Sci. Appl. **4**(8), 62–73 (2013)
19. Ikeda, T., Yamamoto, K.: Development of social recommendation GIS for tourist spots. Int. J. Adv. Comput. Sci. Appl. **5**(12), 8–21 (2014)
20. Mizutani, T., Yamamoto, K.: A sightseeing spot recommendation system that takes into account the change in circumstances of users. Int. J. Geo-Inf. **6**(10), 303 (2017). https://doi.org/10.3390/ijgi6100303
21. Okuma, T., Yamamoto, K.: Study on a social media GIS to accumulate urban disaster information: accumulation of disaster information during normal times for disaster reduction measures. Socio-Informatics **2**(2), 49–65 (2013)
22. Murakoshi, T., Yamamoto, K.: Study on a social media GIS to support the utilization of disaster information: for disaster reduction measures from normal times to disaster outbreak times. Socio-Informatics **3**(2), 17–31 (2014)
23. Yamamoto, K., Fujita, S.: Development of social media GIS to support information utilization from normal times to disaster outbreak times. Int. J. Adv. Comput. Sci. Appl. **6**(9), 1–14 (2015)
24. Asukai, S., Yamamoto, K.: A recommendation system regarding meeting places for groups during events. J. Geo-Inf. **7**(8), 296 (2018). https://doi.org/10.3390/ijgi7080296
25. Saito, Y. Fujihara, Y., Murayama, Y.: A study of reconstruction watcher in disaster area. In: Proceedings of the ACM Conference on Human Factors in Computing Systems 2012 (CHI 2012), Austin, Texas USA, pp. 811–814. SIGCHI (2012)
26. Sato, M., Kanda, Y., Takizawa, Y., Matsuoka, J., Murayama, Y.: Use of live streaming for barrier-free in a university. In: Proceedings of the Multimedia, Distributed, Cooperative, and Mobile Symposium 2017, Sapporo, Hokkaido, Japan, pp. 1553–1556 (2017)

Development of Real-Time Evacuation Support System (RESS) to Reduce Human Damage in Natural Disasters

Makoto Kitsuya, Ryota Tsukahara, and Jun Sasaki^(✉)

Iwate Prefectural University, 152-52 Sugo, Takizawa, Iwate 020-0693, Japan
{g231s008,g031p102}@s.iwate-pu.ac.jp, jsasaki@iwate-pu.ac.jp

Abstract. In Japan, there are many natural disasters such as river flood and tsunami caused by typhoons, heavy rains and earthquakes. In this case, the residents have an evacuation time to evacuate to shelters after evacuation alerts from a governmental office. The authors reported in a previous paper the development and evaluation of the Regional Information Sharing System (RISS) in order to reduce human damage in natural disasters. But, the actually required and important information to reduce human damage in a regional natural disaster was still unclear. This paper shows an evacuation time-line model and indicates that the actually required and important information in such a case are the location information of Support-required People (SRP) and supporters, and the current shelter's detail condition. Based on this concept, we newly developed the Real-time Evacuation Support System (RESS), which can share the information on the location of SRP and supporters, and shelter conditions in real time. Further, we present a case study of the prototype system for Kamaishi City in Iwate Prefecture, Japan. We conclude that the developed system will be helpful for local residents to accurately understand the state of the SRP and supporters, and evacuation shelters and reduce the risks of human damage in natural disasters.

Keywords: Evacuation support · Shelter condition · Real-time system · Mapping system · Information sharing system

1 Introduction

In recent years, various natural disasters have occurred throughout the world. In the case of flood and tsunami disasters caused by typhoons, heavy rains, and earthquakes, residents in a disaster-affected area have some time to evacuate to a shelter after an evacuation alert is received from a governmental office.

A delay in evacuation may result in a significant number of casualties. Weathernews Inc. reported the relationship between evacuation delay and human risk during the 2011 Great East Japan Earthquake and following tsunami disaster [1]. The report shows the evacuation start time of both (a) the survivors and (b) the dead and missing residents after an earthquake. There is a significant difference between (a) and (b): 71% of the

© IFIP International Federation for Information Processing 2021
Published by Springer Nature Switzerland AG 2021
Y. Murayama et al. (Eds.): ITDRR 2020, IFIP AICT 622, pp. 14–25, 2021.
https://doi.org/10.1007/978-3-030-81469-4_2

survivors evacuated within 120 min; by contrast, for the deceased (confirmed dead or missing), only 22% evacuated within the same time. Therefore, an early evacuation is extremely important for decreasing the risk to human life.

The report also indicated that the people who arrived at the emergency shelters decreased their risk of becoming a casualty. Three-quarters of the survivors evacuated to the emergency shelters; however, in the case of the dead and missing, only one-quarter made it to a shelter. During such an emergency, more people may be saved by providing information on the location of the available shelters and the evacuation conditions of the neighborhood.

Another problem is a change in the destination shelter after an evacuation starts. Such a problem occurred when typhoon Hagibis hit Japan on October 12, 2019. The Meteorological Agency issued an evacuation advisory because a huge rainfall and river flooding had been forecasted. At the time, some shelters in Kanagawa [2] and Fukushima prefecture [3] exceeded their capacity and refused to accept additional evacuees. The rejected evacuees were forced to move to another acceptable shelter despite the dangerous conditions. To avoid such a problem, evacuees should know where the optimal shelters with sufficient space are located before starting their evacuation.

Evacuation support for elderly and disable people, who cannot evacuate oneself, is also serious problem in emergency situations. The cabinet office of Japan published the statistics of damage to elderly people in the 2011 Great East Japan Earthquake. The statistics shows that the number of deaths in the disaster is 15,812, and 10,360 of them, about two-thirds of the whole deaths, is elderly people who cannot evacuate alone at the time of a disaster. We defined such a people as Support-required People (SRP) [4]. It is important that the supporters who support the evacuation of such people with sharing the information of the SRP, supporters and shelters' condition, and take evacuation action promptly.

2 Related Studies

Owing to technical improvements and the popularization of mobile devices and information communication systems, people can now receive up-to-date information easily and quickly from related websites. Once a disaster occurs, an evacuee can access the disaster information published on the websites to decrease the risk of injury.

Many studies have shown that the integration of a geographic information system is effective for a disaster risk reduction. Nakajima et al. [5] built an evacuation guide system based on GPS-capable cellphones, which provides evacuation route guidance on maps for massive evacuations. Rahman et al. [6] proposed a location-based early disaster warning and evacuation system using OpenStreetMap (OSM). They used OSM, a free and rapidly growing open-source map of the world, to share disaster data, such as the type of disaster, the probable disaster-affected area, and the shortest path to a shelter. Itoi et al. [7] proposed an offline mobile application for automatic evacuation guidance in an outdoor environment. They developed an automatic evacuation guidance scheme to estimate the state the evacuees and applied it to the application, which presents a suitable evacuation path.

Regarding to using Social Media in the case of disaster, there are some papers. For example, Hilts et al. (2014) proposed to use of Social Media for U.S. Public Sector

Emergency Manager [8] and Abdllah et al. (2017) discussed about the issues on information spreading by Twitter in the case of the disaster [9]. Regarding to the decision making in emergency, Cesta et al. (2014) proposed the training for the decision making in crisis based on plan adaptation [10]. Further, Bernabé et al. (2018) also studied the impact of warning situations for decision making in transportation companies through social media [11].

Above problems are related with the "public support" in an emergency case. In an emergency case, the "public support" has a limitation because of the budget and human resource limitation. Therefore, voluntary evacuation by citizen is important for emergency, and it is necessary for all citizens to share disaster information promptly. Additionally, the above studies did not mention the information sharing on the SRP and supporters, and shelter conditions during a natural disaster. In our previous study, we proposed the Regional Information Sharing System (RISS) and evaluated the effect by multi-agent simulation [4, 12]. But, the actually required and important information to reduce human damage in a regional natural disaster was still unclear.

This paper shows an evacuation time-line model and indicates that the actually required and important information in such a natural disaster are the location information of SRP and supporters, and the current shelter's detail condition. Based on this concept, we newly developed the Real-time Evacuation Support System (RESS) which can share the information on the location of SRP and supporters, and shelter's detail conditions. Further, we present a case study of the prototype system for Kamaishi City in Iwate Prefecture, Japan. We conclude that the system will be helpful for local residents to accurately understand the state of the SRP and supporters, and evacuation shelters and reduce the risks of human damage in a natural disaster.

3 Evacuation Time-Line Model

Japanese government organizations have a mechanism to send information from disaster warnings to evacuation orders according to the level of natural disasters. The information level and behavior to be taken are shown in Table 1. This information level changes not only with the magnitude of the disaster, but also with time. So, as our behavior will change according to the time, so we should make a time-line model to best behavior in the case of natural disasters.

In the Level 3 on Table 1, the evacuation is started from the SRP (Support-required People), who is vulnerable people for disasters and required assistance to evacuate, and supporters who assist SRP, and then the general evacuees will evacuate. In those situation, the location information of SRP and supports, and the condition of shelters are very important. The information of shelters includes the location, the state of open or closed, the capacity and current number of evacuees for the capacity. Those information will be changed moment to moment and it should be provided real-time to the every evacuees. In particular, due to the recent situation of the new coronavirus (COVID-19), the capacity of evacuation centers is often limited to half of the normal number, and information on the current number of evacuees for the capacity is very important. There are some cases that ordinary evacuees may need to evacuate to their homes or cars instead of to shelters in such a restricted case.

Table 1. Evacuation Time-Line Model.

Level	Information	Behavior
5	Disaster	Take the best action to save your lives
4	Evacuation order	Evacuate everyone quickly from dangerous places
3	Evacuation preparation order	For SRP (Support-required People) and supporters; evacuate to shelters from dangerous areas For Others (GE: General Evacuees): prepare for evacuation
2	Disaster alert	Confirm evacuation behaviour
1	Disaster warning	Prepare for disaster prevention according to weather information

4 Proposed System

Figure 1 shows our proposed Real-time Evacuation Support System (RESS). In this system, IT volunteers, etc. manage the disaster information and the evacuation shelter information in the area collected from government organizations, social media (radio, TV etc.) and Social Network Services (SNS) in the internet. Then, they send those information to regional residents as early as possible. It is assumed that this system will be used at the initial stage of a disaster and at the available stage of the power supply and communication facilities. Namely, our proposed system RESS is assumed to be used in the case of level 3 and 4 in Table 1.

When level 3 information (evacuation preparation information) is issued, the supporter confirms the location of the SRP and will go to evacuation support. Other supporters confirm the location information of the SRP and the supporters, and if there is not supporter to support the SRP, he/she goes to the SRP. Next, when level 4 is issued, all evacuees including general evacuees go to the evacuation shelter. If the shelter capacity is in over capacity, the general evacuees go to own home, relative's home or other comparatively safe place such as hotels or cars.

For safety evacuation, the system integrates actually required and important information and provides those information in real time onto a smartphone map of needed people in the area. With our proposed system, supporters and evacuees can check the location of SRP and available shelters and decide where to evacuate by themselves, and thus reach an optimal shelter quickly and safely. Since there was no such a mechanism before, it was difficult to share promptly the location information between a supporter and other supporters as well as SRP and shelter's detail condition. So, we developed newly following functions.

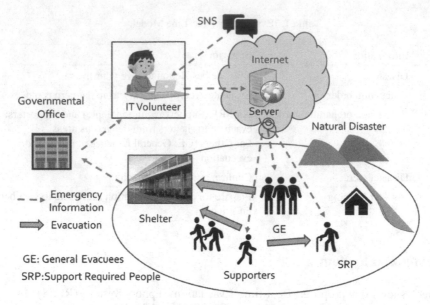

Fig. 1. Proposed Real-time Evacuation Support System (RESS).

4.1 Location Visualize Function of SRP and Supporters

In Japan, each local government office is obliged to compose and keep a list of SRP (Support-required People) as a document. For example, in Kamaishi city on Iwate Prefecture in Japan, there are 2,636 SRP, each name, age, address, contact address, family structure and information of two or three responsible supporters are written in the list of SRP.

Figure 2 and Fig. 3 show the developed structure of the location visualize function and an example of the smartphone display in the system. The markers of Fig. 3(a) show the positions of supporters which obtained as the location information of their smartphones by GPS (Global Positioning System), and an evacuation shelter and a SRP's house location which can be obtained based on the latitude and longitude information in the address of registered SRP and evacuation list prepared by local government office. When a user taps each marker, the application display modality screen shows its detailed information as shown in Fig. 3(b). The supporters can confirm the evacuation shelter information such as address and the number of current evacuees and the capacity. When evacuation is completed, the marker of SRP is removed from the map by registering. When the supporter launches the application, the application seeds location information that is obtained using GPS on smartphone to the database every 5 s. By creating markers based on those data, supporters can grasp each other's position.

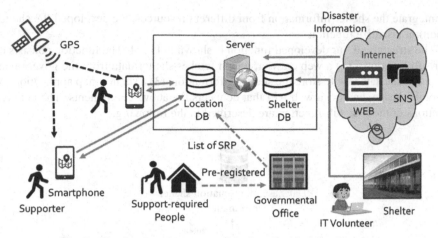

Fig. 2. The developed structure of the location visualize function.

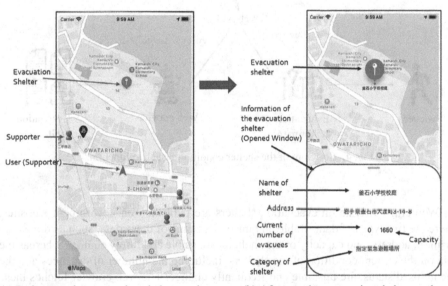

(a) Before tap the evacuation shelter marker   (b) After tap the evacuation shelter marker

Fig. 3. An example of the smartphone display in the developed system.

4.2 Shelter Condition Visualize Function

The Japanese government provides different disaster-related information depending on the local level. For example, the city government provides the addresses of the shelters, the prefectural government provides the current number of evacuees and the open/closed statuses of the shelters, and the national government provides early alerts about disasters and is required to declare an evacuation. However, such data are not integrated, and thus it is difficult for general evacuees to use the information during an actual evacuation.

To integrate the shelter information from different resources, we developed the shelter condition visualize function.

The structure of our developed function is shown in Fig. 4. The function consists of four sub-functions: (1) a web crawler, which fetches shelter data from the government website, (2) a database to store the shelter information, (3) a shelter map application for a mobile device, and (4) a web API that connects the above components. The detailed functions of the four sub-function are described in the following.

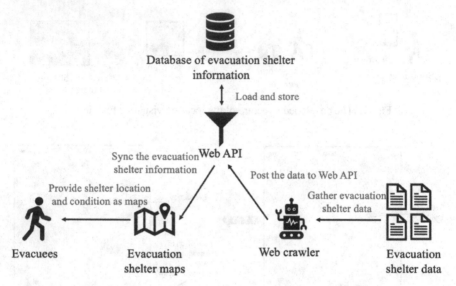

Fig. 4. Structure of the shelter condition visualize function.

(1) Web crawler: Data on evacuation shelters are published on government websites. There are two types of data: stable and unstable. Some of these data, such as the name, location, address, and capacity of the shelters, are stable and rarely change, whereas the data on the current condition of the shelters, including the number of evacuees and the open/closed status, are unstable and frequently change. The web crawler fetches these two types of data at different intervals for each type: at 1-day intervals for stable data under typical conditions and at 1-min intervals for unstable data during an emergency. By fetching data based on this method, the system can provide information in real time.
(2) Database: The database stores evacuation shelter data, such as the name, location, capacity, and number of evacuees from the web crawler through the web API. If the web API requests to receive data, the database responds.
(3) Shelter Maps Application: Our system provides shelter information as a smart phone map. The map includes markers that are placed on the location of the shelters. If the user of our system clicks a marker, the tooltip extends the shelter information such as the name, open/closed status, address, and rate of occupancy. Furthermore, the color of the marker represents the current occupancy rate of the shelter, as shown in Fig. 5. When the color of the marker turns red, it indicates that the occupancy has increased.

We believe it will be easy to understand for general evacuees. The map and markers will automatically update if the data in the database are affected, and thus users can check the shelter information in real time.

0%   0–20%   21–40%   41–60%   61–80%   81–100% Over 100%

Fig. 5. Relationship between color of the marker and the occupancy rate. (Color figure online)

(4) Web API: The web API connects the three subsystems mentioned above. In the relationship among the web crawler, web API, and database, the web crawler fetches the updated data and posts the data to the web API. The database then stores the data posted from the web API. Regarding the relationship among the Shelter Maps App, the web API, and the database, the Shelter Maps App requests map-related resources from the web API, and the web API transfers the request to the database. The database then passes the requested data to the Shelter Maps App through the web API.

The developed, consisting of the sub-functions described above, provides the shelter conditions for evacuees in real time. In the next section, we describe the prototype system and its behavior based on a simulation using actual data from a regional disaster.

4.3 Case Study

In this section, we introduce a case study and implementation of the prototype shelter condition visualize function. For the case study and use of the prototype, we collected data from a past disaster, i.e., typhoon Hagibis in 2019.

Kamaishi city, Iwate Prefecture, Japan, was selected as the case study area because the data required for this research were obtainable. Kamaishi is located in northeast Japan, faces the Pacific Ocean on the east, and has a population of 32,000 and a total area of 440 km^2. The city has been damaged by numerous tsunamis: during the Sanriku Earthquake in 1896, Sanriku Earthquake in 1933, and Great East Japan Earthquake in 2011, 4,985, 409, and 1,046 people died or went missing in the city, respectively. Moreover, other disasters such as floods caused by typhoons have occasionally occurred in the city.

Owing to these events, the city manages multiple disaster shelters and publishes its data on a website. We focused on typhoon Hagibis, which hit on October 12, 2019 and collected shelter-related data on the typhoon. The data used for the prototype system were obtained from the following websites:

1. Unstable data including the open/closed status and the current number of evacuees of the shelter are published on the Iwate Disaster Prevention Information Portal by Iwate Prefecture [13] in HTML format.
2. Some stable data, including the shelter name, address, longitude/latitude, and types of disasters to be dealt with, are published on Designated Emergency Evacuation Site Data by the Geospatial Information Authority of Japan [14] in CSV format.

3. Other stable data, including the capacity of the shelters, are published by Iwate Prefecture [15] in PDF format.
4. In addition, data on welfare shelters, i.e., shelters for people who need extra help such as the elderly and disabled people, are published by Kamaishi city [16] in HTML format.

We developed and used a web scraper to gather data written in Node.js and Nightmare.js [17]. As a result, we obtained shelter-related data for a total of 226 shelters from the start of the disaster on October 12, 2019 to the closing time of the last shelter on October 28, 2019.

We developed the prototype shelter condition visualize function and used the collected data in the case study. We used the following programming languages and frameworks to develop the prototype:

1. For flexible software combining the web API and database, the Hasura GraphQL Engine [18] was used.
2. For the Shelter Maps App, Vue.js [19], a reactive front-end framework, and Leaflet [20], an open-source JavaScript library for mobile-friendly interactive maps, were applied.

We did not develop the web crawler to collect the shelter-related data in real time. In addition, to maintain confidentiality, the capacity of evacuees and the actual evacuee data from the welfare shelters could not be contained in the prototype function data. Instead, we simply set the green markers to indicate welfare shelters on the map of the prototype system.

An example of a display image of the prototype Shelter Maps App is shown in Fig. 6. The positions of the markers show the shelter location based on the latitude and longitude information. The color of the markers presents the number of evacuees per shelter at a particular time. The users can see which shelters exceeded the capacity limit, allowing them to avoid going to these locations, and instead evacuating to one of the shelters presented by a blue marker.

When a user clicks a marker, the tooltip extends. The tooltip contains information on the name, address, current number of evacuees, and capacity of the shelter. This function helps users check these current condition data and make a decision regarding where to evacuate.

We confirmed that both the desktop and mobile versions of the Shelter Maps App operate without any problems. However, the function is currently under development and has some missing functions. For example, the Shelter Maps App should show the user's current position and the optimal evacuation path to the safe shelter on the map. The web crawler is not yet used in the prototype system, and thus we should implement, test, and confirm that the system works well during an actual disaster.

We are planning to add these missing functions and update the prototype function. Further, we will introduce the Shelter Maps App to actual regional areas and verify whether the users can actually evacuate safely and quickly to the optimal shelter in the case of a disaster.

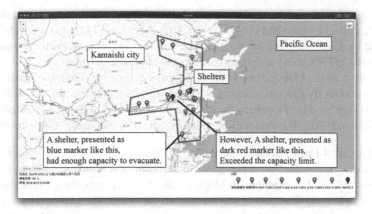

Fig. 6. Example of a display image of the prototype Shelter Maps App. (Color figure online)

5 Discussion

5.1 Location Visualize Function of SRP and Supporters

The developed location visualize function can show the positions of supporters, SRP and evacuation shelters. The information of SRP can be obtained based on the SRP list prepared by local government office. However, the list is usually not disclosed to protect personal information. In the case of disaster, the list needs to be quickly provided in available condition to supporters. When the supporters use the application, the application needs to get the location information on each supporter. So, the location information of every supporters should be "ON" condition so that it can be obtained using GPS.

5.2 Shelter Condition Visualize Function

Conventional research [5–7] has shown that sharing disaster-related information through visual methods, such as maps, is more effective than using text-based methods. However, these studies did not consider some limitations, such as the capacity of the shelters and the dynamic transition of the conditions during an actual disaster evacuation. Our newly developed function provides information on the capacity of the shelters and the changing conditions in real time. We expect that the developed function will be useful under not only real disasters but also evacuation drills because it can provide conditions on both real shelters and virtual shelters in a simulation. Further, the proposed method can be adopted in other areas that require information on the shelter conditions. For example, a government can create a new shelter construction plan or assignment plan for current shelters based on real experiences or disaster simulations. However, the function is still in the development stage, and there are two issues that should be resolved: (1) data reusability and (2) data format standardization.

Data Reusability. It is necessary to transfer a large amount of data that are difficult to reuse, such as the location and capacity of the shelters, into digital information. Regarding the data that are difficult to reuse, there are some available examples, such as data on the capacity of the shelters, published as PDFs, and data on the open/closed status of the shelters, expressed as HTML text. However, the HTML text is currently only surrounded by a <p> tag and has no semantics. In the case of the developed prototype, we parsed the HTML texts and found a designated regular expression, and converted the information into a PDF file manually to be used as data in a database because there is no way to correctly recognize text in a PDF. If the data that are difficult to reuse are converted beforehand into a general format such as CSV or JSON, or as published data on a standard web API, the data will be much easier to obtain using a web crawler.

Data Sharing and Data Format. Currently, data sharing between government staff members in evacuation shelters and in government offices is typically conducted using a paper-based method. For example, in Morioka city, Iwate, Japan, the current population of a shelter is sent by Fax, using the format. In this case, the city-level government (Morioka city office) receives the Fax, and then transcribes it on a spreadsheet tool such as Excel. The spreadsheet is then sent to the prefecture-level government (Iwate Prefecture office) by Fax again. Thus, there is a large time lag when sharing the information, which does not occur in real time. To solve this problem, we believe that digitizing the format for government communication during an emergency will be an effective approach. As a tool for digitalization, web-based and cloud-based spreadsheet tools such as Google Sheet will be suitable in terms of usability and availability. We expect that such a digitized format will increase the speed of the data sharing and increase the opportunities of evacuees to obtain the latest information as a result. We also plan to propose an optimal data input/output format using Google Sheet for government organizations in Japan.

6 Conclusion

In this study, we described the importance of early evacuation in the case of natural disasters in regional areas. Then, this paper showed an evacuation time-line model and indicated that the actually required and important information were the location information of Support-required People (SRP) and supporters, and the current shelter's detail condition. To realize an early evacuation, the evacuees need to know the shelter conditions in detail and real time. But, there was a problem that the shelter information was not integrated on government websites, people could not determine the best shelter for evacuation. To solve the problem, we newly developed the location visualize function which could share the information on the location of SRP and supporters, and shelter conditions in real time. We also presented a case study of the prototype shelter condition visualize function for Kamaishi City in Iwate Prefecture, Japan. We concluded the function would be helpful for local residents to accurately understand the state of evacuation shelters in detail.

By using our proposed Real-time Evacuation Support System (RESS), which is integrated the location visualize functions of SRP, supporters and shelter conditions, every evacuees can easily check the necessary information in real time on a map and can evacuate in the optimal way. As a result, we believe the system will contribute to reduce the risks of human damage in natural disasters.

References

1. Weathernews Inc.: The Great East Japan Earthquake: Tsunami Survey (Survey Results). http://weathernews.com/ja/nc/press/2011/pdf/20110908_1.pdf. 8 Sept 2011
2. NHK News Web: Some evacuation shelters are full of evacuees and can't be accommodated in Hayama-cho, Kanagawa. https://www3.nhk.or.jp/news/html/20191012/k10012125301000.html. 12 Oct 2019
3. NHK News Web: 13 evacuation shelters are having trouble accepting people in Iwaki-shi, Fukushima. https://www3.nhk.or.jp/news/html/20191013/k10012127731000.html. 13 Oct 2019
4. Sasaki, J., Kitsuya, M.: Development and evacuation of Regional Information Sharing System (RISS) for disaster risk reduction. Inf. Syst. Front. Springer (2020). ISSN 1387-3326
5. Nakajima, Y., et al.: Disaster evacuation guide: using a massively multiagent server and GPS mobile phones. In: 2007 International Symposium on Applications and the Internet. IEEE (2007)
6. Rahman, K.M., Alam, T., Chowdhury, M.: Location based early disaster warning and evacuation system on mobile phones using OpenStreetMap. In: 2012 IEEE Conference on Open Systems. IEEE (2012)
7. Itoi, J., Sasabe, M., Kawahara, J., Kasahara, S.: An offline mobile application for automatic evacuation guiding in outdoor environments. Sci. Phone Apps Mob. Devices 3(1), 1 (2017). https://doi.org/10.1186/s41070-017-0013-1
8. Hilts, S.R., Kushma, J., Plotnick, L.: Use of social media by U.S. public sector emergency managers: barriers and wish lists. In: Proceedings of the 11th International ISCRAM Conference (2014)
9. Abdullah, N.A., Nishioka, D., et al.: Why I retweet? Exploring user's perspective on decision-making of information spreading during disasters. In: 50th Hawaii International Conference on System Sciences (HICSS-50) (2017)
10. Cesta, A., Cortellessa, G., Benedictis, R.D.: Training for crisis decision making-an approach based on plan adaptation. Elsevier Knowl.-Based Syst. 58, 98–112 (2014)
11. Bernabé-Moreno, J., Tejeda-Lorente, A., Porcel, C., Herrera-Viedma, E.: Leveraging localized social media insights for early warning systems. Int. J. Inf. Technol. Decis. Making (IJITDM) 17(1), 357–385 (2018)
12. Kitsuya, M., Sasaki, J.: Proposal of evacuation support system and evaluation by multi-agent simulation in a regional disaster. In: Murayama, Y., Velev, D., Zlateva, P. (eds.) ITDRR 2019. IAICT, vol. 575, pp. 45–54. Springer, Cham (2020). https://doi.org/10.1007/978-3-030-48939-7_5
13. Iwate Prefecture: Iwate Disaster Prevention Information Portal. https://iwate.secure.force.com/PUB_VF_HinanList
14. Geospatial Information Authority of Japan: Designated Emergency Evacuation Site Data. https://hinan.gsi.go.jp/hinanjocjp/hinanbasho/koukaidate.html
15. Iwate Prefecture: Evacuation Shelters and Designated Emergency Evacuation Sites Data. https://www.pref.iwate.jp/kurashikankyou/anzenanshin/bosai/kokoroe/1004197.html
16. Kamaishi city: Welfare Shelters Data. http://www.city.kamaishi.iwate.jp/kurasu/bosai_saigai/hinanbasho/detail/1190992_2227.html
17. Segment: Nightmare. http://www.nightmarejs.org
18. Hasura Inc.: Hasura. https://hasura.io
19. Evan You: Vue.js. https://vuejs.org
20. Vladimir Agafonkin: Leaflet. https://leafletjs.com

Visualization of Tweets and Related Images Posted During Disasters

Sanetoshi Yamada[1], Keisuke Utsu[2], and Osamu Uchida[3](✉)

[1] Research and Information Center, Tokai University, Hiratsuka, Kanagawa, Japan
S.Yamada@star.tokai-u.jp
[2] Department of Communication and Network Engineering, Tokai University,
Minato, Tokyo, Japan
utsu@utsuken.net
[3] Department of Human and Information Science, Tokai University, Hiratsuka, Kanagawa, Japan
o-uchida@tokai.ac.jp

Abstract. To minimize damage during disasters, rapid collection and delivery of accurate information are essential. From this perspective, the use of social media, especially Twitter, in the case of a disaster has attracted worldwide attention. On the other hand, it is known that the number of tweets explodes at the time of a large-scale disaster. For example, at the time of the 2018 northern Osaka earthquake, more than 270,000 tweets containing the word "earthquake" were posted during the 10 min immediately after the quake. Therefore, it is essential to analyze the characteristics of tweets in order to make effective use of Twitter at the time of a disaster. In this study, we develop a system to simultaneously visualize the content of disaster-related tweets as well as the attached images that are related to their textual content. The purpose of constructing the system is to encourage prompt decision-making from local government and rapid evacuation actions by disaster-affected residents in the event of a disaster. From the visualization results using data from tweets posted during Typhoon Hagibis in 2019, it is shown that the proposed system is useful in the event of a disaster. It is also found that good results can be obtained by using datasets consisting of tweets posted during other disasters.

Keywords: Disaster · Disaster mitigation · Twitter · Visualization · Co-occurrence network

1 Introduction

In recent years, Japan has been hit by several natural disasters. In particular, extensive damage resulted from the 2017 northern Kyushu heavy rain disaster [1], the 2018 northern Osaka earthquake [2], the 2018 western Japan heavy rain disaster (2018 Japan Floods) [3–5], and Typhoon Hagibis [6] in 2019. In order to minimize the damage caused by such large-scale disasters, it is crucial to collect and transmit information quickly and accurately. From this perspective, the utilization of social media, especially Twitter,

© IFIP International Federation for Information Processing 2021
Published by Springer Nature Switzerland AG 2021
Y. Murayama et al. (Eds.): ITDRR 2020, IFIP AICT 622, pp. 26–35, 2021.
https://doi.org/10.1007/978-3-030-81469-4_3

has been attracting worldwide attention [7–12]. At the time of the Great East Japan Earthquake in March 2011, many residents in the affected areas used Twitter to collect information about the tsunami, evacuation centers, and public transportation services [13–16]. Nishikawa et al. showed that many tweets, including the Japanese hashtag " #救助" (meaning "#rescue"), were posted for rescue requests during the 2018 Japan Floods [4]. The following text is an example of a tweet posted after the 2016 Kumamoto earthquake struck (originally written in Japanese): "There is no food or drink at Ubuyama Junior High School. The people there are in real trouble. Please send them food. Please help them. They need disposable diapers because there are many seniors." Tweets like this can help not only the victims but also government agencies and disaster volunteer groups to get a better understanding of the situation and make the right decisions.

On the other hand, it is known that the number of tweets explodes at the time of a large-scale disaster. For example, on the day of the Great East Japan Earthquake, about 33 million tweets were posted. When Hurricane Sandy hit the U.S. East Coast in 2012, many people used Twitter to share disaster-related information; more than 20 million tweets that included the words "sandy," "hurricane," "#sandy," and "#hurricane" were posted between October 27 and November 1, 2012 (https://twitter.com/Twitter/status/264408 082958934016). At the time of the 2018 northern Osaka earthquake, more than 270,000 tweets containing the word "earthquake" were posted during the 10 min immediately after the earthquake [2]. Therefore, it is essential to analyze the characteristics of tweets in order to make effective use of Twitter at the time of a disaster. From that point of view, in previous work, we have analyzed tweets at the time of a disaster [1–6, 17]. However, our research so far has focused only on tweet text. It is clear that analysis of the images attached to tweets is also critical in order to further utilize tweets in the event of a disaster [18–20].

In this study, we developed a system to simultaneously visualize the content of disaster-related tweets and the attached images, which are related to the textual content of the tweet. The purpose of constructing the system is to encourage prompt decision-making from local governments and the rapid evacuation of residents from disaster-affected areas.

2 Tweet Data for Analysis

This study mainly considers tweets related to Typhoon Hagibis, which caused severe damage in a widespread area of eastern Japan in October 2019. This typhoon killed more than 80 people, more than 3,000 buildings were utterly destroyed, and a further 28,000 were partially destroyed. The typhoon inundated many rivers in areas of eastern Japan. Figure 1 shows an example of a tweet posted during Typhoon Hagibis. We primarily focus on the flooding of the Chikuma River, which runs through Nagano Prefecture, which caused extensive damage to the river basin. Then, we used the Twitter API to collect original tweets (non-retweeted tweets) that were posted between October 12 to 13, 2019 and contained the word " 千曲川" (Chikuma River). A total of 64,819 tweets were collected, and of these, 4,755 had images attached. We then deleted tweets that appeared to be quotes from news articles, finally obtaining 4,209 tweets to analyze. Figure 2 shows the trend in the number of these tweets posted at ten-minute intervals.

The number of tweets rose sharply at around 20:50 on October 12. The Chikuma River in Nagano city, the capital of Nagano Prefecture, flooded around this time. The number of tweets soared at around 6:50 on October 13, when the extent of the damage was actively reported in the morning news on TV.

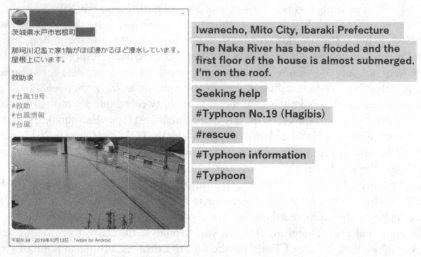

Fig. 1. An example of a tweet posted during Typhoon Hagibis in 2019

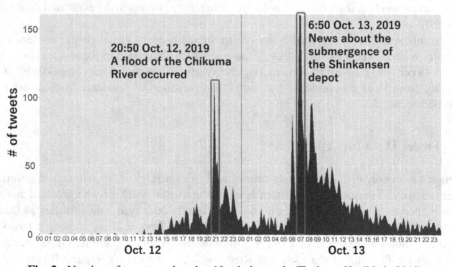

Fig. 2. Number of tweets analyzed at 10 min intervals (Typhoon Hagibis in 2019)

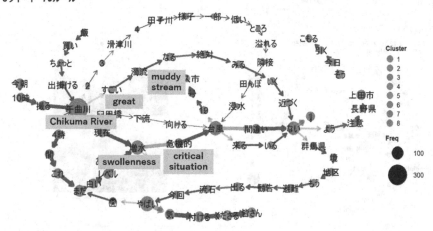

Fig. 3. Example of co-occurrence network of tweets (Typhoon Hagibis in 2019)

3 Visualization of Tweets

3.1 Visualization of Tweets Using a Co-occurrence Network for Comprehending Posted Content

In this study, we used a co-occurrence network as a method of comprehending the content of tweets. Figure 3 shows the co-occurrence network created from one hour of tweet data, starting from 14:00 on October 12, 2019. The size of the circle indicates the frequency of occurrence of particular words, the thickness of the arrow indicates the frequency of co-occurrence, and the opacity of the arrow indicates the magnitude of the co-occurrence rate, $CR(A \rightarrow B|B)$, of words A and B, where

$$CR(A \rightarrow B|B) = \frac{Fr(A \rightarrow B)}{Fr(B)} \qquad (1)$$

Here, $Fr(A)$ and $Fr(A \rightarrow B)$ denote the frequency of the occurrence of the word A and the frequency of co-occurrence of two words $A \rightarrow B$, respectively. From Fig. 3, it can be seen that there were posts about the river conditions, containing text such as "千曲川" (Chikuma River) → "すごい" (great) → "濁流" (muddy stream) and "増水" (swollenness) → "危機的" (critical situation). The flooding of the Chikuma River occurred at around 20:50, but it is speculated that it was in a dangerous state even around 14:00.

In the co-occurrence network, it is difficult to comprehend the relationship between the preceding and succeeding words when one word has multiple connections.

Especially in this study, since "千曲川" (Chikuma River) appears in every tweet, it is difficult to comprehend how the words that co-occur before and after "千曲川" (Chikuma River) are connected. Therefore, a cluster analysis was performed using the frequency of the occurrence of the words in each tweet, and the words were then grouped.

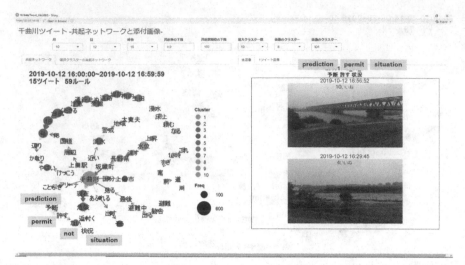

Fig. 4. Screenshot of the proposed system Typhoon Hagibis in 2019, 16:00 on October 12, 2019)

3.2 Simultaneous Visualization System of the Co-occurrence Network and Images Attached to Tweets

We consider a method to visualize the type of images attached to tweets in an easy-to-understand manner. First, in order to make it easier to understand the relationship between the textual tweet content and the attached images, we collected images attached to tweets in which the words in each cluster are included in the text. We also created a system that displays the co-occurrence network and the attached images at the same time.

Figure 4 shows the co-occurrence network created from the tweet data during the one hour period that began at 16:00 on October 12, 2019, as well as the attached images related to the words in the cluster, including " 余談" (prediction), " 許す" (permit), and " 状況" (situation). At the top of the image, the original time that the tweet was posted and the degree of attention (number of retweets and favorites) that the image received are displayed. By looking at the state of the river in the picture, the meaning of "a situation that is difficult to predict (an unpredictable situation)" can be understood more intuitively. We were also able to find two posts from the phrase "an unpredictable situation." In this way, this system can find similar images from the words in the tweet and display them all together. Figure 5 shows the analysis results created from the tweet data for the one-hour period that began at 7:00 on October 13, 2019. This was around the time when the number of tweets increased as the typhoon had passed, and the extent of the damage became apparent. In particular, it can be seen that many people were shocked by the submergence of the Hokuriku Shinkansen, with many taking photos of TV news images and posting them. Figure 6 shows the results created from the tweet data for the one-hour period that began at 23:00 on October 12, 2019. Although the number of tweets during this time was not large, information on evacuation shelters had been released, and it can be said that it is a useful visualization to encourage the evacuation of residents.

Our system can display not only the overall result of the co-occurrence network but also only the words that are directly connected to the words within the selected cluster.

In addition, the system can choose one post from the attached images and display the tweet text simultaneously. In addition, the target date and time, the lower limit of the co-occurrence rate, the lower limit of the frequency ranking, the maximum number of clusters, and the cluster number for displaying images can be set. With these functions, it is possible to interactively analyze and visualize the object that the user is paying attention to.

3.3   Tweets Visualization Results of Other Disasters

We verified the usefulness of the visualization system constructed in this study by visualizing tweets posted during the 2018 northern Osaka earthquake and the 2018 Japan Floods.

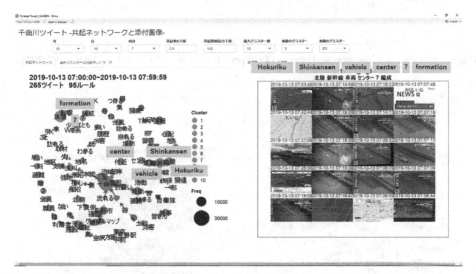

Fig. 5.   Screenshot of the proposed system (Typhoon Hagibis in 2019, 7:00 on October 13, 2019)

Figure 7 shows the visualization results from tweets posted during the 2018 northern Osaka earthquake (June 18, 2018, 8:00). From the co-occurrence network, there were tweets about the quake, which contained text such as " 震度" (seismic intensity)→" 6弱" (weak 6) and " 深さ" (depth (of the epicenter)) → 10 → km, and tweets about the damage, which contained text such as " 水道管" (water pipe) → " 破裂" (burst) and. " 高槻駅" (Takatsuki Station) → " 水" (water) → " 漏れ" (leaking). In particular, the situation where passengers flooded the platform attracted attention due to the significant damage that resulted in the suspension of train operations and water leaks at stations across Osaka Prefecture.

Figure 8 shows the tweet visualization results from tweets posted during the 2018 Japan Floods (July 6, 2018, 19:00). From the co-occurrence network, it can be seen that tweets about the announcement of the heavy rain special warning were posted in Hiroshima, Okayama, and Tottori prefectures at 19:40, containing text such as " 特別"

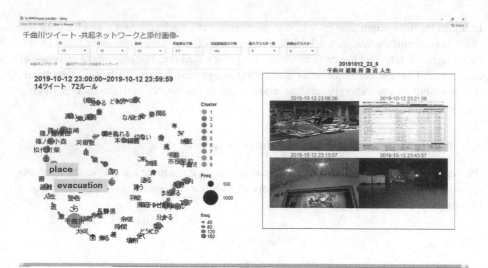

Fig. 6. Screenshot of the proposed system (Typhoon Hagibis in 2019, 23:00 on October 12, 2019)

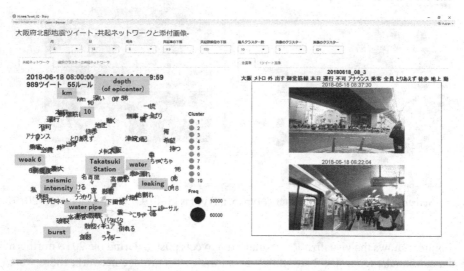

Fig. 7. Screenshot of the proposed system (2018 northern Osaka Earthquake, 8:00 on June 18, 2018)

(special) → "警報" (warning) → "発表" (announcement). Besides, it can be seen that there were also posts urging residents to take action to evacuate, e.g., "Take action to save lives." It can also be seen that images were posted comparing the normal conditions of the Kamo River in Kyoto City with pictures taken following the increase in the water on that day. The original tweets of these images were posted at around 10:00, and they were still being retweeted even 9 h later and received considerable attention.

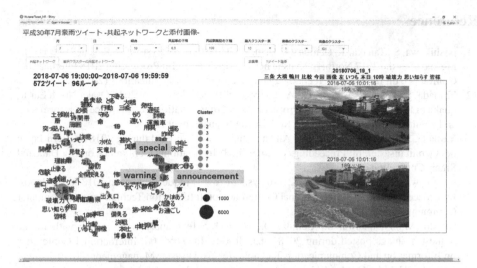

Fig. 8. A screenshot of the proposed system (2018 Japan Floods, 19:00 on July 6, 2018)

4   Discussion

From the analysis results for the three disasters, there was a difference in the shooting locations of the attached images. In tweets posted during Typhoon Hagibis in 2019, many pictures of the river were posted, but in tweets posted during the 2018 Japan Floods, images showing not only the state of the river but also the state of the submerged part of the city were also posted. There were few images of people in typhoons and heavy rain, but in tweets posted during the 2018 northern Osaka earthquake, there were many posts from places where people were gathering, such as stations and amusement parks.

Since the characteristics of each disaster could be visualized appropriately, the system constructed in this study is considered useful for the analysis and visualization of tweet data.

5   Conclusion

This study developed a system to simultaneously visualize the contents of disaster-related tweets and the attached images that are related to the textual content. From the visualization results using data from tweets posted during Typhoon Hagibis in 2019, it was shown that the proposed system is useful in the event of a disaster. It was also found that good results can be obtained by using datasets consisting of tweets that were posted during other disasters. We are engaged in research pertaining to tweet classification and mapping at the time of disasters [16], efficient disaster information collection [21], and construction of disaster information sharing system using Twitter [22–24]. We plan to expand on the findings obtained in the present study in these subsequent investigations.

References

1. Nishikawa, S., Tanaka, T., Uchida, O., Utsu, K.: Time trend analysis of "# Rescue" tweets during and after the 2017 Northern Kyushu heavy rain disaster. In: Proceeding 2018 International Conference on Information Technology and Computer Communications (2018)
2. Yamada, S., Utsu, K., Uchida, O.: An analysis of tweets during the 2018 Osaka North Earthquake in Japan - a brief report. In: Proceedings of 5th International Conference on Information and Communication Technologies for Disaster Management (2018)
3. Yamada, S., Utsu, K., Uchida, O.: An analysis of tweets posted during 2018 Western Japan heavy rain disaster. In: Proceedings of 2019 IEEE International Conference on Big Data and Smart Computing (2019)
4. Nishikawa, S., Uchida, O., Utsu, K.: Analysis of rescue request tweets in 2018 Japan floods. In: Proceedings of 2019 International Conference on Information Technology and Computer Communications (2019)
5. Kondo, M., Nishikawa, S., Uchida, O., Utsu, K.: Text analysis of tweets with rescue request hashtags posted during 2018 Japan floods. In: Proc. 6th International Conference on Information and Communication Technologies for Disaster Management (2019)
6. Utsu, K., Uchida, O.: Analysis of rescue request and damage report tweets posted during 2019 Typhoon Hagibis. IEICE Trans. Fundam. E103-A(11), 1319–1323 (2020)
7. Uchida, O., Utsu, K.: Utilization of social media at the time of disaster. IEICE ESS Fundam. Rev. 13(4), 301–311 (2020). (in Japanese)
8. Imran, M., Castillo, C., Diaz, F., Vieweg, S.: Processing social media messages in mass emergency: a survey. ACM Comput. Surv. 47(4), Article 67 (2015)
9. Simon, T., Goldberg, A., Adini, B.: Socializing in emergencies - a review of the use of social media in emergency situations. Int. J. Inf. Manage. 35(5), 609–619 (2015)
10. Meier, P.: Digital humanitarians: How Big Data Is Changing the Face of Humanitarian Response. CRC Press, Boca Raton (2015)
11. Castillo, C.: Big Crisis Data. Cambridge University Press, Cambridge (2016)
12. Dragović, N., Vasiljević, Đ., Stankov, U., Vujičić, M.: Go social for your own safety! review of social networks use on natural disasters – case studies from worldwide. Open Geosci. 11(1), 352–366 (2019)
13. Toriumi, F., Sasaki, T., Shinoda, K., Kazama, K., Kurihara, S., Noda, I.: Information sharing on twitter during the 2011 catastrophic earthquake. In: Proceedings of 22nd International Conference on World Wide Web Companion, pp. 1025–1028 (2013)
14. Peary, B.D.M., Shaw, R., Takeuchi, Y.: Utilization of social media in the East Japan earthquake and tsunami and its effectiveness. J. Nat. Dis. Sci. 34(1), 3–18 (2012)
15. Wilensky, H.: Twitter as a navigator for stranded commuters during the great East Japan earthquake. In: Proceedings of 11th International Conference on Information Systems for Crisis Response and Management, pp. 695–704 (2014)
16. Uchida, O., et al.: Classification and mapping of disaster relevant tweets for providing useful information for victims during disasters. IIEEJ. Trans. Image Electron. Vis. Comput. 3(2), 224–232 (2015)
17. Yamada, S., Utsu, K., Cho, K., Uchida, O.: Analysis and visualization of attention area of tweets during disasters: In: Proceedings of 6th International Conference on Information and Communication Technologies for Disaster Management (2019)
18. Alam, F., Ofli, F., Imran, M.: Processing social media images by combining human and machine computing during crises. Int. J. Hum.–Comput. Interact. 34(4) (2018)
19. Mozannar, H., Rizk, Y., Awad, M.: Damage identification in social media posts using multimodal deep learning. In Proceedings of 15th International Conference on Information Systems for Crisis Response and Management (2018)

20. Imran, M., Alam, F., Qazi, U., Peterson, S., Ofli, F.: Rapid damage assessment using social media images by combining human and machine intelligence. In: Proceedings of 17th International Conference on Information Systems for Crisis Response and Management, pp. 761–773 (2014)
21. Utsu, K., Manaka, A., Nakafuri, K., Uchida, O.: Web application prototype for collecting disaster-related information focusing on tweets immediately after retweeting news posts. In: Proceedings of 4th International Conference on Information and Communication Technologies for Disaster Management (2017)
22. Uchida, O., et al.: A Real-time information sharing system to support self-, mutual-, and public-help in the aftermath of a disaster utilizing twitter. IEICE Trans. Fundam. E99-A(8), 1551–1554 (2016)
23. Kosugi, M., et al.: Improvement of twitter-based disaster-related information sharing system. In: Proceedings of 4th International Conference on Information and Communication Technologies for Disaster Management (2017)
24. Kosugi, M., et al.: A twitter-based disaster information sharing system. In: Proceedings of 4th International Conference on Computer and Communication Systems (2019)

Preliminary Evaluation of Information Sharing in COACHES*

Chihiro Takada[1], Yurika Takeuchi[1], Mari Kinoshita[2(✉)], and Mikifumi Shikida[1]

[1] Kochi University of Technology, Kochi, Japan
shikida.mikifumi@kochi-tech.ac.jp
[2] University of Kochi, Kochi, Japan
kinoshita@cc.u-kochi.ac.jp

Abstract. Because of geographical, topographical and meteorological conditions, Japan is subject to frequent natural disasters such as typhoons, torrential rains and heavy snowfalls, as well as earthquakes and tsunami [4]. A team of University of Kochi launched a novel information management system COACHES (Community Oriented Approaches for Comprehensive Healthcare in Emergency Situations), which enables the efficient and quality provision care and relief to the all evacuees [7, 10]. In this paper, we evaluated prototype its web service information sharing among relief workers from the perspective of evacuees through questionnaires and interviews. We found that in order for COACHES to be operational in the field, evacuees need the ability to limit the type of relief workers who can see their information and the types of information they can release.

Keywords: Disaster support · Evacuee support · Rapid healthcare assessment · Information sharing · Web service

1 Introduction

Japan is located in the Circum-Pacific Mobile Belt where seismic and volcanic activities occur constantly. Although the country covers only 0.25% of the land area on the planet, the number of earthquakes and active volcanoes is quite high. In addition, because of geographical, topographical and meteorological conditions, the country is subject to frequent natural disasters such as typhoons, torrential rains and heavy snowfalls, as well as earthquakes and tsunami [4].

In 2011, more than 18,000 people died or went missing due to the Great East Japan Earthquake. There is also a high probability of the occurrence of largescale earthquakes in the near future including impending possibilities of Nankai Trough Earthquake and Tokyo Inland Earthquake. As such, natural disasters remain a menacing threat to the safety and security of the country [4].

Shelters are established in the event of such a large-scale disaster. Shelters can be defined as a displaced neighborhood of convenience, providing physical shelter as well as social and medical services [11]. In fact, records show that approximately 410,000

Y. Murayama et al. (Eds.): ITDRR 2020, IFIP AICT 622, pp. 36–48, 2021.
https://doi.org/10.1007/978-3-030-81469-4_4

people in Iwate, Miyagi, and Fukushima prefectures, and 470,000 people in total across Japan, lived in shelters after the Great East Japan Earthquake [5].

However, in the Great East Japan Earthquake, there were many problems arising during the disaster: affected people suffered health problems; aged people were forced to stay home because they could not adapt themselves to the evacuation shelters in some cases, relief supplies were not provided sufficiently to home evacuees in many cases; and there were reported problems for provision of information, relief supplies, and services for wide area evacuees who evacuated to other prefectures or municipalities [4].

Mr. Fujita said that currently, many of the shelters have no privacy and often have poor sanitary conditions. Under such circumstances, the staff of the shelter need to provide medical and health care to the evacuees. In addition, when the damage is particularly severe and the central disaster hospitals and mainstay medical institutions in the affected area do not function, or are too busy, medical care in the evacuation centers becomes important for a certain period of time [6].

In addition, the Disaster Relief Law stipulates that evacuation shelters should provide food and water through cooking and other means. For this reason, many evacuation centers distribute relief supplies.

However, in the immediate aftermath of the disaster, because of the chaos on the ground, there was a situation in which the production capacity of the suppliers could not keep up with the supply of goods due to overlapping procurement, or because of the concentration of orders to specific suppliers [8].

In addition, many of the survivors have chosen to evacuate from their homes instead of using the evacuation centers. According to a survey conducted by the Cabinet Office on the victims of the Great East Japan Earthquake, about 70% of the respondents had not visited an evacuation center [3].

Evacuees in shelters have some level of support system in place, including medical personnel and relief supplies, which makes it easier for them to receive assistance. In contrast, those who choose to evacuate at home tend not to be able to receive adequate support [9].

In order to address these issues, the University of Kochi School of Nursing in collaboration with the Kochi University of technology has launched a novel information management system COACHES (Community Oriented Approaches for Comprehensive Healthcare in Emergency Situations), which enables the efficient and quality provision care and relief to the all evacuees. We proposed a prototype of web service for the COACHES, which enables a secure and user-friendly data collection and reference in disaster settings [7, 10].

In this paper, we use the prototype of COACHES [7, 10] to conduct a preliminary evaluation of information sharing among relief workers from the perspective of evacuees through questionnaires and interviews, and present the findings from the results.

2 Related Research

A related study is an ICT-based shelter management system [2]. This system uses ICT to collect information on evacuees, create and disseminate lists of evacuees including their relief needs, and manage the evacuees. An electronic triage system has also been proposed [1].

The system will use the evacuee's own NFC cards for personal identification, and if they don't have one, the shelter will distribute NFC wristbands provided by the shelter. However, under this system, when evacuees come to an evacuation center, staffs have to go through the procedure of asking the receptionist if they have an NFC card and handing out wristbands to those who don't have one. The procedure would not be so complicated if the number of evacuees in shelters had settled down, but immediately after a disaster occurs, the number of evacuees in shelters is large and the situation is chaotic, so there is a possibility that people may line up at the reception desk. In addition, personal information, such as name and address, is required, so consideration must be given to those who may not feel comfortable entering this information. Also, the results of the electronic triage are displayed by the color of the light on the wristband with LEDs, which is visible to other people and does not provide sufficient privacy considerations.

3 Coaches

We proposed a prototype of web service for the novel information management system COACHES (Community Oriented Approaches for Comprehensive Healthcare in Emergency Situations), which enables a secure and user-friendly data collection and reference in disaster settings [7, 10]. An overview of this is presented in this chapter.

3.1 Flow of Use

This system is intended to be used by evacuees who have been evacuated to shelters or evacuated at home, as well as healthcare professionals and Relief workers (Non-Medical Support) who provide support.

– Evacuees
  QR codes for personal identification are routinely stored at evacuation centers, town halls, and disaster prevention warehouses, and are distributed to evacuees at evacuation centers and town halls in the event of a disaster. QR codes are distributed on wristbands and are intended to be carried at all times. Evacuees will present QR code to relief workers, if necessary. Following is information about evacuees to be recorded.

• Health conditions

  • Gender
  • Approximate age category
  • Physical status
  • Physical symptoms

- Vital signs

  - Body temperature
  - Pulse
  - Respiratory rate
  - Blood pressure (diastolic and systolic)

- Triage results
- Support history

  - Meal service (Time and place)
  - Receiving relief supplies (time, place, distribution group, category (foodstuffs, daily necessities, etc.), photos)
  - Bathing (Time and place)
  - Medical examination (Time, doctor in charge, remarks)
  - Legal/Welfare consultation (Time, responders, content (e.g., moving into a hypo-thetical home, inheritance issues, etc.)

- Shelter entry and exit records

- Healthcare professionals
  First, healthcare professionals examine evacuees who has received the QR code, read the QR code, and record health conditions and vital signs. The vital signs recorded at this time will be used for primary triage. Then, healthcare professionals can view and edit the health conditions and vital signs by scanning the QR code of the evacuees at the time of examination. Also, when the QR code is scanned, the medical examination is recorded. The blue arrows in Fig. 1 indicate flow of use by healthcare professionals. Healthcare professionals have access to all information about the evacuees that is recorded in COACHES.
- Relief workers (Non-Medical Support)
  First, relief workers register their support, such as food services and distribution of relief supplies, with the COACHES (Distribution group, Category (Foodstuffs, Daily necessities, etc.), Photos, etc.). Then, when providing support, they scan the QR codes of evacuees receiving support. Also, when the QR code is scanned, details of support are recorded. Unlike healthcare professionals, relief workers are not allowed to edit information on evacuees. The orange arrows in Fig. 1 indicate flow of use by relief workers. Relief workers have access to evacuees' support history and shelter entry and exit records.

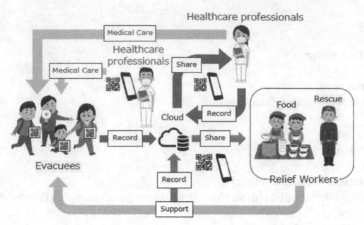

Fig. 1. Flow of use (Dark arrows point to the flow of data and light arrows point to the flow of support.)

3.2 The Prototype Screens

Figure 2 is a screen that displays the health condition of evacuees. Figure 3 is a screen that displays the vital signs of evacuees. Figure 4 is a screen that displays a history of the support received by evacuees and a record of their entry and exit from the shelter. Relief workers can only see Fig. 4 [7, 10].

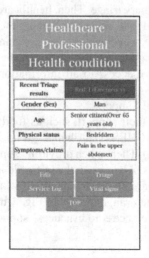

Fig. 2. Health conditions

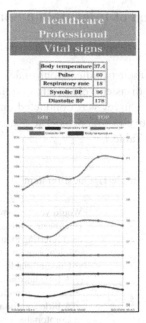

Fig. 3. Vital signs

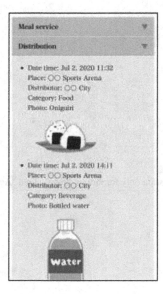

Fig. 4. Service Log

4   Preliminary Evaluation of Information Sharing in COACHES

4.1   Survey Method

In this study, seven students in their twenties (four males and three females) who had never experienced a large-scale disaster were briefed on the system using prototype of COACHES, and a questionnaire survey was conducted on information sharing among relief workers from the perspective of evacuees. The content of the questionnaire to be used in this process is shown in Table 1.

Table 1. Question item

Q1	Would you be comfortable with relief workers (e.g., Healthcare professionals, Psychological counselors, etc.) referring to the information you have entered for efficient support? · Uncomfortable · A little uncomfortable · Neither uncomfortable nor comfortable · A little comfortable · Comfortable
Q2	Do you think you want to limit the types of relief workers who can view your information? · Agree · Agree a little · Neither agree nor disagree · Disagree a little · Disagree
Q3	Do you think you want to limit your information that relief workers can view? · Agree · Agree a little · Neither agree nor disagree · Disagree a little · Disagree
Question only for those who answered "Agree" or "Agree a little" in Q2	
Q4	Are you willing to share your information with following types of relief workers? · Healthcare professionals · People distributing relief supplies (Meal, Daily necessities, etc.) · Shelter reception · Psychological counselors · Legal counselors · Care workers

(*continued*)

Table 1. (*continued*)

Question only for those who answered "Agree" or "Agree a little" in Q3	
Q5	Are you willing to share following your information with healthcare professionals? · Triage results · Gender · Approximate age category · Physical status (Pregnant, Disabilities, etc.) · Physical symptoms (Fever, Injury, etc.) · Vital signs (Body temperature, Pulse, Respiratory rate, Blood pressure (diastolic and systolic)) · Meal service log · Receiving relief supplies log · Bathing log · Shelter entry and exit log · Medical examination log · Legal/Welfare consultation log
Q6	Are you willing to share following your information with relief workers? · Meal service log · Receiving relief supplies log · Bathing log · Shelter entry and exit log · Medical examination log · Legal/Welfare consultation log

4.2 Survey Result

The answers to Q1 of Table 1 ("Would you be comfortable with relief workers (e.g., Healthcare professionals, Counselors, etc.) referring to the information you have entered for efficient support?") are shown in Fig. 5.

The results were four people who answered "A little comfortable" and three people who answered "Comfortable".

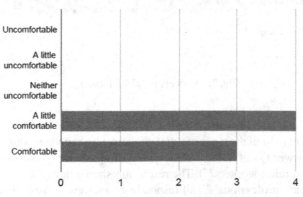

Fig. 5. Answers to Q1 of Table 1

The answers to Q2 of Table 1 ("Do you think you want to limit the types of relief workers who can view your information?") are shown in Fig. 6.

The results were four people who answered "Disagree a little", two people who answered "Agree a little" and one person who answered "Agree".

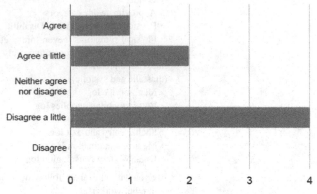

Fig. 6. Answers to Q2 of Table 1

The answers to Q3 of Table 1 ("Do you think you want to limit your information that relief workers can view?") are shown in Fig. 7.

The results were five people who answered "Disagree a little" and two people who answered "Agree a little".

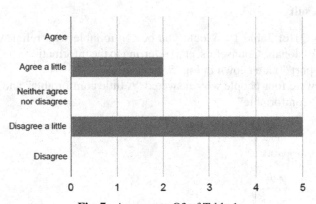

Fig. 7. Answers to Q3 of Table 1

The three people who answered "Agree" or "Agree a little" on Q2 of Table 1 ("Do you think you want to limit the types of relief workers who can view your information?") were asked to answer Q4 of Table 1 ("Are you willing to share your information with following types of relief workers?"). The results are shown in Fig. 8.

For "Healthcare professionals", all respondents answered "Yes". For "People distributing relief supplies (Meal, Daily necessities, etc.)", "Psychological counselors",

"Legal counselors" and "Care workers", two people answered "Yes". For "Shelter reception", all respondents answered "No".

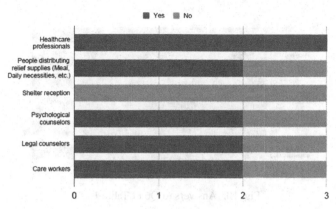

Fig. 8. Answers to Q4 of Table 1

The two people who answered "Agree a little" on Q3 of Table 1 ("Do you think you want to limit your information that relief workers can view?") were asked to answer Q5 of Table 1 ("Are you willing to share following your information with healthcare professionals?"). The results are shown in Fig. 9.

The results were all respondents answered "Yes" to all items.

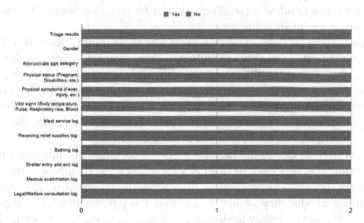

Fig. 9. Answers to Q5 of Table 1

In addition, we asked them to answer Q6 of Table 1 ("Are you willing to share following your information with relief workers?") as well. The results are shown in Fig. 10.

For "Meal service log" and "Receiving relief supplies log", all respondents answered "Yes". For "Bathing log", "Shelter entry and exit log", "Medical examination log" and

"Legal/Welfare consultation log", one person answered "Yes", but other person answered "No".

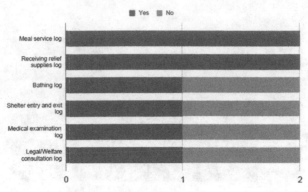

Fig. 10. Answers to Q6 of Table 1

4.3 Discussion

The results of this survey showed that many people who viewed COACHES from the perspective of evacuees were willing to have their information shared with relief workers. However, some respondents wanted to limit the types of relief workers who see the information and the types of information that are released. Therefore, we found that evacuees are willing to allow their information to be seen, but wanted to control the extent to which it was made public.

In questions about the types of relief workers who share information (Q4 of Table 1), all respondents indicated that they are willing to share their information if they were a healthcare professional. Also, all respondents indicated that all healthcare professionals would be allowed to share all of the information recorded in COACHES. In contrast, some respondents did not want to share their information with relief workers except healthcare professionals. In particular, all respondents indicated that they did not want to share their information with receptionist at the shelter.

This result may be due to the fact that respondents could not imagine what kind of person would be in charge of the shelter's reception area. Healthcare professionals and psychological counselors are people with credentials and expertise, so evacuees can have some image of what they are like. In addition, it is possible that some respondents decided that it was not necessary to show the information to shelter's receptionist.

In questions about the types of information shared (Q5 and Q6 of Table 1), All respondents indicated that "Meal service log" and "Receiving relief supplies log" were acceptable to share. In contrast, some respondents did not want to share "Bathing log", "Shelter entry and exit log", "Medical examination log" and "Legal/Welfare consultation log". Respondents were interviewed in this regard. Despite wanting to limit the type of information shared, respondent who indicated that all information in COACHES is willing to share with relief workers were concerned that they did not know what information was being shared, rather than that there was information they did not want to be shared.

That respondent said "I think I would feel more comfortable sharing the information if I was presented with what the information would be used for." Also, Respondent who said they were only willing to share "Meal service log" and "Receiving relief supplies log" said "I was willing to share "Meal service log" and "Receiving relief supplies log" on the survey because there were many types of relief workers and they did not know exactly which information would be shared with whom, so they answered A and B that they were willing to share." Both opinions indicated that evacuees wanted to know which information was being shared with whom and for what purpose. We think this result because evacuees want to minimize the amount of information about themselves that is shared.

The above indicated that some evacuees would like the scope and type of information about themselves to be the minimum required. Also, we found that some people asked for an explanation in advance of what information would be shared and for what purpose. The results suggest that in order for COACHES to be operational in the field, there needs to be a function that allows evacuees to limit the types of relief workers and the types of information they release, as well as a system that allows evacuees to see what information is being shared and for what purpose.

5   Conclusion

In this paper, we used the prototype of COACHES [7, 10] to conduct a preliminary evaluation of information sharing among relief workers from the perspective of evacuees through questionnaires and interviews, and presented the findings from the results. The results showed that while evacuees were less resistance to have their information shared with relief workers, some wanted to limit the type of supporters and type of information shared, with some wanting the minimum type of relief workers who can view the information shared and type of information shared, even if there was no directly identifiable information, such as names and addresses, that could be used to identify individuals.

These results suggest that in order for A to be operational in the field, evacuees need a system to limit the relief worker to share their information and a system to limit the type of information they share. In the future, we aim to clarify which relief workers need which information and to implement a function to restrict information. We will also consider a system that allows evacuees to check what information is being shared and for what purpose. In addition, we plan to conduct a survey of people who have experienced the disaster and healthcare professionals.

Acknowledgement. The work was supported by JSPS KAKENHI Grant Number JP20K11132 and the University of Kochi Strategic Research Promotion Project (R1 Theme3) given to MK.

References

1. Akasaka, K., Kanisawa, K., Kanemaru, T., Isshiki, M., Abe, K.: A proposal on refuge management system by electronic triage for persons requiring special assistance at large-scale disaster. In: Proceedings of Multimedia, Distributed Collaboration and Mobile Symposium 2018, pp. 277–282 (2018)
2. Akasaka, K., Osone, R., Amagi, Y., Yamaguchi, T., Abe, K.: Development and evaluation of refuge management system using ict at the time of large scale disaster. Trans. Inf. Process. Soc. Japan, Consum. Devices Syst. 7(3), 15–25 (2017)
3. Director General for Disaster Management Cabinet Office, Government of Japan: Report on the Implementation of Comprehensive Measures for Evacuation (2013)
4. Director General for Disaster Management Cabinet Office, Government of Japan: Disaster Management in Japan (2015)
5. Director General for Disaster Management Cabinet Office, Government of Japan: Shelter Management Guidelines (2016)
6. Fujita, T.: Medical support (shelter). J. Jpn. Soc. Intern. Med. 99(10), 216–218 (2010)
7. Kinoshita M., Shikida M. Measuring Personal Damage in a Large-Scale Disaster: A Review of the Reports Published by the Japanese Fire and Disaster Management Agency on the Great East Japan Earthquake and Tsunami Disaster Medicine and Public Health Preparedness. in-press (2021)
8. Kuwahara, M., Wada, K.: Recording and quantitative analysis of the flow of emergency relief supplies in the great east japan earthquake analysis of the flow of emergency relief supplies handled by the national and prefectural governments. Japan Transp. Tourism Res. Inst. 16(1), 42–53 (2013)
9. Sato, S., Maeno, T., Takai, M., Owada, Y., Oguchi, M.: A development of an application to support distribution of relief supplies to victims in a large-scale disaster. In: Proceedings of Multimedia, Distributed Collaboration and Mobile Symposium 2018, pp. 716–720 (2018)
10. Takada, C., Takeuchi, Y., Kinoshita, M., Shikida, M.: Development of a web service to support the community oriented approaches for comprehensive healthcare in emergency situations. In: Proceedings of International Joint Symposium on Artificial Intelligence and Natural Language Processing, pp. 244–249 (2020)
11. Veenema, T.G., Rains, A.B., Casey-Lockyer, M., Springer, J., Kowal, M.: Quality of healthcare services provided in disaster shelters: an integrative literature review. Int. Emerg. Nurs. 23(3), 225–231 (2015)

Application of Disaster Management Information for the COVID-19 Pandemic

Wei-Sen Li[(✉)], Ming-Wey Huang, Wen-ray Su, Yanling Lee, Yi-Ching Liu,
Ke-Hui Chen, and Chi-Ling Chang

National Science and Technology Center for Disaster Reduction, New Taipei City, Taiwan

Abstract. Since end of 2019, because of the worldwide spread of COVID-19,
the whole world has been struggling for solutions to mitigate adverse impacts and
worsening situations, which demonstrate very dynamic characteristics requiring
high integration among government agencies to make decisions and deliver operation. Within countries around the world, most of disaster management agencies are
the primary institutions working with health agencies to cope with health emergencies. To comparing disaster management with public health management, there are
lots of common grounds like procedures to deal with emergency and allocations
of resources. However, the differences between the two fields offer an opportunity
for mutual leaning on best practices of emergency management. For example,
in case of disaster event, for better response and control, commanding officials
usually dispatch several teams and concentrate resources as much as possible to
effectively respond to emergency. According to reports on containing COVID-19
spread, whenever any decisions should consider social distancing first that limits
operational space because of safety reason. This paper explores possible collaboration between disaster management with public health management and discusses
direction about how to apply information of disaster risk management for public health events. More focal topics concentrate on data processing of population
distribution and information integration.

Keywords: COVID-19 · Disaster management · Public health management ·
Information intelligence

1 Examples of Collaborations Between Disaster Management and Public Health

COVID-19 has infected 100 million people and caused 3 million deaths [1] that not just
bring global health crisis, but also all kinds of interruptions to operations of governments and business, livelihood, education, and other activities. Before massive vaccina-
tion could deliver herd immunity, "Social distancing" and "Quarantine" are two basic
approaches to contain the spread for buying more time to develop effective "antidote"
to solve this global crisis. Looking history of public health emergencies, Spanish flu
in 1918, SARS in 2003 and H1N1 in 2009 have given lessons to the world in handling global pandemics through assistance science and technology. From Spanish flu to

Y. Murayama et al. (Eds.): ITDRR 2020, IFIP AICT 622, pp. 49–56, 2021.
https://doi.org/10.1007/978-3-030-81469-4_5

COVID-19, besides medical research to find out treatments and vaccines, how to effectively conduct "Social distancing" and "Quarantine" that demands monitoring developing situations, comprehensive information integration, risk communication, emergency operation, information facilitation and other measures which help decision making. All possible measures mentioned above are the same ones for disaster management covering phases of mitigation, preparedness, response and recover.

Since human beings are the primary target to protect by risk reduction of natural hazards or pandemics, common grounds of identifying social and physical vulnerabilities are to build up cross-cutting collaborations in sharing of information, technology operation principles, resources, and experiences. For example, seismic disaster reduction, disaster managers need patterns of population distribution which help to highlight disaster hotspots in case of large-scale earthquake and provide a risk profile to decision maker to deliver a drill or respond to emergency. Likewise for containing spread of pandemic, density and distribution pattern of publication are also key indicators to pinpoint high-risk communities and propose strategy to build "firewall" for isolating infections. Therefore "Human-centric" countermeasures can establish good connections for inviting more synergies from disaster managers and public officers.

Traditionally, disaster managers apply census for exploring social and physical vulnerabilities. Among all categories of census data, population is the one of the most applicable information to estimate exposure and risk of both urban and rural areas. After collecting original population data and expanding the information on a GIS platform, it offers a map of population distribution. To increase the resolution of population distribution map, it requires additional processes to make the map more informative for application in disaster risk management. A case done by the National Science and Technology Center for Disaster Reduction (NCDR) is a good practice of data processing on population distribution.

Having collaboration with government, NCDR integrates census and tax information to make maps for seismic risk identification. The population data of census can tell numbers, ages, genders, and address of demographic structure. Tax information of residential housing can tell floor areas to accommodate residents. Making estimates of population distribution by deriving equations between numbers of population and floor areas that leads to the first version of population distribution map of Taiwan. The map assists in understanding seismic profile for making plans of risk reduction and emergency preparedness. The Fig. 1 is the product delivered by NCDR based on 2010.

Cesus [2]. For delivering the population density map (PDM) with better geo-spatial resolutions, a mesh with grid size of 500 m by 500 m is applied to divide the whole Taiwan into 13,2712 grids.

By overlapping the map with ground motion, casualty estimate, building damage estimate, soil liquefaction, etc. (See Fig. 2), the integrated map will give a comprehensive risk distribution for both planning phase and emergency operation. In case of an earthquake, the NCDR system would use real shake maps to estimate impacts, possible casualty, damage and interruptions to lifeline system and critical infrastructure. For study on Dengue, the map has been applied for tracing the spread and highlighting prioritized areas to disinfect. The PDM overlaps with investigations of Aedes aegypti that can identify hotspots requiring disinfection.

After typhoons or floods, some water-born diseases like pathogenic Leptospires and melinidosis are the two major concerns of public health, especially in flooded areas. To send warning to the possibly affected areas, the Center of Disease Control (CDC), Taiwan, in collaboration with NCDR, would use the PDM, floods map and rain forecast to give public health guidance to follow.

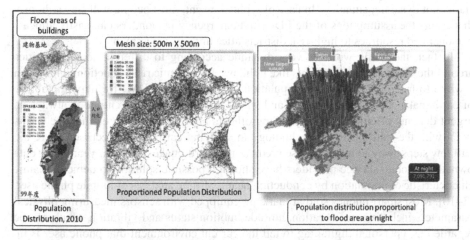

Fig. 1. Population density map based on grid approach by using 2010 Census.

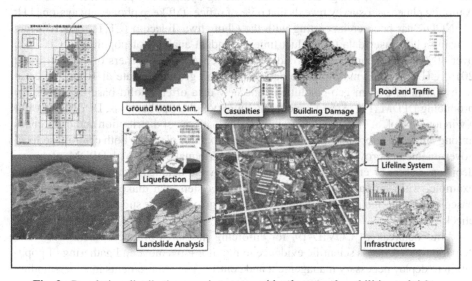

Fig. 2. Population distribution map integrates with relevant vulnerabilities and risks.

2   Unique Demands for Containing COVID-19 Speared by Applying Data and Information Prepared for Disaster Management

Examining the characteristics and assumptions of the PDM mentioned in Sect. 1, the PDM can only static distribution of population based dwelling facts and assume the distribution is proportional to floor area. Therefore, the PDM is ideal for risk analysis of static, not dynamic, situation. In case of typhoon event, most people will stay at homes that meets the assumptions of the PDM and emergency responders can easily allocate personal and resources to high-risk districts after impacts assessment.

In fact, the living world is very dynamic according to different social activities around the clock or specific events like holidays. For seismic risk reduction, it has been a while to try to catch dynamic population density map (DPDM) for unpredictability of earthquake. To know how many and where people highly concentrate is always an urgent demand of emergency responding officers after a large-scale earthquake strike. Even with the-state-of-the-art technology in studying earthquake precursor, there are still few steps away to make precise prediction of earthquake. In recent years, user data owned by mobile service providers have shown a possible solution to depict dynamic characteristic of population by conducting near real-time analysis of mobile phone user, [3–10]. Most smart phones sold at mark are equipped with sensors measuring physical parameters including geo-location, altitude, motion status and vibration which can be regarded as a personal digital tag to tell the current environment that phone user is in. If mobile service providers can share the users' information without intruding personal privacy, it does make a huge leap in understanding dynamics of population movement. A mobile phone user survey reveals that 65% of office staff keep phones always-on [11].

NCDR has been collaborating with the Chunghwa Telecom (CHT) over 10 years in using phone user data to conduct time-dependent analysis of population. CHT has over 40% market share and its broadest service covers most corners of Taiwan. From 2019, CHT provides more precise data, which can give an update at 10-min interval with 500 m-by-500 m geo-resolution. The new data offer a solid base to NCDR for producing DPDM (Fig. 3) and conducting more possible applications. DPDM can offer a window to look at 7/24 population movement, patterns of distribution and differences among areas. By adopting DPDM, NCDR helps to make plans for both central and local governments and provide scenarios for national earthquake drill. With DPDM, planners, decision makers or emergency responders can have a detailed picture of impacts. For example, when an earthquake strikes, NCDR's system can make impact assessment based on 10-min-ago population distribution that gives primary suggestions for casualty check.

After outbreak of COVID-19, for enforcing measures of Social distancing" and "Quarantine", it needs scientific evidence to monitor movement and gathering of population to deploy necessary management and control. The requirements in understanding population for containing COVID-19 are similar to seismic risk reduction that demands dynamic characteristics of population movement. NCDR immediately convened a taskforce for working out solutions aimed at pandemic control. During developing maps for COVID-19 monitoring, it requires indicators to define levels of mass crowd gathering for signaling warnings. As specified the collaboration between NCDR and CHT has been 10 years, it builds a good database for a long-term observation which can provide a baseline for compassions of population density.

- **Time domain resolution: every 10 minutes**
- **Spatial domain: 500m x 500m, with gender**
- **Coverage: urban and rural areas**

Fig. 3. The dynamic population density map (DPDM) of Taipei Metropolitan area produced by NCDR.

3 Applying the Dynamic Population Density Map (DPDM) for Mass Crowd Control During Holiday Under COVI-19

As requests by disaster managers and emergency responder, in case of sudden-onset events like earthquake or social disturbance, where densely populated areas are to identify hotspots to make plan for, check out or respond to.

Under guidance of COVID-19, lots of social activities are either cancelled or downscaled to satisfy demands for keeping social distancing since beginning of 2020 Chinese New Year Festival. When the 4-day spring break came in the early April 2020, lots of Taiwanese residents took this opportunity for having domestic tours, visiting families or tomb sweeping. From news footages of over-crowded tourist spots, the Central Epidemic Command Center (CECC) launched messages through the Public Warning System (PWS) to warn citizens in these over-crowded areas and suggest on-the-way derivers avoid visiting the over-populated areas. Figure 4 showed the population changes during April 1st−5th. To illustrate levels of mass crowd the NCDR taskforce choose 3-week averaged time-dependent data as the baseline, the grey line in Fig. 4, for qualitative analysis.

To answer requests proposed by CECC to evaluate mass crowd movement, NCDR taskforce decided applying DPDM to provide geo-spatial and time-dependent factors for monitoring population movement. The following items are key elements to create an effective platform of monitoring:

1. Where and how to identify crowd movements through adopting management tools

   • The system should display and estimate locations and numbers of crowds.
   • Indicators identify the density of crowds could exceed allowable capacity or not.
   • Time-dependent increments helps to forecast the increasing or decreasing trends.
   • Channels inform citizens of taking actions.

2. Quick solutions by applying near-real-time dynamic population data

   • Non-privacy information produced by mobile service provider is to monitor the movements.
   • The analysis should be based on sufficient resolutions of time, every 10 min, and space, 500 m × 500 m grids.

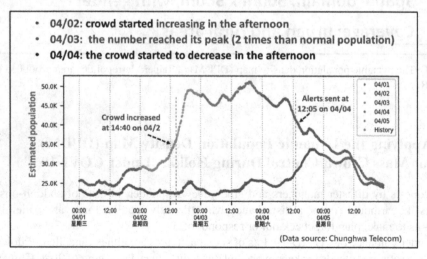

Fig. 4. The population movement during spring break in Hengchun Township.

4 Conclusions

To better engage disaster managers and public officers for better information share to cope with future and compound disasters, the following suggestions are proposed:

1. The cross-cutting usage of information should be the trend under all-hazards approach that can meet compound disasters like earthquake or flood response under influence of COVID-19. Data and information should provide multiple functions for diverse emergencies.
2. Disaster managers or researchers should extend collaboration with other community that can introduce innovation and build integration. Therefore, a mechanism or platform should be designed to routinely engage key stakeholders.
3. At information age, how information can be well transferred and understood by the public is an essential measure for emergency management, no matter disaster or epidemic. From current practices and observations, a clear and direct risk communication always requires scientific-based tools to produce correct information intelligence. And the last mile is to deploy effective and efficient channels to reach end users. The target end users could be citizen, disaster managers, emergency responders or decision makers. According to the actions taken by individual end users, information intelligence should be designed to offer clear guidance such like timing or procedures.

References

1. COVID-19 DASHBOARD. https://covid-19.nchc.org.tw/?language=en. Accessed 30 Mar 2021
2. Wu, B.-R.: Application of a mesh-based earthquake impact assessment tool on emergency preparedness and policy support. In: The 7th International Workshop on Natural Disaster Reduction Management among Japan-Taiwan-Korea (2016)
3. Bagrow, J., Wang, D.P., Barabási, A. L.: Collective response of human populations to large-scale emergencies. PLOS ONE 6(3), e17680 (2011). https://doi.org/10.1371/journal.pone.0017680
4. Basseville, M., Nikiforov, I.V., et al.: Detection of Abrupt Changes: Theory and Application, vol. 104, Prentice Hall Englewood Cliffs (1993)
5. Bengtsson, L., Lu, X., Thorson, A., Garfield, R., von Schreeb, J.: Improved Response to disasters and outbreaks by tracking population movements with mobile phone network data: a post-earthquake geospatial study in Haiti. PLoS Med 8(8), e1001083 (2011). https://doi.org/10.1371/journal.pmed.1001083
6. Brockmann, D., Hufnagel L., Geisel, T.: The scaling laws of human travel. Nature 439, 462–465 (2006)
7. Chandola, V., Mithal, V., Kumar, V.: Comparative evaluation of anomaly detection techniques for sequence data, data mining. In: ICDM'08. Eighth IEEE International Conference on IEEE, pp. 743–748 (2008)
8. Chen, J., et al.: Fine-grained prediction of urban population using mobile phone location data. Int. J. Geogr. Inf. Sci. 32(9), 1770–1786 (2018)
9. DesRoches, R., Comerio, M., Eberhard, M., Mooney, W., Rix, G. J.: Overview of the 2010 Haiti earthquake. Earthquake Spectra, 27(1), S1-S21 (2011).

10. Gething, P.W., Tatem, A.J.: Can mobile phone data improve emergency response to natural disaster? PLoS Med **8**(8), e1001085 (2011). https://doi.org/10.1371/journal.pmed.1001085
11. Inside.   https://www.inside.com.tw/article/19692-taiwan0employees-are-on-call-247. Accessed 04 May 2020

Applying Information Technology for Cross Border Disaster Risk Reduction Through Public Private Partnership Amidst COVID-19

Yanling Lee[1]([✉]), Wei-Sen Li[1], Yi-Chung Liu[2], Ke-Hui Chen[1], Chi-Ling Chang[1], and Kenji Watanabe[3]

[1] APEC Emergency Preparedness Capacity Building Center and National Science and Technology Center for Disaster Reduction, New Taipei City, Taiwan
[2] National Science and Technology Center for Disaster Reduction, New Taipei City, Taiwan
[3] The Nagoya Institute of Technology, Nagoya, Japan

Abstract. The crisis of humankind, the COVID-19 pandemic, brought the threats but the opportunities toward collaboration on disaster risk reduction (DRR) through public private partnership (PPP) over sustainable development goals (SDGs) at global landscape. Under the direct impact to the social-cultural, political and economic interests, we are in time for change. In the past decade, the concept of PPP has been widely applied to facilitate supply chain resilience after the 2011 the Great East Japan Earthquakes and Tsunami on business continuity planning (BCP). The highlight in 2019 is to implement PPP on climate extremes capacity building programme "Plant Back Better (PBB)" initiatives for Livelihood Continuity Planning (LCP) through the smart technology and climate-smart agriculture across the border for international collaborations. How to look out each other in distance will be the future challenge amidst COVID-19. Consolidating 10 years of implementation findings, this paper developed a cross-border PPP approach on utilizing smart technology for better governance on emergency preparedness and building a stronger partnership engagement on real-time basis. On the digital transformation era, this paper illustrated how we came across the barrier of language, cultural difference and border-control to deliver the DRR mission through PPP amidst the COVID-19 crisis on a common operational picture for emergency preparedness, response and recovery.

Keywords: Emergency preparedness · DRR · PPP · BCP · SDGs · COVID-19

1 Background Development of Public Private Partnership for Collaboration

1.1 A Milestone for Promoting the Public Private Partnership for Emergency Preparedness

Asia-Pacific Economic Cooperation (APEC) [1] region suffered from 70% of global natural disasters over USD100 billion in related losses annually [2]. Since the 2011

© IFIP International Federation for Information Processing 2021
Published by Springer Nature Switzerland AG 2021
Y. Murayama et al. (Eds.): ITDRR 2020, IFIP AICT 622, pp. 57–72, 2021.
https://doi.org/10.1007/978-3-030-81469-4_6

Great East Japan Earthquakes and Tsunami [3], global value chains (GVCs) [4] and supply chain resilience continued to be discussed from a variety of dimensions. APEC took note of a string of costly earthquakes and extreme weather and called for projects on sustainable growth in the world's most natural disaster-affected region to improving business resilience from 2011. The networking engaged APEC collaboration on cross-cutting issues and kick-off a series of project on Business Continuity Planning (BCP) [5] (SMEWG [6], EPWG [7]), Digital Resilience in 2013 (SMEWG, EPWG), 2015 Critical Infrastructure Resilience and Safety [8] (CTWG [9], EPWG), the 7 Principles for Supply Chain Resilience in 2017 (TPTWG [10], EPWG), and Financial Risk Financing (FMP [11]-DRFI [12], EPWG) across boundary.

Meanwhile, through public and private partnership (PPP) [13], APEC invested in promoting BCP for disaster resilience and delivered train-the-trainer workshops on the project output "Guidebook on SME Business Continuity Planning in APEC" [14] based on ISO22301 [15] but SMEs/MSMEs [16] user friendly. The guidebook illustrated 10 easy steps for SMEs/MSMEs on implementing BCP available online in 7 languages, English, Chinese, Spanish, Japanese, Thai, Indonesian and Vietnamese covering 40% of the world population [17]. With the fruitful outcomes and deliverables, APEC Emergency Preparedness Capacity Building Center (EPCC) [18] host "APEC Summit on Resilience" in Nagoya, Japan at Nagoya Institute of Technology (NiTech) [19] to brainstorming the next step for DRR in April 2017.

1.2 Information-Based Preparedness and Scenarios

The concept of information-based preparedness and scenarios for cross-border PPP has been addressed as the concluding summary of APEC Summit on Resilience. It explored the idea of "Operational Framework for Regional Collaboration on Resilience" for strengthening global supply chains through PPP as shown in Fig. 1 [20]. Connecting the "business" to a "Business Continuity Management (BCM)-based supply chain", is aimed at keeping the deadline of shipment on time through cross-border join virtual operation, exercises and drills. It is anticipated to synergise work on regional BCP/BCM efforts for multi-sectorial collaborations at regional level.

In this context, developing information-based preparedness and scenario tools became top priority to ensure stakeholders are on the same page for emergency preparedness. Agreed upon on Geo-spatial distribution maps of lifeline systems, event scenarios, and critical infrastructure resilience in a Wi-Fi readiness environment can help to implement active PPP involvement and voluntary efforts, we pictured a framework for conducting the train the trainer workshop in real-time or near real-time basis for building a keen PPP at the regional level. Streamlining the interdisciplinary countermeasures and cross-cutting issues, the real-time situation assessment for scenario simulation or emergency response/preparedness can take advantage of cloud computing/technology for information exchange and sharing in a timely manner.

Under the Coronavirus Disease 2019 (COVID-19) Pandemic impact [21] in 2020, the tangible and intangible productions and services are interrupted due to lockdown, border control and quarantine in a great deal. The cross-border PPP approach for disaster risk reduction (DRR) on virtual operations and drills turnout to be a no-touch solution for delivering emergency preparedness and response. To further support cross-border cascading disasters interactive with COVID-19, the long-term objectives are set to deliver a board spectrum activities from policy making to capacity build at the regional level through smart technology. Thus, engaging regional institutes to deliver the virtual single operational picture for emergency response and preparedness on supply chain resilience is the ultimate goal for promoting BCP amidst COVID-19 spreading.

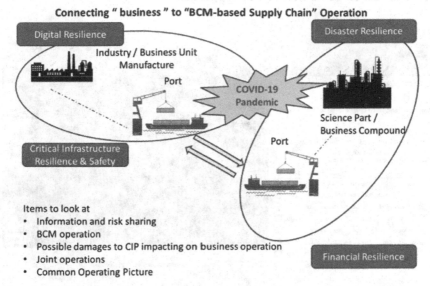

Fig. 1. Operational framework for regional collaboration on resilience, Source: APEC EPCC

2 Cross-Border PPP Approach for New Normal on Climate Extremes

2.1 Plant Back Better for Food Security

The 2019 United Nations' report on Sustainable Development Goals (SDGs) [22] revealed the impact on the climate related disasters. From 1998 to 2017, seventy-seven percent of the estimated direct economic losses (US$3 trillion) are from disasters. It is about a 1.5 time rise compared to the one from 1978 to 1997. Estimated 1.3 million death toll for climate related and geophysical disasters. How to provide the rapid growing global population with economic access to sufficient, safe, nutritious and quality food as well as better livelihoods of millions of rural people, mainly small farmers, particularly women on the vegetable plantation? APEC recognized the urgent need of resilient infrastructure, early warning systems, emergency-actionable plans and countermeasures for better preparedness and recovery to tackle the constant threat of extreme events, earthquakes, floods and natural disasters. Thus, APEC called for climate adaptation countermeasures. In 2019, EPCC demonstrated the Plant Back Better (PBB) initiative [23] as one of the cross border PPP model to function as the countermeasure of food security over climate extremes to boost microeconomic momentum. The PBB project mainly focused on promoting capacity building by adopting smarter and disaster-resistant plantation of flowers and vegetables in the rural area on local knowledge over the local social network.

2.2 APEC PBB on Cross-Border PPP Approach

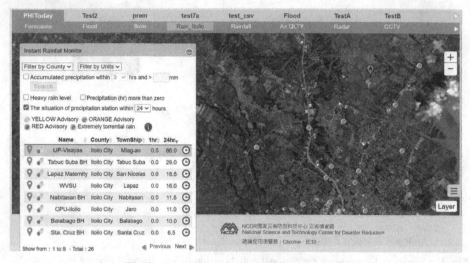

Fig. 2. Hazard sensor network, Source: NCDR

To further engaging key stakeholders as a whole society for implementing PBB and map out a pathway of sustainable and resilient developments, the Iloilo City Government has installed 26 multi-hazard sensor network in partnership with Taiwan's National Science and Technology Center for Disaster Reduction (NCDR) [24] (Fig. 2). APEC EPCC for delivering regional capacity building engaged a cross-border PPP project over Taiwan New South-bound Policy [25] and the Iloilo City Government in the Philippines to constantly look out its APEC PBB project [26] and monitored the situations of natural disasters the situation of natural disasters and climate extremes in the long run.

2.3 Cross-Border PPP Approach on Climate Smart Agriculture for Food Security in Barren Land Amidst COVID-19

PBB project targeted on vegetables and flowers plantation on quick harvests, cash crops and nutrition. To link with the food security priority to support the daily SMEs and MSMEs' activities for a living, PBB initiative incorporates the implementation of the best practices and toolkits [27] for sharing local knowledge and utilising regional resources to facilitate Livelihood Continuity Plan (LCP) before or after disasters and climate extremes since 2018.

In 2020, amidst COVID-19, World Bank indicated that COVID-19 has slowed economic growth, increased unemployment, and raised poverty and hunger. The global output is estimated to shrink by 5.2% in 2020 [28], with a downside estimate of about 8% contraction should the lockdowns continue into the second half of the year. International Labour Organization highlighted the decline in world gross product could lead to an additional 25 million people unemployed worldwide. Hunger will increase, with the number of people facing acute food insecurity doubling to about 265 million by the end of 2020 [29]. These deprivations are likely to hit children, women, and the elderly, as well as least developed countries (LDCs) [30] and other vulnerable developing countries, harder.

How to provide the rapid growing global population with economic access to sufficient, safe, nutritious and quality food as well as better livelihoods of millions of rural people, mainly small farmers, particularly women on the vegetable plantation while COVID-19 spreading? The PBB pilot community in Iloilo City shown its resilience while COVID-19 spreading for border control, lockdown and quarantine. On its continuous harvests (Fig. 3) received from PBB Facebook, PBB pilot community upgraded its role on sharing its harvests. From receiving assistance to delivering assistance, a self-sufficient climate smart agriculture community functioned in the critical moment amidst COVIDE-19 as a food provider outreaching the helping hands to the people in need and sustain the LDCs' activity, circular economy [31] as well as SMEs/MSMEs activities in the Philippines while lockdown for COVID-19.

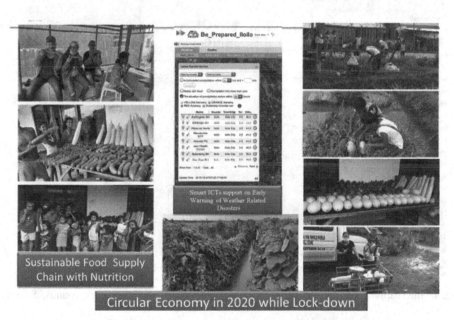

Fig. 3. APEC plant back better initiative, Source: NCDR & APEC EPCC

To echo United Nations' Food program [32], PBB community continued to share nutritious food, love, healthy life style and hope amidst COVID-19 pandemic spreading.

PBB as a living project helps the most vulnerable people to strengthen their capacities to absorb, adapt, and transform in the face of shocks and long-term stressors amidst COVID-19 lockdown.

3 Capacity Building Through PPP Amidst COVID-19

3.1 New Globalisation for PPP - 2020 International Training Workshop

Youth can play an important role in disaster preparedness and response. To further build up the youth capacity at the regional level to deploy the multi-hazard approach on geological and hydro-meteorological hazard, Tzu Chi Foundation (Tzu Chi [33], International NGO) and NCDR collaborate to organize the 2020 International Training Workshop (2020ITW) - Youth Leadership Camp on Disaster Risk Management [34], the 15th ITW, focusing on capacity building for disaster preparedness to seek the new globalisation model for capacity buildings on cross-border PPP approach. The workshop targeted at meeting college junior, senior, graduate and post-graduate international students majoring in disaster management or relevant disciplines who are enthusiastic fast learners with mobility and creativity to join the training. The international participants from 21 countries with broad-spectrum backgrounds are depicted in Fig. 4.

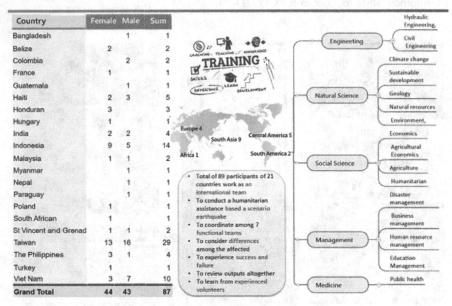

Fig. 4. International participants of 21 countries with broad-spectrum backgrounds, Source: NCDR.

Through scenarios simulation and on-site hands-on operations, 2020ITW are designed to empower future leaders to involve in science and technology on decision making and deployment. The challenging missions during the whole event, including smart DRR through strategic process, is the highlights of the training. Scenario-based information intelligence in delivering humanitarian assistance is critically important to ensure quality decision-making in the case of emergency operations.

3.2 A Large-Scale Earthquake Scenario

Take the case of magnitude 7.1 earthquake in Miaoli County, the Shihtan Fault movement [35], depicted in Fig. 5 as a scenario that hits the central Taiwan nearby HsinChu Science Park [36] where the world-leading semiconductor company, Taiwan Semiconductor Manufacturing Company Limited (TSMC) [37], located for 2020ITW Youth Camp on-site training. The scenario of estimated damage (to building, to public and critical infrastructure), casualties, demands of short-term sheltering, population distribution (and estimation by mobile phone data) are provided to the trainees for planning and action in GIS [38] based information (Fig. 6). We utilized the situation assessment smart technology, Decision-making Support System for Emergency Operation Center (EOCDSS) [39] in Taiwan for central operation (Fig. 7). We have another lesson learnt and plan for the staff safety for remote workers, work at home with also monitor the staff families' safety.

Peak ground acceleration (PGA)@ 7.1 magnitude

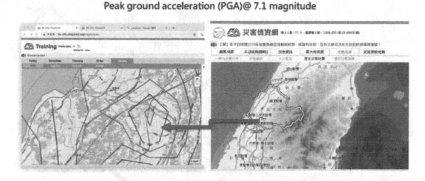

**M7.1 Quake of Shihtan Fault Impact Miaoli County獅潭斷層規模7.1_苗栗縣
Response to D0+2hr ~ 7 Days**

Fig. 5. A large-scale earthquake scenario, Source: NCDR

3.3 Incorporate United Nations' Cluster Approach into 2020ITW

2020 ITW embedded the concept of Cluster Approach [40]. The expected goals of the 4-day training program are aimed at capacity building on: 1) Understanding of disasters from impacts to operations, 2) Observing the needs of the affected people, 3) Picturing the "situation awareness" as if trainee is one of the affected people after an earthquake and could suffer from its aftermaths; alternatively, trainee play a role of leader by formulating feasible solutions and allocating resources to tackle each challenge, 4) Streamlining the data, photo and information collected for situation assessment through Information and Communication Technology (ICT) [41] devices and consolidating them into a GIS-based system for emergency response and risk communications, 5) Mobilizing the tangible and intangible resources for emergency preparedness, 6) Integrating team efforts on the scenario simulation for operations, and 7) Delivering effective and efficient operation.

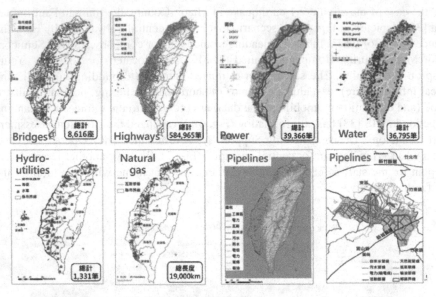

Fig. 6. Geo-spatial distribution maps of lifeline systems, Source: NCDR

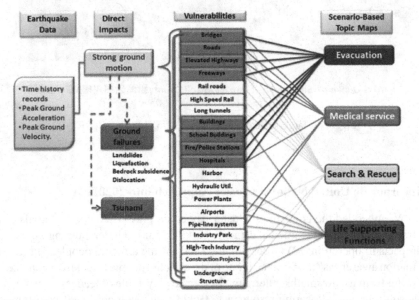

Fig. 7. Components of information-based preparedness and scenarios, Source: NCDR

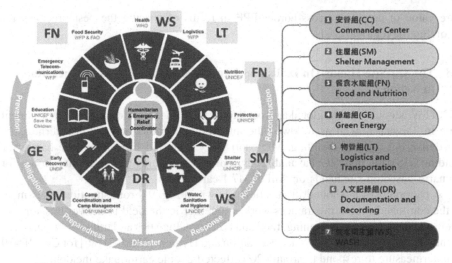

Fig. 8. UN cluster approach and 2020ITW, Source: UN OCHA [42] & NCDR

3.4 Applied Smart ICTs Through PPP for DRR

Taiwan is a very dynamic mobile market with strong coverage and intense competition among its five operators. A collaborative framework of 38 government agencies for sending the public warning messages through mobile system operators covering 29.29 million of 4G subscribers [43] set an example for PPP for DRR. It is free of charge for 4G subscribers in Taiwan to receive 22 types of warning messages such as the big thunderstorm, earthquake, debris flow, dam discharge, pandemics as well as the international outbreak, road closure, terrorist attack, suspension of school or public services at both central and local level by the end of October 2020. NCDR initiated the Cell Broadcast System (CBS) project, a public warning system, in 2016 to kick-off and maintain the operations of the Cell Broadcast Entity (CBE) and consolidate the real-time data received from government authorities into the Cell Broadcast Center (CBC) for mobile system operators to further sending the warning message through mobile to their 4G subscribers.

Only one channel for communications cannot target all the people living in Taiwan. Despite Short Message Service (SMS) sending through CBS, Taiwan took multiple approaches to send public warning message through radio, television, email, internet, loudspeakers, counter liquid-crystal display (LCD) panel of 7–11 convenience stores and social media such as google alert, Facebook and line [44, 45]. The message sent in SMS, GIS-based, visual image, chart, sound and graphic can to some overcome the language barrier to service the diverse of population and activities in Taiwan to pay attention to the potential risk involved if emergencies. Taiwan took the advantage of the existing digital capacity for networking and developed contingency plans for COVID-19 preparedness and response. A part of daily life in Taiwan to receive all-hazard including pandemic public warning through multi-media communication channels for emergency preparedness and response can be expected. Getting ready to people to people connectivity via smart technology and team-up to contribute to the global society is the core value in preparing cross-border PPP in terms of sharing the best practices for resolving the regional crisis.

3.5   The On-Site Hands-On Drills and Exercises Through Virtual Operation in Action

2020ITW adopt a local to global approach to utilize smart technology and environment here in Taiwan as well as followed the international guidelines and countermeasure for delivering capacity building. Microsoft story map and Line group are handy for sending GIS data. In a Wi-Fi available environment, the trainees divided into groups for scenario-based on-site hands-on drill of M7.1 earthquakes.

A panorama of a whole drill in actions shown in Fig. 9. From situation assessment at the command center, the trainees worked together in the field to deliver missions on shelter management and planning, food and nutrition, logistics and transportation, documentation and recording and Water, Sanitation and Hygiene (WASH) [46] for COVID-19 countermeasure to respond to around 200 affected people earthquake incident.

Fig. 9. Cluster approach in action for 2020ITW drills and exercises, Source: NCDR

4 Global Social Change

4.1 Cross Border PPP Approach for DRR on Common Goals

In 2020, managing risks and impacts of natural disasters under COVID-19 pandemic spreading is inevitable. The international society seeks for collaboration over competition amidst COVID-19 pandemic. We incorporate the appropriate PPP approach for collaboration [47] and using ICT Technology into the information-intelligence knowledge platform to provide the single common operational picture for emergency response by adopting open data approach for scenario-based join drills, exercises or operations. Mobilising regional science and technology & research and development for capacity building at the local level, it is very challenging on transferring knowledge and the best practices to share information. Provide solution package and toolkits on challenges are critical to succeed the daily emergency preparedness for better emergency preparedness. This approach shared how to apply information technology for cross-border PPP admits COVID-19 spreading. Wi-Fi [48] Readiness and Cloud Computing/Technology [49] are two pillars to sustain the regional virtual operation and local drills and exercises in action. The best practices of the team efforts (BCP, PBB and 2020ITW) provide valuable information and reference as well as fruitful and inspiring outcomes in conjunction of further perspectives of cross-border PPP approach over the future DRR challenges.

Nowadays, we are more or less connect each household by internet, social media for emotional demand powered by code. Robot, internet or AI technology came to help to provide remote medical service with zero-touch or no-touch policy amidst COVID-19 for mental and physical health in communities even across the border. Wi-Fi readiness is critical. Virtual operation for operational risk management to ensure business continuity for financial resilience for a living is the long-term goal amidst Covid-19. Connecting people through science and technology is inevitable amidst COVID-19. Smartphone is an easily accessible device in connecting the urban and rural community as well as in distance across the borders.

4.2 Cross Border PPP Approach for DRR on MOU

Legal Harmonization and Environment Enablement
Increasing threats from the infrastructure resilience draw our attention for future resilience. Emergency preparedness and recovery rely on daily operations of water and energy supply, telecommunication and etc. To resolve the structural issues and harmonise the cross-border legal framework, MOUs are critical for building consensus on common goals and enable the environment for change. In this context, boosting economic activities on SDGs is fundamental for DRR to uphold livelihoods, business continuity and supply chain connectivity. To gauge implementation of the region's disaster-resilient trade and investment, public sector involvement is crucial to shielding local economic platforms such as business operations, employment and legal flexibility environment over disruptions after a disaster. Taking account of human behaviour as a core value to involve science and technology, Fig. 10 illustrated how to engage cross border PPP approach for DRR at regional level for capacity building, emergency preparedness and

pandemic crisis. Building common goals and partnerships under MOU is the top priority to kick-off the cross-border PPP in the context of **whole of society's participation.**

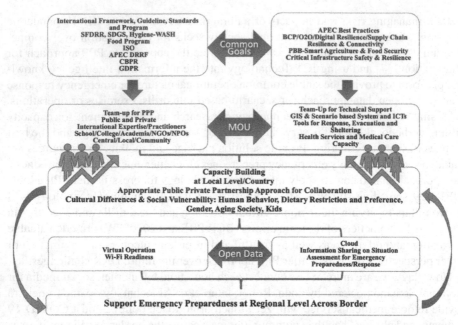

Fig. 10. Cross-border PPP approach for DRR

4.3 Cross Border PPP Approach for DRR on Open Data

Infrastructure Readiness for Smart Appropriate Technology

We utilize innovative ICT tools as well as big data and open data for vulnerability assessment at the regional level for emergency preparedness. It is convenient to apply on cascading disaster interactive with COVID-19 spreading. The consolidated picture of emergency and pandemic provide a comprehensive picture for preparedness, response, search and rescue as well as recovery. While adopting cross-border PPP approach, the effective investment from the public and private sectors for integrating information into a single operational for multi-hazard and pandemic can ensure synergy and avoid crowding out effect [50] to provide all-hazard approach including pandemic decision-making support. Thus, building a robust GIS-based system to incorporate COVID-19 into emergency preparedness is cost-efficient and operation effective for the global community in the sense of supply chain resilience. The critical beneficiary of a cross-border PPP approach will be stakeholder involvement among the public and private sectors in achieving the SDGs.

In the case of PBB project, we use Facebook for connecting Taiwan and the Philippines to deliver real-time emergency preparedness, response and recovery according to the local availability of easy access on smartphone device. In the case of 2020ITW, we adopt Line and Window Story Map for communication in Taiwan. Understanding the appropriate technology in terms of easy access and availability at the local community is critical to be embedded science and technology into daily life operation. It contributed to the sufficient transmission of the data and feedback from the field for study, assessment and circle of experience learning and local knowledge sharing to better off regional operation for capacity building as a whole. On demand, regional science and technology research and development can better fit in the local capacity building in support of local capacity building for secure livelihoods and sustainable growth in disaster-affected areas and beyond.

4.4   Future Perspectives - Challenges or Opportunities

Social Coherence

The investment in efficient BCP can effectively confront emergencies even countries at a relatively low-income level. The emergent COVID-19 became critical which jeopardised the daily operation in the marketplace. Quarantine, regulations, border control, lockdown to great extent change the business conduct for operation and human behaviour. Cyber Security also listed as a priority for Cross-border PPP Approach. Cyberworld does not abide by any rules or guidelines. Fake news, adverse comment or input can jeopardize the partnership and collaboration in a great deal. Panic escalated while the fake news or rumor spreading. The in-time real-time truth and facts are the cure and solution to calm down the general public. Challenges and hard works fall at building trust and bridge the gap of social value difference and the level of economic development including income, racial or gender discrimination, language barrier, cultural difference and conflict while conducting cross-border PPP.

Protecting Privacy Information and Space for Social Good

Cyber security issue draws the attention of the global society on how to regulate a better internet environment for human good and business friendly. It is more than critical for us to ensure the use and abuse of modern technology. Thus, APEC CBPR [51] and EU GDPR [52] provide us clear guidance on cross-border activity in sharing information. Most of the activities interrupted by the COVID-19 measures such as border control, movement restrictions, home/community isolation, business operation control, media and public relations, remote education, remote working, can be tackle by IT technology application. Base on APEC CBPR and EU GDP develop a voluntary GIS-based information-sharing network on emergency preparedness and COVID-19 measures (particularly measures related to emergency preparedness) for pursuing facilitative measures and strengthening regional connectivity and resilience.

Build Back Stronger for Recovery Through Cross-border PPP Approach for DRR over New Normal

Globalization is a trend for nowadays social and economic benefits in synergising the global resources for sustainable development especially in the digital world. Although the COVID-19 spreading has seen a dramatic decline in trade, investments and the movement of people, a new type of globalisation is emerging, the "new globalisation" for "new normal". The change is based on systematic changes of digital services, research and development, data, ideas, and other intangibles for sharing information and resources over crisis across the border for PPP under APEC.

To sum up, for succeeding cross-border PPP Approach, we need to pay special attention to improve the governance by ensuring: 1) consensus on common goal and interests in respect of culture difference, gender, language and etc.; 2) whole society participation; 3) stakeholder empowerment; 4) accountable local practitioners endeavour; 5) effective coordination across units of governments (public sector); 6) effective coordination across levels of INGOs, NGOs [53], academia, community, SMEs and MSMEs (private sector); 7) technical competency of the bureaucracy; and 8) smart use of technology (effective ICTs tools, Cloud and Wi-Fi readiness.

Better governance, smarter technology and stronger partnership networking are three elements toward a cross-border PPP approach for DRR. Make it as simple as possible for users and lower the entry barrier to call for greater participation and contribution to enhance global resilience. Taiwan's experiences and best practices can contribute to resolving the situation of the climate extremes amidst COVID-19 spreading. Predisaster deployment on local knowledge is not only cost efficient and operational effective. Regional science and technology can help vulnerable areas to promote capacity building with synergies. Constantly looking out each other in distance, consolidating 10 years of best practices on capacity building of BCP and PBB, the cross-border PPP approach on utilizing smart technology do effectively connect the world for better governance on emergency preparedness. Team up on cross-border PPP approach is cost efficient to bridge local into the international communities. Cross-border PPP for DRR is a cost effective and efficient strategy for resilience in delivering emergency preparedness, response and quick recovery from disaster impacts while COVID-19.

References

1. Asia-Pacific Economic Cooperation (APEC) homepage. https://www.apec.org/. Accessed 31 Dec 2020
2. World Bank. https://www.apec.org/Groups/SOM-Steering-Committee-on-Economic-and-Technical-Cooperation/Working-Groups/Emergency-Preparedness. Accessed 31 Dec 2020
3. The 2011 Great East Japan Earthquakes and Tsunami. https://en.wikipedia.org/wiki/2011_T?hoku_earthquake_and_tsunami. Accessed 31 Dec 2020
4. Global value chains. https://www.oecd.org/industry/ind/global-value-chains.html . Accessed 31 Dec 2020
5. Business Continuity Planning (BCP) completion report. https://www.apec-epwg.org/media/2353/2c0ca0199ba34676c3a21032d8e03918.pdf. Accessed 31 Dec 2020
6. Small and Medium Enterprises Working Group (SMEWG). https://www.apec.org/Groups/SOM-Steering-Committee-on-Economic-and-Technical-Cooperation/Working-Groups/Small-and-Medium-Enterprises. Accessed 31 Dec 2020
7. Emergency Preparedness Working Group (EPWG). https://www.apec.org/Groups/SOM-Steering-Committee-on-Economic-and-Technical-Cooperation/Working-Groups/Emergency-Preparedness. Accessed 31 Dec 2020

8. 2014 Workshop on Enhancing Critical Infrastructure and Resilience in the Asia-Pacific Region. https://www.apec-epwg.org/our-work/epwg-meetings-events/2014-workshop-on-enhancing-critical-infrastructure-and-resilience-in-the-asia-pacific-region/. Accessed 31 Dec 2020

9. Counter-Terrorism Working Group (CTWG). https://www.apec.org/Groups/SOM-Steering-Committee-on-Economic-and-Technical-Cooperation/Working-Groups/Counter-Terrorism. Accessed 31 Dec 2020

10. Transportation Working Group (TPTWG). https://www.apec.org/Groups/SOM-Steering-Committee-on-Economic-and-Technical-Cooperation/Working-Groups/Transportation. Accessed 31 Dec 2020

11. Finance Ministers Process (FMP). https://www.apec.org/Groups/Other-Groups/Finance-Ministers-Process. Accessed 31 Dec 2020

12. Disaster Risk Financing and Insurance (DRFI). https://www.apec-epwg.org/media/2647/14_epwg1_008a.pdf & https://www.financialprotectionforum.org/news/apec-finance-ministers-welcome-cooperation-with-drfip. Accessed 31 Dec 2020

13. Public Private Partnership Best Practices. https://www.apec.org/Publications/2016/04/Public-Private-Partnership-Best-Practices. Accessed 31 Dec 2020

14. APEC: Guidebook on SME Business Continuity Planning. https://www.apec.org/Publications/2013/09/Guidebook-on-SME-Business-Continuity-Planning. Accessed 31 Dec 2020

15. The International Organization for Standardization (ISO): https://www.iso.org/obp/ui/#iso:std:iso:22301:ed-2:v1:en. Accessed 31 Dec 2020

16. Small and medium enterprises (SMEs)/micro small and medium enterprises (MSMEs). https://data.oecd.org/entrepreneur/enterprises-by-business-size.htm. Accessed 31 Dec 2020

17. Lee, Y., Watanabe, K., Li, W.-S.: Enhancing Regional Disaster Resilient Trade and Investment ? Business Continuity Management (2019). https://link.springer.com/chapter/https://doi.org/10.1007/978-3-030-18293-9_10. Accessed 31 Dec 2020

18. APEC Emergency Preparedness Capacity Building Center (EPCC). https://www.apec-epwg.org/media/2372/8331464076020fe73446e8a421899c22.pdf. Accessed 31 Dec 2020

19. Nagoya Institute of Technology (NiTech) home page (2019). https://www.nitech.ac.jp/eng/. Accessed 31 Dec 2020

20. APEC Summit on Resilience and Capacity Building. https://www.apec-epcc.org/news/news-releases/connecting-the-business-dots-to-a-bcm-based-supply-chain/. Accessed 31 Dec 2020

21. COVID-19. https://en.wikipedia.org/wiki/COVID-19_pandemic. Accessed 31 Dec 20120

22. United Nations (UN): The 2019 UN report on Sustainable Development Goals (SDGs), UN: https://unstats.un.org/sdgs/report/2019/. Accessed 31 Dec 2020

23. APEC EPCC: Building Resilient Community Through Plant Back Better Initiative ? Guiding Principles and Best Practices (2020). https://link.springer.com/chapter/https://doi.org/10.1007/978-3-030-48939-7_9. Acessted 31 Dec 2020

24. NCDR homepage. https://ncdr.nat.gov.tw/oriNCDR/home.aspx?WebSiteID=873f5b27-b86d-4d5c-a356-c369768bffe9. Accessed 31 Dec 2020

25. Taiwan New South-bound Policy. https://nspp.mofa.gov.tw/nsppe/. Accessed 31 Dec 2020

26. PBB project and activities. https://www.apec-epcc.org/programs-and-events/programs/plant-back-better-pbb/. Accessed 31 Dec 2020

27. APEC EPCC: Plant-Back-Better Toolkit (2020). https://www.apec.org/Publications/2020/04/Plant-Back-Better-Toolkit. Accessed 31 Dec 2020

28. World Bank. https://www.worldbank.org/en/news/press-release/2020/06/08/covid-19-to-plunge-global-economy-into-worst-recession-since-world-war-ii. Accessed 31 Dec 2020

29. International Labour Organization and World Food Program: https://www.wfp.org/news/covid-19-will-double-number-people-facing-food-crises-unless-swift-action-taken. Accessed 31 Dec 2020

30. United Nations: least developed countries (LDCs). https://www.un.org/development/desa/dpad/wp-content/uploads/sites/45/publication/ldc_list.pdf. Accessed 31 Dec 2020
31. World Bank. https://blogs.worldbank.org/psd/circular-economy-can-support-covid-19-response-and-build-resilience. Accessed 31 Dec 2020
32. World Food Program. https://www.wfp.org/resilience-building. Accessed 31 Dec 2020
33. Tzu Chi Foundation Homepage. http://www.tzuchi.org. Accessed 31 Dec 2020
34. 2020ITW. https://ncdr.nat.gov.tw/oriNCDR/Conference_workshop_Content.aspx?WebSiteID=873f5b27-b86d-4d5c-a356-c369768bffe9&ID=46&SubID=62&ItemID=0&TypeID=0&keyword=&ConferenceID=35 . Accessed 31 Dec 2020
35. The Shihtan Fault movement. https://en.wikipedia.org/wiki/1935_Shinchiku-Taich?_earthquake#Earthquake. Accessed 31 Dec 2020
36. HsinChu Science Park homepage. https://www.most.gov.tw/folksonomy/list/a365d856-3247-4937-8c76-0488f488d6ee?l=en. Accessed 31 Dec 2020
37. Taiwan Semiconductor Manufacturing Company Limited (TSMC) homepage. https://www.tsmc.com/english. Accessed 31 Dec 2020
38. Geographic Information System (GIS). https://www.usgs.gov/faqs/what-a-geographic-information-system-gis?qt-news_science_products=0#qt-news_science_products. Accessed 31 Dec 2020
39. Decision-making Support System for Emergency Operation Center (EOCDSS) homepage. https://eocdss.ncdr.nat.gov.tw/web/. Accessed 31 Dec 2020
40. United Nations. https://www.humanitarianresponse.info/en/coordination/clusters/what-cluster-approach. Accessed 31 Dec 2020
41. Information and Communication Technology (ICT). https://www.oecd-ilibrary.org/science-and-technology/information-and-communication-technology-ict/indicator-group/english_04df17c2-en. Accessed 31 Dec 2020
42. United Nations Office for the Coordination of Humanitarian Affairs (UN OCHA). https://www.unocha.org/. Accessed 31 Dec 2020
43. Number of mobile cellular subscriptions in Taiwan from 2000 to 2019. https://www.statista.com/statistics/501135/number-of-mobile-cellular-subscriptions-in-taiwan/. Accessed 31 Dec 2020
44. Lee, Y., Watanabe, K., Li, W.-S.: Enhancing Regional Digital Preparedness on Natural Hazards to Safeguard Business Resilience in the Asia-Pacific (2017). https://www.springerprofessional.de/en/enhancing-regional-digital-preparedness-on-natural-hazards-to-sa/15258690. Accessed 31 Dec 2020
45. Lee, Y., Watanabe, K., Li, W.-S.: Public private partnership operational model-a conceptual study on implementing science-evidence-based integrated risk management at regional level. J. Disaster Res. **14**(4), 667?677 (2019). https://www.fujipress.jp/jdr/dr/dsstr001400040667/. Accessed 31 Dec 2020
46. United Nations: WASH. https://sustainabledevelopment.un.org/partnership/?p=1665. Accessed 31 Dec 2020
47. Lee, Y: Enhancing Disaster Resilience Through Public Private Partnership: from Collaborations, Integration to Practices for Business Continuity. (2019). https://nitech.repo.nii.ac.jp/?action=repository_action_common_download&item_id=6467&item_no=1&attribute_id=13&file_no=2. Accessed 31 Dec 2020
48. Wi-Fi. https://en.wikipedia.org/wiki/Wi-Fi. Accessed 31 Dec 2020
49. Cloud Computing. https://en.wikipedia.org/wiki/Cloud_computing. Accessed 31 Dec 2020
50. OECD. https://www.oecd.org/economy/growth/35554787.pdf. Accessed 31 Dec 2020
51. APEC Cross Border Privacy Rules (CBPR). http://cbprs.org/. Accessed 31 Dec 2020
52. European Union - General Data Protection Regulation (GDPR). https://eur-lex.europa.eu/legal-content/EN/TXT/PDF/?uri=CELEX:32016R0679. Accessed 31 Dec 2020
53. Non-governmental organizations (NGOs). https://research.un.org/en/ngo. Accessed 31 Dec 2020

Towards Single Value Coordinate System (SVCS) for Earthquake Forecasting Using Single Layer Hierarchical Graph Neuron (SLHGN)

Benny Benyamin Nasution$^{(\boxtimes)}$, Rahmat Widia Sembiring, Indra Siregar, Ermyna Seri, and Rina Walmiaty Mardi

Politeknik Negeri Medan, Jalan Almamater 1, Kampus USU, Medan 20155, Indonesia
bennynasution@polmed.ac.id

Abstract. The current coordinate system has been the major challenge for the development of earthquake forecasting technology using Single Layer Hierarchical Graph Neuron (SLHGN). First, the accuracy of the longitude value is not distributed equally, and the accuracy gets worse towards the poles. Second, the distance of the same longitude difference varies following the difference of the latitude values. The extreme one is again on the poles, where the longitude value becomes unity. Third, there is no way to have a coordinate of an area. As an alternative the Single Value Coordinate System (SVCS) has been scrutinized and elaborated. The coordinate system treats every area on the earth equally on the equator until the poles. It means that the accuracy is everywhere the same and the calculation of a distance and an area is not dependent on the location (e.g. near the equator, near the North Pole, etc.). At this stage the algorithm for measuring a distance and the conversion from and to the current coordinate system are available. The distance between two locations is directly discovered from the value of the coordinate itself. The coordinate system is fundamentally dedicated to pinpoint an area, not a point. The smaller an area is the more precise the location will be. Using the SVCS, the characteristic of the earth as a spherical shape suits the SLHGN architecture.

Keywords: Earthquake forecasting · Single Layer Hierarchical Graph Neuron (SLHGN) · Single Value Coordinate System (SVCS) · Hierarchical Graph Neuron (HGN)

1 Introduction

The issues related to forecasting an earthquake are not only about when it will occur and how big the tremor will be, but also about where the epicenter will be and which area and how big the area will suffer from it. The research in earthquake forecasting using Single Layer Hierarchical Graph Neuron (SLHGN) that has been started since two years ago has also been working on those challenging issues. Some promising results have shown that the SLHGN would come up with good results. Therefore, the SLHGN has

© IFIP International Federation for Information Processing 2021
Published by Springer Nature Switzerland AG 2021
Y. Murayama et al. (Eds.): ITDRR 2020, IFIP AICT 622, pp. 73–89, 2021.
https://doi.org/10.1007/978-3-030-81469-4_7

been improved to increase the accuracy of its results. Not only the accuracy of the time and the magnitude of the earthquake occurrences, the SLHGN would also attempt to identify the epi centrum and the areas of the impact about several hours prior to the incidence [1–3]. The description of HGN and mHGN can be found in [3–7].

The main barrier why the accuracy of SLHGN is not yet as good as expected, is that the SLHGN has used the current coordinate system that represents a coordinate through longitude and latitude values. Assuming that the earth is a perfect sphere, the value of the longitude would be more and more inaccurate towards the poles, since the longitude value becomes unity. Similarly, the distance between two points of different longitude values but the same latitude value, would become smaller when the latitude value is closer to a pole (90 degree of latitude value).

Furthermore, the ultimate problem that makes SLHGN ineffective when working on earthquake forecasting is that the current coordinate system does not provide a way to represent a coordinate of an area. Originally, an earth coordinate system was proposed for the first time in 1866 [8, 9]. The current coordinate system is only able to represent a coordinate of a point. However, it is very unlikely that an earthquake forecasting system could determine a point on earth where the upcoming earthquake would occur. In fact, most earthquake forecasting techniques measure and calculate the possibility of an earthquake that will hit an area, not a point on earth. Some other researchers have used a grid approach [10].

So, due to some unfortunate characteristics of the current coordinate system, SLHGN has lost some part of its accuracy while recognizing patterns of earthquakes. The first issue is that in most cases the surface of the earth will be transformed into a two dimensional diagram [11]. This transformation would produce two problems for SLHGN: 1) Although in reality they are close to each other, Japan and Hawaii look very far from each other, that is from the east to the west. 2) It is difficult to locate and allocate an observation area close to a pole, because there are a lot of "blank" areas in between.

The second issue is the measurement or the calculation of a distance of two coordinates. There are different formulas (at least two) for calculating a distance. The first one is the formula for the case when both coordinates are in the area around the equator. The other one is the one for the case when the coordinates are far from the equator. This issue raises a number of questions. First, how far from the equator is the formula still valid? Second, which formula will be used, if one coordinate is in the area of the equator and the other one is very far from the equator? Many researchers have tried to figure out all of those problems [11].

The third issue is the mapping of reported earthquake locations into SLHGN architecture. Since the SLHGN needs to be trained with historical data of previous earthquakes, the location of the epicenter and the affected areas need to be stored/taught in the SLHGN architecture. However, it is very complicated to calculate the transformation of longitude and latitude into something like Cartesian coordinates.

These three main issues have been the reason to develop something that can solve those problems, so that the SLHGN would work more accurately and be able to forecast an earthquake.

2   Some Issues When Using Current Coordinate System

The idea of developing the Single Value Coordinate System (SVCS) has been triggered by those above-mentioned issues: 1) inaccurate physical location, 2) inaccurate distance calculations, and 3) not suitable for SLHGN architecture. The next sections discuss them.

2.1   Inaccurate Physical Location

Physical location is important for SLHGN to forecast earthquakes. The location of an epicenter would be used to be fed to the SLHGN during both training phase and forecasting phase. Depending on the accuracy of the results required, there will be a lot of epicenter locations that need to be elaborated and composed. For instance, for 9X9 grid size 81 epicenter locations would be used within SLHGN architecture.

In order to know the coordinate of an earthquake, the location of an epicenter is normally first calculated through the data from at least four seismograph stations that have received the physical wave of an earthquake across the earth crust [12]. To calculate the longitude and the latitude values of the epicenter the data from the four seismograph stations will then be combined with the longitude and the latitude values of each seismograph station [13]. It is known that using a GPS device, the measurement error of coordinates received is around 10 m. Therefore, if there are at least four seismograph stations that have been observed, then there would be around 40 m of coordinate measurement error. Additionally, the physical wave of an earthquake would travel through the crust and sometimes also through the core of the earth. It is possible that the wave would be distorted or the path were swerved that would affect the traveling time and in the end affect the location accuracy [14, 15]. This is another contributing factor to the epicenter measurement error using the current coordinate system.

2.2   Inaccurate Distance Calculations

Another important part for SLHGN architecture is the calculation of a distance between two location points. During a training phase, earthquake data is taken from locations that have regular distances amongst them. Therefore, every distance must be calculated accurately in order to get accurate results. During the real-time earthquake monitoring phase, the data must also be taken from locations with regular distances. So, distance calculation is very important for having accurate results. Unfortunately, the current coordinate system does not offer a fixed formula for calculating a distance. There is a formula for the case when both location coordinates are in the area around the equator only. On the other hand, when the coordinates are far from the equator, another formula must be used. Such an uncertainty would make the distance calculation using the current coordinate system not applicable, because SLHGN will be used for all areas of the earth surface.

Another challenging issue related to distance calculation is the fact that it is not easy to find a targeted location (gained through a distance calculation) in which earthquakes have occurred. Ideally, the whole surface of the earth will be used as locations of the to-be-measured earthquake magnitude.

2.3 Not Suitable for SLHGN

Originally, the type of data that can be fed to the architecture of SLHGN could be one-dimensional, two-dimensional, three-dimensional, or other multi-dimensional data. In case of earthquake forecasting, all the stations of earthquake data are located on the surface of the earth. This is another challenge as the earth itself is a three-dimensional shape, the source of data is located only on the surface. It is true that such kind of data on the surface can be mapped into two-dimensional data [9], but the spherical nature of the earth would not allow that. The reason for this is—for instance—that, in a two-dimensional shape Tokyo and Honolulu would look far away separated, but in reality both are close to each other.

For the SLHGN, in order to allow the data to be fed the same way as the real situation of the data, a kind of spherical structure of data needs to be developed within SLHGN. With such a spherical surface all close neighbors will be treated as close neighbors, and vice versa all far neighbors will be treated as far neighbors. In principle, the SLHGN will treat a seismic location the same as where it is located on the earth. This concept is important when working with time-series pattern recognition. The observed earthquake patterns will be verified by the SLHGN in order to forecast dangerous earthquakes several hours earlier. Different to the previous approach using mHGN that observed local areas, the latest approach observes the whole area of the earth in real-time. In this approach, the accuracy is dependent on the number of faces SLHGN covers earth surface, either with: 32 faces, or 122 faces, or 482 faces, and so on. The details about the number of faces are described in the next section.

3 Single Value Coordinate System (SVCS)

As already discussed, the development of the Single Value Coordinate System (SVCS) is for solving those above-mentioned issues: 1) inaccurate physical location, 2) inaccurate distance calculations, and 3) not suitable for SLHGN architecture.

The inaccurate physical location and inaccurate distance calculation are fundamentally caused by the usage of the transformation of the physical units of seismic wave and electromagnetic wave to a distance. To avoid such a transformation, SVCS attempts to calculate the location and the distance through elaborating the earth surface directly. To this purpose, the first step is finding the composition of polygons that cover the earth surface, and then determine a polygon as the reference area to other polygons. The most suitable composition of the polygons are the following figure (see Fig. 1).

There are 12 pentagons and 20 hexagons (32 faces) that can evenly cover up a spherical shape of the earth. The following is the composition of the polygons represented in a two-dimensional way (see Fig. 2).

The polygons above are marked with letters from A till P, and from AA till PP. Note that hexagons A and AA are located opposite to each other on the surface of the ball. The same applies for B and BB, C and CC, and so forth. As the length of the edge of all hexagons is the same as the length of the edge of all pentagons, all hexagons and pentagons can be decomposed differently. The following figure shows it (see Fig. 3).

To increase the accuracy of locations and distances, every hexagon can be decomposed into 4 (four) smaller hexagons, and every pentagon can be decomposed into 1

Fig. 1. A Football with 12 pentagons and 20 hexagons

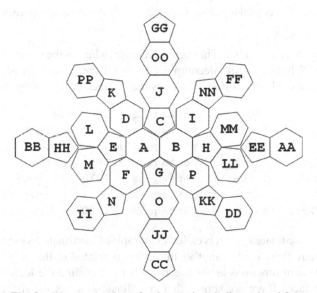

Fig. 2. A representation of polygons in a 2-dimensional form

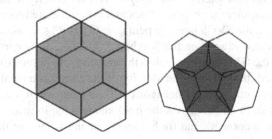

Fig. 3. A decomposition of hexagon and pentagon in different form

small pentagon and 2.5 (two point five) smaller hexagons. So, in total there will still be 12 (twelve) pentagons and 12 * 2.5 + 20 * 4 = 110 hexagons. The number of faces is now 110 hexagons + 12 pentagons = 122 faces. A piece of the ball after the decomposition is like the following (see Fig. 4).

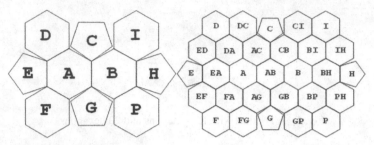

Fig. 4. The condition before (left) and after (right) the decomposition

It can be seen that the number of hexagons increases whereas the number of pentagons stays the same. When the same decomposition to all the pentagons and hexagon is implemented recursively, the following shows the changes of the polygons.

```
32        faces:  12 pentagons + 20 hexagons
122       faces:  12 pentagons + 110 hexagons
482       faces:  12 pentagons + 470 hexagons
1922      faces:  12 pentagons + 1910 hexagons
7682      faces:  12 pentagons + 7670 hexagons
30722     faces:  12 pentagons + 30710 hexagons
122882    faces:  12 pentagons + 122870 hexagons
```

The current coordinate system is called Geographic Coordinate Systems. Beside the coordinate system, there is also another thing that is related to the coordinate system called datum. Datum functions as the mechanism to determine the location of a place on the earth surface. There are some other coordinate systems for specific purposes, they are: geodetic coordinate system and plane coordinate system. All those coordinate systems have a general characteristic that they all rely on geometric calculations which require electronic equipment such as satellites and may generate inaccurate results.

On the other hand, the SVCS uses the pentagon G (see Fig. 2) as the reference area. This pentagon is located exactly on the South Pole and one of its corners points to the North Pole through the GMT mark, which is through the zero degree of longitude value. This corner is marked (big dot) and the identity of the corner is a small letter (a) on the pentagon G. All the pentagons and hexagons will be fixed where the mark is located. As already mentioned, in all pentagons the mark denotes the location of the "a" corner (out of a, b, c, d, and e corners), and for hexagons the mark denotes the location of the "f" corner (out of f, g, h, i, j, and k corners) (see Fig. 5).

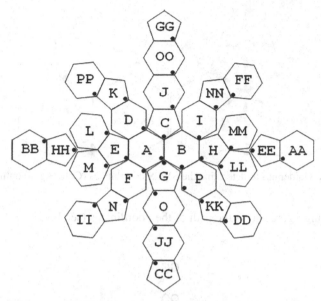

Fig. 5. A representation of polygons in a 2-dimensional form with marks

From the reference area (pentagon G), the SVCS-coordinate of each polygon will be determined and elaborated. The algorithm of the coordinate determination follows the following direction guidelines (see Fig. 6).

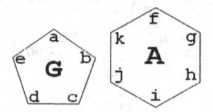

Fig. 6. All marked corners of pentagons and hexagons

In the Fig. 7, the red colors are the reference for determining the values of a coordinate along the side (edge) of polygons (1, 2, 3, 4, 5, 6), whereas the blue colors are the reference for determining the values of a coordinate into or out of a polygon (a, b, c, d, e, f, g, h, i, j, k). The following are two examples of SVCS-coordinates of the pentagon GG and the hexagon I.

```
GG-Coordinate is    0:a>1331221>a
I-Coordinate is     0:b>12>f
```

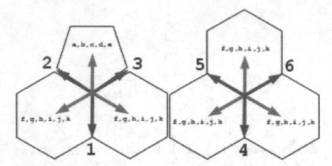

Fig. 7. Guidelines to determine the SVCS coordinates (Color figure online)

The following figure shows the path of the coordinates (see Fig. 8).

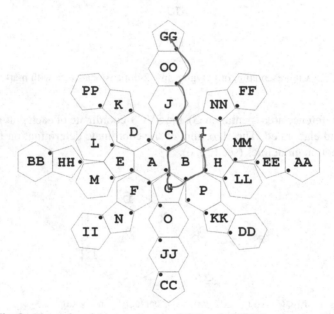

Fig. 8. The paths of the coordinates of GG and of I (Color figure online)

This is the description of those coordinates. As already mentioned, the pentagon G is the (starting) reference of all coordinates of the SVCS. The coordinate of GG starts with zero. The first number of a coordinate shows the level of the polygons. The zero means that the polygons have 32 faces. If the first number is one, the polygons have 122 faces, number two means 482 faces, and so on. After the first number of the coordinate is a delimiter (:), followed by the information about from which corner the coordinate is constructed. In the case of the coordinate of GG, from the pentagon G the path goes through the corner "a", followed by another delimiter (>). After the delimiter, the coordinate of GG shows that the values are determined by the direction of red arrows. Using the above references (red and blue arrows), the coordinate is constructed as: 1331221 followed by another delimiter (>) and finished with a letter either one of these: a, b, c, d, and e corners. In the case of the coordinate of GG, the path goes through the corner "a" of the pentagon GG. Note that values 4, 5, and 6 will only appear in coordinates on level 1 and higher.

Similar to the coordinate of GG, the coordinate of I starts with zero. It means that the polygons have 32 faces. After the first number of the coordinate is a delimiter (:), followed by a letter b, meaning that the path goes through the corner "b", then followed by another delimiter (>). After the delimiter, the coordinate of I shows that the coordinate is constructed as: 12 followed by another delimiter (>) and finished with a letter either one of these: f, g, h, i, j, k. In the case of the coordinate of I, the path goes through the corner "f" of the hexagon I.

The following (see Fig. 9) are the coordinates of all 32 polygons including their distances measured from the pentagon G. Note the s denotes the side (edge) length of a pentagon.

A	→	0:a>>f	: Distance = a + f = 0.85 * s + s = 1.85 * s;
B	→	0:b>>f	: Distance = b + f = 0.85 * s + s = 1.85 * s;
C	→	0:a>1>a	: Distance = a + s + a = 2 * 0.85 * s + s = 2.7 * s;
D	→	0:a>12>f	: Distance = a + 2 * s + f = 0.85 * s + 3 * s = 3.85 * s;
E	→	0:e>1>a	: Distance = e + s + a = 2 * 0.85 * s + s = 2.7 * s;
F	→	0:e>>f	: Distance = e + f = 0.85 * s + s = 1.85 * s;
G	→	0:>>	: Distance = 0
H	→	0:b>1>a	: Distance = b + s + a = 2 * 0.85 * s + s = 2.7 * s;
I	→	0:b>12>f	: Distance = b + 2 * s + f = 0.85 * s + 3 * s = 3.85 * s;
J	→	0:a>133>f	: Distance = a + 3 * s + f = 0.85 * s + 4 * s = 4.85 * s;
K	→	0:a>1221>a	: Distance = a + 4 * s + a = 2 * 0.85 * s + 4 * s = 5.7 * s;
L	→	0:e>133>f	: Distance = e + 3 * s + f = 0.85 * s + 4 * s = 4.85 * s;
M	→	0:e>12>f	: Distance = e + 2 * s + f = 0.85 * s + 3 * s = 3.85 * s;
N	→	0:d>1>a	: Distance = d + s + a = 2 * 0.85 * s + s = 2.7 * s;
O	→	0:d>>f	: Distance = d + f = 0.85 * s + s = 1.85 * s;
P	→	0:c>>f	: Distance = c + f = 0.85 * s + s = 1.85 * s;
AA	→	0:b>133133>f	: Distance = b + 6 * s + f = 0.85 * s + 7 * s = 7.85 * s;
BB	→	0:e>122133>f	: Distance = e + 6 * s + f = 0.85 * s + 7 * s = 7.85 * s;
CC	→	0:d>1221>a	: Distance = d + 4 * s + a = 2 * 0.85 * s + 4 * s = 5.7 * s;
DD	→	0:c>133>f	: Distance = c + 3 * s + f = 0.85 * s + 4 * s = 4.85 * s;
EE	→	0:b>1331>a	: Distance = b + 4 * s + a = 2 * 0.85 * s + 4 * s = 5.7 * s;
FF	→	0:b>12213>f	: Distance = b + 5 * s + f = 0.85 * s + 6 * s = 6.85 * s;
GG	→	0:a>1331221>a	: Distance = a + 7 * s + a = 2 * 0.85 * s + 7 * s = 8.7 * s;
HH	→	0:e>1221>a	: Distance = e + 4 * s + a = 2 * 0.85 * s + 4 * s = 5.7 * s;
II	→	0:d>133>f	: Distance = d + 3 * s + f = 0.85 * s + 4 * s = 4.85 * s;
JJ	→	0:d>12>f	: Distance = d + 2 * s + f = 0.85 * s + 3 * s = 3.85 * s;
KK	→	0:c>1>a	: Distance = c + s + a = 2 * 0.85 * s + s = 2.7 * s;
LL	→	0:b>13>f	: Distance = b + 2 * s + f = 0.85 * s + 3 * s = 3.85 * s;
MM	→	0:b>133>f	: Distance = b + 3 * s + f = 0.85 * s + 4 * s = 4.85 * s;
NN	→	0:b>1221>a	: Distance = b + 4 * s + a = 2 * 0.85 * s + 4 * s = 5.7 * s;
OO	→	0:a>13312>f	: Distance = a + 5 * s + f = 0.85 * s + 6 * s = 6.85 * s;
PP	→	0:e>13312>f	: Distance = e + 5 * s + f = 0.85 * s + 6 * s = 6.85 * s;

Fig. 9. The coordinates of all 32 polygons and their distances (s is the side length)

The following (see Fig. 10) are the coordinates of level 0 and its corresponding level 1 of 10 polygons including their distances measured from the pentagon G.

A	→ 0:a>>f	: Distance = a + f = 0.85 * s + s = 1.85 * s;
A	→ 1:a>12>f	: Distance = a + 2 * s + f = 0.85 * s + 3 * s = 3.85 * s;
B	→ 0:b>>f	: Distance = b + f = 0.85 * s + s = 1.85 * s;
B	→ 1:b>12>f	: Distance = b + 2 * s + f = 0.85 * s + 3 * s = 3.85 * s;
C	→ 0:a>1>a	: Distance = a + s + a = 2 * 0.85 * s + s = 2.7 * s;
C	→ 1:a>16556>a	: Distance = a + 5 * s + a = 2 * 0.85 * s + 5 * s = 6.7 * s;
D	→ 0:a>12>f	: Distance = a + 2 * s + f = 0.85 * s + 3 * s = 3.85 * s;
D	→ 1:a>156565>f	: Distance = a + 6 * s + f = 0.85 * s + 7 * s = 7.85 * s;
E	→ 0:e>1>a	: Distance = e + s + a = 2 * 0.85 * s + s = 2.7 * s;
E	→ 1:e>16556>a	: Distance = e + 5 * s + a = 2 * 0.85 * s + 5 * s = 6.7 * s;;
F	→ 0:e>>f	: Distance = e + f = 0.85 * s + s = 1.85 * s;
F	→ 1:e>12>f	: Distance = e + 2 * s + f = 0.85 * s + 3 * s = 3.85 * s;
G	→ 0:>>	: Distance = 0
G	→ 1:>>	: Distance = 0
H	→ 0:b>1>a	: Distance = b + s + a = 2 * 0.85 * s + s = 2.7 * s;
H	→ 1:b>16556>a	: Distance = b + 5 * s + a = 2 * 0.85 * s + 5 * s = 6.7 * s;
I	→ 0:b>12>f	: Distance = b + 2 * s + f = 0.85 * s + 3 * s = 3.85 * s;
I	→ 1:b>156565>f	: Distance = b + + 6 * s + f = 0.85 * s + 7 * s = 7.85 * s;
P	→ 0:c>>f	: Distance = c + f = 0.85 * s + s = 1.85 * s;
P	→ 1:c>12>f	: Distance = c + 2 * s + f = 0.85 * s + 3 * s = 3.85 * s;

Fig. 10. Ten coordinates in both level 0 and level 1

4   Characteristics of SVCS

In this section, the characteristics of SVCS will be discussed. These characteristics are important for finding the direction from an area to another area, finding the shortest path between areas, and converting a SVCS coordinate from and to a current coordinate system.

4.1   Reversed Coordinates

The SVCS is not only for representing the location of an area, either a pentagon or a hexagon, it is also for representing a direction from the origin to the destination and its distance. Therefore, the SVCS is reversible. Such a characteristic is important for future usages, such as finding a reversed direction, calculating a distance of a complex path, and also finding the shortest path between two areas.

The following (see Fig. 11) are the rules to make a reversed direction of a coordinate. Reversed 1 (!1) is 1, reversed 2 (!2) is 3, reversed 3 (!3) is 2, and reversed 4 (!4) is 4. To get a reversed 5 or reversed 6 it is determined by the previous direction. If the previous direction is 5, then the reversed 5 or reversed 6 is 6, and if the previous direction is 6, then the reversed 5 or reversed 6 is 5. The following shows some examples of coordinates and the corresponding reversed coordinates (denoted by the exclamation mark).

```
J      →  0:a>133>f
!J     →  0:f>221>a
K      →  0:a>1221>a
!K     →  0:a>1331>a
FF     →  0:b>12213>f
!FF    →  0:f>21331>b
BB     →  0:e>122133>f
!BB    →  0:f>221331>e
GG     →  0:a>1331221>a
!GG    →  0:a>1331221>a
```

Fig. 11. Some coordinates and their corresponding reversed directions

4.2 Shorten the Sequence of a Direction

As also applies in other coordinate systems, there are some circumstances that the sequence of a direction can be shorten. Through such a characteristic, there is a possibility that within the SVCS the shortest path of a direction can be found. Additionally, the shortest path is also important to disclose the distance between two areas.

Opposite Direction. The following are rules and samples of shortening the sequence of a direction through opposite directions.

- $23 = !33 = 2!2 =$ empty, for example 0:b>131233>c can be shorten to 0:b>1313>c
- $233 = 3$, or $223 = 2$
- $32 = !22 = 3!3 =$ empty, for example 0:b>131322>c can be shorten to 0:b>1312>c
- $322 = 2$, or $332 = 3$
- $11 = 1!1 = !11 =$ empty, for example 0:b>1112133>c can be shorten to 0:b>12133>c
- $44 = 4!4 = !44 =$ empty, this rule applies for level of polygons>0

Alternative Direction. The following are rules and samples of shortening the sequence of a direction through alternative directions.

- $333 = 22$, for example 0:b>13331>c can be shorten to 0:b>1221>c
- $222 = 33$, for example 0:b>12221>c can be shorten to 0:b>1331>c
- $3333 = 223 = 322 = 2$, for example 0:b>133331>c can be shorten to 0:b>121>c
- $2222 = 233 = 332 = 3$, for example 0:b>122221>c can be shorten to 0:b>131>c
- $33333 = 3322 = 32 =$ empty, for example 0:b>1333333>c can be shorten to 0:b>13>c
- $33333 = 2233 = 23 =$ empty

- 22222 = 3322 = 32 = empty, for example 0:b>3122222>c can be shorten to 0:b>31>c
- 22222 = 2233 = 23 = empty
- 1212 = 31, or 2121 = 13
- 3131 = 12, or 1313 = 21

From a Pentagon Out or to a Pentagon in. The following are rules and samples of shortening the sequence of a direction that goes from a pentagon out or to a pentagon in.

- 0:a>131 = 0:b>12, the same way rules for sides: b, c, d, and e
- 0:a>121 = 0:e>13, the same way rules for sides: b, c, d, and e
- 131>a = 21>e, the same way rules for sides: b, c, d, and e
- 121>a = 31>b, the same way rules for sides: b, c, d, and e

From a Hexagon out or to a Hexagon in. The following are rules and samples of shortening the sequence of a direction that goes from a hexagon out or to a hexagon in.

- 0:f>313 = 0:g>21, the same way rules for sides: g, h, i, j, and k
- 0:f>212 = 0:k>31, the same way rules for sides: g, h, i, j, and k
- 0:f>222 = 0:g>3, the same way rules for sides: g, h, i, j, and k
- 0:f>333 = 0:k>2, the same way rules for sides: g, h, i, j, and k
- 313>f = 12>k, the same way rules for sides: g, h, i, j, and k
- 212>f = 13>g, the same way rules for sides: g, h, i, j, and k
- 222>f = 3>k, the same way rules for sides: g, h, i, j, and k
- 333>f = 2>g, the same way rules for sides: g, h, i, j, and k

4.3 Sequence Modification

There are some other circumstances that the sequence of a direction that is built over a pentagon or over a hexagon can be modified. Through such a characteristic, there is another possibility that within the SVCS the shortest path of a direction can be found.

Over a Pentagon. The following are rules and samples of the modification of the sequence of a direction that is built over a pentagon.

- 1>ae>1 = 131, the same way rules for: ba, cb, dc, and ed
- 1>ad>1 = 1331, the same way rules for: be, ca, db, and ec
- 1>ac>1 = 1221, the same way rules for: bd, ce, da, and eb

- 1>ab>1 = 121, the same way rules for: bc, cd, de, and ea

Over a Hexagon. The following are rules and samples of the modification of the sequence of a direction that is built over a hexagon.

- 3>fg>3 = 333, the same way rules for: gh, hi, ij, jk, and kf
- 3>fh>2 = 3312, the same way rules for: gi, hj, ik, jf, and kg
- 3>fi>3 = 33133 or 31213, the same way rules for: gj, hk, if, jg, and kh
- 3>fj>2 = 3122, the same way rules for: gk, hf, ig, jh, and ki
- 3>fk>3 = 313, the same way rules for: gf, hg, ih, ji, and kj
- 2>fg>2 = 212, the same way rules for: gh, hi, ij, jk, and kf
- 2>fh>3 = 2133, the same way rules for: gi, hj, ik, jf, and kg
- 2>fi>2 = 21312 or 22122, the same way rules for: gj, hk, if, jg, and kh
- 2>fj>3 = 2213, the same way rules for: gk, hf, ig, jh, and ki
- 2>fk>2 = 222, the same way rules for: gf, hg, ih, ji, and kj

4.4 Samples of Directions

The following are two examples of directions (from K to M and from M to K) that have been shortened using above rules. Note that the coordinate of K is actually the direction from G to K and similarly the coordinate of M is actually the direction from G to M (see Fig. 12 and Fig. 13).

```
The coordinate of K, or GK is 0:a>1221>a
The coordinate of M, of GM is 0:e>12>f

The direction of KM =?
KM = KG + GM = !K + M
KM = 0:a>1331>ae>12>f
KM = 0:a>1331312>f
KM = 0:a>13122>f
KM = 0:b>1222>f
KM = 0:b>13>k

The direction of MK =?
MK = MG + GK = !M + K
MK = 0:f>31>ea>1221>a
MK = 0:f>3121221>a
MK = 0:f>33121>a
MK = 0:f>3331>b
MK = 0:k>21>b
```

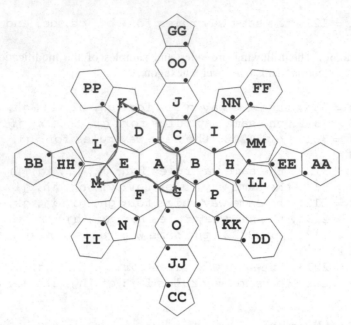

Fig. 12. The paths of the direction KG + GM = KM = 0:b > 13 > k

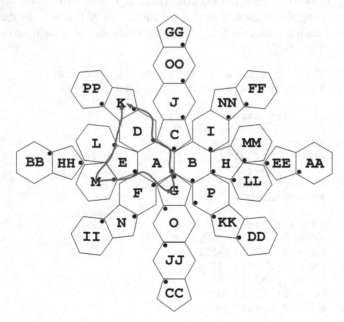

Fig. 13. The paths of the direction MG + GK = MK = 0:k > 21 > b

4.5 Coordinate Conversion

As all the 21 pentagons and 20 hexagons are so composed that they are symmetrical and regularly distributed, for coordinate conversion purposes it is adequate to only focus on a piece of those polygons, that is 5% of the surface. Through this piece of surface, all the areas on the earth surface can be represented. For discussion purposes this piece is named Half Sector (HS). So there will be 20 HSs in total.

The index of HS in the Southern Hemisphere will be between 0 and 9, whereas the one on the Northern Hemisphere will be between 10 and 19. For a location with a longitude value between 0.0 and 35.999 the coordinate will be within HS with index of 0 or 10, for longitude value between 36.0 and 71.999 the coordinate will be within HS with index of 1 or 11, and so on. Note that the HS with index 0 is the same as the HS with index 2, 4, 6, and 8. Similarly, the HS with index 1 is the same as the HS with index 3, 5, 7, and 9. Additionally, the HS with index 1 is actually the vertically mirrored HS with index 0, and the HS with index 10 is actually the 180 degree rotated HS with index 0. Furthermore, within a HS there are subarea indexes between 0 and 4.

As the side borders of a HS can be formulated as a collection of linear lines, as well as the borders within the HS, the coordinate conversion calculation requires linear equations only. So, the two values of longitude and latitude will determine in which HS and in which subarea index the coordinate is located. The following is the image of the HS with index 0 (see Fig. 14).

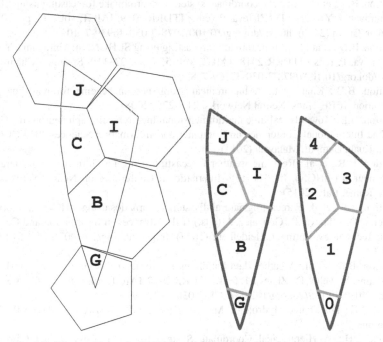

Fig. 14. The position of a Half Sector (HS) index 0 and its subarea indexes

5 Conclusion

The research on a more suitable coordinate system and the development of Single Value Coordinate System (SVCS) has revealed that the issues within the current coordinate system have been scrutinized and solved. The inaccurate physical location is handled through the regular and symmetric structure of polygons on the earth surface. It means that the accuracy is everywhere the same and the calculation of a distance and an area is not dependent on the location (e.g. near the equator, near the North Pole, etc.). Related to inaccurate distance calculation the SVCS offers a single value of a coordinate and using a direction and shortest path approach. The suitability of the SVCS is solved through utilizing the original shape of the earth, which is a spheroid. With such an approach, the hierarchical characteristic of SLHGN would be maintained. At this stage of the SVCS development, the algorithm for measuring a distance and the conversion from and to the current coordinate system have been made available. The SVCS coordinate system has successfully been developed to work on the coordinate and the direction of an area, not a point. The smaller an area is the more precise the coordinate and the direction will be. When SVCS is completed, the characteristic of the earth as a spherical shape will suit the SLHGN architecture.

References

1. Nasution, B.B., et al.: An earth coordinate system for earthquake forecasting using SLHGN. In: Murayama, Y., Velev, D., Zlateva, P. (eds.) ITDRR 2019. IAICT, vol. 575, pp. 107–118. Springer, Cham (2020). https://doi.org/10.1007/978-3-030-48939-7_10
2. Nasution, B.B., et al.: Real-time tornado forecasting using SLHGN. In: Murayama, Y., Velev, D., Zlateva, P. (eds.) ITDRR 2018. IAICT, vol. 550, pp. 97–119. Springer, Cham (2019). https://doi.org/10.1007/978-3-030-32169-7_8
3. Nasution, B.B., Khan, A.I.: A hierarchical graph neuron scheme for real-time pattern recognition. IEEE Trans. Neural Networks, 212–229 (2008)
4. Nasution, B.B.: Towards real time multidimensional hierarchical graph neuron (mHGN). In: The 2nd International Conference on Computer and Information Sciences 2014 (ICCOINS 2014), Kuala Lumpur, Malaysia (2014)
5. Nasution, B.B., et al.: Realtime weather forecasting using multidimenssional hierarchical graph neuron (mHGN). In: The 16th International Conference on Neural Networks (NN 2015), Rome, Italy (2015)
6. Nasution, B.B., et al.: Forecasting natural disasters of tornados using mHGN. In: Murayama, Y., Velev, D., Zlateva, P., Gonzalez, J. (eds.) IFIP Advances in Information and Communication Technology. Springer, Heidelberg (2017). https://doi.org/10.1007/978-3-319-68486-4_13
7. Nasution, B.B., et al.: Weather data handlings for tornado recognition using mHGN. In: Murayama, Y., Velev, D., Zlateva, P. (eds.) ITDRR 2017. IAICT, vol. 516, pp. 36–54. Springer, Cham (2019). https://doi.org/10.1007/978-3-030-18293-9_5
8. VIeux, B.E.: Distributed Hydrologic Modeling using GIS. Kluwer Academic Publishers, Oklahoma (2001)
9. Dutton, G.H.: A Hierarchical Coordinate System for Geoprocessing and Cartography. Springer, Heidelberg (1999). https://doi.org/10.1007/BFb0011617
10. Wheatley, D., Gillings, M.: Spatial Technology and Archaeology: The Archaeological Applications of GIS. Taylor & Francis, New York (2002)

11. Harvey, F.: A primer of GIS: Fundamental Geographic and Cartographic. The Guilford Press, New York (2008)
12. Dehant, V., Creager, K., Karato, S.-I., Zatman, S.: Earth's Core: Dynamics, Structure. Rotation. AmericanGeophysical Union, Washington, DC (2003)
13. Einstein, A.: Relativity: The Special and General Theory. Methuen & Co Ltd. (2002)
14. Lambeck, K.: The Earth's Variable Rotation: Geophysical Causes and Consequences. Combridge University Press, New York (2005)
15. Tipler, P.A., Llewellyn, R.A.: Modern Physics. W. H. Freeman and Company, Basingstoke (2012)

The Muddy Practice of Social Media Crowdsourcing in Bandung City

Muhammad Akram Mansyur[1,2]([✉]), V. M. F. Homburg[2], and J. F. M. Koppenjan[2]

[1] University of Gunadarma, Depok 16424, Indonesia
[2] Erasmus University Rotterdam, 3062 PA Rotterdam, The Netherlands
mansyur@ihs.nl

Abstract. This interpretative case study investigates social media use during three urban floods in Bandung City, Indonesia. The results suggest that social media is widely used by citizens as an alternative means of emergency communication. As for the government, although the implementation of social media in Bandung City Government can be said to be a pioneer in comparison to other city governments, and Bandung governments units were required to implement social media, social media played a very limited role in crisis communication between citizens and government. Reasons for this include fragility in adoption of technology, lack of institutionalization of technology, and a mutual distrust between government and citizens, where citizens prefer to use traditional media to issue complaints and report status updates rather than government agencies. This empirical finding was found based on a multimethod study, using interview data, social media scraping, document analysis and field study as sources of data.

Keywords: Social media · Twitter · Smart city · Government's response · Floods

1 Introduction

Since about a decade, academic and professional literatures have emphasized the notion of the smart city: a metaphor for data sharing over technological infrastructures for the purpose of enabling sustainability, well-being and quality of life for residents living in urban areas. Availability of data such as emission levels, traffic congestion and energy consumption allows residents, policy makers and politicians to develop and/or implement smart, preferably real-time responses to problems residents are faced with [1, 2]. The metaphor of a smart city can be interpreted in various ways with various perspectives. One of those perspectives is that increased availability of data allows for more rationalized decision-making and the use of big data algorithms to support or even automate some aspects of decision making, which is exemplified in the rising popularity of all kinds of dashboards (either or not located in cockpit-like headquarters) with which key measures of relevant urban developments are visualized [3]. A second perspective is that it is increasingly possible to 'crowdsource' relevant development using sensors that are owned by a variety of resident groups, allowing for a much more inclusive form

Y. Murayama et al. (Eds.): ITDRR 2020, IFIP AICT 622, pp. 90–101, 2021.
https://doi.org/10.1007/978-3-030-81469-4_8

of city governance; for instance, residents can use mobile devices to capture and share images of defunct public infrastructures, thereby contributing to a more citizen-centric form of urban governance.

Recently, disaster management practices were discussed in the context of the smart city metaphor [5, 6], thus highlighting the role of networks linking all kinds of sensors (including residents' mobile social media applications) and dashboards for the purposes of disaster recovery. This paper focuses on the Indonesian city of Bandung's responses to seasonal floods, and especially on the implementation and use of social media channels as a medium to inform the disaster management operations. The research question is: what role do social media play in the government response to Bandung floods, and how can this role be explained?

The answer to this research question necessitates an empirical, inductive approach with which actual practices are observed and analyzed from the ground level. The remainder of this paper, therefore, presents an analysis of both secondary (online) data scraped from Bandung-based social media accounts in which eyewitness accounts, questions and requests for assistance were communicated, as well as primary interviews data, and data gathered during fieldwork conducted by one of the researchers in Bandung.

2 Smart City, Disaster Management and Social Media

Scholars have addressed a broad variety of definitions of a smart city, without converging to a consensus yet. In ongoing debates, the focus is actually circling around technology innovation, underlining governance approaches in urban development, and the role of social capital herein [4]. This means that in addition to the integration of sophisticated information and communication technologies (ICTs), the role of society in their continuous interaction with various city actors including government is the key element of the concept of the smart city. Thus, one of the main foci of smart cities as a topic of study and debates is how to promote innovative governance network through smart urban collaboration [1].

In practice, smart cities are becoming a very common trend in urban development over the world, including in Indonesia. The level of resilience of smart cities has become the focus of scholars' research endeavors. One notable line of research is related to smart cities' capability of responding to unexpected predicaments such as natural disasters; smartness in urban governance is considered to have the potential to increase resilience. In the context of smart cities, however, various priorities exist and crisis response and resilience in practice competes with economic development, development of technological infrastructures, and the enhancement of multi-stakeholder partnerships [5].

A 'centralized intelligence'-connotation of the metaphor of a smart city highlights the use of, for instance, meteorological sensors, satellite imaging and computational models to adequately predict river flows and possible floods [6, 7], thereby potentially improving the ability of emergency services to effectively allocate scarce resources to disaster management operations. Researchers have also argued that citizens' spontaneous social media activities are a valuable source of data for emergency services [8], especially for purposes of mapping and rapid assessment [11–16], and some studies have proposed mathematical models that use social media messages as inputs to predict streamflow and flood conditions [9]. Social media is considered to be the accessible and promising real time sensing tool in facilitating people participation in smart city management [10].

However advanced existing model-based approaches to alleviate disasters may be, the crowdsourcing of data at the ground level (implying 'crowdsourced participation') results in many obstacles. Academic literatures have reported limited and/or unequal social media reach, officials' doubts about credibility of social media reports, resource constraints from the side of emergency services, and privacy and security issues as prime obstacles to the use of social media in disaster management [11–13].

In the analysis of social media adoption and use in the context of the Bandung City authorities' response to seasonal floods, we draw concepts selected from the literature mentioned above relevant to our investigation. These literatures sensitize us to various possible obstacles in various perspectives on the concept of 'smart cities'. However, a rigorous explanatory framework of relevant antecedents, conditions and/or implications of social media use for disaster management is lacking. Moreover, it is likely that such an explanation should take local contexts (including but not limited to a country's or city's development classification) into account. Therefore, we designed an interpretative case study to construct a set of patterns with which social media's role in disaster management practices are illuminated and theorized about.

3   Context and Methods

This study is an inductive, qualitative study of the role of social media in disaster management (particularly dealing with seasonal floods) in Bandung Indonesia, a city that has received recognition as one of the more advanced 'smart cities' in South-East Asia. Over half of Bandung's population aged above five years old is an active Internet user, and Bandung's city administration and internal management practices have revolved around e-government programs, e-budgeting and performance management systems for work units and civil servants.

Bandung has invested heavily in measures with which its city government can monitor all forms of city events and disruptions related to traffic, weather conditions, floods and crime. Under the leadership of its mayor Ridwan Kamil (mayor from 2013–2018), Bandung was the first Indonesian city to acquire a Command Centre, with which CCTV feeds and social media feeds were to be integrated in visualizations of traffic congestion and natural disasters. The Command Centre is supposed to be the main control center for all information that relevant and useful for decision-making.

The City of Bandung is subject to impact of seasonal floods, and this study focuses on events and developments during the floods of March 20, 2018, November 26, 2018, and January 13, 2019, all of which were extensively covered in national and local media and discussed on social media. All the floods were classified as flash floods, in the sense that floods were triggered by high rainfall intensities that caused water absorption areas and reservoirs not being able anymore to accommodate large volumes of water. These floods have been compounded by the condition of urban drainage, which has not been able to flow the water properly. This was exacerbated by garbage that had been piled up, and also by the inadequacy of the infrastructure. The people of Bandung often call this form of flood as "Cileuncang Flood."

This empirical study involves data triangulation, making use of interview transcripts, observations, relevant documents and social media accounts. Interviews have been conducted with officials or employees related to the social media services of Public Works Service, Health Service, and Fire Brigade and Disaster Mitigation Service. The other informants are officials and employees from Bandung Command Centre (BCC) under the Communication and Information Service, officials and volunteers at the Indonesian Red Cross (PMI) of Bandung City, managers of a local media, and representatives of (Quick Response Team) TCT Bandung.

For the study of social media, the GetOldTweets, a Python-based application developed by Github was used to capture contents and meta data (time of publishing, message interactions) of Twitter social media messages (from one week prior to the flood up to a week after the flood), using 'Banjir' and 'Bandung' as search terms. Additionally, Gephi was used to analyze and create network graphs.

From all private, NGO, government, mass media and individual officials' accounts studied, conversations were categorized in topics like complaints, suggestions / ideas, assistance requests, updates, and government response. This categorization is developed on the basis of the main topic of the Twitter posts, and the categorization's labeling is tailored in accordance with a number of previous studies [14–16].

Data analysis proceeded iteratively between examinations of data and development of explanatory patterns. Prior research briefly mentioned in section two informed the analysis but a variety of new insights were considered as the analysis continued. Inductive reasoning facilitated the discovery of new theoretical themes and patterns, which eventually coalesced into explanatory statements regarding the role of social media in the government response to Bandung floods. As the process of the analysis of data provided multiple occasions to review the plausibility and consistency of the logic underlying interpretations, the eventual findings and conclusions meet the established criteria for the credibility and authenticity of qualitative, inductive research.

4 Results and Discussion

4.1 Description of Social Media Use During Urban Floods

From the social media scraping, 540 Twitter conversations related to the 20 March 2018 flood were obtained, 484 conversations for the 26 November 2018 flood, and 434 conversations related to 13 January 2019 flood. Not all of these conversations were deemed relevant: some conversations were related to Bandung Regency not Bandung City, and some use the word 'flood' yet in a different context (such as in online marketing efforts for products or services that utilizes a conversation that is being talked about). After filtering, 1497 relevant conversations related to the 20 March 2018 flood were found, 406 related to floods on 26 November 2018, and 211 related to floods on 13 January 2019 (see Table 1).

Table 1. Issue and issuer classification

Flood events	Number of relevant Tweets	Topics	Type of issuer account				
			Private	NGO	Officials	Government	Media
20 March 2018	1497	Complaint	171	1	1	0	27
		Suggestion	137	6	5	2	126
		Request	43	5	0	0	12
		Update	378	23	2	14	418
		Government Response	145	7	2	27	96
26 November 2018	406	Complaint	76	0	0	0	2
		Suggestion	73	0	0	3	37
		Request	13	0	0	0	0
		Update	73	4	0	5	110
		Government Response	3	1	0	18	16
13 January 2019	211	Complaint	44	0	0	0	2
		Suggestion	23	1	1	0	6
		Request	5	0	0	0	0
		Update	70	2	1	2	40
		Government Response	4	1	2	2	16

In general, based on data scraping, a number of observations need elaboration. First, in all three events, updates are the most frequent type of messages, with instances being rain intensity, water inundation level, traffic jams, impacted locations, coverage of locations that were being assisted, and reports on the progress or results of flood responds. Arguably, citizens use social media to raise awareness among fellow citizens or relevant authorities. Traditional media accounts frequently retweet these kinds of messages, giving updates an even bigger outreach.

Second, especially on private accounts, complaints were relatively frequent, which included frustration and sarcasm that questioning the government's performance. It must be noted here that the three floods intersected with the elections for the position of governor of West Java, with Bandung's mayor Ridwan Kamil being one of the candidates.

Third, many 'suggestions' originated in NGOs and expert communities and relate to issues such as reduced water absorption capacity in the North Bandung area. The opinions covered by the media criticized politicians' promises to fix the North Bandung area problems.

Fourth, government accounts were likely to disseminate and document governments' response to floods, such as reports of Health Services' visits to affected areas and Public Works' activities related to fixing clogged waterways, and CCTV-sourced images of puddles, traffic congestion and strong winds. These posts were accompanied by safety messages to the public.

4.2 Themes and Patterns on Social Media Implementation and Use

Overall, the interpretation is that social media is used to a limited degree in relation to flood disaster management operations. Based on analysis of media reports, documents, interview transcripts and observations, a number of themes underlying this observation could be noted that – individually, as well as in combination – provide an explanation for the limited use of social media, which may be interpreted as a stark contrast with the 'smart city'-clamor that is so vividly present in Bandung city's policy talk. The themes are presented below.

Theme 1: Fragile Adoption of Bandung Command Center

During Ridwan Kamil's reign as mayor of Bandung, the Command Center was used for social media analysis. The city acquired funds and invested in a partnership with Mediawave, a third party supplier of social media text analysis and mapping software which enabled sentiment analyses as per geographic region.

A change of political leadership in 2018 led to a change of priorities and the more or less advanced analyses of social media were discontinued, making way for a much simpler analysis of social media activity with more informal reactions to signals on social media. Citizens' reports and complaints were from 2018 on only accepted when citizens explicitly tagged government's social media accounts. As one respondent who is associated with the Command Center stated:

> *"…So, the job of the operator is also to monitors Twitter, because there are also complaints delivered via Twitter. But there are people who cc (tag / mention), and some are not. For people who do marking/tagging (BCC Twitter account), we can simply see it in the notification. For those who don't, it's a hassle"* (Furqon, BCC)

From the data, it became clear that the adoption of the Command Center and implementation of the advances social media monitoring features bore heavily on the then-mayor's Smart City vision, with no efforts put into place to provide more sustainable funding and legal foundation for technology adoption. In this context this demonstrates the fragility of technology adoption were support for specific uses of technologies is heavily dependent on individual (and temporal) support by top leaders, with no institutionalization of that support in more enduring financial and coordinative organizational structures.

Theme 2: Lack of Government Social Media Presence

Although under the heading of Bandung's 'Smart City' initiative, social media were strongly promoted throughout various units, it is believed that the adoption of social media in agencies like Public Work Service, Social Service, Fire Brigade and Disaster

Mitigation unit including BCC evolved rather informally and organically, with agencies setting up and using accounts according to local customs, rules and practices. Arguably as a result, it proved hard for the public to find relevant information disseminated through these channels of communication, and Bandung city government accounts do not appear as popular accounts marked by the public in their posts during flood events. Contents related to recent updates and expressions of complaints about the impact of flood as the top two dominant topic categories were not directed to government social media accounts.

Table 2. Top-10 most mentioned accounts

20 March 2018			26 November 2018			13 January 2019		
Accounts	In-degree	Out-degree	Accounts	In-degree	Out-degree	Accounts	In-degree	Out-degree
youtube	44	0	prfmnews	11	5	ridwankamil	12	0
ridwankamil	17	0	ridwankamil	8	0	youtube	10	0
pembdg	12	0	youtube	7	0	polres_	8	0
humasbdg	10	7	infobdg	5	3	radioelshinta	4	6
bandung	7	0	dpukotabandung	5	7	prfmnews	4	1
prfmnews	6	2	dadanmartapura	4	2	elshintabandung	3	0
aagym	6	0	tct_	4	0	odedmd	2	0
bdg	5	0	lewatmana	3	9	na_nurularifin	2	0
dinsos_	5	0	chandra_p36	2	1	vimuthia	1	3
diskominfobdg	5	0	radioelshinta	2	2	tmcresbdg	1	1

The only government-owned Twitter account that is often targeted by the public was @dpukotabandung during the November 2018 floods, as one of the causes of the floods was a defunct water management infrastructure for which the Public Works Service unit behind @dpukatabandung was responsible.

Interestingly, other government accounts such as @pembdg, @humasbdg, which also appeared as frequently mentioned accounts, especially during the 2018 March flood, were not targeted with complaints, but these accounts were mostly mentioned by other government accounts, particularly village and sub-district office accounts. The accounts of village and sub-district report virtually the local activities of their respective areas to the @humasbdg and @pembdg accounts which belong to the public relations unit and the regional secretariat which are hierarchically higher agencies (see Fig. 1 and Fig. 2). It turns out that this social media behavior is part of the obligations of the Bandung city government organization, where village and sub-district are required to report their activities virtually, one of which is via social media that aim to promote transparency.

This obligation turns out to create the opportunity of dishonest practices in reporting government activities. This is because one of the performance assessments of the village and sub district governments, is assessed by their social media posts. The problem is not every time there are events that require a response from the village and sub-district in the form of activities that can be covered on social media. So that the practice of re-uploading photos of old activities is one of the dishonest strategies of social media managers to overcome their obligations.

Fig. 1. Closer look of @pembdg account in-degree network graph on 20 March 2018 flood

Fig. 2. Closer look of @humasbdg account in-degree network graph on 20 March 2018 flood

Theme 3: Traditional Media as Intermediaries

Above, it was concluded that although many Bandung municipal units did have social media accounts, their online presence was hardly noted by the general public. Instead, Bandung's residents used Twitter as an alternative means of emergency communication when urban floods occurred, and residents seemed to prefer mentioning local media accounts such as @prfmnews, @infobdg, @Radioelshinta, @elshintabandung (the local version of Elshinta), when they share their contents related to flood (see Table 2). This behavior is thought to be a catalyst for local media to grow as an intermediary for issuing complaints and sharing updates. Another factor that is also strongly suspected of driving this activity is the more dynamic social media approach performed by PRFMnews. Admin PRFMnews will reward a sign of recognition to every post that mentions them. In addition, if community posts are related to urban issues, the admin will try to crosscheck the fact by replying the posts and then forward the post by mentioning relevant government accounts through Twitter. This bridging hub role can be seen in the Twitter communication network, especially regarding the November 2018 floods as seen in Fig. 3.

PRFMNews emphasizes its efforts in bridging residents' concerns to relevant stakeholders and simultaneously building intimacy with the community:

"...now, Twitter penetration is faster than other social media accounts, why is that, because we deploy one person, every eight hours. So for social media (management), there are two shifts minimum. The focus is receiving all reports from citizens via Twitter, mentions, DMs (Direct messages) and etc. Later, we will follow up (the reports) with related agencies. That's what makes it (PRFM Twitter growth) so fast. ... Once we get the (floods) report we won't wait long. We directly forward to the relevant party such as Public works Service or Fire Brigade and Disaster Mitigation Service, since here in Bandung there is no regional disaster mitigation unit" (Rifki, PRFM News).

The social media managers for government accounts were aware of the popularity of this local media organization. So, when urban flood occurs, social media managers for government accounts selected the PRFM account as one of the most up-to-date sources of information. As previously described, this information monitoring was done manually, or in "lurking mode", which means the government social media managers monitors the developments of information and current situation through popular media Twitter accounts.

Fig. 3. Closer look of @PRFMNews account in-degree network graph on 26 November 2018 flood

Theme 4: Mutual Distrust Between Government and Citizens

In discussing social media's role in crisis communication, the issue of quality of information and trust therein has been given ample attention [17]. The volume (or even overload) of information exchange on social media has, in the case of Bandung, increased local government's concern about the emergence of fake news, with the Public Work Service unit seemingly being able to better cope with this phenomenon than other units. For instance, The Fire Brigade and Disaster Mitigation Service, which is the leading sector in disaster management in Bandung City, only uses social media according to its rather strict Standard Operating Procedures (SOPs) to distribute information, and chooses not to use social media as a source of relevant information as it fears being deceived by false information, as one of respondents from Fire Brigade and Disaster Mitigation stated:

> *"...Social media is quite helpful for us when dealing with disasters. But there are also negative sides like hoaxes, such as photos or videos that were shared not at the time of the incident... So, our SOP in carrying out disaster management is through telephone... Because, we can directly provide feedback with the reporter, it can be recorded, and the person in charge with the incidents report is clearer."*
> (Robby, Fire Brigade and Disaster Mitigation of Bandung City)

On the other hand, this study also found a tendency for members of local communities to distrust the government. One of the indications found in this study is the growing popularity of local media as a source for government information, rather than using official or semi-official government information. As explained above, the citizens prefer to submit their reports to local media in the hope that these reports can be amplified and put a pressure to the government. The lack of the government's ability to build interaction and engagement arguably negatively impacts citizens' trust in government. Various scholars have argued that the more often virtual interactions are developed, the higher citizens' trust in government could be [18, 19]. This shows the government's failure to manage social media, because, in an emergency situation, government institutions should ideally be the primary sources for people's hopes, because government agencies are considered to be the most resourceful institutions to deal with the impact of disasters [20].

5 Conclusion

This paper reported on the role of social media in the context of disaster management operations in one of South-East Asia's most prominent 'Smart City', Bandung. In the rhetoric of Smart City strategies, social media play an important role as a medium for crowdsourcing, which enables citizens to speak up in a more inclusive participative governance approach. The Bandung City Government seems to be trying to take advantage of people's knowledge of what the community actually experiences by implementing social media. The empirical data, gathered and analyzed using qualitative methods, demonstrate a limited role for social media, due to a number of reasons that in combination provide an explanation for the limited role of social media (1) fragile implementation of a Command Center that was heavily dependent on the temporal political leadership (2) diffusion of social media use throughout the City government's agencies and units, where use of social media is characterized by local enthusiasm, and driven by local rules, conventions and practices, but institutionalization is lagging behind, (3) emergence of traditional media that embrace social media to build intimate relationships with residents and act as alternative channels of communication between citizens and government units and (4) an overall lack of government officials' trust in the authenticity and sincerity of residents speaking up on social media about issues they are confronted with and a lack of citizens' trust in government's willingness to take their communication seriously and act responsively.

From the empirical data, alternative government use of social media could be observed. For instance, social media are used internally by government units to enforce transparency [21] and reporting on social media by government units takes place to conform to performance indicators instead of responding to citizens' needs or requests.

Overall, this paper shows the quirks and challenges of implementing compelling 'smart city' rhetoric applied to disaster management practices in the specific context of Bandung City, where a relatively new technology results in somewhat surprising and unanticipated uses that are both enabled and arguably amplified by the local context in which innovation takes place.

References

1. Meijer, A., Bolívar, M.P.R.: Governing the smart city: a review of the literature on smart urban governance. Int. Rev. Adm. Sci. 82(2), 392–408 (2016)
2. Landry, C.: The art of city making, The Art of City Making, pp. 1–478 (2012)
3. Coletta, C., Evans, L., Heaphy, L., Kitchin, R.: Creating smart cities, Creating Smart Cities, pp. 1–242 (2018).
4. Albino, V., Berardi, U., Dangelico, R.M.: Smart cities: definitions, dimensions, performance, and initiatives. J. Urban Technol. 22(1), 3–21 (2015)
5. Zhu, S., Li, D., Feng, H.: Is smart city resilient? Evidence from China, Sustain. Cities Soc. 50, 101636 (2019)
6. Candelieri, A., Archetti, F., Giordani, I., Arosio, G., Sormani, R.: Smart cities management by integrating sensors, models and user generated contents. WIT Trans. Ecol. Environ. 179, 719–730 (2013)
7. Stephens, E., Cloke, H.: Improving flood forecasts for better flood preparedness in the UK (and beyond), Geographical J. 180(4), 310–316 (2014)
8. Zhang, N., Chen, H., Chen, J., Chen, X.: Social media meets big urban data: a case study of urban waterlogging analysis. Comput. Intell. Neurosci. 2016 (2016).
9. Restrepo-Estrada, C., de Andrade, S.C., Abe, N., Fava, M.C., Mendiondo, E.M., de Albuquerque, J.P.: Geo-social media as a proxy for hydrometeorological data for streamflow estimation and to improve flood monitoring. Comput. Geosci. 111, 148–158 (2018)
10. Batty, M., et al.: Smart cities of the future. Eur. Phys. J. Spec. Top. 214(1), 481–518 (2012)
11. Harrison, S., Johnson, P.: Challenges in the adoption of crisis crowdsourcing and social media in Canadian emergency management. Gov. Inf. Q. 36(3), 501–509 (2019)
12. Ogie, R.I., Clarke, R.J., Forehead, H., Perez, P.: Crowdsourced social media data for disaster management: lessons from the PetaJakarta.org project. Comput. Environ. Urban Syst. 73, 108–117 (2019)
13. Kankanamge, N., Yigitcanlar, T., Goonetilleke, A., Kamruzzaman, M.: Determining disaster severity through social media analysis: Testing the methodology with South East Queensland Flood tweets. Int. J. Disaster Risk Reduction 42 (2020)
14. Wukich, C.: Government social media messages across disaster phases. J. Contingencies Cris. Manag. 24(4), 230–243 (2016)
15. Pogrebnyakov, N., Maldonado, E.: Didn't roger that: social media message complexity and situational awareness of emergency responders. Int. J. Inf. Manage. 40, 166–174 (2018)
16. Vijaykumar, S., Meurzec, R.W., Jayasundar, K., Pagliari, C., Fernandopulle, Y.: What's buzzing on your feed? health authorities' use of facebook to combat Zika in Singapore, J. Am. Med. Informatics Assoc. 24(6) (2017)

17. Brynielsson, J., Granåsen, M., Lindquist, S., Narganes Quijano, M., Nilsson, S., Trnka, J.: Informing crisis alerts using social media: best practices and proof of concept. J. Contingencies Cris. Manag. **26**(1), 28–40 (2018)
18. Sivarajah, U., Irani, Z., Weerakkody, V.: Evaluating the use and impact of Web 2.0 technologies in local government, Gov. Inf. Q. **32**(4), 473–487 (2015).
19. Carter, L., Thatcher, J.B., Wright, R.: Social media and emergency management: exploring state and local tweets. In: Proceedings of the Annual Hawaii International Conference on System Sciences; 47th Hawaii International Conference on System Sciences, HICSS 2014, pp. 1968–1977 (2014)
20. Atkinson, C.L.: Crisis communication in dark times: the 2011 mouse river flood in Minot, North Dakota. Int. J. Commun. **8**(1), 1394–1414 (2014)
21. Bonsón, E., Torres, L., Royo, S., Flores, F.: Local e-government 2.0: social media and corporate transparency in municipalities, Gov. Inf. Q. **29**(2), 123–132 (2012)

Bumikita Mobile Application: The Starting Point of a Children-Centred Approach for Multi Hazard Early Warning System in Indonesia

Mujiburrahman Thontowi[✉]

Charles Darwin University, Darwin, NT, Australia
mujiburrahman@cdu.edu

Abstract. Across the Indonesia Archipelago, children are affected by multiple disasters such as floods, earthquake, tsunami, forest fires and now exacerbated by the Covid-19 pandemic. Children and schools should be protected from disasters. During 1967–2020, 37,430 schools are damaged due to natural disasters in Indonesia. Since, March 16, 2020 virtually days without going to school. This research aims to unfold the convergence of Children Centred Approach and Multi Hazard Early Warning Systems in Indonesia as an effort to build resilience. This research is a case study of the mobile application called BUMIKITA which is translated to OUR WORLD by Save the Children in Indonesia. The location of the research is at the provincial level in Jakarta, West Java, Bali, and West Nusa Tenggara. The mobile app is potential to be developed into a Children Centred Multi Hazard Early Warning System. Currently there is still a few numbers of downloads with about 1000 users within a couple of months. Aggressive promotions are needed with an opportunity to collaborate with government agencies such as the Ministry of Education and Disaster Management Agencies to proliferate the mobile app to be utilized by parents, teachers, and children.

Keywords: Multi hazard approach · Early warning systems · Child-centred approach · Indonesia

1 Introduction

Many children affected by natural disasters in Indonesia. Data from the National Disaster Management Agencies state that 60% to 70% of disaster effected people are women, children and the elderly [1]. Besides facing deaths, injury or becoming displaced because of losing their homes, the access to education is jeopardized by a disaster according to various publication on disaster impact on education. During 1967–2020, 37,430 schools are damaged due to disasters in Indonesia [2]. Covid-19 has worsened the access of children to attain good education. Since March 16, 2020 the start of virtually days without going to school and all classes are online [3]. There is a high exposure to school in disaster prone regions from Single Hazard to Multiple Hazards Early Warnings. Sendai Framework for Disaster Risk Reduction emphasizes the importance of a multi hazard

© IFIP International Federation for Information Processing 2021
Published by Springer Nature Switzerland AG 2021
Y. Murayama et al. (Eds.): ITDRR 2020, IFIP AICT 622, pp. 102–115, 2021.
https://doi.org/10.1007/978-3-030-81469-4_9

early warning system availability. The objective the early warning systems is generally to save lives, but specifically to save children lives through a child-centred early warning system.

Large disaster should be perceived as a momentum for policy change and even as an evaluation to improve the existing early warning System. The current regulations of disaster management law need to be majorly revised. This can be an entry point for government officials the legislative to listen to the voice of children and to amend the law accordingly. Second, this is a good opportunity to develop a platform for children's engagement in the early warning process. One promising development is crowed sourcing such as Hackathon by Humanitarian Open Street Map, Citizen Reporting by Petabencana.id and Bumikita by Save the Children Indonesia. This research aims to unfold the convergence of Children Centred Approach and Multi Hazard Early Warning Systems in Indonesia as an effort to build resilience. Below is the schematic design of a multi-hazard early warning by WMO in 2018 (Fig. 1).

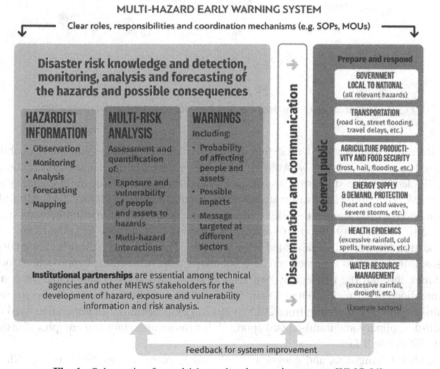

Fig. 1. Schematic of a multi-hazard early warning system WMO [4]

2 Gaps in Children Centred Approach for Multi Hazard Early Warnings

A solid body of literature on Child-Centred Disaster Risk Reduction has gradually evolved in recent years. It serves as a guiding framework for international and national child-rights organizations [5]. The international community's concerns about children centred disaster risk reduction has grown significantly for instance the European Union and ASEAN [6]. 16 articles on child centred disaster risk reduction were gathered from explain from 2012 to 2020 using Scopus database. The following text analysis is developed by using VOS Viewer based on the 16 articles extracted from the title, abstract and key words (Fig. 2):

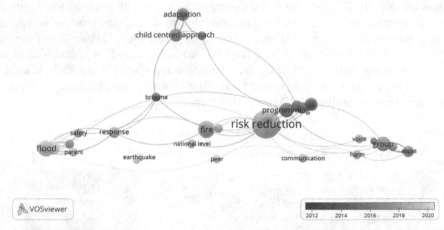

Fig. 2. Text analysis of Children Centred Disaster Risk Reduction (2012–2020)

Referring to the figure, we can find that risk reduction is central to the study of child centred approach. Previously, Amri in 2017, [7] provides an explanation on bridging the divided between studies on disaster risk reduction education and child-centred disaster risk reduction. His disaster studies were conducted from 2001 to 2015. Multiple hazards have been frequently discussed in various researches on natural hazards such as fire [8], typhoon [9] flood [10] and earthquake [11]. Man-made hazards, harm, and abuse to children are also elaborated in these papers. These studies on child centred DRR poses a single hazard approach and have not adopted the multi hazard approach. Efforts to break through the concept of "working in silos" stresses the importance of communication between children and their families before and after disaster by reviewing multi-disciplinary literature from 2015 to 2017 [12]. It becomes an imperative need of multi-disciplinary and multi-hazard approach for future uncertain and complex disaster that children will face.

Cultures, language, and geographic differences contribute to the variety of Child Centred Disaster Risk Reduction. Most of papers explain about child centred disaster risk reduction in Australia, followed by the United States and United Kingdom. In Australia, Towers studied the progress, gaps and opportunities [13]. Then children perception and adaptive behaviors response to seasonal change and extreme weather [14].

Furthermore, research to understand how a disaster resilience program reduce risk and how to increase the resilience of children and households in the region are critical [15] These researches coincide with the Millennium Development Goals and the Sustainable

Development Goals as well as from the Hyogo framework for action to the Sendai framework for action.

Studies focusing on the Asian and African regions specifically for CCDRR are limited. In Asia region, there are best practices from India, the Philippines, and India. In India, the research was developed based on the 2015 South Indian floods [16]. In the Philippines, translating children voices into action for resilience based on Haiyan typhoon [17]. Finally, Indonesian children experienced earthquake disaster in Lombok. The research draws attention to children rights violations such as basic survival, freedom from abuse and exploitation, access to health and education [18]. In South America a research was conducted to listen to Ecuadorian children about disaster [19]. In Africa, a research related to the establishment of a child centred disaster management framework in Zimbabwe was carried out in 2015 [20]. One of the rights which was not discussed in the study is the right to information or warning system for children, even though preparedness activities was reported lacking in schools and minimal involvement of children.

Realizing the gaps of the previous researches, it is important to understand the convergence of Child centred approach and Multi Hazard Approach within the context of Multi hazard early warning systems in Indonesia. Especially, by looking deeper into the digital disaster risk management ecosystem which is central to the Bumikita mobile application. The purposes of this research are as follow:

1. Understand the development, features and convergence of Children Centred Approach and Multi Hazard Approach through the mobile apps Bumikita
2. Map out the feedback for continuous improvements and development the embryo of a children centred multi hazard early warnings
3. Identify the stakeholders in the penta-helix to support the mainstreaming of child centred disaster risk reduction

3 Methodology

A mix method design was deployed in this qualitative method for description based from interviews and focus group discussion. Furthermore, quantitative methods were applied by using a feedback form which distributed via online after 6 socializations webinars and workshops for the apps Bumikita organized by Save the Children Indonesia. The analytics from android apps was collected from seeing the download rate daily from April – October 2020. A total of 340 participants submitted the feedback forms and a total of 2118 times the have been downloaded from android devices from various version such as 435 users in Android 8.1, 178 users in Android 7.1, 686 users in Android 9 and 311 users in Android 10 and 508 users unspecified.

Case Study was used to understand the usage Bumikita apps. The location of this research is at provincial level in Jakarta and Bandung, West Java. Interviews with Government Agencies and Focus Groups Discussion with Save the Children and its partners such as Humanitarian Forum Indonesia. Field research was conducted in Bali and West Nusa Tenggara.

Primary Data was collected through interview with government officials of BNPB, Education Department in Jakarta, Education Department in Lombok and Education Department in Bali. Focus Groups with Save the Children at National Headquarters – Concerning MHEWS and Save the Children at Sub-national Level Lombok – MHEWS. Finally, Observations webinar by Save the Children via Socialization of Bumikita, Voice of Children to International Forum and Voice of Children at National Forum – to Legislator and National Government Agencies (Fig. 3).

Fig. 3. Multi Hazard Map National Disaster Management Agency Indonesia (BNPB) at inarisk.bnpb.go.id

4   Research Findings

This section will discuss about the convergence of a child centred approach and Multi-hazard early warning system. The findings show that the Apps Bumikita is a starting point for a Children Centred Multi Hazard Early Warning System. Currently, there is a few numbers of downloads which is about 1825 users within the first two months with 70% of active accounts. Aggressive promotions are needed. There is an opportunity of collaboration with government agencies such as the Ministry of Education and Disaster Management Agencies to proliferate the mobile app and to be used by children at the later stage. Bumikita is a free online mobile application which provides information about multi hazards in Indonesia.

The features of the apps are: Monitoring zone, Information zone, Leader board, Lets read, How if and People stories. There is a push notification called "REPORT DISASTER" that the user can report and trace all disasters in Indonesia. The feature includes report first an active hazard in your location, a page about education concerning Disaster Risk Reduction and Mitigation; second, "How if" an interactive game play on how to prevent and face an incoming hazard; third, a map to the nearest disaster management agency/post; fourth, a leader board that counts the experience points of the user. Below is the first feature appearance.

The above monitoring of hazards zones and information zones are beneficial to be the foundations of a child centred multi hazard early warning system. It is visually pleasing and appealing to children. Currently, this apps is connected to the earthquake and tsunami warning systems. In the future, it needs to link up to the forest fires from the SIPONGI Apps by the Ministry of Environment and Magma Indonesia from the PGMBG (Fig. 4).

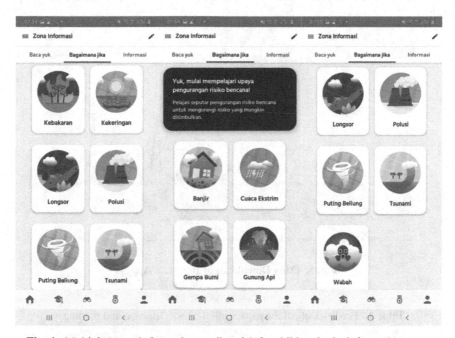

Fig. 4. Multiple hazards for understanding risk for children in the information zone.

Socialization of the Bumikita apps includes 1) meeting with the national disaster management agency on explaining the platform and apps. especially the helpdesk and Bumikita app. Support BNPB for the in the 1 million face mask movement by providing donation of face mask. 2) The usage of YouTube to launch the Apps via a video. 3) The usage of Facebook to share the developments of BUMIKITA apps using a webinar format. An opportunity for children voice to be head by international and national policy makers. The figure below shows the daily downloads of Bumikita Apps.

The rise of downloads is closely related to the activities conducted by save the children such as the apps dissemination. The month of August and September 2020 have a significant increase of user acquisitions. The most users are using the version of Android 9, android 8.1, android 7 and final android 10 still minimal users. A more active participation is needed to be conducted by children before a disaster strike by utilizing the Bumikita Apps.

The introductory workshops on Bumikita are conducted from July to September 2020 with a total of 7 events: 18 July with the Youth Red Cross, 25 July with U-inspire, 26 July PMI DKI, 27 July with Pramuka/Scouts and 30 July with Bali Red Cross. Another activity is a training for Bumikita Champions. Two activities were held to build champions for Bumikita on 17 September – Training for Bumikita Champions and 30 September – Training for Bumikita Champion. Additional Champaign from Youtube upload was also used to promote Bumikita and a guideline of how to use Bumikita apps (Fig. 5).

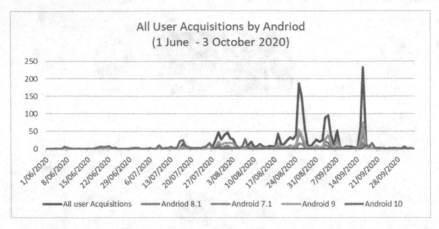

Fig. 5. Daily Downloads of Bumikita App

Table 1. Feedback about the participation on socialization and training

Question	1	2	3	4	5	6	7	Total
	18 July	25 July	26 July	27 July	30 July	17 Sep	30 Sep	
Participants	120	17	94	55	21	21	12	340
How do you feel about participation								
Happy	31	x	23	13	10	5	6	88
Very happy	87	x	70	42	11	15	6	231
Normal	2	x	1	0	0	0	0	3
Do you feel that the materials is useful?								
Useful	24	13	10	13	7	3	5	75
Very Useful	96	4	83	42	14	17	7	263
Normal	0	0	0	0	0	0	0	0

The participants feel happy and useful about the socialization and training of the Bumikita. This needs to be spread to other regions. Socialization for disaster preparedness was also conducted in other locations and other organizations. Interview results with head of education department in Karangasem, Bali explain the importance of the cooperation with Save the Children Indonesia during the Mount Agung Volcano Eruption. Besides teachers training and establishment of contingency plan for education in emergency, evacuation after a warning and disaster simulations. On the other hand, During the FGD results, Bali Red Cross conducted similar activities with schools such as disaster preparedness schools (Sekolah Siaga Bencana), activities with the youth red cross and recruitment of volunteers, before, during and after a disaster. They used various apps to monitor disaster such as the official apps form the government such as Info BMKG, Magma Indonesia and InaRisk. Focus group with Save the children Lombok provided examples of work with children before, during and after the earthquake. They relied on official information from official agencies apps and even using WhatsApp. Lombok island is also a potential region to share the BUMIKITA apps, socializations, and training of champions (Table 1).

Online feedback about the apps. The general review on google play store was positive from people who downloaded the apps. There is a total of 32 reviews with the majority providing 5 stars, 4 starts and 3 starts. There was no review that provided a 1 or 2 starts for the Bumikita apps. For the reviewer that provide a score of 3 and 4 stars stated that: "Sorry I was asked to download. Even though my storage is low" (8 August 2020). "How do you use it, I don't understand, I ASK FOR GOD FORGIVENESS, I'm sorry I uninstalled but I give a star, okay" (19 September 2020). "I was also told to download this app but if you want to be safe from natural disasters all you need to do is pray and throw your rubbish away in an appropriate place, what is so hard about that?" 19 September 2020). A reviewer that provided a 5 start also felt forced to download the app stating that: "For the sake of the webinar, I was forced to install the app, it does not matter for the developer to make money" – 8 August 2020.

While, other he 5 Star comments are very positive and encouraging: "The application is very good… By downloading this apk, you can know some of the actions to take when a disaster is coming… even though you know how to cope with disasters but… At least you can be broader in knowing what actions to take when faced with… (26 September 2020). "Very good, very helpful in understanding risk reduction when a disaster occurs. Besides that, we can also find out what disasters are around us. Ayoo guys.. Really cool" (24 August 2020) "like it alot, I can report the dangers in my area"- 8 August 2020 and "there are XP (experience Point) and the avatar at the start is cute the most exciting is to play what if" – 8 August 2020. The usual one-line comments such as "Very good" – (8 August 2020), "Very satisfied" – (23 June 2020), "Good" (24 September 2020) and "Great" (20 September 2020). The comments from google play store is more open compared to the comments from the webinar socialization and trainings. More open critics should be encouraging by participants especially the children and youth. The feedback from Workshops and Online Webinar Bumikita Features can been seen in the table below (Table 2):

Table 2. Feedback about the participation on socialization and training

Question	1	2	3	4	5	6	7	Total
	18 July	25 July	26 July	27 July	30 July	17 Sep	30 Sep	
Participants	120	17	94	55	21	21	12	340
What features do you like the most? (Can choose more than one)								
Monitoring zone	51	x	32	29	4	8	0	124
Leader board	14	x	11	10	1	8	1	45
Information zone	120	x	73	40	16	13	11	273
Lets read	64	x	38	40	6	13	7	168
How if	40	x	36	17	4	10	2	109
People stories	37	x	24	12	3	8	2	86

Source: Save the Children (2020) modified by Author

First, the most voted features are the information zone, then the let's read and monitoring zone. This is most voted based on their similarities which is the passive usage of the apps. Most users just want to learn about the app first before contributing. The next votes are followed by how if and people stories. This requires more effort and contributions from the user in this case children or youth. This can be part of the crowd sourcing and children participations in disaster risk reduction. Children can also be a content creator using the apps telling stories or reporting disasters. This entails active children participation. The least voted is the leader board, it is probably not well explained during the socializations and training. The video tutorials on YouTube also lacks the detailed explanation about the leader board and experience point concepts.

Digital disaster risk management ecosystem from triple-helix to penta-helix. An effort for mass coverage and adoption of Bumikita. In the past the term tri-helix has been used in Indonesia's research community from describe the three main stakeholders for research innovation in the Bumikita Apps or MHEWS with are the academic institutions (ITB), government (BNPB), and private sector/Industries (Google). The tri-helix emphasise the importance of research to practice. The disaster management have adopted this concept to include additional stakeholders such as the media and community as mayor players in disaster management, hence it is called the Penta-Helix. Innovation of mobile technology withing the disaster science have been relative slowly adopted by the government, due to barriers between the researchers and industry. The lack of government incentives to support private sector in funding research on disaster management or even preparedness. The majority companies still have a mindset of providing donation during a disaster which is more favorable and gains wide media coverage than just a going a Corporate social responsibility try to eliminate the vulnerabilities in a disaster prone region or funding research at universities is still limited. It was a major a significant deal that google funded the project at save the children in Indonesia do develop the Bumikita apps.

Save the Children needs to consider maximizing the use of the media. The addition of media and community makes the cooperation for innovation more complex but on the other hand more participative. The "end users" of the technology being the community can have an important role during the co-planning, co-creating and co-implementing phases. The term "End-users" can be disregard because they become part of the innovation process from the start. While the process is tedious and takes a long time, the usability and usefulness for the community is even more valued. The jargon "people centred" has been used as a label by the government to make the early warning systems seems favorable to the public. Whereas in fact, the participation of the community is vague in the regulations and standard operating procedures. Feedback on the apps becomes an important consideration and act as an accountability.

The media channeling the voice of voiceless who are children. The national media as a channel of information is like a two-edge sword, as a mouthpiece of the government disaster warning dissemination or as a watch dog of government policies and actions. The media is tamed by daily and monthly press conference in the National Disaster Management Agencies Headquarters in Jakarta. Even vast efforts by the national and local government to make Media Forums and Media Volunteers for Disaster Management. At times, the media will attack the government, by going investigative journalism, exposing the weakness, finding cracks in the field, far beyond the national image, like a dog biting its master. Especially media coverage concerning the failure of early warning systems to save lives. Poor journalism has also led to the increase of spread of hoax and fake news. The lines have even been more blurred by the emergence of social media and citizens journalism. The app must be able to create disaster and risk literacy, under the umbrella of media literacy. It should be a weapon to fight against hoax and misinformation. Children and youth using Bumikita can provide important information about disaster from a children perspective.

The rise of social media platform in disaster management is a blessing in disguise. The coverage, participating and engagement of the community presence online is something that cannot done in the past. Before Facebook, twitter and YouTube was invented, the only traditional source of information from broadcast media such as TV and Radio including the printed media such as newspapers and magazine. This type of traditional media is only one way. The social media have created a hyper interaction between the knowledge producers and knowledge consumers. The drawbacks of social media are its spread of unfiltered content, such as the spread of hoax and rumors related to disaster. Even truths or scientific discoveries become bombastic headlines that creates fear and alarms in the community. In some cases, the scientist with their claims are threatened by the law to withdraw the findings and request to apologize to the community for making alarmist claims. Such research like the possibility of an earthquake and tsunami that occurs in the southern part of Java and Bali. Not only the scientist is captured by the law, the community is also in jail because of spreading hoax when an earthquake occurs, and then he spread in Facebook that after the earthquake and tsunami will come and strike the coastal area. This post caused panic in the northern part of Bali, and people run and evacuated to safety. The official report from BMKG is that there is an earthquake but no tsunami warning.

Children need to be aware of hoax about disaster. Especially with the problems with social media as a dissemination of warning is the term "Echo Chambers" "epistemic bubbles" which are used in research related to media. The Echo Chamber of government and its partners such as NGO's who work in the disaster management context. In Jakarta you can hear the term "You Again You Gain" which is a translation from "Loe Lagi Loe Lagi" or the 4L's. Since the humanitarian and disaster management sector is a closely tight groups of people, it's the same people who are concerned about disasters and early warning. While the connections and collaborations are strong, formal and informal information between spread within in the networks. Especially the activist from the 1990's, especially after the fall of the Suharto Era, after the humanitarian workers in conflict and disaster settings are still active until now, with more and more young generation joining the efforts for disaster risk reduction. From becoming students, being volunteers and joining international organizations, attain masters and doctoral degrees and returning to Indonesia to contribute to disaster management in Indonesia. Same type of people from same type of organizations. These people are from government and from non-government institutions. There are reinforcements that makes them feel that what they are going is right. Information spread in these groups and networks but not all of it di disseminate out of the disaster management groups to the wider community. Having a simple post or retweet a government dissemination and warning does not mean that it spreads to all members of the public. Maybe just between you friends and family. Your followers who are not concerned about disaster management will just disregard the post that is plied up in the timeline. In some cases, hoax spread in these groups, but it is quickly negated and followed up by an apology and removing the message or post.

On the other extreme, networks or groups who are not connected to any humanitarian or disaster management sector. The spread of hoax and rumors will spread like wildfire. Sharing and sharing without anyone from the group to verify the fact about the post or message. This becomes fatal since the negation or verifications of the hoax is virtually non-existent. These occur in religious groups, village groups, women's groups, and youth groups. In these senses the efforts which have been done by the government and NGO's, but these efforts have not reached all villages and population at risk. The advancement of technology related to instant messaging have accelerated the spread of hoax from the initial usage of SMS which as a limited broadcast can only send one SMS at a time in the 90's and early turn of the millennium, to the introduction of blackberry messaging (BBM) with a maximal group size of 30 people and now with WhatsApp which can house 256 people. The future can be with even more people having capabilities to broadcast even more such as using Facebook, twitter and other open social media networks, telegram which can have super groups which can include 5000 members of a group. Bumikita Apps can be shared among social media platforms.

5 Conclusion

The convergence of the Children Centred Approach and Multi Hazard Approach is very important. It can be used to revise the multi hazard early warning system. We should start at a young age to make children understand about the risk around them and they should also get involved in monitoring hazards, help disseminate the warning to peers and act accordingly. They will become the future leaders. It's important to empower the children and youth. Bumikita apps is a ground-breaking app for make disaster preparedness a part of the digital ecosystem in Indonesia. It marks the starting point of a child centred-Multi Hazard Early Warning System. Second, the important of feedback from children, parents and teachers to improve the usability of the mobile apps. Finally, understanding the digital disaster risk management ecosystem which involves the 5 major sectors elaborated in the Penta helix with is government, private sector, universities, media, and community (including children).

The recommendations for the mobile apps features and feedback mechanism. Provide additional features for the BUMIKITA APP which is a "Our Surroundings". You need to know if your house is safe, if your school is safe and if your workplace is safe? These questions will make the app more relevant to everyday life. Are our house, school, and work in a disaster-prone region? Weekly updates of disaster such as the AHA center or UNOCHA weekly update. Currently is a be-weekly update of the apps. To be able to access without internet connection since not all village have access in Indonesia. Gamification aspect should be able to access without the internet connection. There should be an offline mode and online mode. The offline mode has limited capacity and features which is understandable. Language is important in terms of communicating risk. The use of local language and foreign language will make the APPS more accessible. In many project sites, the use of local language is more important that using the national language. On the hand, for guess in Indonesia, to have an English version so not for Indonesian. A possible to be scale-ed up to the Asia Pacific Region. The app can target children tourist who are currently traveling in Indonesia and to be replicated in other save the children project sites. To increase the user numbers is by developing the app compatible to both android and apple apps devices. Further, research to get the perception and gain valuable insight to improve the BUMIKITA apps of teachers and children is advisable.

Recommendations for creating awareness about the Bumikita. The recommendation is a larger campaign to spread apps, increase people to download and use in schools. The priority of schools-based Data from DAPODIK (Database of Schools in Disaster Prone Regions from the Ministry of Education). Part of a safe school initiative for teachers to download and promote to students and parents. The apps should target University students and youths to actively download. Possible future cooperation with government agencies such as a cooperation with the National Disaster Management Agencies is rec-ommended. It aims to have access to the INARISK database and link it to Bumikita. INARISK is for adults, but BUMIKITA can be transformed into an INARISK for Kids. It is essential to add information about volcano warning such as short updates of vol-canos that erupted in Indonesia and have the distance to your location or information about hotspot in the notification. BUMIKITA can be a part of government agencies pro-gram in sharing information on disasters such as "go to school program" since many government agencies conduct activities at schools. This is an opportunity to also spread and increase the engagement and establish cooperation with google on earthquake early warning system. We need to consider the usage of social media to increase awareness and improve traffic to the website such as by putting hashtag of #bumikita #savethechildren #savebumikita #MHEWS #Childcentred. This will improve the visibility of the mobile app. This should link up to go to school programs by government and local NGOs and not just spreading in the virtual space but also in the real-world scenario.

Acknowledgements. I would show my appreciations to Save the Children Indonesia for letting me research out Bumikita Mobile Applications and access to meetings, webinars, and data. To my scholarship funding from LPDP under the Ministry of Finance, Republic of Indonesia. Last but not least to my supervisor who provide constant support in Charles Darwin University, Northern Territory, Australia.

References

1. Setiawan, R.: BNBP: 60 Sampai 70 %Korban Bencana Adalah Perempuandan Anak (2019). https://tirto.id/bnbp-60-sampai-70-korban-bencana-adalah-perempuan-dan-anak-dgod. Accessed 24 Apr 2019
2. BNPB: Data dan Informasi Bencana Indonesia (2020). https://dibi.bnpb.go.id
3. World Bank: Education systems's response to Covid-19 Brief (2020). http://pubdocs.worldbank.org/en/857971586182572110/COVID19EducationSectorBriefApril3.pdf. Accessed on 3 Apr
4. WMO: Multi-hazard early warning systems: a Checklist Outcome of the first Multi-Hazard Early Warning Conference (2018)
5. Haynes, K., Tanner, T.M.: Empowering young people and strengthening resilience: youth-centred participatory video as a tool for climate change adaptation and disaster risk reduction. Children's Geographies. **13**(3), 357–371 (2015)
6. Taylor, G.: EU disaster risk reduction in the Asia pacific: Reducing the social vulnerability of children. In: International Disaster and Risk Conference: Integrative Risk Management in a Changing World, Pathways to a Resilient Society, IDRC Davos, pp. 677–680 (2012)
7. Amri, A., Haynes, K., Bird, D.K., Ronan, K.: Bridging the divide between studies on disaster risk reduction education and child-centred disaster risk reduction: a critical review Children's Geographies **16**(3), 239–251 (2018)
8. Mitchell, P., Borchard, C.: Mainstreaming children's vulnerabilities and capacities into community-based adaptation to enhance impact. Climate Dev. **6**(4), 372–381 (2014)
9. Kancharla, R.: Child centred disaster risk reduction (CC DRR)/Resilience (Book Chapter) Disaster Risk Reduction: Community Resilience and Responses, pp. 261–276 (2018)
10. Pooley, K.: Youth justice conferencing for youth misuse of fire: a child-centred disaster risk reduction mechanism. Aust. J. Emer. Manage. **32**(2), 54–59 (2017)
11. Towers, B.: A critical pedagogy of risk: Empowering children with knowledge and skills for DRR. In: Proceedings of the 4th International Disaster and Risk Conference: Integrative Risk Management in a Changing World - Pathways to a Resilient Society, IDRC Davos pp. 703–706 (2012)
12. Wisner, B., et al.: Communication with children and families about disaster: reviewing multi-disciplinary literature 2015–2017. Current Psychiatry Reports **20**(9), 73 (2018)
13. Towers, B., Haynes, K., Sewell, F., Bailie, H., Cross, D.: Child-centred disaster risk reduction in Australia: Progress, gaps and opportunities. Aust. J. Emergency Manage. **t29**(1), 31–38 (2014)
14. Harwood, S., Haynes, K., Bird, D., Govan, J.: Children's perceptions and adaptive behaviors in response to seasonal change and extreme weather in Broome Western Australia. Aust. J. Emer. Manage. **29**(1), 39–44 (2014)

15. Ronan, K.R., et al.: Child-centred disaster risk reduction: can disaster resilience programs reduce risk and increase the resilience of children and households? Australian J. Emer. Manage. **31**(3), 49–58 (2016)
16. Krishna, R.N., Ronan, K.R., Alisic, E.: Children in the 2015 South Indian floods: community members' views. Eur. J. Psychotraumatol. **9**(sup2), 1486122 (2018)
17. Alburo-Cañete, K.Z.: Learning from Haiyan: Translating children's voices into action for resilience (Book Chapter) Issues in Teaching and Learning of Education for Sustainability: Theory into Practice, pp. 36–47 (2019)
18. Beazley, H.: Children's experiences of Disaster: a case study from Lombok, Indonesia (Book Chapter). Natural Hazards and Disaster Justice: Challenges for Australia and Its Neighbours, pp. 185–203 (2020)
19. Carr, A., Abad Merchán, M., Ullauri, N.: Conversations about disasters: listening to Ecuadorian children. Children's Geographies **18**(2), 222–233 (2020)
20. Sillah, R.M.: A call to establish a child-centred disaster management framework in Zimbabwe. Open Access. Jamba: J. Disaster Risk Stud. **7**(1), 148 (2015)

General Knowledge Representation and Sharing for Disaster Management

Philippe A. Martin[1]([✉]) and Tullio J. Tanzi[2]

[1] EA2525 LIM, University of La Réunion, 97490 Sainte Clotilde, France
philippe.martin@univ-reunion.fr
[2] LTCI, Télécom Paris, Institut Polytechnique de Paris, Paris, France
tullio.tanzi@telecom-paris.fr

Abstract. The first part of this article first distinguishes "restricted knowledge representation (KR) and sharing (KS)" and the still seldom researched task of "*general* KR and KS". This parts then highlights the usefulness of the latter for disaster management, and provides a panorama of complementary techniques supporting it. The research question that these techniques collectively answer is: how to let Web users collaboratively build KBs (KR bases) i) that are not *implicitly* "partially *redundant* or *inconsistent*" internally or with each other, ii) that are complete with respect to certain criteria or subjects, iii) without restricting what the users can enter nor forcing them to agree on terminology or beliefs, and iv) without requiring people to duplicate knowledge in various KBs, or manually search knowledge in various KBs and aggregate knowledge from various KBs? In a second part, this article shows the way various kinds of disaster management related information can be categorized or represented for general KS purposes, e.g. terminologies and information objects (these objects are rarely represented via KRs; examples about *Search & Rescue* procedures are given).

Keywords: Disaster management · Knowledge sharing · Ontology

1 Introduction

Disaster management, e.g. disaster risk reduction or *Search & Rescue* operations, requires many resources, e.g. certain kinds of people, search robots, maps, communication tools, detection devices, search procedures and search software. It also depends on many parameters, e.g. the available resources, the nature of the disaster, the terrain and the weather. Ideally, all published information on all these elements would be stored, related and organized on the Web in places and in ways permitting people and software agents to i) retrieve and compare them according to any set of criteria, and ii) complement the stored information in ways that maintain its degree of organization and hence retrievability.

Such an ideal and scalable organization of information implies the building and exploitation of *knowledge representation* bases: *KR bases* or simply *KBs*. KBs store

© IFIP International Federation for Information Processing 2021
Published by Springer Nature Switzerland AG 2021
Y. Murayama et al. (Eds.): ITDRR 2020, IFIP AICT 622, pp. 116–131, 2021.
https://doi.org/10.1007/978-3-030-81469-4_10

KRs (alias, *knowledge*), i.e. *semantic* and *logic-based* representations of information. In this article, KRs is opposed to *data*, i.e. information merely organized by predefined *structural* relations (i.e. partOf ones) and *semantic relations of very few predefined types* (mostly typeOf relations). In KBs, all the types (i.e. relation types and concept types) and their definitions are user-provided: most of the knowledge in many KBs are expressed via the definitions. Document based technologies and data-base systems only handle *data*, although deductive databases are steps towards KBs. A KB is composed of an ontology and a base of facts. An ontology is i) the set of terms used in representations within KBs, along with ii) representations of term definitions, hence semantic relations between the terms. Natural language based documents or databases cannot automatically be converted into *KBs that are well-organized via generalization (and part-of) relations*, if only because they often lack the necessary information for even human readers to derive such relations. This organization – and hence, manually or semi-automatically built KBs – is necessary to support i) *semantic*-based searches, via queries or navigation, and ii) any *scalable* organization or integration of information. This is why methodologies or architectures for building ontologies or ontology based systems, and their advantages, have already often been discussed in relation to disaster management related information. E.g., in July 2020, the digital library of IFIP (International Federation for Information Processing) included 12 articles about ontologies and "risk or disaster or emergency", while the digital library of the ISCRAM conferences ("Information Systems for Crisis Response and Management" conferences) included 46 articles in which "ontology" was recorded as a keyword.

There are some *top-level* ontologies related to disaster management, e.g. SEMA4A [5] (the purpose of which is to help alerting people of imminent disasters) and *empathy* [3] which is more general and integrates some other top-level ontologies. However, as of 2020, there does not appear to be any publicly accessible large *content ontology* about information related to disaster management, let alone KBs in which people or organizations could relate or aggregate information. For instance, even though [14] mentions past "massive efforts e.g. in European projects such as DISASTER (disas-ter-fp7.eu), SecInCoRe (www.secincore.eu), EPISECC (www.epi secc.eu), or CRISP (www.crispproject.eu)", only the second and third project Web pages of this list are now accessible, and the results of these projects are not KBs but reports about planned works and advocated architectures or small models (top-level ontologies). Some other large projects such as the Norwegian INSITU (Sharing Incident and Threat Information for Common Situational Understanding) project (2019–2022) [13] focus more on terminology harmonisation as well as tools for the *collaborative synthesis* of information in classic media (textual documents, databases, maps,…), hence not information synthesis via KBs. The use of classic media make terminology harmonisation useful for lexical searches but this harmonisation is a complex task requiring committees (hence centralization) and it is useful only when its guidelines are followed (which is not easy to do). With KBs, such terminology harmonisation is not necessary: relations of generalisation or equivalence between terms within KBs or across KBs can be added in a decentralized and incremental way by each term provider or knowledge provider. Thanks to these relations, people can use the terms they wish without decreasing knowledge retrievability.

There are two meanings for "knowledge sharing" (KS). *"Restricted KS"* is quite related to *data(base) sharing*: it is about i) easing the exchange of information (data or KRs) between *particular* agents (persons, businesses or applications) that *can* discuss to solve ambiguities or other problems, and ii) the *full or efficient* exploitation of the information by these particular agents. *"General KS"* is about people representing or relating information within or between KBs in ways that maximize the retrievability and exploitation of the information by any person and application. These two meanings are very rarely explicitly distinguished, including by the World Wide Web Consortium (W3C). Regarding KS, the W3C has a "Semantic Web vision of a Web of *Linked data* [17]". As the name may suggest, and as explained in Sect. 2, the vision and techniques proposed by the W3C are mainly focused on *restricted* KS. Risk management related research articles that advocate the use of KBs, e.g. [2] and [4], rely on the W3C approach or techniques. However, they are insufficient for (general) KS in disaster management, if only given the amount of potentially useful information for such a management. This insufficiency is also one reason for the above cited lack of large publicly accessible content ontologies or KBs related to disaster management.

Section 2 summarizes complementary ways to support *general KS* and the above cited ideal. By doing so, Sect. 2 also explains different aspects of the above cited insufficiency. The originality of Sect. 2 is mainly in the synthesis or panorama it-self, more than in the description depth of the cited or introduced techniques, because the first author has separately published on several of these techniques. However, new elements have been introduced and these techniques are original wrt. disaster management related articles. Furthermore, these techniques or ways to support general KS *collectively* answer the following research question: how to let Web users collaboratively build KBs i) that are not *implicitly* "partially *redundant or inconsistent*" internally or with each other, ii) that are complete with respect to certain criteria or subjects, iii) without restricting what the users can enter nor forcing them to agree on terminology or beliefs, and iv) without requiring people to duplicate knowledge in various KBs, or to manually search knowledge in various KBs and aggregate knowledge from various KBs?

Using various examples, Sect. 3, the second part of this article, shows the way various kinds of disaster management related information can be categorized or represented for general KS purposes. Section 3.1 illustrates the representation and organization of a small terminology, and the advantages of performing such tasks. Section 3.2 gives a general model to represent and organize Search & Rescue information; the illustrated originality is the handling of information objects. Section 3.3 gives KRs about automatic explorations of a disaster area, e.g. by a rover; the illustrated originality is the representation of procedures. http://www.webkb.org/kb/nit/o_risk/ gives access to the full representations that these sections illustrate, as well as other ones: representations synthesizing and organizing the important content of three related articles about how to create rovers adapted to a terrain, the biggest article being [15].

2   Complementary Ways to Support General Knowledge Sharing

2.1   Tools to Import & Export Any Kind of Knowledge, Even in User Specified Formal Languages

Knowledge representations (KRs) are logic statements. For graph-oriented models, KRs are concept nodes (i.e. possibly quantified instances of some types) possibly connected by relation nodes (existentially quantified instances of relation types). *The non-predefined terms* in KRs are defined or declared in ontologies by knowledge providers and are identifiers of either individuals (type instances that cannot have instances) or types. Types are either relation types or concept types. Section 3 gives examples.

Regarding KR languages (KRLs), the W3C proposes i) some ontologies of logic models – e.g. RDF for the simplest formulas (the existential quantified conjunctive ones), OWL for the SROIQ description logic, RIF for rule-based more expressive classic logics – and ii) some notations for some models, e.g. the notations RDF/XML, RDF/Turtle and RIF/XML. There are other standards for KR logic models, e.g. Common Logic (CL, the ISO/IEC 1st-order logic model), with various notations for them, e.g. CL/XML (XCL). However, as described by the next two paragraphs, all these KRLs have problems for general KS, hence for general disaster management purposes.

The first problem of these KRLs is their expressiveness restrictions. Although these restrictions ensure that what is represented has particular interesting properties (e.g. efficiency properties), this is at the cost of *preventing* the representation of some information: some KRs are either not written, hence not shared, or written in ways that are *ad hoc*, biased or imprecise, hence in far less exploitable ways. For general KS, using expressive KRs has often no downside since, whichever their expressiveness, KRs can be translated into less expressive ones, often automatically, to fit the need of a particular application, by *discarding* the information that *this* application does not handle or require. On the other hand, KRs designed for particular applications are often unfit (too biased,...) for other ones. Since present or future disaster management is not a fixed list of known applications, expressiveness restrictions limit it.

Another important problem of these KRLs is that they are not high-level in the sense that they do not allow "normalized and easy to read or write" representations for many useful notions such as meta-statements, numerical quantifiers and interpretations of relations from collections. Thus, even when representing similar information, different KRs written in different languages or by different users are difficult to translate and match automatically, and hence to search or aggregate. The use of *ontology design patterns* (e.g. those of [1]) by knowledge providers only very partially addresses these issues and is difficult, hence rarely performed. Furthermore, for different domains or applications, different notions and different ways to write them are useful. Creating or visualizing KRs via the current KR editors is even more restricting in terms of what can be expressed and displayed. E.g., graphics take a lot of space and hence do not allow people to simultaneously see and hence visually compare a lot of KRs (this is problematic for KR browsing and understanding).

One answer to these problems was i) FL [8], a very expressive, concise and configurable textual notation for KRs, and ii) FE [6], a more verbose version of FL which looks like English and hence is more easily read by non-experts. A complementary and more general answer is the creation of an ontology of not only model components for logics but also of notation components for them. KRLO (KRL ontology) [10] is a core for such an ontology: it allows people to specify any KR language they wish. Software modules that exploit such an ontology are currently being designed. With these modules, KB systems will be able to import and export from, to or between any such specified KR languages, and hence also perform certain kinds of KR translations (furthermore, since the rules for these translations are also specified in the ontology, tool users may select the rules to apply and they may also complement these rules).

2.2 General-Purpose Ontologies Merging Top-Level Ontologies and Lexical Ones

Top-level ontologies define types that support and guide the representation, organization and checking of KBs. Lexical ontologies organize and partially define the meanings of common words and relate these meanings to these words. Both kinds (top-level ones and lexical ones) are domain-independent, hence reusable for disaster management. The more types from such ontologies a KB reuse, the easier it is to create and organize its content and the more this content can be retrieved via these types. The more types from such ontologies two independently created KBs share and are based on, the easier the content of these two KBs can be aligned or fully integrated. Since such ontologies are sets of definitions, not assertions of facts or beliefs, inconsistencies between them are signs of conceptual mistakes, e.g. misinterpretations or over-restrictions. Thus, when not fully redundant, such ontologies are complementary and, possibly after some corrections, may be merged without leading to inconsistencies.

The Multi-Source Ontology (MSO) [7] is one step towards such a merged ontology. It already merges many top-level ontologies and a lexical ontology derived from WordNet. More will be added. Unlike for other merges, Web users can cooperatively complement and improve the MSO via the methods described in the next subsection. In accordance with these methods, the top-level of the MSO has already been organized via subtype partitions, and hence has advantages similar to those of a decision tree for knowledge retrieval and inference purposes. Furthermore, the MSO includes KRLO and hence types that are interesting for representing or categorizing procedures or software. As illustrated in Sect. 3.2, this last point is useful too for disaster management purposes.

2.3 KB Servers that Support Non-restricting KB Sharing by Web Users

For general KS, a KB should not include two statements logically inconsistent with one another, since classic logics – and hence most inference engines – cannot handle KBs that are logically inconsistent. Yet, different users of a shared KB may want to enter statements that happen to be inconsistent with each other. For general KS, the avoidance of inconsistencies in a shared KB cannot be done by the owner(s) of each shared KB *accepting or not* each statement submitted to the KB: this not only de-feats the purpose ("*general* KS"), this is also a too slow and arbitrary process to be scalable. Automatically dispatching submitted statements into various KBs for each one to be internally consistent, is also not scalable: with such a method, the number of required KBs and redundancies between KBs can grow exponentially.

The solution starts by associating each term *and each statement* to its source (document or author). For terms, this is now standard practice: the W3C advocates the systematic use of URLs, with the possible use of abbreviations for the sources, but there are other more flexible and scalable solutions. For statements, making this association is recognizing that facts in KBs are actually *beliefs*; this may be formalized using meta-statements that contextualize statements according to who created them or believe in them. (Unfortunately, the W3C has not yet made recommendations regarding this last point and OWL does not handle meta-statements). In such KBs, statements may be seen as either "beliefs" or "definitions". Since these last ones are tied to a term, they cannot be false, i.e. they are true "by definitions": the meaning of the term is whatever its definitions specify. E.g., assuming that pm identifies a particular user in a KB, then pm has the right to create the term `pm:Table` (this term identifier uses the term prefixing syntax usable in most W3C KRLs) and define it as a type for flying objects rather than as a type of furniture. Thus, *definitions* need not be contextualized to avoid inconsistencies.

Contextualizing *beliefs* may avoid direct inconsistencies but is not sufficient to avoid conceptual conflicts nor relate possibly conflicting or partially redundant statements. E.g., a relation between the statements "according to user X, birds fly" and "according to user Y, healthy adult carinate birds can fly" is necessary to state whether the second statement is a correction (by Y) of the first statement, or if the first statement is a correction (by X) of the second statement. Such a relation can then be exploited by each user (according to preferences and application requirements) for manually or automatically selecting which statement should be exploited by an inference engine if it has to choose between the two. For knowledge retrieval purposes, a choice may not have to be made since, when the two statements are potential answers to a query, returning both, connected by their relation, may be a good and informative result. One user-specified strategy of automatic exploitation strategy may be: "when statements conflict and when their authors are all trustable, select the most corrected statements according to their inter-relations and then, if conflicts remain, give the result of the inferences for each selectable combination of non-conflicting set of statements".

The above approach is further detailed and implemented in the *shared KB editing protocol* of the WebKB-2 server [9]. It handles any KB sharing conflict via the addition of relations to the KB. E.g, terms or relations which are made obsolete by their creators but used by other agents are not fully removed but contextualized in a way that indicates i) for terms, who are their new owners, and ii) for relations, who does not believe in them anymore. Regarding additions to the KB, the main rule is that, when the addition of a statement to the shared KB would lead to a potential conflict or implicit redundancy with already stored statements, the protocol asks for the new one to *be directly or indirectly related* to each of those stored ones by a relation of one of the following types: "`pm:non-corrective_=>`", "`pm:non-corrective_<=`",   "`pm:corrective_=>`", "`pm:corrective_<=`",   "`pm:corrective_reformulation`", "`pm:corrective_exclusion`", "`pm:corrective_alternative`" and "`pm:statement_instantiation`". Since these relation types *either* specialize the *generalized implication relation type* "pm:corrective-or-non-corrective_= >", (which is transitive) *or* its exclusion (the type "`pm:implication_exclusion`", alias "pm:=> !"), i) the protocol leads all the statements of the KB to be organized into a hierarchy based on this generalized relation type, and ii) all the potentially redundant or conflicting statements are (directly or transitively) connected via this generalized implication relation or its exclusion. These last two points are useful for inferences, checks and quality evaluations of the KB. Since people can use the above cited relations even when an inference engine is not able to detect potential conflicts or implicit redundancies, people may use such relations between informal statements within a KB or a semantic wiki. Thus, the approach may *also* be used to organize the content of a semantic wiki and avoid or solve edit wars in it. To conclude, this approach works with any kind of knowledge, does not arbitrarily constrain what people can represent and store (within the constraints of any automatically enforceable topic or KB scope), and keeps the KB organized, at least insofar as the used inference engine can detect inconsistencies or redundancies.

2.4 KB Servers that Support Networked KBs

As hinted in the first paragraph of the introduction, the amount of information that can be valuable for risk management is huge (and can be used for many other purposes). That information cannot be stored into a single *individual KB* (alias, *physical KB*), i.e. a KB which i) has an associated KB *server* storing it, and hence, ii) unlike a *networked* KB (alias, *virtual* KB), is not composed of a network of individual KBs exchanging information or forwarding queries via the KB servers associated with these KBs. As also hinted in the introduction, the W3C does not make any recommendation about networked KBs, it solely advises the authors of KBs to relate the terms of their KBs to those of some other KBs. Yet, the more knowledge is added to independently or semi-independently developed KBs, i) the more implicit redundancies and inconsistencies they have between them, ii) the harder it is to fix these problems, and iii) each user that wants to reuse these KBs has to (re-)do this work.

For reasons similar to those given in the previous (sub-)sections, for a networked KB to be scalable and interesting for general KS purposes, i) its total content, i.e. the sum of its component KBs, should be as organized as if it was stored in an individual shared KB with the properties described in the previous subsection, ii) neither the repartition of the KRs amongst the KBs, nor adding one's own individual KB to a networked KB, should depend on a central authority (automated or not), and iii) no user of the networked KB should have to know which component individual KB(s) to query or add to. Hence, *ideally*, i) there would exist at least one networked KB organizing all KRs on the Web, and ii) additions or queries to one KB server would be automatically forwarded to the relevant KB servers. In distributed or federated databases, the protocols that exchange information or forward queries exploit the fact that each individual database has a known and *fixed* (small) schema. These database schema based protocols cannot be directly adapted to networked KBs since the counterpart of a database schema in a KB is its ontology, which is generally large and *often modified* by the KB contributors. Many architectures advocated in disaster management related articles, e.g. those of [2] are based on – or related to those of – distributed or federated databases. Extending the classic peer-to-peer protocols by taking into account the ontologies of the component individual KBs is also not scalable: i) this either implies a "database schema based"-like solution (and then the ontologies can hardly be modified) or a centralization mechanism, and ii) this does not address potential implicit redundancies and inconsistencies between KBs.

To satisfy all the above cited constraints, the solution proposed by [8] is based on the notions of "(individual KB) scope" and "nexus for a scope". The rest of this section presents the underlying ideas of a recently extended version of this solution. An *intensional scope* is a specification (via a KR) of the kinds of objects (terms and KRs) that the server handling an individual KB is committed to accept from Web users. This scope is decided by the owner of the shared individual KB. An *intensional core scope* is the part of an intensional scope specifying the kinds of objects that a server is committed to accept even if, for each of these kinds of objects, another intensional core scope on the Web also includes this kind of objects (i.e., if at least another server has made the same storage commitment for this kind of objects). An *extensional scope* is a structured textual document that lists each formal term (of the ontology from the individual KB) using a normalized expression of the form: "<for-mal-term-main-identifier>__scope<URL_of_the_KB>". This format permits KB servers to exploit Google-like search engines for knowing which KBs store a particular term. A *(scope) nexus* is a KB server that has publicly published its intensional and extensional scopes on the Web, and has also specified in its non-core intensional scope that *it is committed to accept storing the following kinds of terms and KRs whenever they do not fall in the scope of another existing nexus*: i) the subtypes, supertypes, types, instances of each type covered by its intensional scope, and ii) the direct relations from each of these last objects (that are stored in this KB only as long as no other nexus stores them). (The WebKB-2 server that hosts the MSO is a nexus that has at least the MSO has intensional scope. Thus, this server can be used by any networked KB as one possible nexus for non-domain specific terms and KRs.) Then, "the *joining* of an individual KB (server) to a networked KB" simply means that the KB server is being committed not only to be a nexus for its intensional scope but also to perform the following tasks whenever a *command (query or update)* is submitted to the KB server:

- The first task is, insofar as the intensional scope allows it, to *handle this command internally* via the KB sharing protocol of WebKB-2 or another protocol with better properties. For efficiency reasons, when an object is in the core intensional scope but is related to other objects that are not in it, each of these other objects should be associated to the URL of another KB server that has this object within its core intensional scope.
- The second task is to forward this command to the KB servers which, given their scopes, may handle it, at least partly. These servers are retrieved via the above cited URLs and/or exploitation of a Google-like search engine.

Via this propagation, the commands are forwarded to all nexus that can handle them, and no KB server has to store all the terms of all the KBs, even for interpreting the published nexus scopes. To counterbalance the fact that some KR forwardings may be lost or not correctly performed, i.e. that this "push-based strategy" may not always work, each KB server may also search other nexus having scopes overlapping its own scopes and then import some KRs from these nexus (this is the complementary "pull-based strategy"). Thus, KB servers with overlapping scopes have overlapping content but this redundancy is not implicit and hence not harmful for inference purposes.

3 Examples of Representations for General Knowledge Sharing

In this section, for concision and clarity purposes, the FL notation [8] is used, not a W3C KRL notation. Regarding identifiers, the difference is minimal: the namespace prefixing separator is "#" (as in pm#Table) instead of ":" (as in pm:Table), since ":" is instead used to delimit relation nodes, as in most frame-based KRLs.

3.1 Organization of a Small Terminology About Disaster Risk Reduction

In 2017, the UNDRR (United Nations office for Disaster Risk Reduction) has defined a "terminology about disaster risk reduction [16]" which is here referred to as "UndrrT". [11] is a Web document that represents UndrrT via the FL KRL and, as illustrated by Fig. 1 and Box 1, organizes it into a subtype hierarchy using i) subtype partitions or exclusions, whenever possible, ii) the top-level concept types of the MSO, and iii) a few additional types when really needed for categorization purposes. This Web document is also structured into sections and subsections according to some of the MSO types, in a systematic and non-subjective way. All these points make the *terms and relations between the terms* in UndrrT *much easier to understand and retrieve (via queries or by following relations)* than in the UNDRR document where they are listed in alphabetic order and only informally defined.

The above first and second points also support some automatic checking of the way these terms are *specialized or used in KRs*, to detect whether some of their meaning has been misinterpreted. E.g., instances of undrrT#Disaster_risk_management can only be *sources* of relations the signature of which has undrrT#Disaster_risk_management or one of its supertypes as the first parameter. Since one of these supertypes is pm#Process, and since the MSO provides many types of relations from pm#Process (e.g. pm#object, pm#parameter, pm#duration, pm#agent, pm#experiencer, etc.), these relations can be used from instances of undrrT#Disaster_risk_management.

Representing UndrrT via the MSO also highlighted important ambiguities that the sometimes lengthy informal definitions associated with the terms did not help resolve. E.g., are the types undrr#Exposure, undrr#Vulnerability and undrr#Resilience supposed to be subtypes of pm#Characteristic_or_dimension_or_measure or of pm#State? In [11], the first option has been chosen because it eases the use of such types in KRs but other users of UndrrT may have used such terms as if they represented states. The two interpretations are exclusive: they cannot be reconciled. Thus, such ambiguities clearly limit general KS.

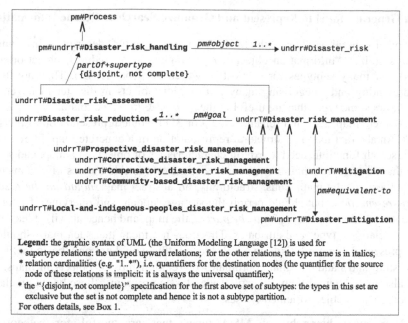

Fig. 1. UML-like representation of the relations represented with FL in Box 1

Box 1. Commented extract of the FL representation of the UNDRR terminology (same content as in Fig. 1: this extract does not include relations for informal definitions and annotations but here has many comments explaining the meaning of the used abbreviations and FL expressions).

```
//Comments are prefixed by "//" and here in italics; the FL namespace separator is '#', not ':'.
pm#undrrT#Disaster_risk_handling   //"pm#undrrT#": the type, created by pm, was implicit in UndrrT
  /^ pm#Process,   //"/^" or "/⌐": supertype relation in FL
  pm#object: 1..* undrr#Disaster_risk,   //"1..*": one or several
  \.part:   //"subtype relation" and "part relation between the instances of the connected types"
    e{ //In addition to be destinations of "\.part", the next two types are exclusive: "e{...}"
      undrrT#Disaster_risk_assesment
      (undrrT#Disaster_risk_management   //"(...)": isolation of relations starting from this type
        pm#goal: 1..* (undrrT#Disaster_risk_reduction
                        pm#parameter: 0..* undrrT#Disaster_risk_reduction_strategy_or_policy ),
        \. //"\." or " \⌐": subtype relation in FL
          //No "e{ ...}" here since the following subtypes are not necessarily exclusive
          undrrT#Prospective_disaster_risk_management   //This type and its next four siblings
          undrrT#Corrective_disaster_risk_management   // are direct subtypes of
          undrrT#Compensatory_disaster_risk_management   // undrrT#Disaster_risk_management
          (undrrT#Community-based_disaster_risk_management
            \. undrrT#Local-and-indigenous-peoples_disaster_risk_management )
          (undrrT#Mitigation   //Since this type name is ambiguous, pm adds a clearer one
            = pm#undrrT#Disaster_mitigation           // via this equivalence relation
          ) __[author: pm]   //pm believes that the last subtype relation is true even though
                              // it is not in UndrrT (neither explicitly not implicitly)
      ) //End of relations from undrrT#Disaster_risk_management
  }. //End of the exclusion set and of all relations
```

3.2 A General Model to Represent and Organize Search & Rescue Information

Unlike other general ontologies, the MSO provides a type for "description instruments or results" (alias, "information objects", e.g. languages, procedures, object-oriented classes) *and* many subtypes for it, most of which are from KRLO. They are useful for representing and categorising many information objects in disaster management. Box 2 shows some types that are useful in the *Search & Rescue* domain.

A concrete map, e.g. on a screen, is a 2D or 3D graphic representation of physical objects. An abstract map is a structural representation of a concrete map. In *Search & Rescue*, search functions need to exploit characteristics of objects in a map, and search agents that do terrain mapping or discover victims or possible indices of victims need *to add* objects to the map. Thus, structurally, an abstract map *should not be a set of pixel representations* but should permit the storage, update and querying of i) object representations that *are, were or may be part of* the map, and hence also ii) at least their partOf relations, types and attributes. This does not mean that such maps should be fully represented *using relations*, in a KB. Indeed, this would not only be an inefficient way to store and handle spatial coordinates or relationships of objects in maps, this would also make them difficult to exploit via classic programs, those based on classic structures such as object-oriented classes.

Box 2. Subtype hierarchy of MSO types that are useful for categorizing description-related types in *Search & Rescue* representations.

```
//For clarity purposes, an informal representation is used below, not a representation in FL:
//  an indented list is used for showing subtype relations between types,
//Still for clarity purposes, from now on in boxes and figures, the source prefix of each
//  type identifier is left implicit (-> all types come from the MSO).
//Below, in this box, bold characters are used for referring to terms that are listed in Box 3.
Description_instrument-or-result-or-container
  Description_instrument-or-result                 //Alias Information_object
    Semantic-representation_instrument-or-result   //E.g. Principle_of_Coriolis_acceleration
      Semantic-representation_instrument           //E.g. Java_semantic, Logic_semantic, Type
      Semantic-representation_result               //E.g. Semantic_of_a_KB, Semantic_of_a_program
    Structural_representation_instrument-or-result
      Abstract_representation_instrument-or-result
        Abstract_representation_instrument
          Abstract_process-structure               //E.g. While_loop, Petri-Net_structure_element
            Abstract_function                      //E.g. each method in Box 3
          Abstract_data_type                       //E.g. Object_oriented_class, Array, Integer
          Abstract_representation  //E.g. Path_representation and each term in bold in Box 3
          Abstract_language-or-language_element  //E.g. Java_abstract_grammar
        Abstract_representation_result             //"Abstract_representation_instrument instance"
          Search_algorithm
            Graph-traversal_and_path-search_algorithm //E.g. the A* algorithm
      Concrete_representation_instrument-or-result
        Concrete_representation_instrument         //E.g. Java_concrete_grammar, Character
        Concrete_representation_result             //E.g. Java_concrete_function
  Description_container                            //E.g. File, Software, Web_server, KB_server
```

Hence, such maps should remain *abstract data structures* but should be represented or implemented in *much richer structures* than "Simple Vector Graphics (SVG) or 2D/3D arrays" (the kinds of structures used in current abstract maps). *Ideally*, for each physical object, such maps would store identifiers or pointers of the object *in a KB*, and this KB would support semantic queries on the physical objects.

Box 3 contains a generic representation of all such abstract maps useful for *Search& Rescue*, i.e. a list of relations between such maps and some other kinds of objects.

Box 3. Commented FL representation of object-oriented classes for *Search & Rescue.*

```
//The types in bold characters (in italics or not) are Abstract_representation types. The types in
// in italics (and not in bold) are information object types that are not Abstract_representation types.
//The other types (except for "Thing") are subtypes of Characteristic_or_dimension_or_measure.
//Variable names are prefixed by "?", as in many other KRLs.
//As in the previous boxes, when comments at the right of some code line are spread on multiple lines,
// each expression in a line is mostly focused on the code of that line.

Abstract_map /^ Abstract_representation,          //Representation of a class for maps
 _{ attribute: 1 Map_scale,                 //The scale of a map should be associated to it
            1 Temporal-point-or-region_coordinate ?timeStamp,   //When the map was valid
            1..3 Spatial-point-or-region_coordinate;           //A 2D/3D point/area
   part: 1..* Physical_object_representation_in_an_abstract_map;   //Object parts
          //This set can be implemented via a 2D/3D array or an SVG structure
   method: Abstract_map__objects_possibly_at       //———— For retrieving objects in (a portion of) a
           (1 Abstract_map, 1..3 Spatial-point-or-region_coordinate,    // map (specified here),
            0..* Type ?typeOfAtLeastOneOfTheSearchedPhysicalObjects,    // wrt. their types
            0..* Attribute ?attributeOfAtLeastOneOfTheSearchedPhysicalObjects) // or attributes, e.g.
               // health, social value, etc. The next line specifies the types in the returned set
           -> .{1..* Physical_object_representation_in_an_abstract_map};   //-> The retrieved objects
   method: Abstract_map__values_of_objects_possibly_at    //———— For knowing the values of objects
           (1 Abstract_map, 1..3 Spatial-point-or-region_coordinate,   // in (a portion of) a map
            0..* Type ?typeOfAtLeastOneOfTheSearchedPhysicalObjects,   // given the types&attributes
            0..* Attribute ?attributeOfAtLeastOneOfTheSearchedPhysicalObjects,  // of searched objects
            1..* Temporal-point-or-region_coordinate ?valuesDuringThisTimePeriod,  // at a given time,
            0..* Environmental_context ?environmentalContextOfTheSearch)   // wrt. the weather, ...
           -> .{0..* Representation_of_the_value_of_a_physical-object};   //-> The retrieved values
   method: Abstract_map__best_paths_from_somewhere_to_at_least_1_object //———— For knowing the best
           (1 Abstract_map                          // paths to take (in a map),
            1..3 Spatial-point-or-region_coordinate ?fromPlace,   // from a place to
            1..3 Spatial-point-or-region_coordinate ?regionOfSearchedObjects,  // another, to find
            0..* Type ?typeOfAtLeastOneOfTheSearchedPhysicalObjects,   // objects of given
            0..* Attribute ?attributeOfAtLeastOneOfTheSearchedPhysicalObjects,  // attributes, at
            1..* Temporal-point-or-region_coordinate ?valuesDuringThisTimePeriod,  // a given time,
            0..* Environmental_context ?environmentalContextOfTheSearch,   // wrt. the weather, ...,
            0..* .{Thing, 1..* Type ?typeOfAttributeOfTheThing,   // given constraints on the
                   0..1 Value ?maxValue, 0..1 Value ?minValue   // types+values of the objects
                  } ?constraintsDuringTheSearch,             // to find, while minimizing
            0..* Type ?typeOfAttributeToMinimizeForBestPaths,   // some attributes (e.g. Battery use)
            0..* Type ?typeOfAttributeToMaximizeForBestPaths,   // & maximizing others (e.g. Safety)
            0..1 Abstract_function ?fctToSelectBestPaths,   // and/or using a function to do so;
            0..1 Integer ?MaxNumberOfBestPaths,             // a maximum number of best paths and
            0..* Search_algorithm ?preferredSearchAlgorithm)   // a given algorithm may also be used
           -> 0..* .{1..* Spatial-point-or-region_coordinate};   //-> The computed best paths
 }.

Physical_object_representation_in_an_abstract_map
 _{ attribute: 0..1 Reference_to_a_semantic_representation, //Identifier of (or pointer to) a KB object
                // that represents this physical object
            1 Representation_of_the_location_of_a_physical-object,
            0..* .{ 1 Physical-object_attribute, 0..1 Certitude_of_a_value };
   part: 0..* .{ 1 Physical-object_representation_in_an_abstract_map ?embeddedObject,
                 0..1 Certitude_of_a_value };
   part of: 0..* .{ 1 Physical-object_representation_in_an_abstract_map ?embeddingObject,
                    0..1 Certitude_of_a_value };
   method: Physical_object_representation_in_an_abstract_map__value
           (1 Physical_object_representation_in_an_abstract_map,
            1..* Temporal-point-or-region_coordinate ?valueDuringThisTimePeriod,
            0..* Environmental_context_of_a_search)
           -> 1 Representation_of_the_value_of_a_searched_physical-object
 }.

Representation_of_the_location_of_a_physical-object
 _{ attribute: 1..3 .{ 1 Spatial-point-or-region_coordinate, 0..1 Certitude_of_a_value } }.

Representation_of_the_value_of_a_physical-object
 _{ attribute: 1 Quantitative-or-qualitative_social_value_of_something, 1 Certitude_of_a_value }.
```

This representation can be viewed as a generalization or "minimal general specification" of *abstract data structures* for such maps. More comprehensively, Box 3 is a top-level ontology – hence a minimal general specification, model or listing – of functions, and of the most interesting kinds of objects that they could exploit, which are useful for *Search & Rescue*. Three important and combinable functions are represented:

- one to *retrieve objects* (generally, *people*, but this is irrelevant for a generic specification) in (a portion of) a map, given some of their types or ranges for their attributes, e.g. a range for the expected health or social value of actual or potential victims at certain places in a map (since, for example, an often used strategy is to first try to save the healthier and most socially valuable victims),
- one to *compute values* (possibly with some associated certitude coefficients) for particular attributes of particular objects in a map, given other parameters such as the environmental context (weather,…) and when the rescue begins and/or when the objects can or could be retrieved (since, for example, some victims may be difficult to save by the time they are found),
- one to *compute the best paths* (possibly given strategic rules and/or a search algorithm) *from a starting place to others* (this may be a whole area to explore) *for finding objects of given attributes*, with additional attributes to maximize (e.g. the safety of the rescuing agents and of the victims) and others to minimize (e.g. the power consumption of a rover used for exploring a disaster area).

In object-oriented (OO) programming, functions are often associated with some of the objects they exploit by being represented as methods of the class of these objects. This kind of association helps organizing and normalizing the code, and is mainstream. Since this association is worth representing and since the content of Box 3 is intended to be a minimal general specification of important primitive functions for *Search & Rescue*, FL has recently been extended to allow the use of the syntax used in Box 3. This syntax is not only close to those of frame-based or graph-based KRLs, including Turtle and JSON-LD, but also *close to UML notations and OO-like notations*. The use of "_{" and "}" as delimiters permits the use of this syntax which slightly departs from the usual one in FL (but FL often uses "." and "_" as prefixes for specifying particular meanings, e.g. ".{" and "}" are the default delimiters for collections in FL). However, the represented KRs are not just OO classes, if only because genuine relations are used, not attributes of classes that are local to them. Here are two advantages of associating functions to information structures via a relation of type "method":

- This allows the use of an intuitive and compact OO-like *naming scheme* for functions: see the "_" within the names where OO programming languages would allow the use of "." for compactness and modularity reasons.
- Combined with the use of UML cardinalities (e.g. "1..3", "0..*") in the parameters of these functions or methods, such a graph-based specification clearly generalizes – or abstracts away – implementation particularities. Indeed, with programming languages, the structures (or *classes* in OO languages) are tree structures, and the functions do not use cardinalities nor have successive default parameters; this generally forces the users of these languages to i) cut the semantic graph into pieces when representing it via such structures, ii) make the relations *implicit*, iii) choose a rather arbitrary embedding

order between the graph elements, and iv) implement various similar versions of a same function, based on particular aggregations of datatypes for the parameters.

3.3 Representations About Automatic Explorations of a Disaster Area

This subsection shows how the task of *systematically exploring* a disaster area (e.g., by a rover, to search for victims) can be represented *at a high-level*: the reuse of the functions from the previous subsection is not shown. The focus is to show how tasks or procedures can be represented *via KRs*, at a high-level.

Box 4 shows an example systematic search procedure written in a procedural language. Such procedures can most often be automatically converted into pure functions, hence in a declarative way. Such functions can be directly represented in a KRL that handles functions (e.g. KIF and FL) and hence included in a KB. There, functions can be organized via generalization relations and also generalized by more classic KRs, e.g. logical formulas representing rules. Box 4 is just an example procedure. Figure 2 (next page) shows some relations (a partOf one and several subtype ones) between top-level tasks in *Search & Rescue*. Such relations are useful for categorization purposes, e.g. to organize and exploit a library of functions useful for *Search & Rescue*. Such a library may for example organize functions which represent different ways of performing similar tasks. The library – and hence programs reusing it – may also include a function that selects the most relevant of these different ways for a particular environmental context given as a parameter. Box 5 shows some further subtype relations from one of the tasks mentioned in Fig. 2 and, to do so, uses FL.

Box 4. Commented procedure for a systematic search by a rover, one based on an infinite loop in which the rover simply decides to go ahead or not.

```
while ( true )   //Infinite loop. Below, "()" indicates a function call (the parameters are not specified)
{ if   ( further_exploring_is_not_useful() )   //To decide that, the methods of Section 3.2 are used
    { come_back_to_base(); break; } //"break": the loop is broken when the rover has returned
  else if ( going-ahead-and-then-come-back-to-base_is_not_possible() )   //Via the methods of Section 3.2
           come_back_to_alternative_route (); //E.g., given battery levels, obstacles, mechanical problems
        else  go_ahead();
}
// Two example cases for a rover exploring underground spaces and fails, under debris and ruins:
// * The rover cannot continue on a particular path (e.g. because it would risk getting stuck):
//   it returns in the opposite direction to a point where it can continue its exploration,
//   an intersection with a not yet explored path.
// * The rover has explored the last path (-> "normal" end of mission) or
//   cannot continue exploring (e.g. because it has not enough energy): it returns to its base.
```

Box 5. FL categorization of the "Safe_path_backtracking" process or task mentioned in Fig. 2

```
Selecting_a_path /^ Process,        //reminder: here, only type names are used (not type identifiers)
part of: 0..* (Search_and_rescue /^ Process),
\. (Selecting_a_safe_path \. (Selecting_a_safe_and_recently_explored_path \. Safe_path_backtracking) ),
\. partition
   { Path_selection_when_going_ahead_is_possible_and_useful
     (Path_selection_when_going_ahead_is_not_possible_or_not_useful \. Safe_path_backtracking)
   }.
```

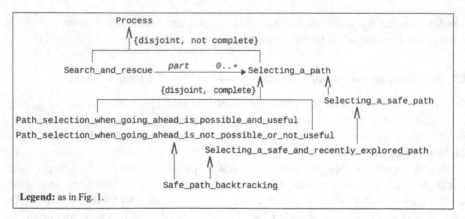

Fig. 2. UML-like representation of some relations between tasks involved in *Search & Rescue*

4 Conclusion

The first kinds of contributions of this article were i) its highlighting of the insufficiencies of *restricted KS* – hence, the waste of efforts and opportunities that not using *general KS* is for supporting generals tasks such as disaster management – and ii) its panorama of complementary techniques supporting *general KS*. Since this field is still seldom researched, for the techniques to be complementary, this panorama draws on techniques previously developed by the first author. Although some new research elements have been included, the originality of this panorama is mainly in the synthesis it makes since the presented techniques together provide a rather complete approach for supporting general KS efforts useful for disaster management, while still allowing the reuse of advances in the well researched field of restricted KS. Together, these techniques answer the following research question: how to let Web users collaboratively build KBs i) that are not *implicitly* "partially *redundant or inconsistent*" internally or with each other, ii) that are complete with respect to certain criteria or subjects, iii) without restricting what the users can enter nor forcing them to agree on terminology or beliefs, and iv) without requiring people to duplicate knowledge in various KBs, or to manually search knowledge in various KBs and aggregate knowledge from various KBs?

The second kinds of contributions of this article were i) KRs showing how complementary kinds of disaster management related information can be represented for general KS purposes, and ii) highlights of the interest of creating or reusing such KRs. The focused example domains were i) the UNDRR terminology, ii) a general model to represent and organize *Search & Rescue* information, and iii) procedures or tasks for automatically exploring a disaster area.

The authors of this article will continue to add KRs to the MSO of the WebKB-2 server for supporting disaster management. WebKB-2 will continue to be improved to ease its use for general KS in disaster management.

References

1. Dodds, L., Davis, I.: Linked Data Patterns – A pattern catalogue for modelling, publishing, and consuming Linked Data. Web document (56p): http://patterns.dataincubator.org/book (2012).
2. Dobrinkova, N., et al.: Disaster reduction potential of IMPRESS platform tools. In: Murayama, Y., Velev, D., Zlateva, P., Gonzalez, J.J. (eds.) ITDRR 2016. IAICT, vol. 501, pp. 225–239. Springer, Cham (2017). https://doi.org/10.1007/978-3-319-68486-4_18
3. Gaur, M., Shekarpour, S., Gyrard, A., Sheth, A.: empathi: an ontology for emergency managing and planning about hazard crisis. In: 2019 IEEE 13th International Conference on Semantic Computing (ICSC), pp. 396–403 (2019)
4. Kontopoulos, E., et al.: Ontology-based representation of crisis management procedures for climate events. In: ICMT 2018 (Workshop on Intelligent Crisis Management Technologies for Climate Events), at ISCRAM 2018, Rochester NY, USA (2018)
5. Malizia, A., Astorga-Paliza, F., Onorati, T., Díaz, P., Aedo Cuevas, I.: Emergency Alerts for all: an ontology based approach to improve accessibility in emergency alerting systems. In: ISCRAM 2008, Washington DC, USA, pp. 197–207 (2008)
6. Martin, P.: Knowledge representation in CGLF, CGIF, KIF, Frame-CG and Formalized-English. In: Priss, U., Corbett, D., Angelova, G. (eds.) ICCS-ConceptStruct 2002. LNCS (LNAI), vol. 2393, pp. 77–91. Springer, Heidelberg (2002). https://doi.org/10.1007/3-540-45483-7_7
7. Martin, Ph.: The Multi-Source Ontology (MSO) of WebKB-2. Web document (2004). http://www.webkb.org/doc/MSO.html
8. Martin, Ph.: Towards a collaboratively-built knowledge base of&for scalable knowledge sharing and retrieval. HDR thesis (240 pages; "Habilitation to Direct Research"), University of La Réunion, France (2009). http://www.webkb.org/doc/papers/hdr/
9. Martin, P.: Collaborative knowledge sharing and editing. Int. J. Comput. Sci. Inf. Syst. (IJCSIS) 6(1), 14–29 (2011)
10. Martin, Ph., Bénard, J.: Creating and using various knowledge representation models and notations. In: ECKM 2017, Barcelona, Spain, pp. 624–631 (2017)
11. Martin, Ph.: Representation and organization of the UNDRR terminology. Web document (2020). http://www.webkb.org/kb/nit/o_risk/UNDRR/d_UNDRR.fl.html
12. OMG (Object Management Group): OMG Unified Modeling Language Superstructure Specification, version 2.1.1. Document formal/2007-02-05, Object Management Group (2007). http://www.omg.org/cgi-bin/doc?formal/2007-02-05
13. Munkvold, E.B., Opach, T., Pilemalm, S., Radianti, J., Rod, J.K.: Sharing information for common situational understanding in emergency response. In: European Conference of Information Systems (ECIS), Uppsala, Sweden (2019)
14. Snaprud, M., Radianti, J., Svindseth, D.: Better access to terminology for crisis communications. In: Murayama, Y., Velev, D., Zlateva, P., Gonzalez, J.J. (eds.) ITDRR 2016. IAICT, vol. 501, pp. 93–103. Springer, Cham (2017). https://doi.org/10.1007/978-3-319-68486-4_8
15. Tanzi, T., Bertolino, M.: 3D simulation to validate autonomous intervention systems architecture for disaster management. In: Murayama, Y., Velev, D., Zlateva, P. (eds.) ITDRR 2019. IAICT, vol. 575, pp. 196–211. Springer, Cham (2020). https://doi.org/10.1007/978-3-030-48939-7_17
16. UNDRR (United Nations Office for Disaster Risk Reduction): Report of the open-ended intergovernmental expert working group on indicators and terminology relating to disaster risk reduction (2020). https://www.preventionweb.net/publications/view/51748
17. W3C (World Wide Web Consortium): Semantic Web. Web document (2020). https://www.w3.org/standards/semanticweb/

Information Technology Based on Qualitative Methods in Cyber-Physical Systems of Situational Disaster Risk Management

Igor Grebennik[1]([⊠]), Oleh Hutsa[2], Roksana Petrova[1], Dmytro Yelchaninov[3], and Anna Morozova[1]

[1] Kharkov National University of Radio Electronics, Kharkiv, Ukraine
`{igor.grebennik,roksana.petrova,anna.morozova}@nure.ua`
[2] Education and Research Institute Karazin Business School, Kharkiv, Ukraine
`oleh.hutsa@karazin.ua`
[3] National Technical University "Kharkov Polytechnic Institute", Kharkiv, Ukraine
`Dmytro.Yelchaninov@khpi.edu.ua`

Abstract. Specialists now make the most of information and communication technologies at all stages of disaster risk management. These technologies, along with the ever-increasing number of Internet of Things devices, can assist in disaster risk reduction or emergency response decisions. At the same time, the existing Cyber-Physical Systems of natural disaster risk management are based on mathematical methods. But mathematical (quantitative) methods have a number of drawbacks, therefore, expert (qualitative) assessments are the only means of solving many control problems due to the ease of use for predicting almost any situation, including in conditions of incomplete information. Research aimed at developing a general methodology for managing disaster response shows that it is possible to view response management as a process and production management problem. Based on this view, process and production management system technology can be used to develop a common framework for a disaster risk management system. A model of situational management of such systems based on qualitative methods is proposed. The model will allow the creation of automatic cyber-physical systems for disaster risk management. At the same time, the proposed model is devoid of the shortcomings of mathematical models and is close to the human way of expressing knowledge.

Keywords: Cyber-physical systems · Information and communication technologies · Internet of Things devices · Disaster risk management system · Qualitative methods

1 Introduction

Today, to build resilience to natural disasters, professionals make the most of information and communication technologies (ICT) at all stages of disaster risk management

– reduction, preparedness, response and recovery. Along with the ever-increasing number of Internet of Things (IoT) devices, these technologies can aid decision-making in disaster risk reduction or emergency response [1]. The result of technologies is Cyber-Physical Systems (CPS), which is the name for a combination of the IoT and System Control. So rather than just being able to "sense" where something is, CPS adds the capability to control the "thing" or allow it to interact with physical world around it [2].

That said, disaster risk management (like disaster response management) can be viewed as a process and production management problem. Based on this point of view, technologies applied in process and production management systems can also be used for a disaster risk management system, which also includes an adaptive (situational) decision-making system [3].

As a method, situational management is based on the assumption that all the necessary information about managing an object that people managed poorly or not very poorly before creating a control system can be obtained from direct observation of their work or from their verbal explanations. Moreover, the object management model can be obtained on the basis of special processing of texts in natural language, which describes a fairly large experience of people [4–6].

The concept of situational management boils down to the following [7]: each type of specific situation should have its own control procedure (scenario) with its own criteria and decision-making methods. The situational control method is used when the complexity of the control object and the particularities of the problem being solved do not allow constructing a mathematical model and setting a traditional problem, as well as when control is carried out mainly in conditions of uncertainty and poor structure of the problem. In this case, it becomes necessary to use heuristic procedures and use high-quality information.

The situational management system (SMS) use Intelligent control algorithms, which imply the rejection of the need to obtain an accurate mathematical model of an object, orientation to the use of "hard" (simple, usually linear) algorithms for generating control actions, and the desire to use synthesis methods known to the developer at any cost, previously positively recommended for other, simpler classes of objects [8].

The situational management method is one of the most relevant and promising methods that allow for a wide class of systems to solve the search problem (in the process of adaptation) of algorithms for disaster risk management systems, in particular CPS.

2 Analysis of Recent Research and Publications

The relevance of the problem raised is confirmed by a sufficient number of publications. In [1], the use of ICT is considered, but only for organizing the dissemination of information, which, according to the authors, increases the efficiency of operations in emergency situations and increase public awareness.

The materials [2] describe the Smart Emergency Response System (SERS) capitalizes on the latest advancements in cyber-physical systems (CPS) to connect autonomous aircraft and ground vehicles, rescue dogs, robots, and a high-performance computing mission control center into a realistic vision. The system provides the survivors and the emergency personnel with information to locate and assist each other during a disaster.

SERS allows organization to submit help requests to a MATLAB-based mission center (i.e. on a set of mathematical models). The command and control center optimizes the available resources to serve every incoming requests and generates an action plan for the mission. The Wi-Fi network is created on the fly by the drones equipped with antennas. In addition, the autonomous rotorcrafts, planes, and ground vehicles are simulated with Simulink (also on a set of mathematical models) and visualized in a 3D environment (Google Earth) to unlock the ability to observe the operations on a mass scale.

So, in [9], the issue of constructing a situational management strategy, relevant for managing complex objects in uncertain environments, when the lack of a strategy is associated with the possibility of default of operational (reactive) decisions, is considered. A method is proposed for constructing a strategy in situational management systems, which opens up the possibility of implementing algorithms such as "situation – strategy – decision".

But the construction of a strategy for transferring an object from the current situation to the target is carried out according to a mathematical model in the form of a situational network in which the degree of preference for a solution is determined by some objective, expert-defined function that has a quantitative expression.

In [10], a situational approach to the management of organizational and technical systems (OTS) was considered during the planning of operations (military operations). A variant of the functional model of the situational approach to the management of OTS is developed. To classify the signs of problem situations (technological relationships), the authors use the declarative knowledge of experts in the form of an oblique matrix, but then, when modeling problem situations, they use an efficiency criterion that has a quantitative expression. The proposed model, in essence, is automated only in the part of modeling problem situations – a description of the current situation prevailing at the control object is submitted to the OTS by the decision-maker (DM).

The review article [11] considers theoretical aspects related to the formation of effective management of the behavior of complex socio-economic objects in an unstable environment. It is noted that situational management of complex objects and fuzzy control algorithms, the organization of which is based on the application of accumulated experience and data obtained by interviewing highly qualified specialists in a given area, can most fully satisfy these requirements. The formation of decision support systems (DSS) on a situational basis and using fuzzy control algorithms is proposed as a promising form of management organization. The result of the work of such a DSS is a lot of output rules (products) for managers, providing various fuzzy (qualitatively expressed) values of the controlled parameters.

In [12], it is stated that the general task of situational management of complex objects is decomposed into the following tasks: decision management when detecting or predicting a problem situation in the process of managing objects and planning management of objects based on the decision made. The scheme of solving these problems is presented: determining the target situation corresponding to the mode of functioning of the managed object in the form of a decision-making task; the choice of a way to achieve the target situation in the form of a task of the direct control of an object. However, it is proposed to use mathematical models of Mayer, Lagrange or Bolza from the classical control theory as a DSS.

In [13], strategy of effective decision-making in planning and elimination of consequences of emergency situations is proposed and discussed. A system of partial indicators that characterize the prevented damage from emergency situations is proposed. To find the optimal resource allocation corresponded to the predicted disaster, the quantitative method of ideal point is used.

The staging work [14] presents the concept of a regional information and analytical system for emergency situations. The three-level architecture of such a system and the functions of its main components are described. The goals and peculiarities of the structural modules for the regional information and analytical system for the prevention and elimination of emergencies are detailed.

The article [15] proposes a universal model to assess the impact of external influences on the system based on the theory of utility (quantitative method). Also information technologies providing the procedure for assessing the risks and consequences of natural disasters in socio-economic systems are considered.

Despite the declared goal of [16] - the development of a management system that integrates the use of the IoT for the detection, prevention and management of natural risks, it is about the implementation of a computerized integrated system only for assessing the costs and benefits in some natural risk situations. The methodology that has been put in place is able to compare the costs of prevention, including the costs of the detection system, analysis and reporting, and an estimate cost to contain damage, with the benefits deriving precisely from the damage avoided.

The work [3] describes technologies for creating a networked Critical Infrastructure system. It is a complex socio-technical system with time-varying boundaries and topology, in which dynamic, uncertain and stochastic factors are present throughout the disaster management process. The article presents a study aimed at developing a general methodology for disaster response management to view the response management as a process and production control problem. Based on this point of view the control system technology is employed to develop a general framework for the disaster response management system, which also incorporates an adaptive decision system. It is proposed to use a methodology called FBS framework, which is a DSS, as part of the formalism for the development of the static part of the object model for the networked Critical Infrastructure system, and also to use the Petri Net as another part of the formalism to develop the dynamic part of the object model. It is proposed to divide the formalization of the control object model into static and dynamic parts and interactions between them. However, mathematical models are used to make decisions, and the Petri Nets methodology proposed for modeling dynamics has extremely low expressive qualities in comparison with existing similar methods.

At the same time in [17] it is emphasized that despite the widespread of mathematical methods in the solution of management tasks, it cannot be assumed that formal methods of modern mathematics will be the universal means of solving all problems arising in this area. Mathematical (quantitative) methods have several drawbacks related, on the one hand, with the necessity of high qualification of developers of such control systems, and on the other hand, errors induced by mathematical models, which have been used. In connection with the limited possibilities of application in management mathematical methods, lack in many cases of statistical and other information as well as reliable methods for the determination of conformity of mathematical models of real office objects, expert (qualitative) assessment is the only means of solving many tasks. The advantages of expert ratings include ease of use to predict almost any situation, including in the conditions of incomplete information.

The material presented in [18] is closest to the goal of this study in the context of the use of SMS based on qualitative methods for automated (and in some cases automatic) process control.

A review of the publications suggests that:

- the vast majority of the proposed solutions is based on mathematical models (quantitative methods), with their inherent errors;
- such systems are automated only in terms of modeling the control object;
- decision-making or entering a description of the situation requires decision-making;
- the main source for creating object management models for SMSs is the knowledge of experts who use terminology in their subject area, i.e. overwhelmingly qualitative data;
- disaster response management can be seen as a process and production management problem.

3   Purpose of the Study

In quantitative methods, an implicit assumption is made that a person once measures a certain quantitative parameter, and the obtained value is the only one reflecting the preference of the DM. However, studies by psychologists [19], as well as the practical experience of using these methods, allow one to doubt the correctness of this assumption. As it is known, the DM is not an accurate measuring device that does not allow errors in quantitative measurements [20]. Psychophysics gives quantitative confirmation of a person's inaccuracy in measuring physical parameters (weight, length, and so on). As a result, the direct assignment of quantitative criteria weights is always carried out with errors [21].

The need to take errors into account in quantitative measurements is rightly pointed out in [22]. In psychological experiments [19], it was shown that human "heuristics and biases" lead to significant errors in the information received (for example, when quantifying events probabilities).

Therefore, the development of the proposed model is based on the use of quality information - expert knowledge obtained from experts in terms of their subject area.

If we talk about expert knowledge, then they can be conditionally divided into two types [23]. One of them – facts, information, theories, problems, etc., is called **declarative knowledge** and is most often displayed in tabular form. They answer the question "What is this?" with their help, you can evaluate the results obtained in the course of any activity (process). Another type is the human ability to solve problems, compose music, treat patients, find faults in cars and devices, etc. called skill or **procedural knowledge**, displayed in the form of process diagrams. This knowledge answers the question "How to do this?" And with their help you can get the required results.

Let us consider in more detail the presentation forms and the content of expert knowledge most suitable for the requirements of the developed model.

Declarative knowledge is the knowledge base for DSS. It is possible to build such a DSS using the ORCLASS method (ordinary classification of alternatives) [20] from a set of verbal decision analysis methods developed under the guidance of academician O. Larichev. The basic principles of verbal decision analysis are formulated as follows:

- *use to describe the problem of definitions and wordings of estimates of decision options in the form that is natural for the DM, his advisers and active groups, without any conversion of such verbal formulations into quantitative meanings;*
- *building a decision rule based on logical, qualitative transformations of verbal variables, while observing the psychological and mathematical correctness of these transformations.*

The ORCLASS method is based on three concepts - an alternative, a criterion (and its values) and a class having the following semantic meaning:

- **alternatives** – data sets (research results). For the model under development, these are sets of process indicator values;
- **criteria** – a set of characteristics that distinguish alternatives from each other. For the model under development, this is a set of process indicators;
- **criteria values** – a set of all possible values of all criteria, while for each criterion they are ordered from best to worst. For the developed model, these are the values of the process indicators;
- **classes** – having their own unique characteristics, ordered (from best to worst) parts of the general list of all possible alternatives (for example, diagnoses, causes of malfunctions, rating or rating categories of something or someone, etc.).

The ORCLASS method allows:

- for any set of process indicators and their values, rank (sort by predefined classes) according to the principle "better – worse" any number of sets of process indicator values, i.e. build a decision rule;
- using the decision rule to unambiguously determine which of the classes belongs to any of the sets of values of process indicators received at the DSS input.

The decision rule (Table 1) is a table containing all possible alternatives, arranged in lexicographic order from the best (having the best values of all process indicators) to the worst (having the worst values of all process indicators) alternatives, each of which is assigned a class, to which it belongs.

Procedural knowledge of the combined model presented in Fig. 4 is the knowledge base for the process executors and the software and hardware complex (SHC) necessary for the full implementation of the process control goals. Expert knowledge is displayed using one of the process modeling methods, namely BPMN (Business Process Model and Notation) [25]. BPMN is a specification of the language of graphic elements for displaying processes in modeling workflows occurring in the system under study. The resulting process model is a network of graphical objects that depict actions (tasks, subprocesses) associated with control flows (see Fig. 1).

Table 1. Fragments of the decision rule for DSS in Nuclear Emergency Management (process indicators from [24]).

N	Thyroid cancer	Other cancers	Positive effects	Negative effects	Costs	Political cost	Classes
1	Best	Best	Best	Best	Best	Best	Strategy 0
2	Best	Best	Best	Best	Best	Middle	Strategy 0
3	Best	Best	Best	Best	Best	Worst	Strategy 1
...	...	...	...	...	...	...	...
364	Middle	Middle	Middle	Middle	Middle	Best	Strategy 2
365	Middle	Middle	Middle	Middle	Middle	Middle	Strategy 2
366	Middle	Middle	Middle	Middle	Middle	Worst	Strategy 2
...	...	...	...	...	...	...	...
727	Worst	Worst	Worst	Worst	Worst	Best	Strategy 3
728	Worst	Worst	Worst	Worst	Worst	Middle	Strategy 4
729	Worst	Worst	Worst	Worst	Worst	Worst	Strategy 4

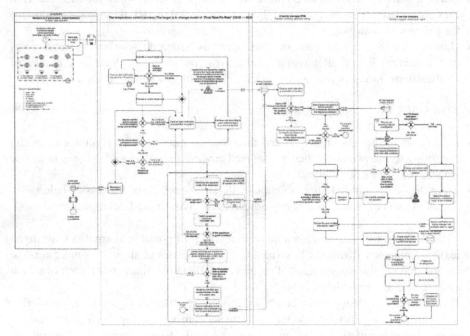

Fig. 1. An example of a process diagram of interaction with the IoT devices in BPMN notation.

Actually, the full specification of the language is difficult enough for non-specialists to understand and redundant to display most processes. Therefore, in the developed model, it is proposed to use the so-called DSL (Domain Specific language), namely, a set of graphic elements of the **language of visual modeling of regulations** (LVMR) [26]. The language is developed on the basis of BPMN and currently contains only 14 graphic elements (of which 2 are most often used), corresponding to BPMN elements, but having either more limited or modified functionality, which is determined by the specifics of the display of process regulations.

The minimum set of elements and their specific properties allow LVMR:

- to be a formal metamodel of knowledge representation about process regulations in any subject area in the form of logic circuits;
- automatically check received circuits not only for syntax but also for semantics.

LVMR, as well as BPMN, is intuitive – as practice shows, the experts with whom we had to work almost immediately begin to "read the diagram" despite the age and degree of technical education.

Analyzing the structure and content of the described forms of knowledge representation, we can draw the following conclusions:

- declarative knowledge with the implementation mechanism represents the level of decision-making – the choice of strategy, including monitoring (*Observe*) and evaluation of process indicators, as well as the choice of a process execution scheme corresponding to the current set of process indicators (*Orient*);
- procedural knowledge is an action plan in the form of a process diagram (*Act*), including the adoption of operative (tactical) decisions "stitched" in a diagram in situations corresponding to the current set of process indicators (*Decide*).

The interaction of knowledge representation forms is shown in Fig. 2.

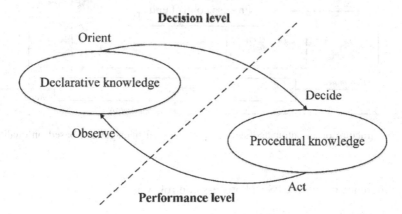

Fig. 2. An example of a process diagram of interaction with the IoT devices in BPMN notation.

The model presented in [18] determines the structure of an automated control system based on qualitative methods, including the following elements (see Fig. 3):

- **Process status evaluation unit** – DSS, which determines to which class the set of values of the process indicators received at the input belongs. DSS is built on the basis of a decision rule developed using the ORKLASS method of verbal analysis;
- **Library process diagrams** – process diagrams containing descriptions of actions in situations and related to classes that are defined in DSS. Schemes developed by LVMR;
- **Process control unit** – executors of the process and SHC, operating in accordance with the selected process scheme;
- **Experts** – make changes to the decision rule and process schemes in case of deviation of the process result from the expected ones or to compensate for the environmental impact;
- **Resources** – a set of resources (process executors, SHC, raw materials and components) supplied to the inputs of the process control unit and the process depending on the class to which the current set of process indicator values belongs.

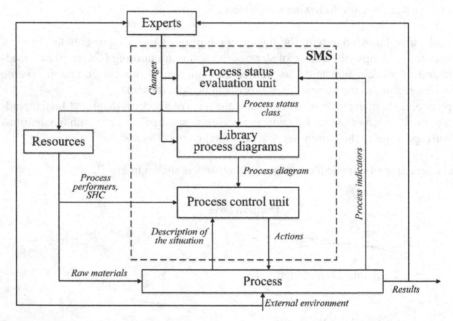

Fig. 3. The structure of an automated system of situational management based on qualitative methods.

The difference between CPS and process control systems is as follows:

- the role of the process control unit is performed by a computer complex;
- the IoT devices act as executors and participants in the process.

In Fig. 4 shows the structure of an automated Cyber-Physical System for situational disaster risk management based on qualitative methods, taking into account the above differences.

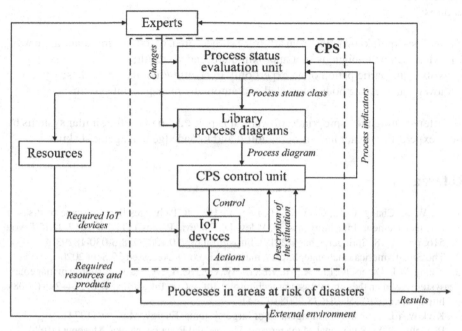

Fig. 4. The structure of an automated cyber-physical system for situational disaster risk management based on qualitative methods.

The structure shown in Fig. 4, includes the following elements:

- **Process status evaluation unit** – DSS, which determines to which class the set of values of the process indicators received at the input belongs. DSS is built on the basis of a decision rule developed using the ORKLASS method of verbal analysis;
- **Library process diagrams** – process diagrams containing descriptions of actions in situations and related to classes that are defined in DSS. Schemes developed by LVMR;
- **CPS control unit** – a computing complex operating in accordance with the selected process diagram;
- **IoT devices** – process executors, functioning in accordance with the selected process scheme and supplying data on the current situation;
- **Experts** – make changes to the decision rule and process schemes in case of deviation of the process result from the expected ones or to compensate for the environmental impact;
- **Resources** – a set of resources, including the IoT devices, necessary for solving problems, depending on the class to which the current set of values of the process indicators belongs.

4 Conclusions

A model of an automated Cyber-Physical System for situational disaster risk management based on qualitative methods has been developed, which has the following features:

- based on expert knowledge in an arbitrary subject area, expressed in a qualitative way;
- produces an unambiguous (not approximate/rounded) result;
- involves the participation of an expert only in creating/modifying models;
- allows you to create both automated and automatic management systems;

After creating the appropriate software, it is possible to make the similar systems by users-expert who do not have programming and knowledge management skills.

References

1. Li, W.-S., Chang, C.-L., Chen, K.-H., Lee, Y.: How ICT changes the landscape of disaster risk management. In: Murayama, Y., Velev, D., Zlateva, P. (eds.) ITDRR 2017. IAICT, vol. 516, pp. 12–18. Springer, Cham (2019). https://doi.org/10.1007/978-3-030-18293-9_2
2. The SmartAmerica Challenge. https://smartamerica.org/. Accessed 30 Sept 2020
3. Zhang, W.J., Deters, R., Liu, X., Tu, Y.L., Li, W., Chai, C.-L.: A disaster response management system based on the control systems technology. Int. J. Crit. Infrastruct. 4(3), 274–295 (2008). https://doi.org/10.1504/IJCIS.2008.017441
4. Klykov, Y.I.: Situational management of large systems. Energy, Moscow (1974)
5. Pospelov, D.A.: Situational Management: Theory and Practice. Nauka, Moscow (1986)
6. Rakov, V.I.: System analysis (initial concepts): a textbook for students of higher educational institutions. Publishing House Academic Natural Sciences, Moscow (2012)
7. Moglyachev, A.V.: Cognitive analysis of situational management in the field of tariff regulation of water supply and sanitation in the region. Bull. Samara State University Econ. 12(62), 82–86 (2009)
8. Vasiliev, V.I., Ilyasov, B.G.: Intelligent management systems. Theories and practice: a training manual. Radio Engineering, Moscow (2009)
9. Gulmamedov, R.G.: The method of constructing a strategy in situational management systems. Inf. Manag. Syst. 6, 36–39 (2011)
10. Yampolskii, S.M.: A situational approach to the management of organizational and technical systems in the planning of operations. High Technol. Space Res. Earth 2 8, 62–69 (2016)
11. Melekhin, V.B., Shikhalieva, N.S.: Theoretical aspects of effective management of the behavior of socio-economic objects in an unstable environment. Internet J. Naukovedenie 4(23), 1–12 (2014). http://naukovedenie.ru Accessed 30 Sept 2020
12. Yedilkhan, D., Uskenbayeva, R.K., Kurmangaliyeva, B.K.: Situational management for process implementation of working operations of the business. In: 54th Annual Conference of the Society of Instrument and Control Engineers of Japan (SICE), pp. 292–297 (2015). https://doi.org/10.1109/SICE.2015.7285573
13. Grebennik, I., Reshetnik, V., Ovezgeldyyev, A., Ivanov, V., Urniaieva, I.: Strategy of effective decision-making in planning and elimination of consequences of emergency situations. In: Murayama, Y., Velev, D., Zlateva, P. (eds.) ITDRR 2018. IAICT, vol. 550, pp. 66–75. Springer, Cham (2019). https://doi.org/10.1007/978-3-030-32169-7_6

14. Grebennik, I., Khriapkin, O., Ovezgeldyyev, A., Pisklakova, V., Urniaieva, I.: The concept of a regional information-analytical system for emergency situations. In: Murayama, Y., Velev, D., Zlateva, P. (eds.) ITDRR 2017. IAICT, vol. 516, pp. 55–66. Springer, Cham (2019). https://doi.org/10.1007/978-3-030-18293-9_6

15. Grebennik, I., Semenets, V., Hubarenko, Y.: Information technologies for assessing the impact of climate change and natural disasters in socio-economic systems. In: Murayama, Y., Velev, D., Zlateva, P. (eds.) ITDRR 2019. IAICT, vol. 575, pp. 21–30. Springer, Cham (2020). https://doi.org/10.1007/978-3-030-48939-7_3

16. Beltramo, R., Cantore, P., Vesce, E., Margarita, S., De Bernardi, P.: The Internet of things for natural risk management (Inte.Ri.M.). In: IntechOpen (2018). https://doi.org/10.5772/intechopen.81707

17. Hutsa, O.M., Yelchaninov, D.B., Porvan, A.P., Yakubovskaya, S.V.: Decision support systems in project management based on qualitative methods. News NTU "KhPI". Seriya Syst. Anal. Manag. Inf. Technol. 3(1225), 82–88 (2017). https://doi.org/10.20998/2413-3000.2017.1225.15

18. Hutsa, O.M. Yelchaninov, D.B., Peresada, O.V., Dovgopol, N.V.: Automation of processes in socio-economic systems based on situational management. In: Linde, I., Chumachenko, I., Timofeyev, V. (eds.) Information Systems and Innovative Technologies in Project and Program Management: Collective Monograph, pp. 138–150. ISMA, Riga (2019)

19. Kahneman, D., Slovic, P., Tversky, A.: Judgment Under Uncertainty: Heuristics and Biases. Cambridge University Press, Cambridge (1982)

20. Larichev, O.I.: Verbal Decision Analysis. Nauka, Moscow (2006)

21. Borcherding, K., Schmeer, S., Weber, M.: Biases in multiattribute weight elicitation. In: Caverni, J.-P. et al. (eds.) Contributions to Decision Research, pp. 3–28. Elsevier, Amsterdam (1995)

22. Von Winterfeldt, D., Fischer, G.W.: Multiattribute utility theory: models and assessment procedures. In: Wendt, D., Vlek, C. (eds.) Utility, Probability and Human Decision Making, pp. 47–86. Reidel, Dordrecht (1975)

23. Larichev, O.I.: Theory and decision-making methods, as well as the Chronicle of events in the Magic countries: Textbook. Logos, Moscow (2000)

24. Hämäläinen, R.P., Mats, R.K., Lindstedt, K.S.: Multiattribute risk analysis in nuclear emergency management. Risk Anal. 4(20), 455 468 (2000)

25. Business Process Model and Notation (BPMN). Version 2.0.2. https://www.omg.org/spec/BPMN/2.0.2/PDF. Accessed 30 Sept 2020

26. Hutsa, O.M.: Knowledge-Oriented Technologies for Solving Organizational Problems in Business: Monograph. Ltd "Company SMIT", Kharkiv (2015)

Creating a List of Works on Reconstruction of Infrastructure Elements in Natural Disasters Based on Information Technologies

Igor Grebennik(⊠), Valerii Semenets, Yevhen Hubarenko, Maryna Hubarenko, and Maksym Spasybin

Kharkiv National University of Radio Electronics, Nauky Avenue 14, Kharkiv 61166, Ukraine
{igor.grebennik,valery.semenets,evgen.gubarenko,maryna.solona, maksym.spasybin}@nure.ua, igorgrebennik@gmail.com

Abstract. The paper formulates the problem of forming a list of recovery measures to restore elements of the region's infrastructure from the consequences of natural disasters by automating the identification of problem areas and places that require repair. It is proposed to process information from unmanned aerial vehicles or high-resolution satellite images, using specially trained neural networks, to check the transport infrastructure and the integrity of power lines. Checking the integrity of the transport infrastructure is necessary to ensure that the repair crew can approach the place of rupture or breakdown. If there is no way to get to the repair site, the repair team should be reassigned to another location to keep downtime to a minimum. A neural network has been built and trained, which allows to determine the places of the rubble, fix their coordinates and plot on the map, as well as send the operator photographs of the areas that have raised doubts to correct the information. The neural network allows to determine the location of breaks in power lines and the integrity of the towers. A strategy for compiling a list of repairs is described, which takes into account the places of necessary repairs, access to them, repair time, travel time, time to eliminate congestion and the number of teams available. The results of computational experiments are analyzed.

Keywords: Information technologies · Disasters · Work scheduling · Neural network · Deep learning

1 Problems Related with Reconstruction of Infrastructure and Public Utility Objects Following Natural Disasters

Natural disasters are almost always accompanied by significant damages to property and human casualties. Major natural disasters may result in a complete destruction of the region's economy and take dozens (or even hundreds) of lives [1]. Thus, according to a humanitarian organisation Christian Aid (https://www.christianaid.org.uk), among all natural disasters in 2019, seven caused more than USD 10 billion of damage each [2]. The largest devastating impact of the disasters was felt in the USA, Japan, China and India.

© IFIP International Federation for Information Processing 2021
Published by Springer Nature Switzerland AG 2021
Y. Murayama et al. (Eds.): ITDRR 2020, IFIP AICT 622, pp. 144–159, 2021.
https://doi.org/10.1007/978-3-030-81469-4_12

The greatest damage of USD 25 billion was caused by forest fires in October–November in the U.S. state California. Experts usually take into account insurance as well as other direct compensational payments to people and companies affected by disasters when calculating the amount of total losses. Two second greatest damages of USD 9 billion and USD 15 billion, total losses reaching USD 24 billion, were caused by Typhoon Faxai and Typhoon Hagibis correspondingly in September and October in Japan.

Statistically the number of man-made disasters hardly differs from the number of natural disasters [3], however, natural disasters cause considerably greater damage to both economy and population. It is worth mentioning that there is a clear tendency of a decreasing occurrence of man-made disasters, the reasons behind this are improved safety protocols and regulations, introduction of new technologies and automation of security systems, etc. [4].

As for natural disasters, the damage they cause increases steadily [5]. Even such minor and casual things as rain or snow may turn into serious problems, for instance, flooding or snowdrift.

The task of public services, rescue and maintenance teams is to reach as quickly as possible those locations, where people may be in need of first aid. Their task also encompasses restoration of main infrastructure objects and, if possible, complete revival of consumption levels, namely, assurance of steady public services supply, functioning hospitals, schools, nurseries, public transportation and other public, logistical and infrastructure objects.

Post-disaster recovery process is rather complex and non-trivial even for typical phenomena. International organisations invest a lot of effort into development of international assistance mechanisms for countries and regions affected by disasters. Thus, the 2015 Sendai Conference saw the presentation of the Framework for Disaster Risk Reduction [6] aiming to generalise the experience of the Global Facility for Disaster Reduction and Recovery (GFDRR) as well as various partner organisations, including the World Bank, United Nations Development Programme, European Union and governments of separate countries within the organisations. Even though the precision of data in the document was not guaranteed and its conclusions were meant as recommendations, this document was an important step towards creation of formalised criteria and principles of damage assessment, reduction of consumption levels as well as reduction of needs during natural disasters and their consequences; these criteria and principles should enable quantitative assessment of needs related to post-disaster recovery and development of universal strategies of impact management. Development of such assessment is a regular procedure, however, every country relies on its own preferences and understanding of the situation, which does not provide an objective perspective for other countries. Moreover, experience of the past decades shows that development of an adequate assessment requires not only absolute values of disaster impact presented in, for instance, monetary equivalent, but also understanding of the level of the country's commitment to implement recovery measures and accordance of these measures with the further development plan. As a result, all over the world there is a high demand for elaboration of universal approaches adopted by the international community. This approach helps to formulate the vision of the recovery, develop the strategies, define the priorities and finalise the plans, it also includes the description of financing, realisation and monitoring of the recovery process.

One of the problematic issues is motivating other countries to provide humanitarian aid. Humanitarian aid may take the following forms [7]:

- financial aid – provision of financial assistance, letting the government of the affected country spend the money on its sole discretion. Such assistance may also be targeted or addressed;
- food aid – in some cases provision of food assistance is more important than financial aid, enabling the population to survive;
- technical aid – provision of various specialised technical means, accessories and consumables, etc. It is not uncommon that disaster impact management requires the use of some kind of specific equipment that is available only to a limited number of countries with other countries possessing only small amount of it or not being able to afford it completely;
- technological aid – provision of expertise and technologies to manage the disaster impact and to revive the economy and improve the environment;
- political aid – in the modern world of fierce competition, sanctions, protectionism and aggressive politics coming from both other countries and corporations, a country, which has lost its competitive advantages because of natural disasters, may not be able to recover without the help and protection of major political players;
- qualified experts and labour force – provision of highly qualified teams of technicians, rescuers or pilots may considerably reduce the time required for the first aid and safe lives.

One should also keep in mind the psychological aspects. Given a sharp drop of consumption level, one needs time to re-adjust and get accustomed. Unfortunately, not everyone is ready for such changes, which, as a rule, take place abruptly. Considering additional stress related to the proximity of death, loss of relatives and friends, sense of helplessness and despair, there might appear spontaneous outbreaks of violence, which could then turn into mass pogroms and acts of civil disobedience, magnifying overall negative impacts. 15 years ago at the end of August 2005 Hurricane Katrina hit New Orleans [8]. The city of approximately half a million of people (484,674 in April 2000) had to be nearly entirely evacuated. Katrina had left in her wake what one reporter called a "total disaster zone" where people were "getting absolutely desperate" [9]. Apart from that, there were the New Orleans marauders. Violence, killing and plundering became normal for New Orleans. The federal government was forced to deploy the National Guard and military units with combat experience in order to prevent the spread of violence and protect the remaining civil population and members of rescue and repair teams. Officials repeatedly made harsh statements against marauders, whereas news from New Orleans terrified the whole country [10]. 15 years have passed, but there are still some city districts remaining unrecovered.

Another situation of mass hysteria and insanity is exemplified by the following incident. On 4 August 2020 in the port of the city of Beirut, an explosion took place. It resulted in more than 200 deaths, 6500 injuries, USD 10–15 billion in property damage, and leaving an estimated 300,000 people homeless [11]. Help came from numerous countries, international organisations and private individuals. However, as early as 6 August the city was shaken by protests, as a result of which hundreds of people were affected; protests not only increase the number of the affected, but also hinder the conduction of the repair works.

A person finding him/herself in a critical situation and under severe stress may act unpredictably and aggressively. Therefore, the task of the country as a whole as well as local authorities in particular is to safe the citizens and ensure at least minimum level of consumption as soon as possible.

Steady supply of electric power is required to re-start the functioning of most of public utilities, service sector and production. Access to the source of steady and available electricity defines the consumption level and the quality of life; formally it is quite possible to meet the basic needs of food and shelter without using electric power (in a critical situation), but no society is able to function and maintain an acceptable consumption level without it over a long period of time. A drastic drop of consumption level means lack of food, medications and personal hygiene items, etc., resulting thus in massive human casualties.

Even during emergencies electric power has to be delivered to hospitals, first aid units, temporary shelters (flophouses), dining facilities and many more. For that reason, consumption level of electric power is generally taken as one of the indirect indicators of current consumption level and economic situation generally. Following the quarantine measures in order to prevent the spread of Covid-19 taken by numerous countries of the world, one of the parameters indicating the stop of the production and general economic processes was the level of electric power consumption. Analytical agencies report a considerable slowdown in the growth rate of global electricity consumption within 2019 (+0,7% compared to 3%/year between 2000–2018) [12]. The forecast for 2020 predicts up to 10% reduction of electricity consumption in some areas of the world [13].

The task of public services, rescue and technician teams is to reach as soon as possible the rubble, where there might be people trapped, restore main infrastructure objects and, if possible, ensure stable delivery of public utilities. Therefore, one may define the time and the number of technician teams as critically limited resources; such technician teams often have certain specialisation, namely, fire and ambulance services, natural gas, road repair services, power system object maintenance and other teams. Each of the abovementioned specialisations requires specific equipment and means that such teams are hardly interchangeable.

Time required for restoration may be reduced through improved management efficiency and quality of repair work organisation. Clear coordination of various technician teams, real-time situation monitoring and application of methods and algorithms enabling optimal solution finding may all contribute to the decision-making process and relieve extra burden from the responsible individuals.

2 Sequencing of an Action Plan in Case of Natural Disasters

As a rule, local authorities are in charge of reconstruction management. The work plan may be presented as a sequence of actions listed on Fig. 1.

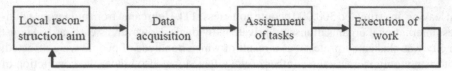

Fig. 1. Reconstruction work sequence

Local aims are often set depending on the experience of the authorities that are in charge of the reconstruction works in the region. This approach accelerates the decision-making process and increases the management flexibility, decreasing, at the same time, overall efficiency and coordination of decisions that are to be made. However, experience of various international organisations should not be disregarded. They were established in order to reduce the risks of disaster occurrence and deal with their consequences, these international organisations conduct information activity, assist in assessing the degree of disaster preparedness and, in worst cases, provide humanitarian help. They also assess disaster risks, develop measures, protocols and methods of risk reduction and publish current dynamics. The organisation of natural disaster management should be based on international experience and make the most of modern technologies as well as computing capabilities of analytical centres.

Figure 2 illustrates the sequence of a decision formation and making when aligned with analytical and coordination centres.

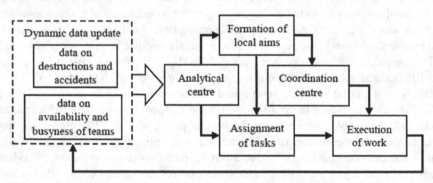

Fig. 2. Modified sequence of reconstruction work

Its main feature is constant update of data on the region's state, one may assume that information on malfunctions, breakdowns, accidents, traffic jams and other issues arrives constantly with varying delays. The analytical centre makes a decision based on the current amount of information, risks and neural network findings concluded from previous emergencies. Once local aims are set for every available technician team, control is then taken by the coordination centre, its main purpose is to provide information support to the team so that it has access to any needed consultation and information on peculiarities of repair works or routes.

Once the repair works are done, information is transmitted to the analytical centre, where the decision is made to send the technician team to the closest point based on the complete picture of repair works time minimisation.

Figure 3 presents a city map including objects that require repair (icon with crossed tools) and places, where routes had to be blocked (triangles with exclamation marks). The number of technician teams is smaller than the number of breakdowns, therefore all repair tasks are to be distributed in such a way that the total repair works time is minimised. Total time includes travel time, time spent on the repair itself and time to report task completion as well as receiving the new one.

Coordinates of breakdowns as well as information on the possibility of reaching corresponding locations are taken as input data to start the analysis. Most probably, city plan as well as all possible routes are prepared in advance, information on actual situation has to be added timely. "Thatch your roof before the rain begins". Unfortunately, not everyone is guided by this principle.

Fig. 3. Example of mapping the places that require repair and road blockage

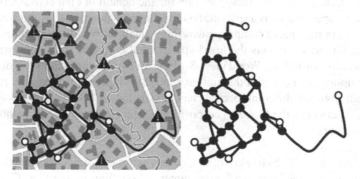

Fig. 4. Presentation of information as a graph

In essence, information is presented in the form of a graph (Fig. 4) with its vertices set either as breakages (white circles on Fig. 4) or route ramifications (black circle). When data is presented as a graph, this task takes the form of the travelling salesman problem with a number of restrictions.

3 Ways of Obtaining Input Data

Another aspect, which is at the same time the weakest point of the suggested model, is the system of obtaining up-to-date information. In order for the analytical centre to start functioning as described above, there must be available data on the exact location of breakages and routes that technician teams will be able to take. Most promising ways of acquiring these data are ground inspections, satellite surveillance and aircrafts. Let us examine strengths and weaknesses of every one of them.

Ground inspections. In other words, this is actual presence at the site or traffic jam. This is the most secure, but also the most costly way. This approach may lead to unreasonable waste of time and resources, disorientation and other related problems when it is not coordinated from one centre. Given efficient management, precise coordination and other ways of obtaining information, this approach is an indispensable way of checking, correcting and clarifying the information received. It is also worth mentioning that some kind of data may only be acquired through personal presence and special verification.

Satellite surveillance. Ultra-high quality imaging is required to correctly determine the status of routes and locations of alleged breakdowns. Ultra-high spatial resolution is considered the pixel size range of 0,3 m to 1 m. Satellite data are easier to process and analyse thanks to wide-area coverage, no flight distortion and availability of rational polynomial coefficients. Current market of ultra-high quality imaging encompasses more than 20 satellites belonging to different countries and operators. They all have their own advantages and solve particular tasks. Let us look at some of them [14]:

- TripleSAT 1–4 spacecraft – is a Chinese spacecraft constellation launched into orbit by 21AT company in 2015 (1–3 satellites) and 2019 (4th satellite). Their distinctive feature is that they are in the same orbit at the distance of 4 s from one another and can therefore take images of the same territory with small time difference;
- SuperView-1 spacecraft – is an orbit constellation of Chinese satellites with ultra-high spatial resolution of 0,5 m – these function for the benefit of civil consumers;
- Kompsat-3A spacecraft – is a spacecraft constellation belonging to South Korea. SIIS (Smart Eyes in the Space) company owns three satellites with ultra-high resolution;
- WorldView-3 spacecraft – is the first hyperspectral commercial satellite with ultra-high resolution of 0,3 m. WorldView-3 films up to 680 thousand sq. km per day enabling up-to-date data with the highest spatial resolution. Furthermore, this is the only satellite with 30 different spectral channels, including 8 SWIR (short-wavelength infrared). It also has the highest geo-positioning precision of 1–2 m without using reference points.

Cost of imaging is USD 6–10 per sq. km, which is several times cheaper than aerial imaging. As can be seen, even data from commercial satellites may suffice. Considering the fact that there are numerous military satellites in the Earth orbit, and some countries are willing to share their data in case of emergency, satellite surveillance may become an important source of information.

However, there is also a range of disadvantages that question the appropriateness of satellite surveillance:

Disaster zone imaging time – usually disaster zones spread over hundreds, if not thousands of square kilometres taking several days in order to film them, which makes it an unacceptable delay. Furthermore, the higher the quality, the smaller the area of filming, which results in longer waiting time;

Weather conditions – clouds, fog, smog, and other factors, which may distort the images or make imaging not possible;

Time to reach the orbit – satellites are constantly moving, they will therefore require time to reach the necessary imaging location.

- Aerial survey. An alternative to satellite surveillance is imaging from an aircraft. There are several types of aerial survey [15]:
- Low oblique aerial photography – an aerial imaging with the camera axis set parallel to the ground surface (or forms a small angle). Low-altitude aerial photography is considered imaging at an altitude of 10 to 150 m above ground level.
- High oblique aerial photography – imaging parallel to the ground surface at an altitude of 150 m above ground level and more.
- Short-range oblique aerial (view) photography – an aerial imaging with the camera axis set at an angle of 25–65° to the ground surface, at an altitude of 10 to 150 m above ground level.
- Long-range oblique aerial (view) photography – at an angle of 25–65° to the ground surface at an altitude of 150 m above ground level and more.
- High vertical (vertical, topographic, nadir) photography –an aerial imaging with the camera axis forming an angle of 90° (or close to it) to the ground surface, in other words, vertically down, at an altitude of 150 m and more above the ground level.

If there are enough aircrafts to launch, they may be able to provide and regularly update actual information on the emergency area and enable the start of repair works.

Figure 5 shows an interaction scheme between the operator and the object taking the images, in this case the focus is on the use of an unmanned aerial vehicle (UAV). A UAV transmits the data via communication towers or satellites to the server, where the interaction with the operator takes place. The operator checks the data received and transmits control signals through available UAV communication channels. The scope of the transmitted data is difficult to estimate, because a UAV sends not only images and video, but also additional information in order to ensure the correct flight.

Currently, solutions are being developed in order to reduce the volume of the transmitted data by means of applying artificial intelligence elements to process the data and make corresponding decisions. During a 4–6-h flight there are about 2 terabytes of data generated [16]. In order to make a decision based on the collected data, it is necessary to process this whole information and retrieve relevant parts.

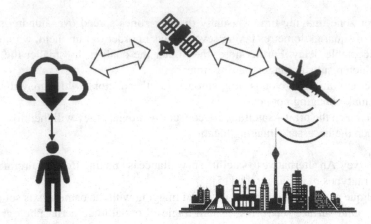

Fig. 5. Interaction scheme between an unmanned aerial vehicle and operator

Figure 6 shows the application scheme of artificial intelligence elements at various stages of obtaining information.

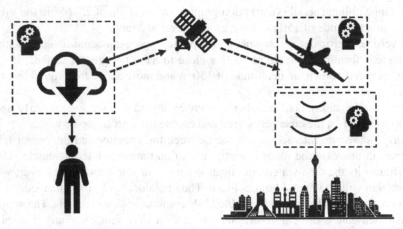

Fig. 6. Interaction scheme between an unmanned aerial vehicle and operator with the application of artificial intelligence elements

Let us look closely at every stage:

1. Obtaining and processing image and video data. Recorded data do not always contain useful information, the purpose of this data is not mapping, but checking the accessibility of the route and the state of certain infrastructure objects, for instance, integrity of power lines and utility poles. Therefore, transmitting large amount of data is not required, what is, however, necessary is analysing the image and forwarding the information on the state of objects. It should also be possible to transmit the image depicting the identified anomaly, be that a breakage or blockage on the route,

for further verification. This will undoubtedly reduce the amount of data transmitted and allow for faster data collection and management decisions.

2. Aircraft control, this area of the artificial intelligence application is already considered standard practice. In an emergency situation, the UAV must be able to independently solve tasks related to flight support, respond to objects, select modes, type and altitude of survey to ensure the best operating conditions for image recognition and analysis algorithms. In this case, the operator is only required to adjust the control and assign the initial targets.

3. Third point is applying AI to process the obtained data and solve the tasks related to work planning, route selection and decision making under conditions of risk and uncertainty.

4 Approaches to Image Processing and Data Acquisition

Deep Learning, as a research area of machine learning [17], is recommended as the basis for the approach to recognise such heterogeneous and non-trivial objects as roadblocks, power line or utility poles breaks. Deep Learning encompasses multiple layers of an artificial neural network, where the current layer takes the output of the previous layer as input. This methodology applies non-linear transformations and high-level model abstractions. It was first known as hierarchical learning [18] and was used to identify images. Deep Learning generally considers two main factors: non-linear processing over several layers or stages and learning with or without supervision [19].

Controlled or uncontrolled learning is related to creation of a controlled or uncontrolled system.

Figure 7 presents an example of a trained neural network functioning, blockages and suspicious areas are marked on the image. The image was taken after the hurricane, as can be seen, fallen trees blocking the road in three places were marked with red rectangles, if we analyse suspicious areas, they turn out to be either shadows from houses or trees or small debris scattered along the road.

The idea is that the UAV control system takes a separate picture of every suspicious area and forwards it to an operator for additional verification.

Fig. 7. Example of an obtained city image and identification of blockages or suspicion of blockages

The neural network can learn from previously made decisions and consequently adapt to current situations. Once areas of blockages have been identified, information on their location will be superimposed on a route plan or graph, as shown in Fig. 8 as can be seen, the system is able to process an image, identify areas of blockages and their coordinates, generate additional requests concerning suspicious areas to the operator, and provide initial data to solve the task of repair work planning.

Fig. 8. Marking the route plan.

In order to make the operator's work more comfortable and avoid replication of incorrect information, different approaches to user authentication are proposed [20]. It is important to understand that working under stress creates unique conditions, and the user simply may not have the time or opportunity to undergo standard authentication.

Apart from locating the blockages, it is necessary to verify the integrity of power lines and utility poles. Figure 9 and Fig. 10 illustrates how a neural network identifies poles and power lines.

Fig. 9. Power transmission line recognition result

Fig. 10. Poles recognition result

Images were recognised by a neural network with the Mask R-CNN architecture. Unlike object detection, segmentation determines the silhouette object, which allows to check their integrity more accurately. Unfortunately, available images of power lines taken by UAVs did not suffice to train the neural network, and it was therefore decided to use images from terrestrial photography.

Now there is no standardised learning base for such a neural network. Therefore, a small dataset was formed from internet images, and each image was labelled by VGG Image Annotator (http://www.robots.ox.ac.uk/~vgg/software/via/).

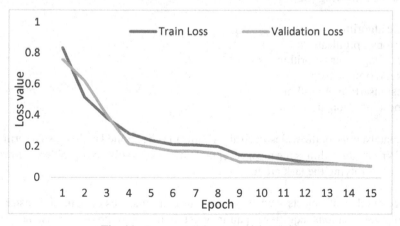

Fig. 11. Loss graph for recognising poles

Figure 11 and Fig. 12 illustrate a reduced recognition loss with decrease in the number of epochs for poles (Fig. 11) and power transmission lines (Fig. 12).

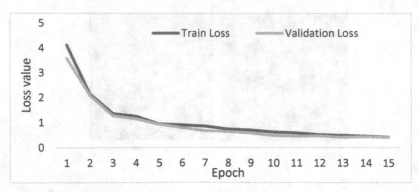

Fig. 12. Loss graph for recognising power transmission lines

It is possible to carry out electric power system reengineering based on the acquired data on its current state [21], improving thereby the overall efficiency of the system.

5 Creation of a Repair Work List

The next stage is distribution of tasks between technician teams. The formulated task is known as the travelling salesman problem. There are numerous mathematical methods to find both an exact and an approximated solution to the problem. Among the methods providing an exact solution, best known are brute-force search and branch-and-bound algorithms).

Main disadvantage of these methods is their high temporal and capacitive complexity, which is important to keep in mind if there is a large number of points. Heuristic methods which, in fact, simplify the brute-force search method, thereby reducing the working time, list the following [22]:

- genetic algorithm
- ant colony optimisation
- nearest neighbour algorithm
- Clarke-Wright algorithm
- nearest insertion algorithm
- cheapest insertion algorithm

Unfortunately, none of the widespread algorithms may be applied in their usual form. The Clarke-Wright algorithm is the most acceptable method to solve our problem. However, conditions to solving the task are to be outlined:

1. Large number of objects – when it comes to consequences of natural disasters, the number of locations requiring repair may list thousands of items; for instance, Fig. 8 illustrates the area of about 0,3 sq. km, but even within such a small radius there were 3 critical zones and 4 places of suspected blockage identified. Therefore, one should look closely before choosing an algorithm with quickly increasing working time;

2   Uncertainty, risks and dynamic information updates – numerous objects may require additional verification, data on many objects may not be proceeded yet, but information keeps updating. The algorithm should be able to distribute the tasks among technician teams basing on lacking information and taking into account those risks that might be hidden in not yet inspected areas. For example, the further away from the epicentre of destruction, the less likely it is that the route will be blocked.

3   Lack of consistency in the implementation of the optimal strategy – in continuation of the previous point, the system allocates work at a specific point in time, based on known information and risk assessments, the optimal (or acceptable) strategy is selected. However, as the technician teams move or complete their tasks, the information is updated, which makes the optimal strategy subject to major changes. Repeated changes to the strategy may lead to a highly inefficient renovation sequence, causing harm and increasing the overall renovation time.

4   Variety of technician teams – in this paper we mention only two different types of teams that are involved in solving the task: to repair electric power equipment and to clean the routes. Actually, the number of specialised teams may reach dozens, making not only the task of work allocation, but also the task of image processing a lot more complicated, as it is then necessary to determine the nature of work and recommend a corresponding team.

5   Interconnection between the repair works – the work of some teams affects the capabilities of other teams, which makes it difficult to find the best strategy.

6   Conclusions

The paper formulates and justifies the task of creating a list of tasks for technician teams of varying specialisations.

It describes the problems that public services have to deal with in the aftermath of natural disasters. Examples show that the main task of public services is to restore as quickly as possible minimum living standards, otherwise, the situation may grow out of control.

A model for developing a sequence of actions in dealing with the consequences of natural disasters was proposed. This model implies the use of systems for the automated allocation of work to technician teams and collection of up-to-date information. This will reduce the time spent on organisational measures and coordination of reconstruction work.

The strengths and weaknesses of different ways of acquiring data on the extent and nature of damage have been discussed. In particular, the paper looks at terrestrial photography, satellite surveillance and aerial survey. It should be noted that sometimes, in order to obtain information, it is helpful to use not only images in the visible range, but also infrared, ultraviolet, radiological, radioactive, and ultrasound etc. This will bring more information and more correct conclusions.

Neural network models trained on the principle of deep learning have been proposed.

The first neural network is responsible for determining traffic congestion. It allows to find the optimal routes. In the paper, existing solution were used to demonstrate the neural network operation.

The second neural network is responsible for recognising poles and determining their integrity. The proposed network is capable of recognizing poles with an accuracy of about 90%.

The third neural network recognises power transmission lines with an accuracy of about 80%. To create the second and third neural networks, the Mask R-CNN architecture was used with retraining the last CNN layer.

When formulating the task of compiling a list of repair works we compared it to the travelling salesman problem. However, standard methods do not solve this task due to various limitations and peculiarities, including: limited time, uncertainty, dynamics, specialisation of teams, variety of tasks, etc. It is also recommended to use the following parameters to compile the list: coordinates of the repair site, possible routes, repair time, travel time, time to eliminate blockages, and number of available teams.

References

1. Grebennik, I., Khriapkin, O., Ovezgeldyyev, A., Pisklakova, V., Urniaieva, I.: The concept of a regional information-analytical system for emergency situations. In: Murayama, Y., Velev, D., Zlateva, P. (eds.) ITDRR 2017. IAICT, vol. 516, pp. 55–66. Springer, Cham (2019). https://doi.org/10.1007/978-3-030-18293-9_6
2. CRED: Natural Disasters 2019. Institute Health and Society UClouvain, Brussels (2019)
3. Grebennik, I., Semenets, V., Hubarenko, Y.: Information technologies for assessing the impact of climate change and natural disasters in socio-economic systems. In: Murayama, Y., Velev, D., Zlateva, P. (eds.) ITDRR 2019. IAICT, vol. 575, pp. 21–30. Springer, Cham (2020). https://doi.org/10.1007/978-3-030-48939-7_3
4. Grebennik, I., Reshetnik, V., Ovezgeldyyev, A., Ivanov, V., Urniaieva, I.: Strategy of effective decision-making in planning and elimination of consequences of emergency situations. In: Murayama, Y., Velev, D., Zlateva, P. (eds.) ITDRR 2018. IAICT, vol. 550, pp. 66–75. Springer, Cham (2019). https://doi.org/10.1007/978-3-030-32169-7_6
5. UNDRR: Global Assessment Report on Disaster Risk Reduction, United Nations Office for Disaster Risk Reduction (UNDRR). Imprimerie Centrale, Geneva (2019)
6. GFDRR: Post-Disaster Needs Assessments, Guidelines, vol. A, United States of America (2013)
7. DG ECHO: Humanitarian Shelter and Settlements Guidelines. Mtia, Iraq (2018)
8. Insurance Information Institute: Hurricane Katrina: The Five-Year Anniversary, New York (2010)
9. HISTORY: Hurricane Katrina. A&E Television Networks. https://www.history.com/topics/natural-disasters-and-environment/hurricane-katrina. Accessed 8 Sep 2020
10. Worthen, K.R.: The storm called America: Hurricane Katrina as a discursive, University of Florida, USA (2018). Figure and the rhetoric of trauma
11. Lebanon's government to resign over blast. BBC. https://www.bbc.com/news/world-middle-east-53720383. Accessed 16 Oct 2020
12. Enerdata: Global Energy Statistical Yearbook 2020. https://yearbook.enerdata.net. Accessed 1 Oct 2020
13. International Energy Agency: Global Energy Review 2020. IEA, Paris (2020)
14. INNOTER: Kosmicheskie snimki sverhvyisokogo razresheniya. https://innoter.com/articles/kosmicheskie-snimki-sverkhvysokogo-razresheniya/. Accessed 10 Oct 2020
15. Paine, D.P., Kiser, J.D.: Aerial Photography and Image Interpretation, 3rd edn. Wiley, Hoboken (2003)

16. Pogorelov, G.I., Kulikov, G.G., Abdulnagimov, A.I., Badamshin, B.I.: Application of neural network technology and high-performance computing for identification and real-time hardware-in-the-loop simulation of gas turbine engines. Procedia Eng. **176**, 402–408 (2017)
17. Deng, L., Yu, D.: Deep learning: methods and applications. Found. Trends Sig. Process. **7**(3–4), 197–387 (2013)
18. Mosavi, A., Varkonyi-Koczy, A.R.: Integration of machine learning and optimization for robot learning. In: Jabłoński, R., Szewczyk, R. (eds.) Recent Global Research and Education: Technological Challenges. AISC, vol. 519, pp. 349–355. Springer, Cham (2017). https://doi.org/10.1007/978-3-319-46490-9_47
19. Bengio, Y.: Learning deep architectures for AI. Found. Trends Mach. Learn. **2**, 1–127 (2009)
20. Nechiporenko, A., Gubarenko, E., Gubarenko, M.: Authentication of users of mobile devices by their motor reactions. Telecommun. Radio Eng. **78**, 987–1003 (2019)
21. Grebennik, I., Ovezgeldyyev, A., Hubarenko, Y., Hubarenko, M.: Information technology reengineering of the electricity generation system in post-disaster recovery. In: Murayama, Y., Velev, D., Zlateva, P. (eds.) ITDRR 2019. IAICT, vol. 575, pp. 9–20. Springer, Cham (2020). https://doi.org/10.1007/978-3-030-48939-7_2
22. Pamosoaji, A.K., Dewa, P.K., Krisnanta, J.V.: Proposed modified Clarke-Wright saving algorithm for capacitated vehicle routing problem. Int. J. Ind. Eng. Eng. Manage. (IJIEEM) **1**(1), 9–15 (2019)

The Ianos Cyclone (September 2020, Greece) from Perspective of Utilizing Social Networks for DM

Stathis G. Arapostathis[✉]

Harokopio University, Kallithea, 17671 Athens, Greece

Abstract. Main purpose of current research is to present evolutions in previous presented approaches of the author for manipulating social media content for disaster management of natural events. Those innovations suggest the adoption of machine learning for classifying both photos and text posted in social networks along with hybrid geo-referencing. As case study the author chose the Ianos cyclone, occurred between Italy and Greece, during September 2020. The geographic focus of the research was in Greece where the cyclone caused 4 human losses and damages in the urban environment. A dataset consisted of 4655 photos, with their corresponding captions, timestamps and location information was crawled from Instagram. The main hashtag used was #Ianos. Two data samples, one for each type, were classified manually for calibrating the classification models. The classes regarding photos were initially: (i) related and (ii) not related to Ianos, while the general classification schema for photos and text was: (i) Ianos event identification, (ii) consequences, scaled according to the impact of each report, (iii) precaution, (iv) disaster management: announcements, measures, volunteered actions. Author's approach regarding classification suggests the use of convolutional neural networks and support vector machine algorithms for image and text classification respectively. The classified dataset, was geo-referenced by using commercial geocoding API and list-based geoparsing. The results of the research in current status are at an initial level, a subset of data though of automatically or manually processed information is presented in four related maps.

Keywords: Machine learning · Disaster management · Social media · Volunteered Geographic Information · Ianos cyclone

1 Introduction

Social network data is an important part of data science. The enormous rhythm of data produced by social media users, forced the scientific world to research on innovative methods for utilizing them in benefit of a plethora of scientific disciplines. In Geography, social network data analysis is strongly associated to the phenomenon of Volunteered Geographic Information (VGI) which is described as the "act of normal citizens, produce geographic information" [1]. Through that point of view, social networks are considered as an "unconventional" VGI source [2, 3] with many potentials in almost

© IFIP International Federation for Information Processing 2021
Published by Springer Nature Switzerland AG 2021
Y. Murayama et al. (Eds.): ITDRR 2020, IFIP AICT 622, pp. 160–169, 2021.
https://doi.org/10.1007/978-3-030-81469-4_13

every spatial-related scientific discipline. Despite any point of view, there is published research regarding its' applications in medicine [4, 5], politics [6], sentiment/marketing [7] and natural disasters. Especially, regarding the latter, the emergence of new innovative tools for DM has brought up a plethora of related re-search that aspires to contribute to DM related to floods [8–11], fires [12], earthquakes [13, 14] and other disastrous events including hurricanes [15].

According to author's latest research findings [3], the main challenges regarding effective social network data manipulation for DM needs, are accumulated in four main groups. A. Classification B. Geo-referencing, C. Visualization, D. Automation. For each one of those groups there is ongoing research. In particular, various classification schemas have been proposed [9, 16] that aspire to extract all the valuable information available through social media. The classification schemas in general may vary depending on data types which can be images, text or video. Moreover, geo-referencing is an important aspect which still faces challenges mostly in terms of enhancing the precision [3, 17]. This research provides some advancement by utilizing a hybrid approach which makes use of both commercial map APIs (google maps geocoder) and conventional list-based geoparsing approaches [18].

In addition, visualization is still a challenge considering that the processed information should be delivered to all citizens, despite their level of literacy, who may potentially face a disastrous event. Finally, automation is a key component that can convert all of those theoretic approaches to operational at real time. Current research provides significant advancements in automation as well, by employing machine learning techniques for both image and text, minimizing thus the whole data processing time to very few minutes.

Case Study

The case study used, was the recent Mediterranean cyclone (medicane) entitled as Ianos. That cyclone occurred during middle of September initially in Italy, between Sicily and Ionian Sea. In Greece, strong storms and floods occurred while the wind's speed reached the 150 km/h. Main affected areas were initially the Ionian Islands: Zante, Kefallinia, and Ithaca. The cyclone affected, sequentially, the prefectures of West Greece, Peloponnese while in Thessaly caused among others 4 human losses.

Eventually, the medicane moved south, to the prefectures of Attica, Cyclades and Crete. Apart from human losses, the port of Zante had serious damages, while in Thessaly, in the area of Mouzaki, 2 bridges were completely destroyed. The main rail network which connects Athens and Salonica was cut in central Greece. In some areas the total rainfall was over 140 mm/h. Hundreds of people were captured within the muds, others were trapped within their cars, many trees fell and thousands of houses were flooded, while few of them collapsed. About three thousand local businesses applied for receiving financial aid from the government. The fire brigade received more than a thousand requests for help. Many areas remained without electricity for days. The floods invoked the Copernicus emergency service in Thessaly (Fig. 1).

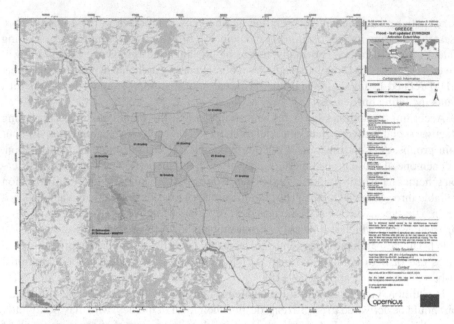

Fig. 1. Rapid mapping activation of the Copernicus emergency service [19].

2   Data and Material Used

An archive of 4649 Instagram photos along with their corresponding descriptive text-information consisted of captions, timestamps and location information (if available) was used. The data were scrapped through the use of a crawler [20].

Data processing was performed in R environment. Main packages used include the "mxnet" for image classification, "rtexttools" for classification of the captions, and "ggmap" along with various other scripts, developed by the author, for georeferencing. QGIS was used for creating the maps. Data manipulation approaches of the presented work can be found at author's github (https://www.github.com/stathisar).

3   Methodology

The main steps of the methodology were divided to the following parts: Initially, the data were crawled while all the metadata for each photo (caption, location, timestamp) were stored in a.json file-format. Sequentially, the json format was con-verted to data-frame and was exported as.csv file, while various pre-processing functions were applied to each text row for reasons of more effective processing.

The second part of the methodology was related to classification. In specific: a classification schema was defined for both image and text data, while the related training datasets, based on data samples were created. In specific, images were initially divided into two basic categories: related to Ianos cyclone and other photos, while the first of the two categories was further sub-classified manually. Regarding text information the categories included: (i) Ianos event identification, (ii) Consequences, quantified to a 5-degree range scale, (iii) Precaution info and (iv) Disaster management: announcements from authorities, measures, volunteered actions. The author suggests Convolutional Neural Networks(CNN) for image and Support Vector Machines (SVM) for text classification, provided through the Mxnet and Rtexttools R packages respectively. Classification especially of photos is at an early stage in current status of the research, limited to the creation of an initial CNN model (https://www.github.com/stathisar).

The next step was related to georeferencing (Fig. 2). The author had presented an innovative method [18] which provides credible results mostly at a municipality level. That method has been advanced to a hybrid approach which employs both geoparsing techniques and commercial geocoding APIs. In specific, all the photos that had location information were geo-referenced through the well known google maps API, while the rest of the text information was processed for detecting geolocations within each caption's text (Fig. 3). That approach increased, in some cases the accuracy; confronting thus with the general known problem of not accurate georeferencing of social media data [3, 17]. As the process is still at a development stage, manual checks and adjustments of the processed info were needed in order to verify the correctness and improve accuracy of the initial results.

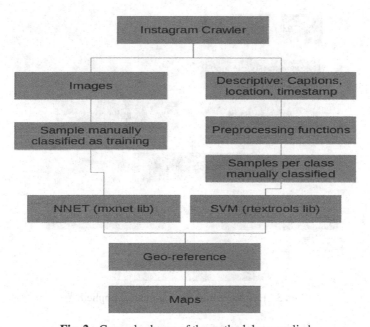

Fig. 2. General schema of the methodology applied

Eventually, the final part of the methodology was related to visualizing the processed output. In current status, the author presents three maps, with information related to: Ianos identification (Fig. 5) in various geographic areas, tracked consequences (Fig. 4), and DM information (Fig. 6). Moreover, a fourth map, displays the geographic positions of three indicative related to Ianos photos (Fig. 7).

Table 1. Basic description of consequence ranged scale used.

Value	Basic description
I	Simple identification, almost zero consequences
II	Big rainfall, measurements of the rainfall without any damages reported
III	Small damages in premises
IV	Big damages, destroyed property and elements of the urban and physical environment. People missing or injured
V	Human loss

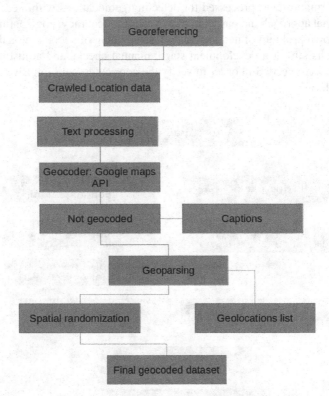

Fig. 3. Hybrid georeferencing method applied

4   Results

Figure 4 displays the location of point observations that represent the consequences, as those reported in Instagram posts. The point values and colors are scaled: The more close to red and bigger each point is the more serious the impact, while the red is related to human loss (Table 1).

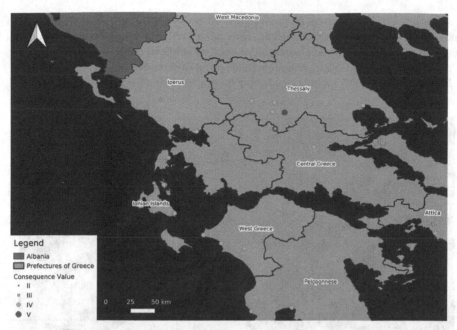

Fig. 4. Point consequence scaled information, extracted though Instagram.

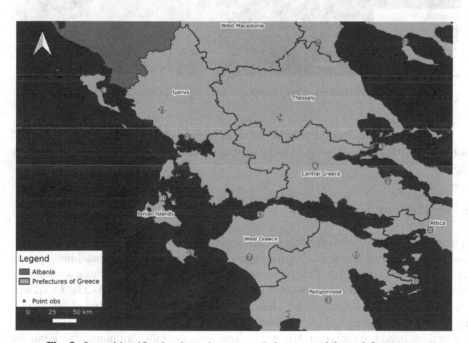

Fig. 5. Ianos identification in various areas: Info extracted through Instagram.

Figure 5 displays clusters of geo-referenced posts regarding the identification of Ianos. Even data processing, in current stage, is still ongoing it can be easily seen that there was information posted about the presence of Ianos, in many areas.

Moreover, the map in Fig. 6 demonstrates point observations that are related to: Precaution and DM: instructions from the authorities, volunteered actions etc.

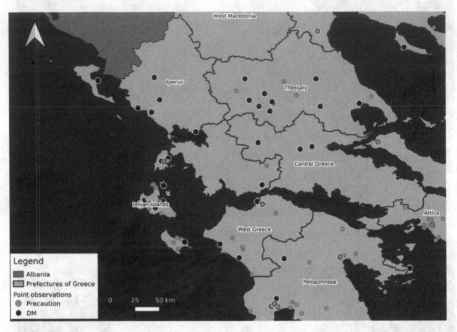

Fig. 6. Point observations of precaution and DM info, extracted through Instagram

Finally Fig. 7 displays the location of three indicative Instagram photos, classified as related to Ianos. Each image's location was mentioned within their corresponding captions.

5 Discussion, Conclusions

In general, automated classification is quite a complex process. There is a wide conversation in international research regarding the capabilities of various machine learning algorithms, while their classification seem to vary according to topic, classification type (binary/multiclass) and data types and properties (i.e. text length) [21–23]. Moreover, specific machine learning algorithms have been emerged as more capable of "generalizing" in a sense of using a general model for all similar classification tasks. Those cases and options need further research in order to evaluate the most optimum algorithms for social network data processing for DM needs.

In addition, initially the author, tried to calibrate the SVM model by using training dataset, created from other natural disastrous event of floods and storms, without any success. The correct classification percentage was less than 40%. By re-feeding the algorithm though, accuracy increased radically. Calibration of the models is still on-going, while the author performed manual corrections in order to have a credible result presented in current status. The initial findings though are promising.

Moreover, even the time needed for training the algorithms and finally perform the classification is, comparatively to manual procedures, significantly less, further research is needed for having models that can operate effectively for similar events.

Regarding georeferencing, even there are promising results by using the hybrid approach there are still quite a few challenges ahead. Initially, there is always the very logical assumption in [24] according to which, the location of a post does not necessarily reflect the post's information. Machine learning for clearing ambiguities could be an effective way, thinking though a real-time system there are a lot of steps towards a desired level of credibility and accuracy. Credibility after all, is vital for the applicability of the methods in DM.

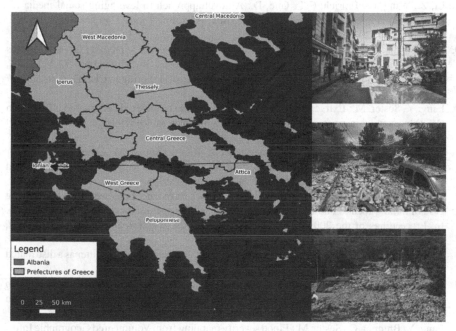

Fig. 7. Images related to Ianos cyclone, posted in Instagram along with their location

The future steps of current research are related to calibrating both image and text classification models and completing the classification automatically. Moreover the optimization of georeferencing is also a mandatory future task. Eventually the general disciplines of author's research are always aligned to generalizing and providing real-time applicability.

References

1. Goodchild, M.F.: Citizens as sensors: the world of volunteered geography. GeoJournal **69**(4), 211–221 (2007)
2. Annis, A., Nardi, F.: Integrating VGI and 2D hydraulic models into a data assimilation framework for real time flood forecasting and mapping. Geo Spat. Inf. Sci. **22**(4), 223 (2019)
3. Arapostathis, S.G.: Fundamentals of volunteered geographic information in disaster management related to floods. In: Flood Impact Mitigation and Resilience Enhancement. IntechOpen (2020)
4. Gorayeb, A., et al.: Volunteered geographic information generates new spatial understandings of covid-19 in Fortaleza. J. Lat. Am. Geogr. **19**(3), 260–271 (2020)
5. Depoux, A., Martin, S., Karafillakis, E., Preet, R., Wilder-Smith, A., Larson, H.: The pandemic of social media panic travels faster than the COVID-19 outbreak (2020)
6. Asghar, M.Z., RahmanUllah, A.B., Khan, A., Ahmad, S., Nawaz, I.U.: Political miner: opinion extraction from user generated political reviews. Sci. Int. (Lahore) **26**(1), 385–389 (2014)
7. Stojanovski, D., Chorbev, I., Dimitrovski, I., Madjarov, G.: Social networks VGI: Twitter sentiment analysis of social hotspots. In: European Handbook of Crowdsourced Geographic Information, p. 223 (2016)
8. Li, Z., Wang, C., Emrich, C.T., Guo, D.: A novel approach to leveraging social media for rapid flood mapping: a case study of the 2015 South Carolina floods. Cartogr. Geogr. Inf. Sci. **45**(2), 97–110 (2018)
9. Arapostathis, S.G.: Tweeting about floods of Messinia (Greece, September 2016) - towards a credible methodology for disaster management purposes. In: Murayama, Y., Velev, D., Zlateva, P. (eds.) ITDRR 2018. IAICT, vol. 550, pp. 142–154. Springer, Cham (2019). https://doi.org/10.1007/978-3-030-32169-7_11
10. Feng, Y., Sester, M.: Extraction of pluvial flood relevant volunteered geographic information (VGI) by deep learning from user generated texts and photos. ISPRS Int. J. Geo Inf. **7**(2), 39 (2018)
11. Kankanamge, N., Yigitcanlar, T., Goonetilleke, A., Kamruzzaman, M.: Determining disaster severity through social media analysis: testing the methodology with South East Queensland Flood tweets. Int. J. disaster Risk Reduct. **42**, 101360 (2020)
12. De Longueville, B., Smith, R.S., Luraschi, G.: "OMG, from here, I can see the flames!" A use case of mining location based social networks to acquire spatiotemporal data on forest fires. In: Proceedings of the 2009 International Workshop on Location Based Social Networks, pp. 73–80, November 2009
13. Crooks, A., Croitoru, A., Stefanidis, A., Radzikowski, J.: #Earthquake: Twitter as a distributed sensor system. Trans. GIS **17**(1), 124–147 (2013)
14. Yang, C., Tian, W.: Social media geo-sensing services for EO missions under sensor web environment: users sensing information about the Ya'an earthquake from Sina Weibo. In: 6th International Conference on Agro-Geoinformatics, pp. 1–6. IEEE, August 2017
15. Feng, Y., Brenner, C., Sester, M.: Flood severity mapping from Volunteered Geographic Information by interpreting water level from images containing people: a case study of Hurricane Harvey. arXiv preprint arXiv:2006.11802 (2020)
16. Gründer-Fahrer, S., Schlaf, A., Wustmann, S.: How social media text analysis can inform disaster management. In: Rehm, G., Declerck, T. (eds.) GSCL 2017. LNCS (LNAI), vol. 10713, pp. 199–207. Springer, Cham (2018). https://doi.org/10.1007/978-3-319-73706-5_17
17. de Bruijn, J.A., de Moel, H., Jongman, B., Wagemaker, J., Aerts, J.C.: TAGGS: grouping tweets to improve global geoparsing for disaster response. J. Geovis. Spat. Anal. **2**(1), 2 (2018)

18. Arapostathis, S.G.: Automated methods for effective geo-referencing of tweets related to disaster management. In: Proceedings of GeoMapplica International Conference 2k18, 23–29 June 2018, Syros, Mykonos (2018)
19. Copernicus Emergency Homepage. https://emergency.copernicus.eu/. Accessed 3 Oct 2020
20. Instagram crawler Homepage. Accessed 3 Oct 2020
21. Suliman, A., Nazri, N., Othman, M., Abdul, M., Ku-Mahamud, K.R.: Artificial neural network and support vector machine in flood forecasting: a review. In: Proceedings of the 4th International Conference on Computing and Informatics, ICOCI, pp. 28–30, August 2013
22. Al-Smadi, M., Qawasmeh, O., Al-Ayyoub, M., Jararweh, Y., Gupta, B.: Deep recurrent neural network vs. support vector machine for aspect-based sentiment analysis of Arabic hotels' reviews. J. Comput. Sci. **27**, 386–393 (2018)
23. Hernandez-Suarez, A., et al.: Using Twitter data to monitor natural disaster social dynamics: a recurrent neural network approach with word embeddings and kernel density estimation. Sensors **19**(7), 1746 (2019)
24. Huiji, G., Barbier, G.: Harnessing the crowdsourcing power of social media for disaster relief. IEEE Intell. Syst. **26**(3), 1541–1672 (2011)

Cyber-Security in Digital Metering Value Chain for Mountain Landslide Warning

Mari Aarland[1], Jaziar Radianti[2], and Terje Gjøsæter[2(✉)]

[1] NC-Spectrum, Kviteseid, Norway
mari.aarland@nc-spectrum.no
[2] CIEM, University of Agder, Kristiansand, Norway
{jaziarr,terjeg}@uia.no

Abstract. The Norwegian Water Resources and Energy Directorate (NVE) are initiating a digitalization process that involves the use of a digital metering value chain and cloud computing. The main objective of this study is to investigate how NVE can ensure cyber-security in digital meters and the cloubased metering value chain for mountain landslide warning. The study is based on a qualitative approach including methods like document analysis and semi structured interviews used as input to a risk analysis based on the ISO 31000 standard. The risk analysis covered three different scenarios from NVE. Those three scenarios were internal, external Norwegian, and transnational value chains for metering landslide warning. The results of the risk analysis showed that the largest risk was loss of metering data caused by failures in complex digital value chains combined with the risk of human error. We concluded that the risk is significantly higher for the transnational digital value chains, and that the recommended risk mitigation is a combination of organizational and technical countermeasures.

Keywords: Risk assessment · Digital value chain · Critical infrastructure

1 Introduction

The paradigm shifts of digital transformation that the society is experiencing comes with both opportunities and challenges. Amongst these challenges, cyber-security is very prominent, in particular in critical infrastructure. Critical infrastructures are defined by EU as [1, p. 3]:

> "an asset, system or part thereof located in Member States which is essential functions, health, safety, security, economic or social well-being people, and the disruption or destruction of which would have a significant impact in a Member State as a result of the failure to maintain those function."

A report from the Norwegian Institute of International Affairs (NUPI) highlights that the digital transformation in critical infrastructure poses greater vulnerabilities, and that cyber-security becomes an even more important aspect to prevent unwanted

Y. Murayama et al. (Eds.): ITDRR 2020, IFIP AICT 622, pp. 170–182, 2021.
https://doi.org/10.1007/978-3-030-81469-4_14

attacks on system weaknesses [2]. Digital transformation in critical infrastructure is the process of implementing new technology in order to better collect, analyze and gather decision-making information [3].

The main contribution of this paper is to present a preliminary study on the risks involved in the digital transformation for The Norwegian Water Resources and Energy Directorate (NVE), specifically in their landslide warning system. NVE is an organization responsible for critical infrastructure, amongst them the critical infrastructure called mountain landslide warning [4].

Digital transformation in this critical infrastructure involves implementing digital sensors and cloud computing in a digital metering value chain to support decision making, which is the most important aspect to mountain landslide warning [3]. A digital value chain is a structure of deliveries between organizations where the delivery either is of a digital service, software or hardware. The digital value chain is characterized by three factors [5]:

1. Error occurs unexpectedly, and the error may spread instantly.
2. A service which is a part of the digital value chain is cross-sectorial, where the service is also subjected beneath different jurisdiction and supervisory regimes.
3. It is difficult to map out the vulnerability for the entire digital value chain.

The mountain Aknes based in Geiranger, is an unstable mountainside that could potentially send 54 million cubic meters of rock down towards the water, which could result in a tsunami wave as high as 85 m. NVE's task is to conduct 24/7 surveillance of high-risk mountains like Aknes and inform the public about any changes to ensure the safety and security of the Norwegian population [6]. In addition, NVE is also responsible for other activities connected to mountain landslide warning. They are responsible for notifying the community if any circumstances change for the worse, this implies that the preparedness level is changing. They are also in charge of implementing countermeasures to prevent any harm upon life, environment and other valuable assets [7].

However, implementing new technology does not come without risk. Incidents or attacks on such high-risk objects could potentially harm up to 10 municipalities, making the digital metering value chain a critical infrastructure [6]. In order to protect such a critical infrastructure, this paper aims to highlight the challenges by conducting a risk assessment of the digital and cloud-based metering value chain for mountain landslide warning. Digital value chains today are already complex and vulnerable. According to a Norwegian Official Report (NOU) from the Norwegian government, the digital value chain is one of the main contributing factors for not being able to determine an organization's digital risk [8].

The rest of this article is organized as follows. Section 2 present previous studies in context of digital supply chain and background on risk management, Sect. 3 describes our risk analysis approach, Sect. 4 outlines the risk analysis process and results, Sect. 5 contains discussion, and our conclusions are presented in Sect. 6.

2 Previous Studies and Study Context

2.1 Previous Studies

Previous studies have examined the advantages and values of using cloud infrastructures for delivering business services. Mohammed et al., [9] for example, have reviewed and analyzed the grid and cloud market services, projects, tools and technologies, using value chain theories. The "value chain" term itself was made popular by Porter, who initially intended to introduce a template to analyze the value chain of manufacturers, which has to do with the increasing connectivity between value components and how the value is created and delivered [10]. Later, it has been used as value chain thinking, to analyze many interconnected value components and value creations, and has been adopted into broader applications such as digital value chains, and various contexts in information-communication technology settings such as cloud computing [9, 11].

Stanoevska-Slabeva et al. [11] look at the grid value chain models by including the linkages among the grid stakeholders or the value networks involving the flow of goods and revenues, flow of knowledge and other intangible benefits such as cobranding. It is presented as role-based value chain. The cloud services are not so much in the pictures, although the framework has introduced some Information Technology elements.

Mohammed et al., e.g., propose a highly-connected three-layer cloud value chain model consisting of *business-oriented support services* (value added services, brokers and resellers, financial services, market place), *primary services* (hardware services, middleware services, grid middleware services, software services and data-content services), and *cloud-oriented support services* (technology operators, consultancy services, etc.). In these two frameworks, the focus is mostly on the economic and business aspects of the supply chain. Giannakis et al., [12] proposed a novel cloud-based supply chain management system framework, by examining different *cloud service models* (i.e., Software as a service (SaaS), Platform as a service (PaaS) and Infrastructure as a service (IaaS)) and *cloud-based approaches* (e.g., on-demand self-service, broad network access, resource pooling, rapid elasticity, and measured service), then link them to the supply chain responsiveness.

The notion of digital supply chain (DSC) is relatively new, it emerges with the development of new innovative technologies such as big data, cloud computing and internet of things, robotics, sensor technologies and trends such as digitalization and digital transformation. The overview of the application of DSC has been discussed in the literature e.g., by Büyüközkan and Göçer [13] and Ageron et al. [14]. The latter defines a digital supply chain as "the development of information systems and the adoption of innovative technologies strengthening the integration and the agility of the supply chain and thus improving customer service and sustainable performance of the organization". Büyüközkan and Göçer [13] add the features of DSC that include speed, flexibility, global connectivity, real-time inventory, intelligent, transparency, scalability, innovative, proactive and eco-friendly. DSC also involve the new emerging technologies mentioned earlier. In other words, DSC is a combination of supply chain management, technology implementation and digitalization.

The notion of cloud-based smart metering is introduced by Pau et al., [15]. The study emphasizes the architecture of the smart meter based on the cloud platform. Cybersecurity comes into the picture, especially in terms of selection of smart metering, which in this study, support secure and trusted communication among different components. However, the main goal is to demonstrate the architecture that can support different services for management and the automation of future distribution grids but is not linked to DSC. The idea of linking DSC with cybersecurity and disaster management is still limited. Indeed, in the literature, studies are available that link the block-chain technology to the supply chain [16], but mostly focus on how technically to apply blockchain distributed ledger technology to promote secure software and hardware in energy sector setting. Risk analysis is also often not a part of the picture of the DSC.

Our study focuses specifically on the cybersecurity in digital metering value chain and the risk management, which can be an initial effort to contribute to the research gaps in these three main areas: DSC, cybersecurity and risk/disaster management. We take the case from the Norwegian experience in the digital metering value chain.

2.2 Study Context: Risk Management in a Digital and Cloud-Based Metering Value Chain

The National Security Authority in Norway (NSM) points out in their report "Risiko 2020" [17] that one of the risk factors for national security in 2020 is the growing dependency of digital infrastructure and digital value chains that stretches across geographical borders. NVE is dependent upon the digital value chain suppliers to distribute their metering data for mountain landslide warning to satisfy their responsibility as surveillance authority for mountain landslide warning. However, a survey conducted by The Norwegian Center for Information Security in 2019 showed that as much as 69% of the Norwegian population lacked training on digital safety culture based on the last two years. This should be alarming news for NVE. When implementing technology into the digital and cloud-based value chain it changes the infrastructure and it affects the entire value chain. If the Norwegian population is not up to date with the evolving technology, they eventually pose a risk towards the value chain by making human errors [18]. Risk management for a digital value chain only works when the entire chain helps contribute with cyber security activities, and the consequences of poor digital safety culture can potentially lead to loss of life for the population living in the area around the unstable mountain. It is critical that the data collected from the unstable mountain is available at all time, continuously processed and consist of the correct metering value data.

NVE uses an operative national surveillance service that utilizes hydro metrological real-time data from the measuring station on each unstable mountain. The protecting and maintenance of the landslide warning is a collaboration between NVE, State Highway Authority, Meteorological Institute, Bane NOR, Geological Survey of Norway and NVE's Section for Landslide [7]. The digital value chain for metering mountain landslide warning can be divided into three different value chains: Internal, Norwegian supplier and Transnational. Transnational value chain means that an external supplier from another country contributes to the value chain making the value chain cross national borders. These types of value chains can often lead to jurisdictional challenges [5].

The instruments used in the digital and cloud-based value chain is both digital and analogue devices to measure movements in the mountain. Instrument like Global Navigation Satellite System (GNSS), Ground-Based Interferometric Synthetic Aperture Radar (GB-InSAR), Satellite-Based Interferometric Synthetic Aperture Radar (SB-InSAR), laser, total station, extensometer, tension rod, tilt-meter, weather station, borehole instrument, seismic and webcam. The metering data is transmitted with the use of fiber cables, ADSL/DSL, wireless communication and satellite, where the communication goes through routers and switches distributed on the mountain [7].

The measuring instrument sends out data each day with updated information about the condition and any movements that may occur for the unstable mountain. It is essential that data collected is both correct and on time, because of NVE task to conduct 24/7 surveillance. These instruments must perform and be redundant for outer intervention so thorough investigation is needed into which factors that could potentially be the cause to the loss of data that must be presented on the website varmson.no. NVE ensures redundancy with the placement of at least three of more instruments together on the unstable mountain that measures the same risk object. However, these instruments are vulnerable to different types of influence and therefore it is important to identify these vulnerabilities. From earlier studies on these instruments, four main categories can be noted that causes vulnerabilities, these are interference, climatic challenges, maintenance of instruments and destruction of instruments [19].

Fig. 1. Illustration of the transnational digital value chain for mountain landslide warning.

In Fig. 1, the transnational digital value chain is presented. Data is collected from GBInSAR, SB-InSAR and borehole instruments metering data, and this is transmitted from the mountain to Italy where metering data are being processed and transmitted to a cloud server in Oslo. From the cloud server, NVE can collect the metering data and present and publish the analyzed data as alerts to their site called varsom.no. The website varsom.no is operated by NVE in collaboration with the State Highway Authority and Meteorological Institute and is a notification portal that the Norwegian population can use to consider whether it is safe to travel or stay in landslide-prone areas [7]. If this site was to be compromised and give wrong information about the condition on landslide-prone areas, people staying or traveling in these areas may be at risk.

3 Risk Analysis Approach

Risk refers to an unknown outcome related to an activity in the future. The process to mitigate risk is called *risk management* and involves a set of activities to identify, analyze and manage risk. It is common to think of risk as a combination of value, threat and vulnerability better known as the three-factor model [20]. This paper combined the three-factor model with ISO 31000 - Risk Management as the baseline and framework for implementing risk analysis. However, in risk management, the person responsible for conducting the risk analysis will influence the outcome of the analysis. The influence is affected by the person's intuition, also called risk perception. Risk perception describes how we see and understand risk, in other words risk perception is a biased interpretation based on different parameters like experience, knowledge and uncertainty [21].

This study used an *abductive* research approach (forming a conclusion based on the information that is gathered) and combined several qualitative methods to determine how NVE can secure their digital and cloud-based value chain for mountain landslide warning [22]. The main advantage for using an abductive approach was that it allows the data gathered through interview and document analysis to guide the direction of the study. It also allows us to omit sensitive information that would have made the study difficult to publish.

To follow the abductive scheme, semi-structured interviews and document analysis are two qualitative methods that were considered suitable for this study where little or no literature was available. To evaluate risk in a value chain, several informants from different parts of the value chain needed to be interviewed. The selection of informants was done in collaboration with NVE and all informants was introduced to the topic with a summary of the context. The interviews lasted from 40 min up to 2 h. In addition, the risk analysis required that the informants possessed essential knowledge about cyber-security and the metering value chain. Another important factor to why semi-structured interview was the preferable choice was the implementation of risk analysis. In order to reflect the reality in the best possible way, the interview guide had to give room for follow-up questions and allow informants to talk about their own experiences [23].

The interview guide was developed along with the process of conducting interviews. The first two interviews made the foundation for developing the interview guide and adjusting the context from each informant towards their position in the digital and cloud-based value chain. However, some questions remained the same to reflect on different points of view to gather a more holistic understanding on the topic. Each risk perception was captured and combined into making the risk analysis to preserve the holistic approach as realistic as it can be. Whenever contradiction occurred, documents gathered from national threat assessment was utilized as a support on how to evaluate risks in the risk analysis. This was done to reflect the risk perceptions to informants, whether or not they could be affected by their position in the digital value chain. This method also allowed us to some degree to confirm some information from the literature study and reduce the uncertainty towards the results from the risk analysis.

However, uncertainty is always present when reflecting on future risk and also on the potential consequences of cyber-attacks. To minimize this uncertainty an extensive research on potential threats and also earlier incidents was utilized when making the interview guide to develop the answers needed.

4   Risk Analysis and Results

Results from interviews and document analysis works as the foundation for this risk analysis. These methods combined were used as references to score the probability and consequence for each incident. Figure 2 below shows a summary of the risk analysis in the digital and cloud-based metering value chain for NVE. In total 60 incidents were selected together with NVE and evaluated for each link in the value chain shown in Fig. 1 above with four main incidents: loss of connection, unstable access, loss of data, and compromised data. These risks were chosen out of knowledge and experience from the contingency department from NVE. They have collected data from earlier incidents and know what type of events is most likely to occur and how it will impact the value chain. Out of 60 incidents, 14 were evaluated as high-risk incidents, 30 incidents evaluated with medium risk, while the remaining 14 incidents were considered as acceptable risk. Concerning the criteria for evaluating the severity of each risk, this study used mostly qualitative data collected through the documents both handed out from NVE and public threat assessments from national departments. Through eight interviews with informants along the value chain, the outcome of the analysis showed that high risk incidents occurred most often in the transnational supplier. This observation corresponds with statements from informants regarding the lack of control over suppliers in other jurisdictions. Further results from the risk analysis showed similar features to those evaluated as high-risk incidents. These factors can be summed up into six categories: dependency to supplier, insufficient control over supplier and sub-supplier, deficient risk analysis, deficient framework for information security, insufficient user education and insider threats.

Link in the Value Chain	Technology	Internal Supplier	Norwegian Supplier	Transnational Supplier
Data Collection	Digital	2	2	2
Data Transmission	Fiber, ADSL/DSL, Wireless, Satellite, etc	1	5	5
Data Processing	Internet	5	4	5
Data Transmission	Cloud computing	3	4	5
Data Presentation	Varsom.no	3	3	3

Fig. 2. Summary of risk analysis results

Figure 2 represents a summary of the risk analysis results where each value represents a risk acceptance criterion based on NVE internal procedures on level of acceptance. The figure shows that the digital sensors are all within the acceptable risk. This is because the instrument located on the unstable mountain have redundant solutions if one were to fail, and if one of the instruments should be compromised or fail to work other instrument could still measure the same metering data and still be operative. However, for data transmission and data processing the risk is high for both Norwegian supplier and transnational supplier. The reason is the rising uncertainty connected to the suppliers and the limitation to monitor how the data is handled through the other suppliers. The service level agreement was the only way to ensure that metering data from external suppliers still had integrity and that it was available at the given time.

In addition to the limitation of monitoring the metering data, the implementation of cloud computing technology into an already complex and tangled value chain increases the risk of human error. When employees are not able to understand the technology and the following consequences or the technology that they are utilizing, they are posing risk towards the integrity of not only the metering data, but in a worst case scenario, the lives of the population close to landslide-prone area. Several informants also pointed out the challenge that NVE is organized in silos and the communication across sectors is not common. The risk carried by moving the value chain to the cloud was emphasized when three of the informants mention that cloud computing could potentially led to more confidential information being compromised because of not understanding how to share information in the cloud. NVE also had challenges in creating a unanimous overview on how to characterize valuable assets. This causes more challenges when sharing information into the cloud. They also did not agree whether NVE published too much information to the public or not. NVE wants their service to be as transparent as possible, and this had led to a large amount of their data being made openly available on their website. This amount of public information might carry a risk of undesired consequences. Attackers could reconnaissance the public information for making attacks more targeted according to one of the informants. But transparency also creates trust in the population towards their decision-making. Since NVE wishes to maintain the transparency while also protecting their assets, the countermeasures need to be well thought out, and the countermeasures themselves must be seen as a part of a digital value chain for a critical infrastructure.

There is no doubt that human error is still a dominant risk factor for the value chain, one informant said that human error was the leading cause for 20–50% of security breaches. In addition, it was mentioned that the most likely event to occur was the insider. However, informants did not agree upon the human capability for preventing threats. Some believed there is always going to be human error and the only countermeasure is to invest in hardware and software barriers. The argument was that cyber-attacks are today very advanced and targeted, making the detection task beyond challenging, and that the employees needed to be experts in cyber-security, "*just*" to detect a phishing email. Other said human knowledge was irreplaceable. They are the weakest link, but at the same time they are also the strongest safeguard according to several informants. The argument behind this statement was based on an example on monitoring mountain landslide, where the hardware system could be compromised, telling the monitoring center they need to evacuate the area because of high movements in the mountain. In fact, the mountain was steady with no movements, so they investigated why the device was giving false measuring data, and then detected that some device was compromised by another entity.

Overall, the new technology is safer and gives opportunities beyond what was previously imaginable. Still, NVE may feel that they are pushed into the digital transformation because "everyone else is doing it". Some are welcoming the new technology, others not so much. They understand that cloud-computing eventually will change the way they are used to work and that they need much time and knowledge to adjust to this change. One interesting observation on some informants welcoming technology and others not, was the position of these informants. Informants from the monitoring center was skeptical towards new technology because they understood the severity of loss of metering data. Informants working in the regional office was welcoming the new technology and was excited to start using it. Another contributing factor was the knowledge about the technology and how it works. Cloud-computing had at the time (2019) no adequate servers within Norwegian borders, which made it impossible for employees to accept the solution as safe because of their duties to conduct 24/7 surveillance and 0% downtime for their instrument. They could not risk sending their metering data outside Norway where they had no control on how the data was being managed. The only way they could accept a cloud-based value chain was through implementing another on-site solution in the cloud to keep it under surveillance at all times. Implementing yet another system into the digital value chain can potentially create more vulnerability, in addition to expanding the attack surface. But this was according to the informants from monitoring center, the only way they would agree upon a cloud-based value chain, which now is more semi-cloud-based. The solution is a compromise between wanting to digitalize and remaining the same level of security, but solution like this could be more vulnerable because the two systems are not made to communicate with each other, so again they are forced to trust that the suppliers of the cloud service is able to manage the integration.

5 Discussion

Open communication and cooperation throughout the value chain may in some cases be impossible because of trade secrets or other conflicts of interest. However, in order to protect their assets, NVE should consider the organizational countermeasures mentioned in the previous section, in order to obtain a holistic approach rather than a sector-based approach. It is no longer enough to rely on trust in the agreements as their safeguard towards suppliers and sub-suppliers in the value chain. The information flow and communication with suppliers should be prioritized to reduce the risk of attacks with lateral movement from sub-supplier into NVE's server, from where attackers might gain even more access throughout the value chain [5].

To manage the digital and cloud-based metering value chain one cannot simply say that it needs to be managed centralized or decentralized. Because on one hand you can create the holistic overview by centralized management of the value chain but missing important details due to lack of expert knowledge on each part of value chain. On the other hand, you can obtain detailed information about your part of the digital value chain when managing it in a decentralized manner, but this misses the overview of the value chain and minor risk events could potentially cascade into more serious incidents when seen as a part of a the digital value chain. Today they use trust between actors as their main way of ensuring that the value chain is secured. But when informants were asked on how they can ensure that suppliers actually fulfill this requirement, they could not provide good answers. This type of uncertainty causes room for attackers to exploit. It is only a matter of time before a more serious attack happens to the critical value chain, and when it does, should it be handled from a centralized or decentralized perspective? Have NVE communicated sufficiently the risk between the value chain actors, and do the suppliers know their role if they are under attack? The answers to these questions may be found in further research on this topic. It is important that each supplier know their role and are ready to collectively manage an attack on the digital value chain.

Consensus between suppliers in a digital value chain is important, both for knowing what exactly they are working on and for a shared understanding of the importance of cyber security to protect the critical infrastructure. If NVE have trouble defining what type of information should be sensitive and what should be public, the information loses its integrity and confidential information may find its way to the public. Even though this is a result of human error, this could be mitigated by raising awareness towards sensitive information and how to handle these types of data. Humans may be the weakest link as some informants may indicate, but they are also the strongest when it comes to complex decision-making, and this cannot yet be replicated by artificial intelligence. Despite humans being dependent on technology, technology also depends on humans to understand it to operate in the way we intendent it to work. In any case, the digital transformation is inevitable and replaces analogue work whether we like it or not.

Cloud-computing causes interdependencies to an already interdependent value chain. NVE is investing in a solution provided by the suppliers of the cloud service and they thereby invest in another system to be integrated into the cloud. NVE becomes dependent on this one supplier, making it more difficult to change cloud service if needed. NVE need to have a backup plan for the event that the cloud service stops working. They cannot be dependent on cloud suppliers committing to the 0% downtime that NVE is regulated to have.

One of the most important actions to protect NVE's digital and cloud-based value chain is to pay attention on the connection between the existing and new countermeasures to avoid dependencies between safeguards. Dependencies thorough the digital value chain could potentially lead to a domino-effect between stakeholders when an incident occurs. Still, the technology of cloud computing that NVE plan to implement will create dependencies and the focus to implement strict procedures and service level agreements will be important contributing factors to obtain a secure value chain. However, these should not be the only countermeasures. Organizational countermeasures that will be important to prioritize include awareness, training, communication, response, surveillance and anticipation. The technical countermeasures considered efficient for digital and cloud-based value chains are as follows: segregated networks, user restrictions, log analysis, pen-testing, security by design/security by default, end-to-end encryption, computer generated passwords and two-factor authentication.

In addition, a general framework for implementing cyber-security for metering value chain should be considered to ensure secure implementation of cyber-security for suppliers and sub-suppliers. Most importantly, performing risk analysis with a *holistic* approach. The framework could potentially help employees on how to assess sensitive information across sectors and make the assessment more coherent. An important aspect to this framework is that is must be communicated not only to internal employees but also to external actors in the digital value chain. To secure the digital value chain, they first need to focus on how to raise awareness on cyber security and the technology that NVE wishes to utilize. The framework should emphasize that NVE conducts risk assessment and provides courses with focus on cyber security and what responsibility an employee possesses when handling sensitive data. Through risk assessment and preventative activities like log-analysis, penetration testing and intrusion detection systems, NVE will be able to work proactive rather than reactive on cyber security incidents. Even though password policy can sometimes work as a recipe for attackers, NVE must influence employees about the importance of making passwords hard to crack. Multiple factor authentication should be a part of their password policy because they are responsible for critical infrastructure.

Results from the risk analysis will be affected by the knowledge, experience and uncertainty of the person conducting the analysis, but also the chosen approach to the risk analysis [21]. When choosing an approach of risk analysis, one must be aware of the results other risk analysis may lead to. There exists benefits and limitation towards all risk analysis, and one must decide which approach is the most suitable for the answers you seek. For this study, the purpose was to understand how best secure the digital and cloud-based metering value chain for the critical infrastructure mountain landslide warning. Based on extensive research on multiple other risk analysis ISO 31000, NIST Cybersecurity framework, ENISA- Cloud Computing, Security Risk Assessment, NSM Foundational principles in ICT-safety the preferable choice was eventually ISO 31000 because this was the most holistic approach which the study needed in order to understand how to secure the value chain. However, the risk analysis results are based on assumption and assumption always contains uncertainty. It is inevitable to omit the uncertainty when referring to something that may happen in the future. But some historical events and expert knowledge will be the best foundation for the risk analysis. On the other hand, expert knowledge will again be influenced by the risk perception, not only to the expert but also the one conducting the risk analysis.

An unbiased risk assessment should not be the objective of a risk assessment in critical infrastructure. Assets that are critical for some may not be critical for others, and therefore NVE is recommended to cooperate and communicate with their suppliers to understand the different approaches to risk. This can help them into making the risk analysis more realistic by involving each supplier. NVE should be the initiating part and they should be open for sharing their analysis with the value chain so that the suppliers have the opportunity to influence the analysis the way they assess the risks.

6 Conclusions

We find that the risk is significantly higher for the transnational digital value chains. The recommended risk mitigation is a combination of organizational and technical countermeasures. To secure the digital and cloud-based value chains, NVE should invest resources to continuously control suppliers and sub-suppliers. The most important countermeasures will be developing a framework for cyber-security that should be distributed throughout the value chain to ensure implementation of important activities to prevent/protect, detect, handle and act on attacks against the value chain. Trust is an important factor but trust alone is not enough to ensure that the critical infrastructure is protected.

The existing literature on security in cloud-based digital value chains is rather limited, providing a good opportunity for further research in this area. To further investigate the vulnerabilities existing in a chain of suppliers and sub-suppliers would be necessary in order to further elaborate of the activities needed to secure the value chain. This would also help in evaluation of risk levels. It would also be very interesting to explore the concept of resilience as a foundation to secure the digital and cloud-based value chain.

Acknowledgements. Thanks to Janne M. Hagen for good and useful advice on this paper which is a short summary of a master thesis. Thanks also to Arne Bjørn Mildal for contribution to the thesis and to the informants from NVE for bringing insight to this topic. Thanks to Eva Brekka at NC-Spectrum for this opportunity to participate in this research.

References

1. European Commission: Evaluation of council directive 2008/114 on the identification and designation of European critical infrastructures and the assessment of the need to improve their protection. European Commission, Brussel (2008)
2. Gjesvik, L.: Comparing Cyber Security. Norwegian Insitute of International Affairs, Oslo (2019)
3. Proactima: Kartlegging av bruk av tingenes internett (IoT/IIoT) i norsk kraftforsyning, Nr.2/2020, Norges vassdrag- og energidirektorat, Oslo (2020)
4. NVE: Om NVE, December 2020. https://www.nve.no/om-nve/?ref=mainmenu
5. DSB: Risikostyring i digitale verdikjeder, Direktoratet for samfunnssikkerhet og beredskap, Tønsberg, (2020)
6. NVE: Åknes, January 2020. https://www.nve.no/flaum-og-skred/fjellskredovervaking/kontin uerligovervakede-fjellpartier/aknes/
7. NVE: Fjellskred - overvåking og beredskap, Nr. 5/2017, Norges vassdrag- og energidirektorat, Oslo, (2017)
8. NOU 2015:13: Digital sårbarhet - sikkert samfunn, Regjeringen, Oslo (2015)
9. Mohammed, A.B., Altmann, J., Hwang, J.: Cloud computing value chains: understanding businesses and value creation in the cloud. In: Neumann, D., Baker, M., Altmann, J., Rana, O. (eds.) Economic models and algorithms for distributed systems. AS, pp. 187–208. Birkhäuser Basel, Basel (2009). https://doi.org/10.1007/978-3-7643-8899-7_11
10. Simatupang, T.M., Pioonrungroj, P., William, S.: The emergence of value chain thinking. Int. J. Value Chain Manage. **8**(1), 40–57 (2017)
11. Stanoevska-Slabeva, K., Talamanca, C.F., Thanos, G.A., Zsigri, C.: Development of a generic value chain for the grid industry. In: Veit, D.J., Altmann, J. (eds.) GECON 2007. LNCS, vol. 4685, pp. 44–57. Springer, Heidelberg (2007). https://doi.org/10.1007/978-3-540-74430-6_4
12. Giannakis, M., Spanaki, K., Dubey, R.: A cloud-based supply chain management system: effects on supply chain responsiveness. J. Enterp. Inf. Manage. (2019)
13. Büyüközkan, G., Göçer, F.: Digital supply chain: literature review and a proposed framework for future research. Comput. Ind. **97**, 157–177 (2018)
14. Ageron, B., Bentahar, O., Gunasekaran, A.: Digital supply chain: challenges and future directions. Supply Chain Forum Int. J. **21**(3), 133–138 (2020)
15. Pau, M., et al.: A cloud-based smart metering infrastructure for distribution grid services and automation. Sustain. Energy Grids Netw. **15**, 14–25 (2018)
16. Mylrea, M., Gourisetti, S. N. G.: Blockchain for supply chain cybersecurity, optimization and compliance. In: Resilience Week (RWS), pp. 70–76 (2018)
17. NSM: Risiko 2020, Nasjonal sikkerhetsmyndighet, Oslo (2020)
18. NorSIS: Nordmenn og digital sikkerhetskultur, Norsk senter for informasjonssikring, Gjøvik (2019)
19. Romsenter, N.: Vurdering av sårbarhet ved bruk av globale satellittnavigasjonssystemer i kritisk infrastruktur, Norsk Romsenter, Oslo (2013)
20. NOU 2006:6: Når sikkerheten er viktigst, Regjeringen, Oslo (2006)
21. Slovic, P.: The perception of risk. Science **236**, 280–285 (2014)

22. Josephson, J.R., Bharathan, V.: An abductive framework for level one information fusion. In: Information Fusion, Italy (2006)
23. Magnani, L.: Abduction, Reason and Science: Processes of Discovery and Explanation. Springer, New York (2001). https://doi.org/10.1007/978-1-4419-8562-0

Disaster Risk Reduction for All?
Understanding Intersectionality in Disaster Situations

Cristina Paupini[1] and Terje Gjøsæter[2(✉)]

[1] Oslo Metropolitan University, Oslo, Norway
cristpa@oslomet.no
[2] CIEM, University of Agder, Kristiansand, Norway
terjeg@uia.no

Abstract. When designing digital services for citizens in a disaster situation, the diversity of its audience and their particular needs are not always sufficiently taken into account. Variables like digital equipment available, environment, disabilities, socio-economic status, etc., play a significant role in people's ability to access and exchange important information through digital means. In this paper, we will examine some factors that lead to this inequality, and we see that they tend to boil down to a lack of awareness or focus on the diversity of the population, and this affects not only people with disabilities, but also other disadvantaged groups. More broadly, we will examine this in terms of *intersectionality,* and suggest how Universal Design can contribute to mitigate these issues. The issues will be illustrated with example scenarios, using personas for highlighting issues that can affect members of intersectional vulnerable groups in a particularly strong way during a disaster.

Keywords: Universal Design of ICT · Digital citizen services · Intersectionality

1 Introduction

2020 has shown the world that disasters can strike hard and wide. Not all disasters come in the form of sudden but short bursts of chaos followed by a clear recovery phase. The COVID-19 pandemic has demonstrated that resilience comes in many forms, and the way society has managed to cope with the situation has required an enormous effort from everybody. For example, most schools and universities have managed to turn around from in-class teaching to remote digital teaching very quickly, and people in many occupations are working efficiently from home with their own digital equipment and network.

However, the success of this swift transformation is not equally distributed. When digital solutions are chosen, the diversity of its audience is not always considered. Returning to the example of schools and universities, students may get very different support depending on many factors, including their own digital competence and the digital competence of the teachers and parents, digital equipment at home, disabilities, socio-economic status, etc. In this paper, we will examine some factors that lead to this

Y. Murayama et al. (Eds.): ITDRR 2020, IFIP AICT 622, pp. 183–192, 2021.
https://doi.org/10.1007/978-3-030-81469-4_15

inequality, and they tend to boil down to lack of support for the diversity of the population, not only people with disabilities, but also other disadvantaged groups. More broadly, we will examine this issue in terms of *intersectionality*.

In feminist theory, especially the stem starting from black American feminism, "intersectionality" is used to identify the relation between systems of oppression that compose our identities and collocation in the hierarchies of power and privilege [1]. In other words, the concept itself is meant to explore the role that race, class, gender, disability and other axes of power play on women's identities and lived experiences [5]. Intersectionality's focus on the dynamics of power and discrimination has been paramount in introducing discussions on societal disadvantage in political discussions and academic disciplines that were not including it before, such as geography, organizational studies, computer science and more [3].

In 2006, the United Nations ratified the Convention on the Rights of Persons with Disabilities (CRPD) and, among other things, acknowledged intersectionality as an important element in the experience of people with disabilities. The Preamble, for example, recognized that the relationship between different forms of discrimination included "color, sex, language, religion, political or other opinion, national, ethnic, indigenous or social origin, property, birth, age or other status" [8]. In the context of this article, we will adopt the term "intersectionality" as intended in the CRPD, as an intersection of disadvantages in the face of society.

During the COVID-19 pandemic as well as other disaster situations, access to digital tools and platforms can make a big difference. Being unable to use digital tools in a disaster situation can in the worst case mean the difference between life and death. Being left behind during a period of education can have severe long-term effects including difficulties to find employment, as well as serious psychological and physical problems.

The rest of the paper is organized as follows. In Sect. 2, we analyze the term "intersectionality" from the initial definition of Kimberlé Crenshaw to its more modern meanings. In Sect. 3, we present three scenarios that present different realistic but made-up typical examples of situations that highlight issues related to intersectionality, using persona that are similarly realistic but made-up characters that illustrate the issues we wish to highlight. Following each scenario, we will discuss the scenario and how intersectionality affects the situation and the ability of the actors to use the relevant digital tools to cope with the situation. In Sect. 4, we discuss Universal Design of ICT and how it can mitigate problems not only for people with disabilities, but also other issues caused by intersectionality. In practice, UD sometimes boils down to taking into account people with disabilities and accessibility. Here, we argue that we should embrace a broader scope of Universal Design of technology for disaster resilience. Finally, Sect. 5 contains a brief set of recommendations on how universal design can contribute to mitigating the effects of intersectionality and concluding remarks.

2 Intersectionality

Kimberlé Crenshaw coined the term "intersectionality" in 1989, as the argument within her essay "Demarginalizing the Intersection of Race and Sex: A Black Feminist Critique of Antidiscrimination Doctrine, Feminist Theory and Antiracist Politics". The purpose of the term was to describe the interaction of multiple oppressions in one human experience, like the one of a Black Woman. The term itself derives from the analogy Crenshaw decided to use to concretize the concept: Discrimination, like traffic through an intersection, may flow in one direction, and it may flow in another. If an accident happens in an intersection, it can be caused by cars traveling from any number of directions and, sometimes, from all of them [4]. It is often hard to determine which driver caused the most damage or how much the fact that the victim was hit on multiple sides at the same time weighted in the final prognosis. In the same way, Crenshaw argues that Women with intersectional identities, Black Women in the case of her essay, experience discriminations just like accidents at traffic intersections: the injury could be the result of sex discrimination or race discrimination, or, often enough, a combination of the two.

Before Crenshaw's essay, women's studies and feminist theories focused mainly on the effects of gender and sexism, leaving Black and Latino studies to explore and protest the effects of systematic racism and color discrimination. Both fields were adamant in asserting how complex and layered the sets of inequalities our society is organized around is, and were therefore interrogating historical patterns of power and domination [6].

Between the 1970s and the 1980s women of color and activists from the United States and the United Kingdom started voicing critiques about the simplistic and yet widespread political discourse that considered "all women are white and all men are black", centering once again white people's experiences in the discrimination discourse [7]. Especially coming from the 1950s, the only relevant experience women were supposed to be having according to the mainstreaming discourse was related to the lives of White Women and their struggles as wives, daughters and mothers, and tragically distant from the difficulties and discriminations of Black Women [6].

After Crenshaw's essay, the term started being adopted by the whole Black Feminism Movement. It was instrumental to express the concept of multiple oppressions that Black Women had been referring to since the times of slavery using terms such as "interlocking oppressions," "simultaneous oppressions," "double jeopardy," "triple jeopardy" [17].

At the present day intersectionality has transcended the metaphorical role and it has become the definition of the contemporary Feminist Movement and Theory, mostly thanks to its versatility and adaptability to the various fields [2]. It has become common knowledge within the feminist theory that women's experiences are conditioned by multiple intersecting systems of oppression [1] and it is no more feasible to analyze said oppression focusing solely on gender.

Intersectionality theory has been celebrated as the most important contribution that women's studies has made so far and its influence has been extended from the academic to the international human rights discourse [1]. In the year 2000 intersectionality was mentioned by the United Nation's Bejing Platform and the Committee on the Elimination of Racial Discrimination, and it was recognized as a key concept by the U.N. Commission on Human Rights, in its resolution on the human rights of women (2002).

Although it is of crucial importance that the concept of intersectionality is being so widely adopted and adapted, by 'women's studies' and 'feminist theory' (which remain white-dominated discourses) as well as international academic environments and interdisciplinary fields, it is paramount to acknowledge and celebrate its origins in the Black feminist thought [1].

3   Scenarios

In this section, we present three realistic but made-up scenarios that present situations that highlight issues related to intersectionality during disaster situations, using persona that are similarly realistic but made-up characters that help illustrate these issues. Following each scenario, we will discuss how intersectionality affects the situation in the scenario and in particular the ability of the actors to use the relevant digital tools efficiently to cope with the situation.

The first two of the following scenarios are adapted from Gjøsæter, Radianti, and Chen [11], and the third is based on a realistic situation in the current COVID-19 pandemic.

3.1   Earthquake in a City

In Reykjavik in Iceland, a strong earthquake strikes one day in late February, around 2AM in the morning.

Martin lives in a small 12th floor apartment in downtown Reykjavik. He is used to evacuating during fire drills, but this is different. He fights the panic as he awakes, puts on some warm clothes, grabs his smart phone, locks his apartment and quickly walks down the stairs among a crowd of other people, who are equally stressed and worried. He follows the directions from the Red Cross volunteers and manages to reach the shelter in a relatively short time.

His neighbor Alejandra has recently arrived to Iceland from Mexico to work on her PhD. In a panic, she didn't think of taking warm clothes with her as she left the apartment, that was never an issue in her home country. Fortunately, she remembered to grab her smartphone on the way out. She is now very cold, and the noise makes it even more difficult to concentrate on finding safe shelter. There is a woman wearing a Red Cross uniform coming towards her, but Alejandra doesn't understand what she is saying. She tries to find information about what is going on and what to do, but the government's websites and alerts are not in English and there is no time for translating them using apps. After looking around in confusion, Alejandra decides to follow the crowd that is being directed *somewhere* she has no idea of, hoping in a quieter moment to request help.

In this scenario, we can notice a distinct difference between Martin and Alejandra. Martin is used to the place and the weather conditions. Growing up in Iceland has imprinted in him automatic actions, like picking up the winter coat when leaving the house, and these automatisms became crucial in an emergency situation, where his brain is focused on the terrifying things happening.

Alejandra, on the other hand, comes from a country with completely different climatic conditions and is not used to such low temperatures. In addition to the overwhelming emotion of the moment, she is now suffering the consequences of being a newly arrived immigrant in a foreign land, not only for the unfavorable temperature she is facing, but also due to the linguistic barrier she is facing when interacting with Anna and with the official websites of the government. Essentially, she is not sure about what is going on, where is she going, how long is it going to last, what are the safety measures she is supposed to take and so on. Furthermore, the moments she took trying to understand what was going on, both on the phone and looking around, could have been crucial for her survival.

3.2 Fire in a Multi-floor Shopping Mall

Just before closing time, a fire breaks out in the "Galleriet" shopping mall in Bergen, Norway. It was caused by an accident in the kitchen of one of the ground floor snack bars. The fire alarm goes off, and evacuation begins.

Bill is an American tourist on a one day visit from a cruise ship. He is a bit lost but finds a map on the wall. To his dismay, the information is only in Norwegian. He tries using google translate to translate the text, but because of stress he gives up and rather follows the crowd to the nearest exit.

Janne is on the top floor, and she is trying to use a smartphone indoor map of the mall to find the way to the nearest emergency exit. Along the way, she notices Hilde, an overweight person in a wheelchair who is unable to evacuate without assistance and is too heavy for her to carry. She sends a message about the trapped person to the local fire department using twitter, since the noise from the fire alarm is too loud for being able to communicate using the emergency phone number.

Nils in the fire department control center is overwhelmed by all the messages about the rapid development of the fire, but sees the tweet from Janne, calls Petter the fire fighter over the emergency communication network, and Petter makes his way to the top floor and is able to help the trapped person out of the burning building.

In this scenario we can see how three different persons are affected in different ways by the exact same event due to their pre-existent conditions. Bill, as a tourist, does not recognize exactly what is going on in the heat of the moment. Although he understands the need to evacuate the shopping center, he loses important time trying to figure out the indications on the floor map of the building.

Janne, on the other end, is a local and is aware of the existence of the smartphone indoor app and of how to use it. She can save time and direct herself safely to the nearest exit. Hilde, finally, is stuck on the top floor of the building because the elevators are not working, for obvious reasons, and she cannot use the stairs. Additionally, she is not petite enough for Janne to carry her to safety and therefore will have to hope someone at the fire department will see Janne's tweet and the rescuers will be fast enough to save her.

In the scenario we depicted all of the characters managing to reach safety, but it is not hard to imagine how different the results could be in a slightly worse condition, as it is also evident who would be more vulnerable and why.

3.3 Teaching During a Pandemic

On the 11th of March 2020, the Italian government instituted a complete lockdown in order to limit the spreading of the COVID-19 virus. Italy was one of the first countries to implement such a drastic measure in response to the upcoming pandemic. From one day to the other, leaving home was not allowed unless strictly necessary, social interactions were completely forbidden, and all the schools were shut down indefinitely.

Eleonora is a primary school teacher; she graduated two years ago and was trained on the use of digital platforms. She immediately starts contacting her students' parents and trying to maintain contacts and organize alternative activities.

Her headmaster disposes the use of an official platform for the whole school, where teachers and students must interact after logging in with their school credentials. Unfortunately, Eleonora is a temporary teacher and was not granted the credentials to access this platform.

Ciro, one of Eleonora's 7-year-old students, got access to the platform right away, but has to share the computer time with his 4 siblings of 9, 11 and 14. All of them are now requested to join the online lectures and activities in order to keep up with their education.

Ada, their mum, is an essential worker at the local hospital and is absent from the house half day every day. She is extremely stressed by working a high-risk job in the middle of a pandemic, the activities in the hospital are frenetic and she is constantly under pressure, but her mind is also preoccupied about what is going on at home while she is not there.

Meanwhile Giovanna, Eleonora's senior colleague, cannot figure out how to upload the word file with the homework on the school platform. She calls Eleonora to get help, and Eleonora explains to her how to log into the WiFi network.

In this scenario there are several elements at play: the fear and anxiety related to the pandemic and the "invisible enemy", which is an experience none of the characters had ever experienced before, the work hierarchy, that prevents who has the knowledge from acting on it, the social class and economic conditions etc.

Ciro, for example, is extremely young and does not understand precisely what is going on. He is also in a vulnerable social-economic condition and therefore his access to the school's resources is limited; not by the institution, but because of the intersectionality of his condition. Ada, at the same time, is affected as a woman, due to being a single mother of four, as a low-income citizen and under a great amount of pressure due to her work conditions.

Because of their disadvantage, Ciro and his brothers will probably not be able to benefit from the online resources and digital lectures their schools provided. They will most likely lose a whole year of education, with all the consequences that will come with it in an already vulnerable household.

4   Universal Design of ICT

In this section, we examine how Universal Design of ICT can contribute towards reducing the effects of intersectionality.

The need for Universal Design in disaster situations is increasingly clear. Paupini and Giannoumis [14] highlight the importance of Universal Design of ICT in disaster situations and refer to the United Nations Convention on the Rights of Persons with Disabilities (CRPD) where states are obliged to take all necessary measures to ensure the protection and safety of persons with disabilities in emergency situations. It has also been made clear [11, 12] that especially in disaster situations, universal design of ICT can benefit a much broader audience than people with disabilities. They emphasize that while Universal Design of ICT is essential for people with disabilities in a disaster situation, it is also of utmost importance for people with so-called situational disabilities that can occur in a disaster, such as smoke and dust blocking the view, stress affecting our cognitive abilities, noise interfering with our hearing, and so on. However, as indicated in the scenarios above, Universal Design can reach even further when it comes to its potential benefits to a diverse population in a disaster situation.

Universal Design has attained an increasingly broad scope when it comes to research and theory. From the beginning it was clear that Universal Design is intended to provide a design that is useable for all, and as such should clearly consider and support the needs of not only people with disabilities, but also the elderly and people with situational or temporary disabilities, and people of diverse other vulnerable groups.

Conceptually it does not stop there. The closely related terms "design for all" and "inclusive design" makes it even more explicit that Universal Design should include everyone, and Universal Design of ICT should therefore ensure tools and technology that is indeed useable by everyone. Giannoumis and Stein [8] argue that while Universal Design traditionally has been associated with persons with disabilities, a more nuanced understanding should also consider barriers encountered by all socially disadvantaged persons. They further state that "the complex, overlapping, and multidimensional barriers that exist at the intersection of multiple forms of social disadvantage should be at the forefront of how universal design is conceptualized." Therefore, Universal Design should be understood to include intersectionality and social disadvantaged groups both in theory and practice. Access to digital services should be facilitated for all, not only for persons with disabilities.

However, this broad scope is not yet fully and consistently realized on the implementation level. There are clear guidelines like the Web Content Accessibility Guide-lines (WCAG) [13]. These guidelines help ensuring that we have a well-defined way to use Universal Design aimed at disabled persons (and in particular disabled persons with one single well-defined disability), but it is less clear, at least to the average software/web/user interface developer, how to broaden the scope of software development to produce tools that are fully accessible and useable by persons with multiple disabilities as well as persons whose identifies with or belong to other vulnerable groups. Unfortunately, the reality of recent tools and technologies for disaster risk reduction is not very encouraging. One might think that at least people with disabilities have been carefully taken into account in the design of tools and technologies for disaster risk reduction, but that is not always the case, as shown by among others [9, 10, 12, 15, 16, 18].

As shown in the scenarios in the previous section, issues stemming from the diversity of intersectional identities of people involved play a clear role on their chances of survival. As potential effects of intersectionality include low socio-economic status as well as reduced employment and education opportunities, it is clear that Universal Design should take into account a requirement for lightweight tools and technologies able to run smoothly on low-cost or old hardware, pay a particular attention to clear and simple culturally neutral language as well as ensuring that languages of significant minorities are supported, with visual support to the most important information to be conveyed.

In fact, these requirements are already supported by Universal Design guidelines, admittedly to a varying degree of detail. For example, the first Principle of Universal Design is "Equitable use", and the third is "Simple and intuitive use". Readability is also covered in WCAG 2.1 Guideline 3.1 "Make text content readable and understandable". Just like Gjøsæter et al. [11, 12] argue that universal design can be able to mitigate some of the effects of situational disabilities, we think that careful application of the principles and best practices of Universal Design of ICT with intersectionality in mind can have a real and significant impact on the broader issues affecting vulnerable groups in a disaster.

5   Recommendations and Concluding Remarks

Universal design cannot by itself solve societal challenges related to inequality and discrimination. However, universal design can and should contribute to mitigate some barriers that are affecting these vulnerable groups. For example, the following groups can benefit from a Universal Design approach when designing software for disaster risk reduction:

- Persons with multiple disabilities

  - Flexibility is key to handle this type of issues. It is important to provide flexible solutions offering alternative presentations and interaction modes, and to offer alternatives not isolated one by one, but available in combinations and in different contexts.

- Persons affected by linguistic barriers

  - To mitigate linguistic barriers and reach as many as possible with emergency communications, it is important to use simple language, to provide alternatives, including relevant translations into important minority languages, explanatory icons, and explanations of difficult terms.

- Persons of low socio-economic status

  - Apps and web pages for use in disaster situations should be as lightweight as possible, so it can run on cheap or old hardware, because not everyone can afford the latest and most powerful smartphones.

- Persons affected by cultural barriers

  - Make sure that instructions are clear, explicit, logically reasoned, and complete, and not just vaguely implied based on cultural assumptions and assumed prior knowledge and training.

Based on our investigations, as exemplified in the scenarios, it becomes clear that intersectionality can make members of multiple intersectional vulnerable groups particularly at risk in a disaster situation. It is therefore paramount that intersectionality is fully taken into consideration when designing information systems for use in disaster situations.

Following the best practices of Universal Design and Human-Centered Design in implementing software for disaster risk reduction, applying the recommendations above, and ensuring a diverse (across all the relevant dimensions) group of users in user testing, will facilitate software that is contributing to a resilient society for all, and not only for the able-bodied and privileged.

References

1. Carastathis, A.: The concept of intersectionality in feminist theory. Philos. Compass **9**(5), 304–314 (2014)
2. Carbin, M., Edenheim, S.: The intersectional turn in feminist theory: a dream of a common language? Eur. J. Women's Stud. **20**(3), 233–248 (2013)
3. Cho, S., Crenshaw, K., McCall, L.: Toward a field of intersectionality studies: theory, applications, and praxis. Signs **38**, 785–810 (2013)
4. Crenshaw, K.: Demarginalizing the intersection of race and sex: a black feminist critique of antidiscrimination doctrine, feminist theory and antiracist politics. u. Chi. Legal f., 139, (1989)
5. Davis, K.: Intersectionality as buzzword: a sociology of science perspective on what makes a feminist theory successful. Fem. Theory **9**(1), 67–85 (2008)
6. Dill, B.T., Kohlman, M.H.: Intersectionality: a transformative paradigm in feminist theory and social justice. In: Handbook of Feminist Research: Theory and Praxis, vol. 2, pp. 154–174 (2012)
7. Ferree, M.M.: Inequality, intersectionality and the politics of discourse. In: The Discursive Politics of Gender Equality, pp. 86–104 (2009)
8. Giannoumis, G.A., Stein, M.A.: Conceptualizing universal design for the information society through a universal human rights lens. Int. Hum. Rights Law Rev. **8**(1), 38–66 (2019)
9. Gjøsæter, T., Radianti, J.: Evaluating accessibility and usability of an experimental situational awareness room. In: Di Bucchianico, G. (ed.) AHFE 2018. AISC, vol. 776, pp. 216–228. Springer, Cham (2019). https://doi.org/10.1007/978-3-319-94622-1_21
10. Gjøsæter, T., Radianti, J., Chen, W.: Universal design of ICT for emergency management - a systematic literature review and research agenda. In: International Conference on Universal Access in Human-Computer Interaction, Las Vegas, USA (2018)
11. Gjøsæter, T., Radianti, J., Chen, W.: Understanding situational disabilities and situational awareness in disasters. In: 16th International Conference on Information Systems for Crisis Response and Management (ISCRAM) (2019)
12. Gjøsæter, T., Radianti, J., Chen, W.: Towards situational disability-aware universally designed information support systems for enhanced situational awareness. In: International Conference on Information Systems for Crisis Response and Management (ISCRAM) (2020)
13. Kirkpatrick, A., O'Connor, J., Cooper, M.: Web content accessibility guidelines (WCAG) 2.1. W3C Recommendation 5 June 2018 (2018)
14. Paupini, C., Giannoumis, G.A.: Applying universal design principles in emergency situations. In: Antona, M., Stephanidis, C. (eds.) HCII 2019. LNCS, vol. 11573, pp. 511–522. Springer, Cham (2019). https://doi.org/10.1007/978-3-030-23563-5_41

15. Radianti, J., Gjøsæter, T.: Digital volunteers in disaster response: accessibility challenges. In: Antona, M., Stephanidis, C. (eds.) HCII 2019. LNCS, vol. 11573, pp. 523–537. Springer, Cham (2019). https://doi.org/10.1007/978-3-030-23563-5_42
16. Radianti, J., Gjøsæter, T., Chen, W.: Universal design of information sharing tools for disaster risk reduction. In: Murayama, Y., Velev, D., Zlateva, P. (eds.) ITDRR 2017. IAICT, vol. 516, pp. 81–95. Springer, Cham (2019). https://doi.org/10.1007/978-3-030-18293-9_8
17. Smith, S.: Black feminism and intersectionality. Int. Soc. Rev. **91**(11), 1–16 (2013)
18. Tunold, S., Radianti, J., Gjøsæter, T., Chen, W.: Perceivability of map information for disaster situations for people with low vision. In: Antona, M., Stephanidis, C. (eds.) HCII 2019. LNCS, vol. 11572, pp. 342–352. Springer, Cham (2019). https://doi.org/10.1007/978-3-030-23560-4_25

Opportunities and Challenges of ICT in Emergency Processes

Bettina Pospisil[✉] and Walter Seböck

Danube University Krems, Dr.-Karl-Dorrek-Straße 30, 3500 Krems, Austria
{bettina.pospisil,walter.seboeck}@donau-uni.ac.at

Abstract. The aim of this paper is to examine emergency employees' perception of the possibilities and challenges of the implementation of Information and Communication Technology (ICT) in their daily processes. Therefore, interviews with eight emergency services employees from differing organizational and positional backgrounds were conducted over the course of two separate research projects. These semi-structured personal and group interviews were subsequently transcribed, and analysed using Grounded Theory. The authors come to the conclusion, that changing perspectives on technology in emergency processes could help enable better cooperation between emergency employees and technology. The raising of employee awareness, and the provision of sufficient training, is vital to both further the understanding of technology as non-human actor and to focus on their interconnectedness. This enhanced interaction between human emergency employees and non-human technological systems could lead to the improved exploitation of socio-technical opportunities to increase the overall security of our society. This research paper seeks to draw out lessons for ICT-implementation within emergency services by examining the opinions and perspectives of employees from different emergency organizations. In so far, the findings and recommendations of the article will support efforts made by emergency organizations to integrate Information and Communication Technologies into their existing processes.

Keywords: Information and Communication Technology (ICT) ·
Socio-technical cooperation · ICT in emergency processes

1 Introduction

Imagine you are on the road and suddenly emergency sirens start to sound out. In these situations, it is often not clear to many road users what to do. While some keep on driving, others slow down, stop completely or even speed up. These different reactions quickly result in a traffic jam, which makes it difficult for emergency vehicles to move forward, and poses an additional risk of accidents. The use of modern traffic management technologies could clarify what needs to be done by all road users, and thus clear the way for emergency drivers to get ahead of the rest of the traffic quickly and safely.

© IFIP International Federation for Information Processing 2021
Published by Springer Nature Switzerland AG 2021
Y. Murayama et al. (Eds.): ITDRR 2020, IFIP AICT 622, pp. 193–205, 2021.
https://doi.org/10.1007/978-3-030-81469-4_16

As this example shows, Information and Communication Technology (ICT) possess huge potential to improve the processes of emergency organizations, and to raise their level of security. While the term "Information and Communication Technology" per se comprises a broad field of applications and systems, these various devices are able to fulfil a range of tasks at different stages of an incident. Most especially, the provision of additional information is of great importance to emergency organizations. Better information can lead to an improved situational awareness, and to more appropriate security measures, thus promoting an emergency employee's safety [1]. However, emergency organizations constantly hesitate to implement new technologies, often due to employee doubts and fear, and the emergence of significant organizational challenges. Since the non-usage of a technology [2, 3] is also a valid option available to an emergency organization and its employees, human actors must be able to see a definite benefit in implementing technological devices in their processes. Otherwise, they would not see a benefit in changing their existing practices. This paradoxical relationship between emergency organizations and technological systems [4] can be understood as a major obstacle to the exploitation of the potential afforded by technology to emergency organizations.

The aim of this research paper is to, therefore, provide guidance to emergency organizations on how to establish and maintain cooperation between technology and their employees. To address this aim, the authors will investigate the question of how emergency employees perceive the possibilities and challenges connected with the implementation of Information and Communication Technology in their emergency practices. The research problem will be discussed in the context of two different research projects, both focusing on how a new technological system can improve existing emergency processes. While the first device under consideration is a priority system aimed at enabling a faster ride to an accident location, the second is a sensor developed to detect the release of chemical, biological, radiological and nuclear (CBRN) substances.

ICT in the Emergency Management

The National Governor's Association (NGA) has identified four phases of emergency management [5] based on McLoughlin [6]. These are recognized as the traditional four stages of disaster management by various authors in the field, and can benefit in different ways from human interaction with technological systems. The first phase – *mitigation* – refers to the long-term activities undertaken to prevent emergencies or reduce the resulting damage of an emergency. The second phase of *preparedness* covers the short-term activities that are realized before the emergency strikes to enhance the readiness of organizations to respond to it. The third phase is about *response*, and includes activities undertaken immediately after an emergency to provide assistance to those in need. The last phase of *recovery* focuses on short-term as well as long-term activities, put into practice to provide victims with their pre-disaster conditions [5].

Summarizing the findings from various authors [4, 7–10] it can be concluded that technology may be used to support employees at all the different stages of emergency management. In particular, technology can help emergency employees obtain information on: (1) environmental conditions – including causalities, location, cause; (2) available resources, in terms of employees, skills and equipment; and (3) best practices, involving training, testing and continuing education. This information, together with the technologies themselves, can help emergency employees with (4) appropriate communication and information sharing within their organization, and with other external actors; (5) enhanced situational awareness; and (6) improved decision support. Through these tasks, technology enhances (7) organizational agility for disaster management; (8) the engagement of the public; and (9) infrastructure survivability. The technologies used can be very diverse, and range from coordination, communication or training platforms driven by government agencies to monitoring technologies as sensor network systems.

However, these multiple possibilities are often accompanied by several challenges faced by emergency organizations and their employees during the implementation of new technologies Following Rogers and Scally [11], these may be summarized under four broad headings: (1) the unlawful use of technology, (2) workforce resistance, (3) training and budget, as well as (4) balance regarding legislation. While the authors focus mainly on police departments as specific kind of emergency organization, their findings may also be applied to other emergency organizations. The first aspect addresses the possibility of the occurrence of cybercrime. Every technology carries with it new vulnerabilities, resulting in the emergence of new entry points for criminals in the critical infrastructure of emergency systems. This can pose a threat to not just the entire organization and its employees, but also society as a whole. The second topic encompasses the impact that new technologies have on the existing practices, beliefs and working culture of an organization. Since the overall mission of emergency employees is to act fast during complex-incident situations, their requirement is for easy-to-use instruments [8]. This is one reason why emergency employees often resist technological changes in their procedures. As third aspect, Rogers and Scally [11] mention the need for employee training, and budgeting by emergency organizations, to enable the successful implementation of a new technology. Enhancing the amount and quality of training could help reduce the skepticism on the part of emergency employees towards change, making them more aware of the possibilities and risks associated with the introduction of new technologies into their processes. Sakurai and Murayama [7] state that the more information technology becomes a part of emergency management, the more IT resources within the organizations are required to address these applications, and to support this dimension. The fourth topic mentioned by Rogers and Scally [11] is the difficult balance required between technology use and human rights. National and international legislation concerning technology use can have a significant impact on the relationship between an emergency organization and the technology available to its employees, as well as on its overall relationship with society. Thus, the general concerns of society raised in connection with data collection and privacy must be considered, when increasing the usage of technology by emergency organizations.

2   Research Design and Methods

The aim of this research paper is to investigate the perspective of emergency employees towards new information and communication technologies, and to determine how they perceive the possibilities and challenges concerning their incorporation into daily routines and processes. Hence, the paper poses the following research question:

How do emergency employees think about the implementation of novel Information and Communication Technology in their daily practices?

To answer this question, the paper draws on empirical material from two different research projects. Both projects focus on how new technological systems can improve existing emergency processes. While in the first project the technology under consideration is a priority system that is supposed to enable a faster ride to an accident location, in the second project the technology investigated is a sensor, developed to detect the release of CBRN-substances in specific contexts. Following the literature, the first ICT tries to improve the phase of response through the introduction of help of a human-to-human communication device. The second tries to improve the mitigation phase with the help of a sensor. In both research projects, the authors interacted with different employees from various emergency organizations located in Vienna. While the topic of the projects had been the specific technologies, the emergency employees in both projects used the openness of the interview method to talk about their perceptions of the use of information and communication technologies in their daily routines. Information collected was merged and analyzed, leading to the findings of this paper.

To obtain their point of view, problem-centered personal and group interviews [12, 13] were performed during June and November 2019. In the context of six interview-settings, eight persons were interviewed. Discussion partners ranged from chief-officers to operative employees, as well as employees at the interface between different associations and organizations. Their organizational backgrounds ranged from occupations in fire departments, police departments, rescue services as well as within special units. Seven male participants and only one female were interviewed. The semi-structured interview guide utilized included, on the one hand, case examples that encouraged interviewees to narrate and describe the emergency processes within their organizations in order to identify practices and their interlinkage with Information and Communication Technology, and, on the other, open-ended questions to obtain insights into the challenges faced by emergency employees within the context of existing processes. The interviews in their duration lasted from between 60 to 260 min. All of them were recorded and transcribed verbatim. In a final step, the interview data thus collected was analyzed following the approach of Grounded Theory as described by Charmaz [14].

Within the literature, various authors share the opinion that stakeholders such as emergency responders whose behavior is shaped by technology, should be integrated into the processes of technology development and implementation in order to address existing needs and concerns [1, 4, 10]. To give emergency employees the possibility to participate in the process of analysis, the findings of the interviews were presented and further developed in the form of a workshop [15]. The results are presented in this research paper.

The participants gave their written informed consent to their involvement in the study, as well as to the recording of the interviews. The authors gave them the opportunity to withdraw from the study at any time they wanted. Additionally, in order to align further with good scientific practice, the authors signed a confidentiality agreement to protect the participants and their organizations. Thus, they will appear anonymized, and data will only be used if it does not disclose personal information, that makes them identifiable, and if it does not endanger existing security processes.

3 Results

While the interviews initially focused on the daily practices of emergency employees, interview data reveals that they started talking about their relationship with technology on their own. This behavior shows that their opinion of technology has an impact on their daily practices, particularly during emergencies. The interviews shed light on the fact that the most important condition for the implementation of a new technology in daily routines is its acceptance by emergency employees. Although in advanced technological societies, technology is inevitably intertwined with disasters [16], the implementation of specific technological systems and devices in existing processes of emergency management is often accompanied by change [17]. Hence, technology acceptance is contingent on how the organizations and the employees cope with this change. Chan [17] distinguishes three sets of factors that influence the course of technological change and its impact on organizations: technical factors, cultural factors and political factors. While technical factors refer to the nature of technology to be used, cultural factors imply a clash between the assumptions underpinning a certain technology and those held by users within adopting organizations. By political factors, the author refers to the interests at stake in technological change. In order to cope with resistance against change in the workforce, it makes sense to take not only technological but also occupational psychology measures [18]. Nevertheless, technology enables change, but is not its cause. By adapting a certain technology to existing processes, emergency employees, by themselves and through the interaction with the new technology, cause change [19].

While emergency employees are used to changing environments, complex situations and a flexible framework, the interviews showed that they often wish for stability in their overall procedures to reduce this immutable complexity. However, emergency employees are also aware of the fact that technologies can ease day-to-day processes and practices. Our findings show that the interviewees consider Information and Communication Technology at once possibility distinct means by which to improve existing processes, and as a threat to existing processes. These two visions of ICT should not be understood as two opposing perspectives with nothing in between, but as two ends of a straight line upon which the perspective of an employee is situated in the middle, as illustrated in Fig. 1. Moreover, it is not like there is one correct understanding of the role of technology in emergency processes. The perspectives are the result of real experiences with technologies and the changes that occur with their implementation. Thus, each perspective has its legitimacy.

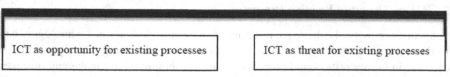

Fig. 1. The perspectives of ICT as opportunity and ICT as threat for existing processes can be understood as the two ends of a line.

3.1 ICT as Opportunity for Existing Processes

Information and communication technologies have the potential to help emergency employees face the challenges encountered during the course of their daily work. In doing so, technological devices can be understood as being allies of the human user, since they broaden the options available to the emergency employee. Technologies can help users through the *gathering of more information* or by facilitating the sharing of information with other actors in the field. This could lead to a better assessment of the situation by all actors involved, and hence to safer incident handling by emergency workers. In this sense, technology can *secure and expand existing capabilities* of emergency employees. Devices with these possibilities include navigation systems, and sensors collecting data. Moreover, ICT can also *simplify existing processes*, either by facilitating process automation or by interconnecting emergency devices like alert units and navigation systems. While the absence of feelings on the part of the technology is usually taken as being a negative characteristic, in some situations it can be beneficial. The technology assesses a situation along certain parameters, leading to a calculated response output. The recommendations based on this process can assist the employee in decision-making processes, especially when facing an ethical dilemma:

> *"In the case of major damage medicine, no distinction is made between child, woman and man. Instead, they look at who has the best chance of survival. That means getting the most out of the situation with the least possible resources. And of course, there are a lot of emotions in us and if I have a child somewhere who is five years old and needs resuscitation, then I have to get three staff members there to resuscitate the child. (...) If 30 others would die because of one life saving, then it is of course not reasonable. And then there must be a system behind it that is objective."*

This example illustrates how technology can support the emergency employee, by recommending practices or by announcing them as the best way to handle certain situations. In doing so, *technologies reduce complexity*, allowing emergency employees to focus on other practices. In some cases, technologies even provide support in legal disputes, for example, through accident data storage. This specific technology can help the employees identify prior behavior in traffic situations. Finally, some respondents mentioned that they see technologies in their processes as being playful instruments from which they can gain new insights and learn new skills.

3.2 ICT as Threat to Existing Processes

In concurrence with the benefits information and communication technologies can afford, emergency employees in some respects also see it as being their opponent. As they work in highly critical and complex situations, they must not make any mistakes and neither should their equipment. Thus, employees work with instruments with so-called high failure safety and reliability. Technologies often seem *more vulnerable* than manual processes, which is, on the one hand, explained by the specific requirements technologies possess, and the materials they are constructed out of (e.g. need electricity, consists partly of glass) and, on the other, by the lack of insight that users have into the functioning of some technical devices. Moreover, every ICT device implies a new gateway for cybercriminals, through which the device could be attacked or taken over, rendering it useless or even dangerous to emergency employees [20]. Thus, there exists a distinct lack of trust in technology. While already mentioned that the lack of emotions on the part of a device can be helpful to employees in certain situations, in others, it can have negative effects. This is especially true during the phase of alerting, wherein *social and emotional intelligence* enables a human to gain insight into the situation of the affected person(s). In this phase, a lot of uncommunicated information hidden between the lines gets lost when information gathering is done by technology. This could then lead to an incomplete assessment of the situation.

Furthermore, each task performed by the technology seemingly leads to the lack of need on the part of the emergency employee to have this ability. For example, a navigation system enables employees to orientate through the city without necessitating them to know the way on their own. Furthermore, these skills are not used and honed anymore, because they are provided by technology, resulting in them getting lost. This process raises employee's *dependency on technology*. In this respect, it is also understandable that some interviewees had the feeling they could come to be replaced by a technological system one day. After all, when dealing with technical tools, it is not just the emergency employees delegating tasks to the devices, but also the devices shaping users' own practices and knowledge [21]. While technology seemingly makes some skills obsolete, it also *demands new skills* in dealing with it. Hence, through the implementation of technologies the requirements for emergency employees are additionally extended to include the acquisition of skills needed to (1) handle technical equipment, (2) assess technical information, and (3) promote self-confidence and assertiveness. Skills in handling technical equipment implies the ability to operate it properly and to use the technical device in the right way. Moreover, if the employee receives information from a monitoring system, this data must also be applied in practice and their meaning must be understood. This evaluation involves the meaningful integration of the additional information. Thirdly, when interacting with technical devices, the emergency employee needs to do so with a high degree of self-confidence and assertiveness. The interviewees agreed that in emergencies decisions should be made by humans and that technology should make recommendations assisting that process. In practice, however, this means that in some situations, emergency employees must actively reject technological recommendations and assert themselves against them. This needs self-confidence and assertiveness, as well as the continuous questioning of technological output. To speak up against the system means *taking on even more responsibility*. It is the requirement of these skills, and the provision of training, that deters some organizations from implementing certain technologies with daily workflow processes:

> "The selection of vehicles was also made intuitively in the past and since it has been computerized, nobody has really dared to change the computer proposal. So according to the motto: the computer will have thought of something. However, this leads to the fact that the whole thing becomes extremely rigid and it is almost only a decision of the computer, which was not the point of the whole story. (...) The willingness to take responsibility, so to speak, to stand against an established system is very low."

Additionally, some emergency employees felt that the huge amount of data collected by technologies could also be used against their persons, thus endangering their right to *privacy*. Finally, some interviewees questioned the usefulness of the implementation of yet another technological system in the workplace.

3.3 Organizations in Between

Overall, we could see that none of those interviewed were free of any kind of concerns pertaining to the use of information and communication technologies in emergency processes. Similarly, however, not one of the interviewees failed to mention the potential benefits that certain technologies brought to their organizations. Our findings show that, as Rogers and Scally [11] state, the working culture bears influence on whether an emergency employee accepts a certain technology or not. While interviewees from organizations that made use of less technology in their processes seemed more concerned about its impact, those employed in organizations with more implemented technologies referred more frequently to the advantages of ICT. Results from research projects show that the target group of blue light organizations in Vienna is very heterogeneous in their relationship to Information and Communication Technology. Some organizations encourage an open discussion of the implementation of common technologies such as navigation systems, and recommend that their employees use technology only if it is absolutely necessary. Other organizations already discuss the implementation of artificial intelligence and other advanced forms of data collection. Yet others have even started to consider new regulations for the individual use of technology to enable better coverage to promote interconnected emergency communication with society.

4   Recommendations

Our findings concerning the perceived positive and negative effects of information and communication technology implementation shed light on the paradoxical relationship between technology and emergency employees described by Yang et al. [4]. Based on these results, and on the existing literature, this research paper makes three interconnected recommendations to support emergency organizations in implementing technology in their daily processes by focusing their attention on the concerns of their employees.

4.1 Awareness and Training

To meet the changing requirements brought about through the continued interaction with ICT, the implementing organization needs to provide training to emergency employees [7, 11]. While already experts in their field of emergency processes [22], emergency workers would benefit considerably from awareness raising and training based on the use of those technological devices deployed in their daily processes. This training should not just focus on the handling of specific technologies to raise employee confidence, but also on the nature of human-computer interactions and the emerging opportunities and challenges. Before speaking of the implementation of a specific technology, first it needs the awareness of the employees that this ICT addresses an important issue, which requires changes in the existing process. If the employee does not see the need to adapt or change his or her behavior to address new challenges, he or she will reject or even trick the system. Thus, raising awareness includes the need for the acquisition of knowledge about a certain technology, as well as an understanding of the specific topic in focus and its practical implications. Moreover, the implementation of ICT into emergency processes has a remarkable influence on how employees think, act and report on their activities [23]. Training should therefore, also raise an employee's awareness of this influence, with emphasis on positive as well as negative effects. Moreover, the training should help the employee *gain an understanding of how to handle and interact with a particular technology*. This – amongst other variables – could help employees in the formation of a trusting relationship with their technological devices [24]. The achieved increases in levels of awareness and knowledge reduces uncertainties, enables employees to make their own informed decisions about technology use, and allows them to deal with the new form of responsibility arising through the interaction with ICT.

4.2 Technology as Non-human Actor

Drawing on the ideas of actor-network-theory (ANT) [25, 26] from science and technology studies (STS), the authors suggest to reconsider the notion of technology as object. Instead, we recommend the development of understanding that technology is more a non-human actor that assists the emergency employees. When taken as being an actor, technology is not only influenced by humans, but also shapes the practices of humans too. Moreover, from an ANT perspective, technologies are not understood as opponents of the human actors, but as actors within the same network [21]. Drawing on this perspective, technological devices can be seen as having particular strengths and weaknesses. For example, the technological characteristic of being emotion-free can be thought of as possessing both qualities in different situations. While in some complex ethical situations, emergency employees can benefit from the emotion free recommendations of technology [27], in others this emotionlessness can lead to the loss of important information [28]. As within every team, it is necessary to have a knowledge of the *strengths and weaknesses of each team member,* to enable the best possible cooperation. Furthermore, focusing on technological devices as aids that assist human actors fulfil tasks enables emergency employees to recognize that technologies are not free of mistakes. In consequence, information obtained from these devices has to be extended and supplemented with their individual experiences and tacit knowledge to combine the strengths of both sets of actors in the process. It is expected that this insight would make it easier for emergency employees to question the recommendations made by technology.

4.3 Cooperation Through Clear Assignment of Tasks

When thinking of technological devices as non-human actors, and of emergency employees as trained experts who interact with these technologies, the last step is to link the skills of both actor groups. To combine the strengths of emergency employees and technology, it is necessary to have clear understanding of assigned tasks. As already suggested by Yang et al. [4], the task of technology is to assist human actors by providing information and facilitating better communication. These tasks would help emergency employees in their decisions, but the decisions themselves should be taken by human actors based on a combination of information, experience, and expert knowledge. This clear assignment of tasks enables organizations to link the skills of both [28]. However, it must be emphasized that, technology needs meaningful human control [29]. Our findings support this aspect, as they demonstrate the need for close cooperation between technology and emergency employees to best meet the requirements of emergencies:

> *"So, imagine it's a family emergency and you call, and you're very excited. It takes feeling and sense to hear what is there. So not just these facts, but to bring this human element into it. And that human feeling – if I shut that off completely, the decisions are usually worse."*

On the one hand, emergency employees can carry technological information forward, with - for example - their experience and skills in social and emotional intelligence. Thus, the skills of emergency employees are needed to apply the output of the technology in the way it makes sense to the present situation and future decisions. On the other hand, technological devices can support and relieve emergency employees with their informational and communication possibilities. As part of regular trainings, not only the employee can be further educated, also the technology can be continuously developed and improved through the practical implications of the employees using them in their daily practices. Nevertheless, imagining technology as assisting actor, and not entrusted with the task of decision-making, could counteract emergency employees' fear of being replaced by technology. However, this fear is comprehensible since it is intertwined with the role technology has in an organization and does not just affect low skilled employees anymore [30]. The replacement of an emergency employee with a technology would end this process of cooperation, and therefore lead to a loss of skills and information, poorer situational awareness, and the insufficient addressing of emergency incidents. Thus, it is necessary to *combine human skills and the potential of machine intelligence with the aim of achieving a "human-technology symbiosis"* [29].

5   Conclusion

Changing the perspective of emergency employees towards the usage of technology in emergency processes could help to enable greater cooperation between these actors and technology. To achieve this aim awareness needs to be raised, and training for emergency employees provided, to further the understanding of technology as a non-human actor and shift the focus on to mutual cooperation through the clear assignment of tasks. These recommendations address the challenges emerging from the implementation of technology, when considered from the perspective of emergency employees.

However, to change the perspective through the provision of recommendations is only effective if the certain technology in focus is (1) useful to the emergency organization and (2) has an acceptable level of vulnerability. The best technology is useless if the potential users do not see any sense in its utilization. Therefore, it is important to involve users in the development of technology, to address their needs and do not develop technology for an end in itself. Moreover, the risks posed by technical applications must be as low as possible in order to be attractive to emergency organizations. A system with open vulnerabilities can do more harm than good to the safety and security of an organization, its employees, and society at a time when cybercrime is continuously on the rise. Considering the process of data collection, emergency organizations opting to implement new technologies must examine more closely the topic of privacy, and take into account the various accompanying legal regulations and societal challenges.

The aim of this paper is to provide support to emergency organizations concerning how to implement information and communication technologies in their existing processes. Therefore, it is necessary to understand disasters in advanced technological societies as socio-technical and thus, technology as associated with disasters in many different ways. Insofar as it is not a human decision to incorporate technology into emergency-situations, since they are already inevitably a part of them, it takes humans to set the course of action to produce the best possible cooperation between humans and non-human actors – emergency employees and technological systems – in specific situations and processes. This would make it possible to exploit the socio-technical opportunities to increase the security of our society.

Methodological Considerations
The interviews on which this work is based were conducted in the context of two different research projects, each focusing on specific technologies for emergency procedures. Therefore, the findings could be biased, as they comprise the opinions of emergency employees to that specific technology. The study presents the perspectives of a diverse range of interviewees, each differing in age and work experience. However, from the eight interview partners only one was female. This could be understood when considering the gender distribution in the field of emergency organizations, which is, especially in the sector of fire and police departments, not balanced. A gender imbalance could lead to a bias, or an overrepresentation of the perspective of male emergency employees, and has to be considered when reading and interpreting the findings. Moreover, the interviewees all work in organizations located in Vienna, so the findings are limited to experiences within an urban area.

Acknowledgments. The authors would like to thank the participants who gave them their time and shared their thoughts. All interviews were conducted in German; the authors translated quotes. The results were developed as part of the projects "Efficient prioritization of emergency vehicles in automated road traffic" and "CBRN City Sensor Network". Both projects are funded by the Austrian security research program KIRAS supported by the Federal Ministry of Agriculture, Regions and Tourism (BMLRT).

References

1. Jackson, B.A., et al.: Protecting Emergency Responders: Lessons Learned from Terrorist Attacks. RAND Corporation, Santa Monica (2002)
2. Wyatt, S.: Non-users also matter: the construction of users and non-users of the Internet. In: Oudshoorn, N., Pinch, T. (eds.) How Users Matter. The Co-Construction of Users and Technology, pp. 67–79. MIT Press, Cambridge (2003)

3. Selwyn, N.: Apart from technology: understanding people's non-use of information and communication technologies in everyday life. Technol. Soc. **25**(1), 99–116 (2003). https://doi.org/10.1016/s0160-791x(02)00062-3
4. Yang, L., Su, G., Yuan, H.: Design principles of integrated information platform for emergency responses: the case of 2008 Beijing Olympic Games. Inf. Syst. Res. **23**(3), 761–786 (2012). https://doi.org/10.1287/isre.1110.0387
5. Donahue, A.K., Philip, G.J.: A framework for analyzing emergency management with an application to federal budgeting. Public Adm. Rev. **61**(6), 728–740 (2001). https://doi.org/10.1111/0033-3352.00143
6. McLoughlin, D.: A Framework for integrated emergency management. Public Adm. Rev. **45**(S1), 165–172 (1985). https://doi.org/10.2307/3135011
7. Sakurai, M., Murayama, Y.: Information technologies and disaster management – benefits and issues. Prog. Disaster Sci. **2**, 100012 (2019). https://doi.org/10.1016/j.pdisas.2019.100012
8. Reddick, C.: Information technology and emergency management: preparedness and planning in US states. Disasters **35**(1), 45–61 (2011). https://doi.org/10.1111/j.1467-7717.2010.011 92.x
9. Perry, R.W., Lindell, M.: Preparedness for emergency response: guidelines for the emergency planning process. Disasters **27**(4), 336–350 (2003). https://doi.org/10.1111/j.0361-3666.2003.00237
10. Rao, R.R., Eisenberg, J., Schmitt T.: Improving Disaster Management: The Role of IT in Mitigation, Preparedness, Response, and Recovery. National Academies Press, Washington, D.C. (2007). http://dx.doi.org/10.17226/11824
11. Rogers, C., Scally, E.: Police use of technology: Insights from the literature. Int. J. Emerg. Serv. **7**(2), 100–110 (2018). https://doi.org/10.1108/ijes-03-2017-0012
12. Witzel, A.: The problem-centered interview. Forum: Qual. Soc. Res. **1**(1) (2000). https://doi.org/10.17169/fqs-1.1.1132. Article no. 22
13. Scheibelhofer, E.: Combining narration-based interviews with topical interviews: methodological reflections on research practices. Int. J. Soc. Res. Methodol. **11**(5), 403–416 (2008). https://doi.org/10.1080/13645570701401370
14. Charmaz, K.: Constructing Grounded Theory. A Practical Guide Through Qualitative Analysis, Sage Publications, London (2006)
15. Rip, A., Robinson, D.K.R.: Constructive technology assessment and the methodology of insertion. In: Doorn, N., van de Poel, I., Schuurbiers, D., Gorman, M.E. (eds.) Early Engagement and New Technologies. Opening Up the Laboratory, pp. 37–53. Springer, Dodrecht (2014). http://dx.doi.org/10.4324/9780429465734-8
16. Hilgartner, S.: Overflow and containment in the aftermath of disaster. Soc. Stud. Sci. **37**(1), 153–158 (2007). https://doi.org/10.1177/0306312706069439
17. Chan, J.B.L.: The technological game: how information technology is transforming police practice. Crim. Justice **1**(2), 139–159 (2001). https://doi.org/10.1177/1466802501001002001
18. Chies, S.: Change Management bei der Einführung neuer IT-Technologien: Mitarbeiter ins Boot holen – mit angewandter Psychologie. Springer Fachmedien, Wiesbaden (2016). http://dx.doi.org/10.1007/978-3-658-11635-4
19. Orlikowski, W.J.: Improvising organizational transformation over time – a situated change perspective. Inf. Syst. Res. **7**(1), 63–92 (1996). https://doi.org/10.4135/9781452231266.n9
20. Pospisil, B., Huber, E., Quirchmayr, G., Seböck, W.: Modus operandi in cybercrime. In: Khosrow-Pour, M. (ed.) Encyclopedia of Criminal Activities and the Deep Web, pp. 193–209. IGI Global, web (2020). http://dx.doi.org/10.4018/978-1-5225-9715-5.ch013
21. Johnson, J.: Mixing humans and nonhumans together: the sociology of a door-closer. Soc. Probl. **35**(3), 298–310 (1988). https://doi.org/10.1525/sp.1988.35.3.03a00070

22. Suryanarayanan, S., Kleinman, D.L.: Be(e)coming experts: the controversy over insecticides in the honey bee colony collapse disorder. Soc. Stud. Sci. **43**(2), 1–26 (2013). https://doi.org/10.1177/0306312712466186

23. Ericson, R.V., Haggerty, K.D.: Policing the Risk Society. University of Toronto Press, Toronto (1997). http://dx.doi.org/10.3138/9781442678590

24. Xu, J., Le, K., Deitermann, A., Montague, E.: How different types of users develop trust in technology: a qualitative analysis of the antecedents of active and passive user trust in a shared technology. Appl. Ergon. **45**(6), 1495–1503 (2014). https://doi.org/10.1016/j.apergo.2014.04.012

25. Law, J.: Actor-network theory and material semiotics. In: Turner, B.S. (ed.) The New Blackwell Companion to Social Theory, pp. 141–158. Blackwell Publishers, Oxford (2009). http://dx.doi.org/10.1002/9781444304992.ch7

26. Michael, M.: Actor-Network Theory. Trials, Trails and Translations. Sage, London (2017). http://dx.doi.org/10.4135/9781473983045

27. Mitchell, R.J., Lewis, S.: Intention is not method, belief is not evidence, rank is not proof. Ethical policing needs evidence-based decision making. Int. J. Emerg. Serv. **6**(3), 188–199 (2017). http://dx.doi.org/10.1108/ijes-04-2017-0018

28. Carver, L., Turoff, M.: Human-computer interaction: the human and computer as a team in emergency management information systems. Commun. ACM **50**(3), 33–38 (2007). https://doi.org/10.1145/1226736.1226761

29. Stephanidis, C., et al.: Seven HCI grand challenges. Int. J. Hum.-Comput. Interact. **35**(14), 1229–1269 (2019). https://doi.org/10.1080/10447318.2019.1619259

30. Wasen, K.: Replacement of highly educated surgical assistants by robot technology in working life: paradigm shift in the service sector. Int. J. Soc. Robot. **2**(4), 431–438 (2010). https://doi.org/10.1007/s12369-010-0062-y

Integration in and Between Earth Observation Research Centers for Achieving Sustainable Development

Todor Branzov, Krassimira Ivanova[✉], and Velichka Milousheva

Institute of Mathematics and Informatics, Bulgarian Academy of Sciences, Sofia, Bulgaria
{kivanova,vmil}@math.bas.bg

Abstract. The digital transformation of society in recent years has led to a qualitatively new leap in the development of natural sciences. Currently, these new technologies allow the collection and processing of a huge amount of information and increase the growth of scientific production, parallel to fusing the boundaries between scientific disciplines. Hence, the created Earth observation centers are a natural prerequisite for facilitating these processes. This article presents our studies on the information system architecture of some of the leading Earth observation research centers, with a focus on capabilities for integration with other scientific infrastructures. We review an original solution based on hybrid service-microservice architecture being implemented in the National Geoinformation Center of Bulgaria, investigating some possible advantages it may provide for integration with other Earth observation centers.

Keywords: Earth observation centers · Information systems architecture · Microservices · Service oriented architecture · IT service management

1 Introduction

The process of Earth observation (EO) gathers information about the physical, chemical, and biological systems of the planet using both remote-sensing technologies and in-situ surveying techniques. It covers all phases of data collection, data analysis, and data presentation aimed to support Earth ecosystem monitoring and management.

Currently, we live in the era of data-driven development. The EO data have already proven their value across many sectors of society, providing vital material for applying decision-making strategies in a broad range of sectors, which can be divided into three main groups – biospheric, economic and societal. Thus, numerous initiatives are currently working toward improving the accessibility, quality, applicability, and reliability of data as an important part of this process.

In 2015 the United Nations General Assembly adopted "The 2030 Agenda" as an urgent call for action by all countries in a global partnership for achieving "better and more sustainable future for all". It is based on 17 global life-changing goals, called Sustainable Development Goals (SDGs) [1]. The integration of geospatial information,

Y. Murayama et al. (Eds.): ITDRR 2020, IFIP AICT 622, pp. 206–215, 2021.
https://doi.org/10.1007/978-3-030-81469-4_17

Earth observations, and other sources of Big Data, combined with modern descriptive and predictive techniques and decision-making strategies are becoming the fundamental solution for the performance of many of the SDGs:

- directly (such as SDG 13: Climate Action);
- or indirectly (such as SDG 2: Zero Hunger).

Another point of view, for successful realization of this integration the Earth observation infrastructures are built in accordance with SDG 17 (Partnerships).

Figure 1 shows the impact of EO systems on the SDGs grouping to three main facets – Biosphere, Economy, and Society. EOs provide accurate and reliable information which is directly necessary for monitoring and management of Biosphere sectors, but also have an indirect influence on the economic sectors and many activities of the society.

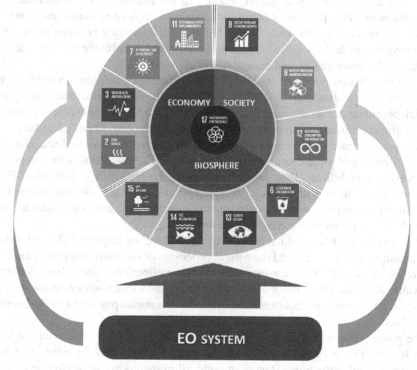

Fig. 1. The impact of EO systems on the SDGs (in accordance with [2])

The benefits of EO as a valuable information source in support of many branches of science, industry, government, and society are already well understood. Because of this many national and international programs focus their efforts on establishing scientific infrastructures for integration of geospatial information and primary geoinformation data from different sources and providers in multidisciplinary, integrated data products

(IGP), using advantages of high-performance and grid computing, big data technologies and the techniques of the Artificial Intelligence.

The digital transformation of society in recent years has led to a qualitatively new leap in the development of natural sciences. Currently, these new technologies allow the collection and processing of a huge amount of information (its volume doubles every five to ten years) and increase the growth of scientific production, which complicates the exchange of scientific ideas. Hence, the created Earth observation centers are a natural prerequisite for facilitating these processes.

A natural specificity of modern sciences is their mathematization, which increases the degree of abstraction of scientific knowledge, expands the possibilities for concentrating scientific information, and greatly increases its capacity. Therefore, the digital mathematical models and data processing tools are an essential part of the service package of each EO center.

The growing complexity of the processes that fall within the scope of research requires an interdisciplinary approach, leading to the emergence of "borderline" and "joint" sciences. This process of integration, i.e. synthesis of sciences and scientific disciplines, combining their methods and blurring the boundary between them, gives the opportunity to build a holistic picture of the world, combining natural sciences, mathematical, philosophical, and general scientific knowledge.

Nowadays, the cooperation between applied mathematics, informatics and information technologies, and another science or scientific discipline gives rise to new disciplines in which obtaining the results from the application of models is impossible without the use of high-performance technology or distributed calculations. In our case, the role of the third part of this cooperation is not one, but a group of sciences and scientific disciplines covered under the common name "*geosciences*", which makes the integration process even more difficult. Thus, this collaboration gave birth to "*Computational Earth Sciences*", which deals with a predictive understanding of Earth systems through the development and application of models, quantitative methods, and computational tools that exploit high-performance computing resources.

At an even higher level of integration, to understand the impacts and relationships between humans as a society and the natural processes of the Earth's system, Guo et al. [3] propose the introduction of a new scientific discipline: "*Big Earth Data Science*", which aims to use data from the observations of Earth and social observation and develop theories to understand the mechanisms of how such a social-physical system operates and evolves.

The paper presents our studies on the information system (IS) architecture of some of the leading EO research centers, with a focus on capabilities for integration with other scientific infrastructures. Having in mind all of the above, we review an original solution based on hybrid service-microservice architecture being implemented in the National Geoinformation Center of Bulgaria, investigating some possible advantages it may provide.

2   The EO Ecosystem

According to [4] "*research infrastructure* means facilities, resources, and related services that are used by the scientific community to conduct top-level research in their respective fields and covers major scientific equipment or sets of instruments; knowledge-based resources such as collections, archives or structures for scientific information; enabling ICT-based infrastructures such as Grid, computing, software and communication, or any other entity of a unique nature essential to achieve excellence in research".

So, one of the key elements in the research infrastructure are knowledge-based resources. The specificity of Earth Observation data is that it comes from a variety of:

- branches – climate, waters, air, soils, geological phenomena, and so on;
- sources – satellite, airborne, and in-situ measurements, crowdsourcing activities records, as well as historical data, stored in earlier databases;
- providers – international agencies, specialized national institutions, scientific organizations, business organizations, NGOs, citizens.

Depending on the degree of complexity of the processing to which the data is subjected, according to [5] the data can be categorized in the following levels (so-called EPOS data levels categorization):

- Level 0: raw data, or basic data (example: seismograms, accelerograms, time series);
- Level 1: data products coming from nearly automated procedures (earthquake locations, magnitudes, focal mechanism, shakemaps);
- Level 2: data products resulting from scientists' investigations (crustal models, strain maps, earthquake source models, etc.);
- Level 3: integrated data products coming from complex analyses or community shared products (hazards maps, catalogue of active faults, etc.).

Except for Level 0, where only software agents for capturing information and storing in a predefined standard form is used, the output of the next levels is called Data Products – where some processing of raw data has to be done, and for which additional modelling services are needed.

These elements – data, data products, software, and services (DDSS) are the production that can be served to the users through the infrastructure of the EO center (Fig. 2).

Fig. 2. DDSS flow from data providers to users

By its nature, DDSS can be given from the providers (DDSS') or produced by the center (DDSS"). We can say that attracting more providers allows the growing of the

EO center horizontally – more kinds of data, from more destinations, etc. On the other hand, often geoscientists are generating products through their research activities, using the resources of the center or in combination with third party resources, and these data products are entered as new resources in the EO center. This pseudo-cycling nature of the resources allows increasing the potential of the center vertically, because:

- for data products – often the new data product is on the next level of complexity in respect to the input data that are used as components;
- for software and services – the situation is similar: more sophisticated modelling tools are built on the base of already existing components.

3   Integration IN and BETWEEN the EO Centers

The analysis of existing geoinformation centers (another term for Earth Observation Centers), made by us in [6] showed a tendency of establishing national centers aimed to gather the information from various sources in the country, along with international agreements for enriching these source data with global observations. On the upper level of the process of integration of the research information and knowledge is the establishing the global aggregation centers, such as GEOSS (https://www.geoportal.org/) and EPOS (https://www.epos-ip.org/), which form sets of coordinated, independent Earth observation, information, and processing systems for strengthening the monitoring of the state of the Earth, where the national and regional centers come as data providers. Especially in EPOS, the data providers are only national and trans-national research infrastructures thus ensuring access to quality-checked data and products, while in GEOSS the providers are more than 150 institutions – international, regional, and national, and from the private sector.

According to the specificity of organizational structure (see [6]) a variety of approaches are used for the achievement of information integration and interoperability. We may distinguish three approaches:

- In the case when a center is governed by a state organization and its operations are closely connected with everyday life (such as prognosis, warnings, etc.), while the research activities play a secondary role as support of the main activities, the centers are built using monolithic architecture. The typical example is GEARS (Ground Enterprise Architecture Services) [7], implementation of which transforms the NES-DIS Ground Enterprise from a set of stand-alone capabilities to an Integrated Ground Enterprise based on common ground services [7]. Another example is ETRIS DZZ – Russian Unified Geographically Distributed Information System for Earth Remote Sensing [8] – the project, which is evaluated by Roscosmos as one of the largest in the field of using the results of space activities in Russia and in the world. ETRIS DZZ unite the entire ground infrastructure within the framework of a new hierarchy with unified technical standards, which ensures the management of the target use of Russian Earth remote sensing spacecraft, the reception of information, its processing and transmission to consumers;

- When a national or trans-national center is built on the basis of an agreement of independent bodies (universities, research centers, business partners) usually some kinds of federated structures are established. The reason is that the federated organization is a hybrid that combines characteristics of centralized (e.g. centralized planning, standardization, etc.) and decentralized organizations (e.g. local leadership, competitive local objectives, etc.) [9] and specifics helps to unravel the situation in which the center has no ownership over data sources, however, it serves as a unifier. As it is mentioned in [10], in this case, the interoperability is achieved through the development of own service buses by each disciplinary community, which cover common/federal "domain" specifications;
- In the case when the disciplinary diversity and the amount of data sources are too many, the center is built as an independent entity. The constituent bodies are not necessarily DDSS providers or this is not their main role. In this case, the realization of cross-domain interoperability using federated architecture is not appropriate, so a middleware structure takes up the tasks for mediation, adaptation, distribution, semantic mapping, and quality checks. Such a "brokering" approach is implemented in GEOSS infrastructure [10].

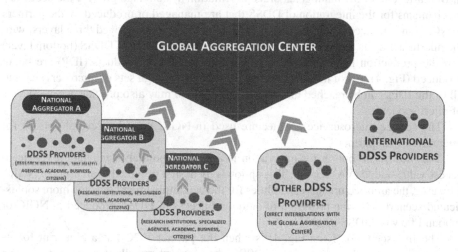

Fig. 3. Integration between centers

So, Fig. 3 stresses this hierarchical process of integration. At the bottom are the primary sources - a variety of ICT and content providers. In terms of the complexity of given sources from the content providers, it varies from raw data (given directly from satellite, airborn, in-situ measurements) or pieces of data (for instance, from crowdsourcing channels that gather sensitive in-time event information) to complex data products (for instance, geomagnetic storm forecast for next 6 h [11]).

In the middleware are the national and regional aggregators, who assimilate these data and data products from some of these primary sources and in turn add new data products as a result of the work of the center. Such integration allows gathering data and models from different scientific disciplines, so, such results as integrated maps of geological, geophysical and seismological data for seismic hazard assessment [12] stand possible.

At the top level are the global aggregators, such as GEOSS and EPOS, which use the primary and middleware providers directly (like GEOSS) or through the national aggregators (like EPOS) as sources of DDSS and ensure integrated multi-disciplinary and trans-national science platforms.

4   Service-Microservice Hybrid Approach to Integration

The appearance of the concept of "microservice" has catalysed changes in enterprise system architecture and pushed for redesign of the software information systems of some of the leading EO centers. Notably, EPOS [13] included the microservices approach as one of the four principles of system development and declared that it will use web services "wherever possible".

Recently, the software information system architecture of the Bulgarian National Geoinformation Center (NGIC) adopted both service and microservice concepts [6]. Since the NGIC aims to foster scientific cooperation between all major EO organizations in Bulgaria, one of the main goals of its information system is to provide the necessary mechanisms for the integration of DDSS that are managed or produced by the partners in NGIC and are needed in joint activities. The architecture employed three layers, with the middle acting as a smart interconnector between the sources of DDSS (bottom layer) and the production layer (top layer) where integrated data products (IDP) are being produced (Fig. 4). All of the "sources" are accessible through sets of microservices and all of the IDPs can be reached through services, which may also provide access to a set of microservices.

The service-microservice architecture used in NGIC provides several options for integration with partner EOC.

The most basic option for integration is accessing publicly available or restricted access value-added (VA) service. This option is by design provided to all users of NGIC. However, the architecture has capabilities for the accomplishment of some more sophisticated scenarios for the provision of outbound access to DDSS produced in NGIC or inbound flow of DDSS needed by NGIC.

The first scenario (1. on Fig. 4) is when the partner EOC has a blueprint for its "accessor" (we use the term as per GEOSS) - the protocol and all other means to receive DDSS from out of its boundaries. If the DDSS is an integrated data product (IDP), i.e. it is a product of some processing in NGIC, a service is built according to both partner's accessor blueprint and internal policies and processes. The partner is provided with access to that service; in case such service exists, that may fulfill the requirements of the accessor, the service is provided, eventually with needed service level agreement alterations. An important subcase of this scenario is when the partner prefers to use microservices to access IDP - then the service provides the API specification to the proper set of microservices; it may also contain some functionalities needed for the business goals of NGIC, e.g. usage accounting.

The second scenario (2. on Fig. 4) is when the partner EOC uses accessors and needs to receive DDSS that is produced by one of the partners in NGIC, i.e. there is no

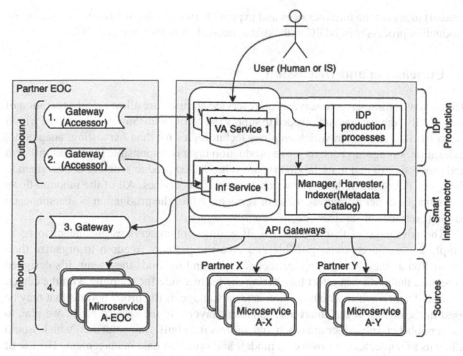

Fig. 4. Scenarios for integration using the service-microservice hybrid architecture

processing or adding value by NGIC. In that case, service is provided that uses the smart interconnector to locate, adapt and deliver to the partner EOC; the NGIC acts as a relay to the source (with little overhead, not related with the value, e.g. again usage accounting). Although from the point of the EOC partner this case is very similar to the previous, it is of importance for NGIC to differentiate, since much more significant resource usage is expected in the first scenario. A subcase of this scenario is when the partner EOC needs to access some module that is actually part of the smart interconnector. For example, one of the requirements for integration with EPOS is to maintain a CERIF metadata catalog (for abstraction we used "Indexer" to denote all of the technologies that have similar functionalities) that may be included in the hierarchy of theirs. That will be provided through a service in the setting of the current scenario.

The first two scenarios covered the outbound flow and the next two will cover the inbound flow. The third scenario (3. on Fig. 4) is when the partner EOC has a blueprint for the protocol and all other means to supply its products out of its boundaries. A service is built in NGIC according to both partner's blueprint and internal policies and processes. That service is used by the smart interconnector to provide the production processes in NGIC with what is needed from the partner EOC. An option is to wrap that service into a microservice, so to keep all of the source access methods consistent with the microservice paradigm. This scenario is the reverse of the first scenario.

The fourth scenario (4. on Fig. 4) is when the partner EOC provides access to its products through microservices. In that case, NGIC uses its API gateway (altered if needed) to access the microservices and to provide through the smart interconnector the production processes in NGIC with what is needed from the partner EOC.

5   Conclusion and Discussion

The reviewed three-layered service-microservice architecture allows clear separation of duties. All of the mechanisms needed to supply the NGIC with "raw materials" are within the smart interconnector, which employs technologies for data harvesting, adaptation, indexation, storage, and delivery. The production layer is responsible for the assimilation and processing of that materials to prepare value-added products, and to deliver them to the users. All of the outbound flows are managed as services. All of the inbound flows are managed either as microservices or services. All of the production is also managed as microservices or services.

The advantage of that approach is its agility - microservices are meant to be as simple and autonomous as possible and give the partners freedom to organize their production as they want, using the technologies and methods they want. It's designed to require the minimum effort for altering the partner side for coupling with the center. Another feature, which in our opinion is an advantage, is the broad options that may be used in the design of the smart interconnector layer – in the case of NGIC we plan to use a publisher-subscriber approach and various data buffering solutions, which would allow us to implement our own data models and optimize data management. The use of both monolith services and small autonomous microservices in production would allow choosing an optimal approach in building each particular IDP.

The main disadvantage of the approach is that most or even all of the tasks for verification and integrity of the connection and the flow are a matter of the center, which generates overhead. Although the partners may prepare some relevant mechanisms, they are not required to do that. The basic case is - we have something useful here, connect and use it at your own risk.

Since that architecture is in process of implementation in the information system of NGIC, we are still approbating and optimizing some of its components.

Acknowledgements. This work is supported by Contract DO1-161/28.08.2018 "NGIC – National Geoinformation Center for monitoring, assessment, and prediction of natural and anthropogenic risks and disasters" under the Program "National Roadmap for Research Infrastructure 2017–2023", funded by the Bulgarian Ministry of Education and Science.

References

1. United Nations: Transforming our world: the 2030 Agenda for Sustainable Development (A/RES/70/1). Resolution adopted by the General Assembly on 25.09.2015, 40 p. (2015)
2. Paganini, M. et al.: Satellite Earth Observations in Support of the Sustainable Development Goals. European Space Agency, 108 p. (2018)
3. Guo, H., et al.: Big earth data science: an information framework for a sustainable planet. Int. J. Digit. Earth **13**(7), 743–767 (2020)

4. European Commission: Legal framework for a European Research Infrastructure Consortium – ERIC Practical Guidelines, 40 p. (2010). https://doi.org/10.2777/79873
5. Bailo, D., Jeffery, K.G.: EPOS: a novel use of CERIF for data intensive science. Procedia Comput. Sci. **33**, 3–10 (2014)
6. Branzov, T., Ivanova, K., Georgiev, M.: Service-microservice basic system architecture model for geoinformation centers. In: Proceedings of XIX International Multidisciplinary Scientific GeoConference, SGEM 2019, vol. 19, no. (2.1), pp. 587–594 (2019)
7. NESDIS Ground Enterprise Architecture Services (GEARS): Concept of Operations, Feb 2015, 48 p. (2015)
8. Romashkin, V.V., Loshkarev, P.A., Fedotkin, D.I., Tokhiyan, O.O., Aref'yeva, T.A., Musiyenko, V.A.: ETRIS DZZ—sovremennyye resheniya v razvitii otechestvennoy nazem-noy kosmicheskoy infrastruktury distantsionnogo zondirovaniya Zemli iz kosmosa. Sovremennyye problemy distantsionnogo zondirovaniya Zemli iz kosmosa **16**(3), 220–227 (2019)
9. Rychkova, I., Zdravkovic, J, Speckert, T.: Challenges of EA methodologies facing progressive decentralization in modern organizations. In: CEUR Workshop Proceedings, vol. 1023, pp. 18–28 (2013)
10. Nativi, S., Craglia, M., Pearlman, J.: Earth science infrastructures interoperability: the brokering approach. IEEE J. Sel. Top. Appl. Earth Obs. Remote Sens. **6**(3), 1118–1129 (2013)
11. NIGGG – Geomagnetic Storm Forecast. http://www.geophys.bas.bg/kp_for/kp_mod_en.php. Accessed 01 Oct 2020
12. Trifonova, P., Metodiev, M., Stavrev, P., Simeonova, S., Solakov, D.: Integration of geological, geophysical and seismological data for seismic hazard assessment using spacial matching index. J. Geogr. Inf. Syst. **11**, 185–195 (2019). https://doi.org/10.4236/jgis.2019.112013
13. EPOS-IP WP6 & WP7 teams: ICS-TCS Integration Guidelines – Handbook for TCS integration: Level-2, 18 p. (2015)

Towards Safety and Security-Related Testing of Crisis Management Solutions

Todor Tagarev[1]([✉]), Petya Ivanova[2], Laurent Dubost[3], and Cyril Dangerville[3]

[1] Institute of Information and Communication Technologies, Bulgarian Academy of Sciences, Acad. G. Bonchev Str., Bl. 2, 1113 Sofia, Bulgaria
tagarev@bas.bg

[2] Procon Ltd., 3, Razluka Str., ap. 20, 1111 Sofia, Bulgaria
petya@procon.bg

[3] Thales Communications and Security S.A., 20-22 Grange Dame Rose, 78141 Vélizy, France
{laurent.dubost,cyril.dangerville}@thalesgroup.com

Abstract. A number of research and innovation projects aim to develop and demonstrate the benefits of novel solutions, in the particular case analysed in this paper – in the field of disaster or crisis management. The focus of the assessment of these solutions is on the benefits they bring by increasing the effectiveness and/or the performance of crisis management actors in a controlled environment. As a rule, little attention is given to safety and security considerations related to their intended use beyond trials and demonstrations, in an actual crisis management context. To speed up market uptake and innovation, this paper presents a technology-based classification of existing and potential solutions and a structure of their possible impact on safety and security. On that basis the authors identify pertinent 'technology-impact' combinations, list some relevant norms and standards for each such combination, and provide the outlines of three illustrative test cases. The paper concludes by a discussion on the implementation of the presented approach.

Keywords: Crisis management · Disaster management · Preparedness · Demonstration · Trial · Safety · Security · Test case · Innovation · DRIVER+

1 Introduction

Modern societies face diverse risks of natural, industrial and human-caused disasters and catastrophes and the related human and economic losses once a disaster occurs [1, 2]. With the growing speed of communication facilitated by modern media, including social networks, citizen's expectations towards public authorities are also on the increase [3, 4]. To respond to these expectations, first responders' organisations, other public authorities and stakeholders need to develop a comprehensive set of capabilities to mitigate risks, prepare for, perform a variety of functions in a crisis, manage the consequences and adapt to climate and other changes [5].

Published by Springer Nature Switzerland AG 2021
Y. Murayama et al. (Eds.): ITDRR 2020, IFIP AICT 622, pp. 216–234, 2021.
https://doi.org/10.1007/978-3-030-81469-4_18

One approach to develop the requisite capabilities is to implement the so-called "capabilities-based planning" [6–8]. A complementary approach involves the development of novel concepts and experimentation with promising technological and other solutions [9, 10].

The latter approach facilitates innovation and allows to speed up the capability development process [11]. Innovations are not always based on most advanced technologies and necessarily expensive; by accounting for context and building on social science insights, they can provide effective and prompt responses and contribute to disaster risk reduction [12].

The DRIVER+ project—Driving Innovation in Crisis Management for European Resilience—built on the idea of experimentation with crisis management concepts and potential solutions for current and future challenges posed by natural disasters, human-caused emergencies, and terrorist threats. It aimed to facilitate the development and market uptake of innovative solutions with account of the operational needs of crisis management practitioners and through their participation in the organisation of trials and demonstrations and the evaluation of the trialled solutions [13].

Crisis management solutions, developed and/or trialled in the DRIVER+ project aim to fill-in identified crisis management gaps, enhance resilience to disaster risks or increase the effectiveness or the efficiency in performing crisis management operations in a resource-constraint framework. Solution providers, often developing innovative ideas or exploiting emerging technological opportunities, aim to demonstrate new effects or more efficient use of limited crisis management resources in a realistic trial setting. Less attention at this stage has been paid to additional considerations that might influence the wider use of a solution in an actual crisis management context.

The aim of the research presented here was to fill in this gap by providing a framework and a knowledge base for safety and security testing of crisis management solutions. This paper starts with the outline of the methodological approach. Section 3 presents a technology-based classification of existing and potential solutions, followed by the structuring of their possible impact on safety and security in Sect. 4. On that basis the authors identify pertinent 'technology-impact' combinations, list some relevant norms and standards for each such combination, and provide the outlines of three illustrative test cases. The paper concludes by a discussion on the implementation of the presented approach.

2 Methodological Approach

The study aimed to set the ground for examining safety and security considerations in the use of solutions in a real crisis management environment. It followed the approach outlined on Fig. 1.

The task is to assist practitioners and solution providers in defining safety and security related requirements to crisis management solutions of interest and demonstrate how to develop respective test cases. Towards that purpose this section of the report provides:

- a classification scheme used to classify crisis management solutions on the basis of the underlying technology used;
- structure of the safety and security considerations, i.e., the type of negative impact a solution may have;

- identification of couples "technology – type of impact" where one has, or can realistically expect, concerns for the safe and secure use of a crisis management solution;
- identification of applicable norms (standards, directives, regulations, etc.) for each "technology – type of impact" couple;
- design of illustrative test cases.

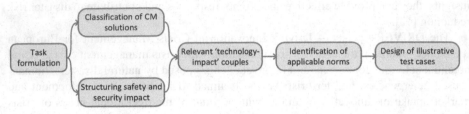

Fig. 1. Safety and security related testing of crisis management solutions: methodological approach.

Each of the enumerated issues is examined in a dedicated section of this paper. The final section outlines the envisioned implementation and future use of this approach to the safety and security related testing of crisis management solutions.

3 Technology-Based Classification of Solutions

To categorise crisis management solutions in terms of the underlying technology and in view of their potential impact on safety and security, we analysed three main taxonomies:

- STACCATO security taxonomy [14];
- CRISP Taxonomy of Security Products, Systems and Services [15];
- EDA Technology Taxonomy [16],

and developed a classification scheme with nine main categories:

1. **Sensors and navigation systems and networks**
   Passive (Optical, IR, magnetic, acoustic, UW, electrical and electro-chemical sensors, magnetometers and magnetic gradiometers, gravity meters and gravity gradiometers) and active sensors (radar, ladar, lidar, sonars, X-ray, Gamma sensors, Active IR sensors), chemical and biological substances detectors, radiological and nuclear detectors, other sensors.
2. **Communications**
   Radio communications and networks; cable communications and networks; mass emergency notification systems; early warning and alerting systems; targeted emergency notification systems; secured, wireless broadband systems; rapidly deployable communication system (rescue services mobile communication system); emergency information hotlines.

3. **Computer-based systems**
   Data bases and database management systems; decision support systems; training, modelling & simulation systems and environments; ...
4. **Specialised software applications**
   Personnel management software; material reserves management software; supply chain management software, information management & dissemination software; privacy and data protection software; electronic tagging systems; volunteers registries and management software, crowd sourcing/crowd tasking systems.
5. **Transportation vehicles and equipment**
   Ground, air, river, and maritime vehicles, ambulances, transportation containers and structures, etc.
6. **Remotely controlled systems and autonomous vehicles and systems**
   Remotely Piloted Vehicles (RPVs) and systems (RPAS), air, ground, surface, subsurface vehicles.
7. **Fire extinguishers and decontamination devices and substances**
   Fire retardants, decontamination devices and substances for radiation sources, biological materials, chemical sources and poisons; other substances.
8. **Specialised disaster management equipment**
   Protective clothing and equipment, (mobile) shelters, Mobile livestock shelters, mobile field hospitals, mobile energy systems and electricity generators, mobile water purification equipment, access control and electronic authentication systems, training ranges, physical obstacles (e.g., to stop flooding), waste management systems, logistics tracking, transportation management systems, other related equipment.
9. **Training and personnel services**
   Education and skills training systems; Psycho-social support systems; Exercises; Manuals; Distance learning (e-Learning, m-Learning); Fatigue and stress observation, analysis and coping system.

4 Types of Potential Safety and Security Impact of CM Solutions

The implementation of crisis management solutions is expected to contribute to reduction of risks and more effective and efficient operations. However, they may have potential undesired side effects on the safety and security of personnel, property, infrastructure and the environment.

International Safety Standards define "safety" as freedom from unacceptable risk of physical injury or of damage to the health of people, either directly or indirectly as a result of damage to property or to the environment. Standards IEC 61508 and IEC 61511-1:2016 refer to this also as "functional safety." In the discussion of crisis management solutions, the analysis of security concerns can start from the definition utilised by the International Society of Automation (ISA), i.e., "security" means prevention and protection from illegal or unwanted penetration, interference with proper operation or inappropriate access to confidential information regardless of motivation (intentional or unintentional) or consequence (result) [17].

Starting from these definitions, and accounting for societal and environmental concerns, this study examines the potential negative impact of crisis management solutions on:

- people, both those involved in crisis management and others who happen to be at or near the crisis scene;
- the equipment and/or the data and information used in crisis management;
- the functioning of critical infrastructures, e.g., energy, transport [18], digital infrastructure and the delivery of essential services, e.g., food, water, financial services [19], etc.
- the environment, i.e., on the animals, the vegetation, air, soil, and water quality.

Respectively, we consider here only direct impact, not taking into account possible cascading effects, e.g., software breech leading to a drone crash and injury of first responders. The reason is that testing will be conducted to assure that a crisis management solution meets the requirements of certain safety and security norms, while potential secondary effects may be studied via more complex models or trial scenarios.

Hence, seven types of negative impact, marked from A to G, are taken into consideration:

- Impact on humans (professional responders and other crisis management personnel, volunteers, service providers, other people in the area of the crisis or its vicinity):

    A. *Physical* (injury, poisoning, blinding, death, …)
    B. *Psychological* impact; impact on the perceptions
    C. Breech of sensitive *personal data*

- Temporary of lasting impact on crisis management materiel, data, and information (equipment, communications, information, …)

    D. Obstructing the use of CM *equipment* (e.g., by physical damage, radio-electronic interference, etc.)
    E. *'CIA'* – impact on the confidentiality, integrity and availability of information (including malicious attempts to manipulate information)
    F. *Impact on critical infrastructures and/or the provision of essential services*
    G. *Environmental impact* (flora, fauna, soil, air, water).

5 Pertinent 'Technology-Impact' Combinations

There are 63 possible combinations among the nine categories of solutions and the seven types of impact (see Table 1 below). Not all combinations are possible, i.e. certain categories of solutions cannot have a particular type of impact (only direct impact is considered here; possible cascading effects are not subject of this study). For example, a software application is highly unlikely to cause physical injury, transportation vehicles and decontamination devices are unlikely to infringe on the confidentiality, integrity and availability of information, etc.

Table 1. 'Technology-impact' combinations.

Potential impact on/	Humans			CM materiel, data, and information		F. Critical infrastructures	G. Environment
Solutions	A. Physical	B. Psychological, perceptions	C. Personal data	D. Materiel	E. CIA of information		
1. Sensors and navigation systems and networks: passive (optical, IR, magnetic, acoustic, UW, electrical and electro-chemical sensors, magnetometers and magnetic gradiometers, gravity meters and gravity gradiometers) and active sensors (radar, ladar, lidar, sonars, X-ray, Gamma sensors, active IR sensors), chemical and biological substances detectors, radiological and nuclear detectors, ...							
2. Communications: Radio communications and networks; cable communications and networks; mass emergency notification systems; early warning and alerting systems; targeted emergency notification systems; secured, wireless broadband systems; rapidly deployable communication system (rescue services mobile communication system); emergency information hotlines							
3. Computer-based systems: data bases and database management systems; decision support systems; training, modelling & simulation systems and environments; ...						X	
4. Specialised software applications: Personnel management software; material reserves management software; supply chain management software, information management and dissemination software; privacy and data protection software; electronic tagging systems; volunteers registries and management software, crowd sourcing/ crowd tasking systems			X		X		

(*continued*)

Table 1. (*continued*)

5. **Transportation vehicles and equipment**: ground, air, river, and maritime vehicles, ambulances, transportation containers and structures, …								
6. **Remotely controlled systems and autonomous vehicles and systems**: RPVs/RPAS, air, ground, surface, sub-surface vehicles								
7. **Fire extinguishers and decontamination devices and substances**: Fire retardants, decontamination devices and substances for radiation sources, biological materials, chemical sources and poisons								
8. **Specialised disaster management equipment**: protective clothing and equipment, (mobile) shelters, mobile livestock shelters, mobile field hospitals, mobile energy systems and electricity generators, mobile water purification equipment, access control and electronic authentication systems, training ranges, physical obstacles (e.g., to stop flooding), waste management systems, logistics tracking, transportation management systems …								
9. **Training and personnel services**: Education and skills training systems; Psycho-social support systems; Exercises; Manuals; Distance learning (e-Learning, m-Learning); Fatigue and stress observation, analysis and coping system								

In Table 1, the cells of such unlikely combinations are marked with grey background colour. The remaining 39 combinations "solution's underlying technology – negative impact on safety and security" are considered pertinent. Respectively, the next section provides standards and other norms for each pertinent combination, followed by provide illustrative test cases for the combinations marked with 'X' in Table 1.

By 'X' in the table are marked "technology-impact" combinations for which this paper presents illustrative test cases.

6   Sample Safety and Security Norms for Pertinent 'Technology-Impact' Combinations

Selected regulations on safety and security of crisis management solutions are presented in Table 2 below.

Table 2. Illustrative set of norms for pertinent 'Technology-Impact' combinations.

Document	Relevance
(1-A) Sensors and navigation systems and networks – Physical impact	
EN ISO 15367-2:2005 (WI=00123043) Lasers and laser-related equipment – Test methods for determination of the shape of a laser beam wavefront - Part 2: Shack-Hartmann sensors (ISO 15367-2:2005).	Power (energy) density distribution, widths and divergence angles of laser beams.
BS EN 50270 Electromagnetic compatibility - Electrical apparatus for the detection and measurement of combustible gases, toxic gases or oxygen	This document applies to apparatus intended for use in variety of settings, including hazardous areas which could contain explosive or potentially explosive atmospheres. It specifies requirements for immunity tests in relation to continuous and transient, conducted and radiated disturbances, including electrostatic discharges, and also for emission tests.
Radiation Protection of the Public and the Environment, IAEA Safety Standards Series No. GSG-8 [applicable to 1-G]	This Safety Guide provides guidance on the implementation of the requirements in the International Basic Safety Standards, IAEA Safety Standards Series No. GSR Part 3, in relation to protection of the public and the environment against radiation risks. It provides generic guidance on the application of the radiation protection principles of justification, of optimization of protection and safety, and of dose limits. The publication covers the protection of the public and the environment in all exposure situations, including in emergency.
(1-B) Sensors and navigation systems and networks – Psychological impact, impact on perceptions	
ISO 27048:2011 Radiation protection — Dose assessment for the monitoring of workers for internal radiation exposure	This standard specifies the minimum requirements for the evaluation of data from the monitoring of those occupationally exposed to the risk of internal contamination by radioactive substances. It presents procedures and assumptions for the standardised interpretation of monitoring data, in order to achieve acceptable levels of reliability. Among others, it addresses assumptions for the selection of dose-critical parameter values; criteria for determining the significance of monitoring results; their interpretation; uncertainties arising from sampling, measurement techniques and working conditions; interpretation of multiple data arising from different measurement methods at different times, handling data below the decision threshold, rogue data.

(*continued*)

Table 2. (*continued*)

(1-G) Sensors and navigation systems and networks – Environmental impact	
Guide for the Selection of Explosives Detection and Blast Mitigation Equipment for Emergency First Responders Preparedness Directorate Office of Grants and Training, Guide 105–07, US Department of Homeland Security, February 2008 [applicable to 1-A, 8-A, 8-D, 8-F]	The Guide presents a broad spectrum of sensing technologies and techniques, with their advantages and disadvantages, of visual detection and blast mitigation equipment, as well as methods and results of the evaluation of concrete products.
(2-A) Communications – Physical impact	
Security in Telecommunications and Information Technology: An overview of issues and the deployment of existing ITU-T Recommendations for secure telecommunications (Geneva: ITU-T – Telecommunication Standardization Bureau, 2015). – 206 pp. [applicable to groups 2, 3 and 4]	This manual provides a broad introduction to the ICT security work of the ITU, with key areas and a discussion of the basic requirements for the protection of ICT applications, services and information, security architectures and management. An 8-page annex provides a list of relevant ITU recommendations and standards.
Directive 2013/35/EU of the European Parliament and of the Council of 26 June 2013 on the minimum health and safety requirements regarding the exposure of workers to the risks arising from physical agents (electromagnetic fields) and repealing Directive 2004/40/EC	This Directive lays down minimum requirements for the protection of workers from risks to their health and safety arising, or likely to arise, from exposure to electromagnetic fields during their work. It covers all known direct biophysical effects and indirect effects caused by electromagnetic fields and provides exposure limit values (ELVs) with scientifically well-established links between short-term direct biophysical effects and exposure to electromagnetic fields.
(2-B) Communications – Psychological Impact, impact on Perceptions	
ISO 22322:2015: Societal security — Emergency management — Guidelines for public warning [applicable to 2-A, 2-F, 2-G]	This International Standard provides guidelines for developing, managing, and implementing public warning before, during, and after incidents.
(2-E) Communications – CIA of Information	
ETSI/TS 119 312 Electronic Signatures and Infrastructures (ESI); Cryptographic Suites	The Technical Specifications provide guidance on selection of cryptographic suites with particular emphasis on interoperability. The present document is based on the specified agreed cryptographic mechanisms of the SOG-IS Crypto Evaluation Scheme [15]. The SOG-IS Crypto WG is in charge of providing requirements and evaluation procedures related to cryptographic aspects of Common Criteria security evaluations of IT products.
(2-F) Communications – Critical infrastructures	
ITU-T K.87 (06/2016) Guide for the	This document outlines electromagnetic

(*continued*)

Table 2. (*continued*)

application of electromagnetic security requirements – Overview [applicable to 2-A and 2-E, 3-E and 3-F]	security risks of telecommunication equipment and illustrates how to assess and prevent those risks, in order to manage information security management systems (ISMS) in accordance with Recommendation ITU-T X.1051. Major electromagnetic security risks addressed in this Recommendation are as follows: natural electromagnetic (EM) threats (e.g., lightning); unintentional interference (i.e., electromagnetic interference, EMI); intentional interference (i.e., intentional electromagnetic interference, IEMI); deliberate EM attacks; information leakage from EM emanation (i.e., electromagnetic security, EMSEC); and mitigation methods against electromagnetic security threats.
(2-G) Communications – Environmental impact	
Maximum Exposure Levels to Radiofrequency Fields —3 kHz to 300 GHz, Radiation Protection Series Publication No. 3 (Australian Radiation Protection and Nuclear Safety Agency, 2002). [applicable to 2-A]	This Standard specifies fundamental limits … that correlate most closely with the established biological effects for which protection is required. Therefore, a set of indicative levels called 'reference levels' have been provided as an alternative means for determining compliance. … This rationale does provide a broad overview of the scientific and philosophical considerations that lead to the derivation of the exposure limits.
Physicians for Safe Technology, Environment and Wildlife Effects, https://mdsafetech.org/environmental-and-wildlife-effects/	A compilation of norms and studies of the harmful effects of radio, microwave communication and magnetic fields on wildlife and the environment.
(3-B) Computer-based systems – Psychological Impact, impact on Perceptions	
Eva Flaspöler et al., The human machine interface as an emerging risk (European Agency for Safety and Health at Work, 2010). [applicable to 4B]	The documents review the literature allowing to foresee multi-factorial risks (e.g. due to combined effects of poor ergonomic design, poor work organisation, mental and emotional demands); complexity of new technologies, new work processes and human-machine interface (HMI) leading to increased mental and emotional strain; poor ergonomic design of non-office visual display unit workplaces; and poor design of HMI (excessively complex or requiring high forces for operation).
(3-C) Computer-based systems – Personal Data	
ISO/IEC 27018:2019 Information technology -- Security techniques -- Code of practice for	This standard establishes commonly accepted control objectives, controls and

(*continued*)

Table 2. (*continued*)

protection of personally identifiable information (PII) in public clouds acting as PII processors	guidelines for implementing measures to protect Personally Identifiable Information in line with the privacy principles in ISO/IEC 29100 for the public cloud computing environment.
(3-E) Computer-based systems – CIA of Information	
ISO/IEC 15408-1:2009 Information technology — Security techniques — Evaluation criteria for IT security	The standard establishes the general concepts and principles of IT security evaluation and specifies the general model of evaluation of security properties of IT products. Parts 2 and 3 defines operations for tailoring functional and assurance components.
(3-F) Computer-based systems – Critical infrastructures	
Directive (EU) 2016/1148 of the European Parliament and of the Council of 6 July 2016 concerning measures for a high common level of security of network and information systems across the Union	This Directive lays down measures with a view to achieving a high common level of security of network and information systems … To that end, this Directive lays down obligations … ; …; establishes security and notification requirements for operators of essential services and for digital service providers; …
(4-B) Specialised software applications – Psychological Impact, impact on Perceptions	
Eva Flaspöler et al., The human machine interface as an emerging risk (European Agency for Safety and Health at Work, 2010). [applicable to 3B]	The documents review the literature allowing to foresee multi-factorial risks (e.g. due to combined effects of poor ergonomic design, poor work organisation, mental and emotional demands); complexity of new technologies, new work processes and human-machine interface (HMI) leading to increased mental and emotional strain; poor ergonomic design of non-office visual display unit workplaces; and poor design of HMI (excessively complex or requiring high forces for operation).
(4-C) Specialised software applications – Personal Data	
Regulation (EU) 2016/679 of the European Parliament and of the Council of 27 April 2016 on the protection of natural persons with regard to the processing of personal data and on the free movement of such data, and repealing Directive 95/46/EC (General Data Protection Regulation, GDPR), *Official Journal* L 119, 4 May 2016	Defines principles relating to and lawfulness, and conditions of processing of personal data
(4-E) Specialised software applications – CIA of Information	
ISO/IEC 27002:2013 "Information technology -- Security techniques -- Code of practice for information security controls"	The standard gives guidelines for organizational information security standards and information security management practices

(*continued*)

Table 2. *(continued)*

[applicable to 3-C, 3-E, 3-F, 4-F, 9-E]	including the selection, implementation and management of controls taking into consideration the organization's information security risk environment.
(4-F) Specialised software applications – Critical infrastructures	
NIST Special Publication 800-53 "Security and Privacy Controls for Federal Information Systems and Organizations", revision 4, April 2014 [applicable to 3-C, 3-E, 3-F, 4-F, 9-E]	The document provides a holistic approach to information security and risk management by providing organizations with the breadth and depth of security controls necessary to fundamentally strengthen their information systems and the environments in which those systems operate—contributing to systems that are more resilient in the face of cyber and other threats.
(5-A) Transport vehicles and equipment – Physical Impact	
CEN/TR 1459-6:2015 (WI=00150078) Rough-terrain trucks - Safety requirements and verification	Explains the risk assessment methodology followed to determine the Performance Level required, for specific safety related parts of control system (SRP/CS) of rough-terrain variable-reach trucks. Part 6 examines the application of EN ISO 13849-1 to slewing and non-slewing variable-reach rough-terrain trucks.
(5-D) Transport vehicles and equipment – Materiel	
ISO 19116:2019 Geographic information — Positioning services [applicable to 5-A, 5-F, 6-A, 6-D, 6-F]	This document specifies the data structure and content of an interface that permits communication between position-providing device(s) and position-using device(s) enabling the position-using device(s) to obtain and unambiguously interpret position information and determine, based on a measure of the degree of reliability, whether the resulting position information meets the requirements of the intended use.
(5-G) Transport vehicles and equipment – Environmental impact	
Directive 2008/68/EC of the European Parliament and of the Council of 24 September 2008 on the inland transport of dangerous goods [applicable to 5-A and 5-D]	The Directive applies to the transport of dangerous goods by road, by rail or by inland waterway within or between Member States, including the activities of loading and unloading, the transfer to or from another mode of transport and the stops necessitated by the circumstances of the transport.
(6-A) Remotely controlled systems and autonomous vehicles and systems – Physical Impact	
Ludovic Apvrille et al., Autonomous Drones for Disasters Management: Safety and Security Verifications, AT-RASC 2015	The paper presents a tool (SysML-Sec/TTool) that can be used for formally verifying the safety and security of an

(continued)

Table 2. (*continued*)

	autonomous drone mission and flight, based on an architecture developed within drone4u project.
(6-D) Remotely controlled systems and autonomous vehicles and systems – Materiel	
CWA 17357:2019 Urban search and rescue (USaR) robotic platform technical and procedural interoperability – Guide [applicable to 6-A]	This CWA provides recommendations to enable interoperability between USaR robotic platforms and the equipment, sensors and tools that are attached to them; principles for enabling USaR robotic platforms to operate in all ground search environments.
(6-F) Remotely controlled systems and autonomous vehicles and systems – Critical infrastructures	
CEN - PREN 16803-2 Space – Use of GNSS-based positioning for road Intelligent Transport Systems (ITS) – Part 2: Assessment of basic performances of GNSS-based positioning terminals [applicable to 6-A and 6-D]	This document proposes testing procedures to assess the basic performance of any GNSS-based positioning terminal for a given use case described by an operational scenario. These tests address the basic performance features Availability, Continuity, Accuracy and Integrity of the Position, Velocity and Time (PVT) information.
(7-A) Fire extinguishers and decontamination devices and substances – Physical Impact	
EN 3-10:2009 Portable fire extinguishers. Provisions for evaluating the conformity of a portable fire extinguisher to EN 3-7 (characteristics, performance requirements and test methods)	European standard EN 3 specifies requirements for portable fire extinguishers. Compliance with the standard is legally required in the EU.
(7-D) Fire extinguishers and decontamination devices and substances – Materiel	
Phillip Carson and Clive Mumford, Hazardous Chemicals Handbook, Second edition (Oxford: Butterworth Heinemann, 2002). – 619 pp. [applicable to the whole group 7]	The Handbook presents a variety of hazardous chemicals, including radioactive chemicals, safety by design principles, operating procedures, transport, impact on the environment, monitoring and protection. It includes selected topics of testing and evaluation.
(7-F) Fire extinguishers and decontamination devices and substances – Critical infrastructures	
CEN/TS 16595:2013 CBRN – Vulnerability Assessment and Protection of People at Risk [applicable also to 7-A, 7-D, 7, 7-G]	This Technical Specification is based on an all-hazards approach, with a specific focus on terrorism and other security related risks. Looking at the combination of threats, vulnerabilities and values to be protected, threats may be terrorist attacks with chemical, explosive and biological agents, or nuclear waste materials, or with conventional means on CBRN plants, causing a similar devastating effect on a

(*continued*)

Table 2. (*continued*)

	potentially large scale. It can serve to guide the development of safety and security test cases.
(8-A) Specialised disaster management equipment – Physical Impact	
Group of standards ISO 13.340 Protective equipment	The group includes standards for protective equipment in general, protective clothing, head protective equipment (helmets, eye-protectors, hearing protectors, ear muffs, teeth protectors and hoods), respiratory protective devices, hand and arm, leg and foot protection, etc.
(8-C) Specialised disaster management equipment – Personal data	
CEN/TR 16670:2014 Information technology – RFID (Radio-Frequency IDentification) threat and vulnerability analysis See also CEN/TR 16674:2014 – Analysis of privacy impact assessment methodologies relevant to RFID	This Technical Report consider the threats, vulnerabilities and mitigation methods associated with specific characteristics of RFID technology in a system. In particular the document should be a tool used by RFID system integrators, to improve security aspects using a privacy by design approach.
(8-D) Specialised disaster management equipment – Materiel	
ISO/IEC 29197:2015 Information technology — Evaluation methodology for environmental influence in biometric system performance	This standard elaborates fundamental requirements for planning and execution of environmental performance evaluations for biometric systems based on scenario and operational test methodologies, respective specifications, baseline performance and procedures for carrying out the overall evaluation.
(8-E) Specialised disaster management equipment – CIA of Information	
CEN/TS 15291:2006 Identification card system – Guidance on design for accessible card-activated devices [applicable to 8-A, 8-D and 8-F]	This document provides guidance for the design and location of card-activated devices and the immediate environment, to facilitate access for the widest possible range of users (all/most members of the community), subject to conditions of adequate privacy and security.
(8-F) Specialised disaster management equipment – Critical infrastructures	
CWA 17260:2018 Guidelines on evaluation systems and schemes for physical security products [applicable to 8-A and 8-D]	This CWA provides guidelines on how to design certification systems and schemes for physical security products and presents a framework in which these systems and schemes can be upheld. Physical security products include products which provide protection of people, property and infrastructure from acts of malicious intent, such as physical attacks.
(8-G) Specialised disaster management equipment – Environmental impact	
Group of ISO standards 13.030.30 Special	See ISO/DIS 16640 Monitoring radioactive

(*continued*)

Table 2. (*continued*)

wastes, including radioactive wastes, hospital wastes, carcasses, electrical, electronic equipment and other hazardous wastes	gases in effluents from facilities producing positron emitting radionuclides and radio-pharmaceuticals; ISO/DIS 22450 Elements recycling –Communication formats for providing recycling information on rare earth elements in industrial waste and end of life products; etc.
(9-A) Training and personnel services – Physical Impact	
ISO 22398:2013 – Societal security — Guidelines for exercises.	This International Standard describes the elements of a generic approach to planning, conducting and improving exercise pro-grammes and projects. It introduces the "exercise safety officer" position for a person tasked with ensuring that any ac-tions during the exercise are performed safely.
(9-B) Training and personnel services – Psychological Impact, impact on Percep-tions	
IASC Guidelines on Mental Health and Psy-chosocial Support in Emergency Settings (Geneva: Inter-Agency Standing Committee, 2007 & 2008).	The Guidelines present good practice in planning, establishing and coordinating a set of minimum multi-sectoral responses to protect and improve people's mental health and psychosocial well-being in the midst of an emergency. The 2008 edition provides a Checklist for Field Use.

This table included in this paper is illustrative. The study did not deliver a compre-hensive list of norms as well; yet, it intentionally included a broad variety of sources, such as international (ISO) and European standards, national standards, potential stan-dards /under development/, i.e., CEN Workshop Agreements (CWAs), EU Directives, regulations, recommendations and guidelines by UN bodies such as ITU and IAEA, good practices identified by industry associations and non-governmental organisations, etc.

A number of these norms are relevant to more than one "technology-impact" combination. Such norms are listed ones, with the respective remark on applicability.

Of general relevance is how testing fits into the development of a strategic crisis man-agement capability, addressed in CEN/TS 17091:2018 "Crisis management – Guidance for developing a strategic capability."

7 Illustrative Test Cases

This section outlines three illustrative test cases for testing safety and security of crisis management solutions that have participated in one or more of the DRIVER+ project trials:

• The Social Media Analysis Platform, trailed in Trial France

- The CrisisSuite solution, trailed in Trials France and The Netherlands, and in the Final Demo
- The Test-bed infrastructure with the Common Information Space, and its embedded security features.

The role and the guidelines for preparing test cases are described in DRIVER+ deliverable D934.21 – Solution Testing Procedure, March 2019 [20].

Test Case 1 "Personal Data Protection in the Social Media Analysis Platform"
The Social Media Analysis Platform is presented in the DRIVER+ Portfolio of Solutions at https://pos.driver-project.eu/en/PoS/solutions/62.

This test case illustrates the couple 4-C, i.e., the potential negative impact of specialised software applications on personal data.

General norms: Regulation (EU) 2016/679.

Specific norms: OASIS/Common Alerting Protocol Version 1.2

During Trial 2 of the DRIVR+ project, the Social Media Analysis Platform (SMAP) solution was identified as requiring a GDRP analysis. The solution collects and exploits Social Media post which are considered as "personal data." The analysis which was conducted with the support of Thales Legal Department is reproduced in the Annex 2 of D942.22 Report on the application of solutions in the Trial 2. In short, this analysis concluded that due to the fact that the purpose of the collection and processing of these personal data was clearly aiming at improving Social Resilience, and thus was in the interest of the persons, they were legitimate, and consequently authorized. Yet, due to the specific nature of the data, some restrictions regarding the access to the data needed to be limited (through authentication of a single user) and their retention over time also. In addition to these measures, the anonymisation of the pseudos (which often contain names in clear) was recommended and implemented. This analysis is a good basis to foresee the requirements which could derive for such a Social Media Analysis Platform if it were to become an operational system.

Test Case 2 "Providing Confidentiality, Integrity and Availability of Information in CrisisSuite"
The CrisisSuite solution is presented in the DRIVER+ Portfolio of Solutions at https://pos.driver-project.eu/en/PoS/solutions/179.

This test case illustrates the couple 4-E, i.e., the potential negative impact of using specialised software applications to exchange information among units participating in a crisis management operation on its confidentiality, integrity and availability.

General norms: The ISO 27000 family of standards.

The CrisisSuite solution. CrisisSuite was trailed three times during DRIVER+ - in two trials and the Final Demonstration. The example which is the most meaningful with regards to the requirements concerning safety and security is the one of the Final Demonstration. In that demonstration, information was shared thanks to CrisisSuite which is deployed at three levels, from EUCPM modules (the tactical level), then at EUCPT level (the operational coordination level), and ERCC, the strategic coordination at European level. The security problems which were faced during the final demonstration related to the right to know (confidentiality) of information: ERCC does not want modules to be able to read the information they share with EUCPT.

During the DRIVER+ Final Demonstration, Warsaw, November 2019, this requirement was implemented by creating two 'crises' in CrisisSuite. This implementation was a work around which actually was satisfying for the table top Trial, but would require other types of implementation if the solution was to be operationally deployed at ERCC, EUCPT and Modules.

Test Case 3 "Security of Digital Infrastructure in the Common Information Space"
The Test-bed infrastructure is presented in detail in the deliverables from Work Package 923 of the DRIVER+ project.

This test case illustrates the couple 3-E, i.e., the potential negative impact of computer-based systems on critical infrastructures; in this case – on the digital infrastructure of a crisis management operation. Although the illustration relates to trial settings, the approach can be of value in testing actual digital infrastructure.

General norms: The ISO 27000 family of standards.

Specific norms: SSL/TLS security protocol.

The Common Information Space (CIS) is a software module of the Test-bed infrastructure which enables the exchange of information between Solutions in DRIVER+ Trials. This CIS can be made available on-line which facilitates on-line testing of solutions, or the use of the on-line Test-bed during a Trial. Making such a software available on-line makes it vulnerable to potential cyber intentional attacks or non-intentional interference. A solution that would either by mistake or malicious intention connect to an instance of the CIS during a Trial could disturb the whole trial by sending unintended messages for example. For this reason, it is very important to fully master what solution is able to connect to the CIS and when. In DRIVER+ this level of security was introduced by distributing security certificates which enforced a strong authentication mechanism on the CIS by encrypted security codes: each solution (of each organization) is issued a security certificate by a Certificate Authority of the Test-bed, and the CIS broker requires every connecting solution to authenticate with such certificate (SSL/TLS protocol). This guarantees that the solutions connecting to the CIS are indeed properly identified and authorized to do so.

Besides, the use of SSL/TLS security protocol on the CIS broker also guarantees the confidentiality and integrity of the messages exchanged within the CIS, i.e. it prevents an unauthorized user to intercept, alter, replace or replay messages maliciously. The next security requirement addressed in DRIVER+ is topic-based access control. Indeed, depending on the sensitivity or criticality of certain CIS topics, only one or more specific solutions should be authorized to publish or read data from these topics. The previous paragraph gives a relevant example where ERCC is exchanging information with EUCPT, which could be done in a specific CIS topic, but does not want the EUCPM modules to read this information. To address this requirement, DRIVER+ provides an access control plugin for the CIS broker that allows to enforce a fine-grained access control policy (defined via the Test-bed's Admin Tool) that consists of rules such as: permit solution X to READ/WRITE from/to topic Y (and deny such rights by default). Although this feature has not been used yet in a Trial, it is available in the Test-bed software repository and tested by the Test-bed infrastructure staff.

In the perspective of an operational use of the CIS, other security measures would be required in order to reduce its vulnerability to potential cyberattacks: the use of one single port to connect to the internet, or the use of a proxy to hide the actual IP addresses of the CIS servers from the outside.

The full securing of the CIS would also depend on the actual physical and logical infrastructure on which the servers would be deployed: the presence of a DMZ zone, firewalls, etc., which can only be examined when all these constraints are known.

8   Conclusions

Assuring safety and security of new crisis management solutions depends on the way practitioners' organisations define their requirements. Solution providers or third parties are expected to warrant that these requirements are met. It is possible also to jointly design and conduct tests to verify the extent to which requirements are met.

The study presented in this paper goes beyond the framework for preparing trials, demonstrations, experiments or tests of innovative crisis management solutions. It is intended to support the process of the uptake of solutions by presenting a framework for dealing with safety and security concerns in the use of crisis management solutions in actual crisis context, which would be of use to both crisis management practitioners and solution providers.

While this framework is comprehensive, the list of normative documents delivered in the study and illustrated above is subject to continuous review, updates and amendment. This also applies to illustrative test cases. An increasing number of test cases and results will contribute to the body of knowledge on the safe and secure use of solutions in actual crisis management context.

Acknowledgement. The research leading to these results was performed by the Centre for Security and Defence Management, Institute of ICT, Bulgarian Academy of Sciences and Thales Communications & Security, France, as part of the DRIVER+ project and has received funding from the European Union's Seventh Framework Programme under grant agreement no. 607798.

References

1. Shi, P.: Hazards, disasters, and risks. In: Disaster Risk Science. IHDP/Future Earth-Integrated Risk Governance Project Series, pp. 1–48. Springer, Singapore (2019). https://doi.org/10.1007/978-981-13-6689-5_1
2. Stäubli, A., Nussbaumer, S.U., Allen, S., Huggel, C., Wymann von Dach, S.: Diverse natural hazards – high human and economic losses. In: Wymann von Dach, S., et al. (eds.) Safer lives and livelihoods in mountains: making the Sendai framework for disaster risk reduction work for sustainable mountain development, pp. 14–19. Centre for Development and Environment, University of Bern, Bern (2017)
3. Chamlee-Wright, E., Storr, V.H.: Expectations of government's response to disaster. Public Choice **144**(1/2), 253–274 (2010). https://doi.org/10.1007/s11127-009-9516-x
4. Jong, W., Dückers, M.L.A.: The perspective of the affected: what people confronted with disasters expect from government officials and public leaders. Risk Hazards Crisis Public Policy **10**(1), 14–31 (2019). https://doi.org/10.1002/rhc3.12150

5. Tagarev, T., Ratchev, V.: A taxonomy of crisis management functions. Sustainability **12**(12), 5147 (2020). https://doi.org/10.3390/su12125147
6. Caudle, S.: Homeland Security Capabilities-Based Planning: Lessons from the Defense Community. Homeland Security Affairs 1, Article 2 (2005). https://www.hsaj.org/articles/178
7. Keim, M.E.: An innovative approach to capability-based emergency operations planning. Disaster Health **1**(1), 54–62 (2013). https://doi.org/10.4161/dish.23480
8. Bradley, D.J.: Applying the THIRA to special events: a framework for capabilities-based planning adoption in local governments. Thesis, Naval Postgraduate School, Monterey, CA (2018). https://www.hsaj.org/articles/14939
9. Nikolov, O.: Distributed training, CAX and experimentation in support of crisis management. Inf. Secur.: Int. J. **27**(2), 138–146 (2011). http://dx.doi.org/10.11610/isij.2713
10. Nikolov, O., Tomov, N., Nikolova, I.: M&S support for crisis and disaster management processes and climate change implications. In: Murayama, Y., Velev, D., Zlateva, P., Gonzalez, J.J. (eds.) ITDRR 2016. IAICT, vol. 501, pp. 240–253. Springer, Cham (2017). https://doi.org/10.1007/978-3-319-68486-4_19
11. Angevine, R.G.: Time to revive joint concept development and experimentation. War on the Rocks (23 January 2020). https://warontherocks.com/2020/01/time-to-revive-joint-concept-development-and-experimentation. Accessed 26 Oct 2020
12. Izumi, T., Shaw, R., Ishiwatari, M., Djalante, R., Komino, T.: 30 innovations for disaster risk reduction. IRIDeS, Keio University, The University of Tokyo, UNU-IAS, CWS Japan, Japan (2019)
13. What is DRIVER+?. https://www.driver-project.eu/driver-project/. Accessed 24 Oct 2020
14. AeroSpace and Defence Industries Association of Europe: STACCATO Final Taxonomy, Deliverable 1.2.2, STACCATO (Stakeholders Platform for Supply chain Mapping, Market condition Analysis and Technologies Opportunities) project (2007)
15. Sveinsdottir, T., et al.: Taxonomy of Security Products, Systems and Services, Deliverable 1.2, CRISP (Project title: Evaluation and Certification Schemes for Security Products) project (2014)
16. European Defence Agency: EDA Technology Taxonomy Overview (n.d.). https://www.eda.europa.eu/docs/default-source/procurement/eda-technology-taxonomy.pdf. Accessed 26 Oct 2020
17. Duran, L.: Safety and Security – Preventing cybersecurity attacks in safety systems. Hazardex (2015). http://www.hazardexonthenet.net/article/105606/Safety-and-Security-Preventing-cybersecurity-attacks-in-safety-systems.aspx. Accessed 26 Oct 2020
18. Council Directive 2008/114/EC of 8 December 2008 on the identification and designation of European critical infrastructures and the assessment of the need to improve their protection. Off. J. L **345**, 75–82 (2008). http://data.europa.eu/eli/dir/2008/114/oj
19. Directive (EU) 2016/1148 of the European Parliament and of the Council of 6 July 2016 concerning measures for a high common level of security of network and information systems across the Union. Off. J. L **194**, 1–30 (2016). http://data.europa.eu/eli/dir/2016/1148/oj
20. Dubost, L., et al.: Solution testing procedure. DRIVER+ Deliverable D934.21. https://www.driver-project.eu/wp-content/uploads/2018/08/DRIVERPLUS_D934.21_Solution-testing-procedure.pdf. Accessed 26 Oct 2020

Mathematical Model of Integral Fire Risk Management

Svitlana Bordiuzhenko[(✉)], Oleksandr Sobol, Yuriy Uvarov, Oleh Stelmakh,
Oleksandr Danilin, and Serhiy Shevchenko

National University of Civil Defence of Ukraine, Kharkiv, Ukraine

Abstract. In the given work the analysis of features of mathematical model of
management of integral fire risk is carried out, and also grouping of administrative-
territorial units of Ukraine on level of integral fire risk by means of the cluster
analysis is carried out. As a result of the analysis, all regions of Ukraine were
divided into 4 groups. This will allow to apply an appropriate model of integral
fire risk management for each group. Further research will be aimed at developing
a method of integral fire risk management, which is expected to be applied to each
group of regions.

Keywords: Mathematical model · Fire risk · Clustering · Correlation analysis

1 Introduction

At present, the actual scientific and applied problem is the development of effective
models of integral fire risk management. An example of these tasks is the minimization
of the risk for a person to die as a result of dangerous events (natural and man-made
events, fires, etc.).

The integral risk characterizes the consequences of dangerous events. One of the
ways to minimize its level is the creation of rescue units (RUs). This approach is in line
with the Strategy for Reforming the Civil Service of Ukraine in Emergencies [1], as
the response time to dangerous events in rural areas can reach even one hour. Thus, the
development of models and methods of integral fire risk management is relevant and
will help solve the above problem.

Modern methods for determining the integral risks of dangerous events are given,
for example, in [2, 3]. In works [4, 5] the analysis of integral fire risks on the territory of
Ukraine is carried out and grouping of administrative-territorial units according to risk
levels by means of the cluster analysis is carried out. Mathematical model of integral
fire risk management and its features are given in [6]. The development of models and
methods of optimal coverage of given areas by geometric objects with variable metric
characteristics is devoted to [7], but this study did not take into account the need to cover
discrete elements of these areas.

In this paper, it is necessary to develop a mathematical model of management of the
integral fire risk.

© IFIP International Federation for Information Processing 2021
Published by Springer Nature Switzerland AG 2021
Y. Murayama et al. (Eds.): ITDRR 2020, IFIP AICT 622, pp. 235–245, 2021.
https://doi.org/10.1007/978-3-030-81469-4_19

2 Presentation of the Main Research Material

Consider the construction of a mathematical model of integral fire risk management. In one of the previous works [8] it was concluded that the integral fire risk depends on the average time of RUs to arrival to the emergency location. At the same time, it is necessary to take into account the impact of the distribution of rescue units on their average travel time to the place of call and assess the impact of the standard time of arrival of rescue units (RUs) to the place of departure of these units.

It was assumed that the average time of RUs to the place of occurrence of the dangerous event and, as a consequence, the average time of localization and elimination of the dangerous event depend on the coverage of the respective territory by the areas of departure of RUs. The specified coefficient is calculated using the following expression:

$$k_{\text{cover}} = \frac{S\left(\bigcup\limits_{q=1}^{N_q} P_q\right)}{S(S_0)},\tag{1}$$

where N_q – the number of existing RUs; P_q – area of departure q-th unit; S_0 – given territory; $S(.)$ – area calculation function.

As an example, Fig. 1 shows the dependence of the average time of RUs to the place of call on the coverage factor for the Kharkiv region, as well as calculated the correlation coefficient and constructed a trend line using the method of least squares. To conduct the study, software was developed in the Java programming language in the IntelliJ IDEA environment using the JavaFX library.

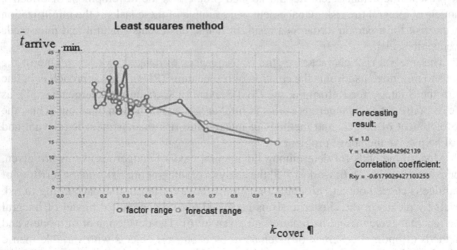

Fig. 1. Dependence of the average travel time to a dangerous event on the coverage factor for the Kharkiv region.

It can be concluded that between the average travel time of rescue units to the scene of an emergency (dangerous event) and the coverage ratio of these units in the Kharkiv region there is an inverse correlation (correlation coefficient is -0.62), and the regression equation the following view:

$$\overline{\tau}_{arrive} = -20,799 \cdot k_{cover} + 35,46. \tag{2}$$

In expression (2) the coefficient at k_{cover} and the free term are measured in minutes. Similar dependencies can be obtained for other administrative-territorial units of Ukraine.

Thus, the following problem arises. Let a certain administrative-territorial unit S_0 be given in the form of a polygon in the global coordinate system (Fig. 2). The region S_0 has discrete elements $V_k, k = 1, \ldots, N_k$, which are settlements. Let $G_l \subset V_k, l = 1, \ldots, L,$ $L < N_k,$ – united territorial communities (settlements), in which it is permissible to create operational and rescue units in accordance with [9, 10].

The settlements in which (next to which) there are potentially dangerous objects and/or objects of the increased danger, we will designate through $S_d \subset G_l, d = 1, \ldots, D,$ $D < L$ (the specified objects can become factors of realization of technogenic risks).

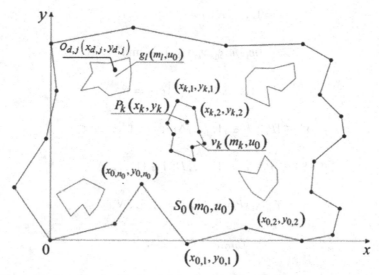

Fig. 2. The region $S_0(m_0, u_0)$ with distrete elements $v_k(m_k, u_0), k = 1, \ldots, N_k,$ and $g_l(m_l, u_0),$ $l = 1, \ldots, N_l.$

It is necessary to cover the area S_0 with the exit areas of rescue units $P_i, i = 1, \ldots, N$ with the exit areas of rescue units.

- minimum area of crossing of exit areas of operative-rescue divisions;
- belonging of departure areas of operative-rescue divisions of area S_0;
- affiliation of settlements $V_k, k = 1, \ldots, N_k,$ as well as settlements $S_d, d = 1, \ldots, D$ areas of departure of operational and rescue units (taking into account other integral risks of emergencies and hazards of man-made nature);

– the travel time of rescue units to the most remote point of the departure area P_i, $i = 1, \ldots, N$ should not exceed the specified T^* (in cities – 10 min; in settlements outside the city – 20 min [8, 9]);
– placement of operational and rescue units is carried out in the united territorial communities (settlements) G_l, $l = 1, \ldots, L$;
– minimum number of operational and rescue units P_i, $i = 1, \ldots, N$.

The mathematical model of distribution of operational and rescue units according to the level of integral risk of emergencies and dangerous events of man-caused nature is as follows [11]:

$$\min_{u \in W} R_3 \left(\overline{\tau}_{arrive}, \ \overline{\tau}_{loc}, \ \overline{\tau}_{liq}, \ N_{fire} \right); \ u = \{m_i; v_i\}; \ i = 1, \ldots, N, \tag{3}$$

where W:

$$\omega\left(m_i, m_j, v_i, v_j\right) \rightarrow \min \tag{4}$$

$$i = 1, \ldots, N; \ j = i + 1, \ldots, N;$$

$$\omega\left(m_i, m_{cS_0}, v_i, v_{cS_0}\right) \rightarrow \min \tag{5}$$

$$i = 1, \ldots, N; \ S_0 \bigcup cS_0 = R^2$$

$$V_k \in \{P_i\}; \ k \in \{1, \ldots, N_k\}; \ i = 1, \ldots, N; \tag{6}$$

$$S_d \in \{P_i\}; \ d = 1, \ldots, D; \ i \in \{1, \ldots, N\}; \tag{7}$$

$$\overline{\tau}_{arrive}(P_i) \leq T^*; \ i = 1, \ldots, N; \tag{8}$$

$$\overline{\tau}_{arrive} = f(k_{cover}); \tag{9}$$

$$u = \{m_i; v_i\} \in \{G_l\}; \ G_l \in \{P_i\}; \ i = 1, \ldots, N; \ l = 1, \ldots, L; \tag{10}$$

$$N \rightarrow \min. \tag{11}$$

In order to assess the negative effects of each type of emergencies of technogenic character, the integral risks of these emergencies were calculated in accordance with the expression (3). The graphic interpretation of integral risks is shown in Fig. 2, with the highest levels corresponding to the integral risk of emergencies due to fires and explosions, $2, 95 \cdot 10^{-6}$ 1/year, and the integral risk of emergencies due to accidents and vehicle accidents (except for fires and explosions) $1, 98 \cdot 10^{-6}$ 1/year. The levels of integral risks of other types of emergencies are less than one order (several orders of magnitude) of the above-mentioned risks.

It should be noted that the analysis of only integral risks of emergencies of techno-genic character for the estimation of the level of technogenic safety in the territory of Ukraine is not sufficiently informative as it does not take into account hazardous events that are not classified. In the mathematical model (3) ÷ (11) expression (3) is the objec-tive function of the problem, with m_i – the coordinates of the vertices of polygons P_i, $i = 1, \ldots, N$ in the local coordinate system, v_i – the parameters of the location of objects P_i (the position of the local coordinate system of the i-th object in the global coordinate system); expression (4) – is a condition of the minimum of mutual intersection of objects P_i and P_j, where is a $\omega(.)$ – ω- function, which is the area of intersection of polygons P_i and P_j; expression (5) – the condition of the minimum intersection of objects P_i with the addition of the region S_0 to the Euclidean space R^2; expression (6) – condition of belonging of settlements V_k, $k = 1, \ldots, N_k$ areas of departure of RUs P_i; expression (7) – condition of belonging of settlements S_d, $d = 1, \ldots, D$ areas of departure of RUs P_i; expression (8) – a condition regarding the arrive time of RUs to the place of call; expression (9) – the relationship between the average arrive time of RUs and the coverage ratio of the region S_0; expression (10) – the condition of placement of RUs in the united territorial communities (settlements) G_l, $l = 1, \ldots, L$; expression (11) – is a condition of the minimum number of RUs.

Administrative-territorial units of Ukraine have features that must be taken into account when developing a mathematical model of the distribution of RUs according to the level of integral risk of emergencies and dangerous events. To do this, we will group the regions of Ukraine by the level of integral fire risk (the main criterion in minimizing the consequences of emergencies and dangerous events) and build regression models that describe the relationship of integral risk with the main factors for each cluster.

The main purpose of cluster analysis [12] is to divide the set of studied objects and features into homogeneous in the appropriate sense of the group or cluster. This means that the task of classifying data and identifying the appropriate structure in it is solved. Methods of cluster analysis can be used in a variety of cases, even in cases where it is a simple grouping, in which it all comes down to the formation of groups by quantitative similarity.

Taking into account the statistics on deaths due to fires and explosions for the last 7 years [13–19], we calculate the integral fire risk [4] and process the results using the software STATISTICA 10. It should be noted that the estimated data do not contain data on the Autonomous Republic of Crimea, Donetsk and Luhansk regions due to the impossibility of obtaining complete statistical information on dangerous events (fires and explosions) in the temporarily occupied territories of Ukraine.

There are two main classifications of clustering algorithms:

1. Hierarchical and non-hierarchical (flat). Hierarchical algorithms build a system of nested partitions, ie at the output of the algorithm is a tree of clusters, with the root as the whole sample and the leaves - as the smallest clusters. Non-hierarchical algorithms build only one division of objects into clusters.
2. Clear and indistinct. Clear algorithms give all sample objects the appropriate cluster number, which means that each object must belong to only one cluster. Fuzzy algo-rithms assign a set of values to each object, which demonstrates the degree to which the object belongs to the clusters. Therefore, each object belongs to each cluster with a certain probability.

We will carry out clustering by a hierarchical method. Hierarchical method - tree clustering. Hierarchical algorithms are based on the idea of sequential clustering. Initially, each object is considered as a separate cluster. In the next step, some of the closest clusters will be merged into a separate cluster.

Using the hierarchical method of cluster analysis, we will divide the administrative-territorial units of Ukraine into groups (Fig. 3), which will be characterized by a similar situation with regard to deaths due to fires or explosions per unit time.

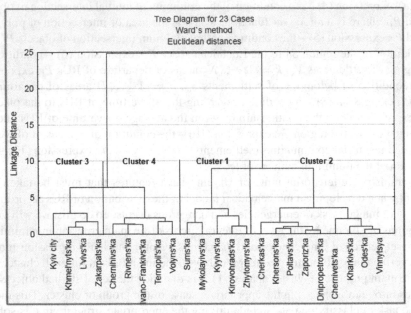

Fig. 3. Vertical tree dendrogram by the Ward method, which shows the distance of the union of the studied areas.

Finally, we take the number of clusters equal to 4, because in the case of a further increase in their number, the clarity of classification is lost (Table 1).

Table 1. Information on the grouping of administrative-territorial units of Ukraine by the number of clusters, which is equal to 4 ($K = 4$).

Groups of clusters at $K = 4$	Regions of Ukraine and Kyiv city	Linkage distance
Cluster 1	Sums'ka, Mykolayivs'ka, Kyyivs'ka, Kirovohrads'ka ta Zhytomyrs'ka regions	8,352732
Cluster 2	Chernivets'ka, Khersons'ka, Poltavs'ka, Zaporiz'ka, Dnipropetrovs'ka, Cherkas'ka, Kharkivs'ka, Odes'ka ta Vinnyts'ka regions	7,410969
Cluster 3	Kyiv city, Khmel'nyts'ka, L'vivs'ka, Zakarpat·s'ka regions	7,20112
Cluster 4	Chernihivs'ka, Rivnens'ka, Ivano-Frankivs'ka, Ternopil's'ka ta Volyns'ka regions	4,466044

Consider the construction of regression models to determine the integral risk of emergencies and dangerous events in groups of administrative-territorial units of Ukraine. These models will allow to obtain the dependences of integral fire risks (the main criterion in the task of minimizing the consequences of emergencies and dangerous events) on the main factors that characterize the response process of RUs for each cluster. To do this, we apply correlation-regression analysis, and assume that the dependences are linear. We will also check the obtained coefficients of linear models for reliability and adequacy.

First of all, let's establish the links between the integral fire risk and the factors that affect it for each cluster (Tables 2, 3, 4 and 5). The analysis of the data given in Tables 2, 3, 4 and 5 allows us to conclude that the risk is directly proportional to the number of deaths, so for further analysis this factor must be excluded from the calculation (correlation matrix coefficients will not change). In each of the matrices you can see the inverse dependence of risk on the number of dangerous events, based on available statistics. In the first and second clusters (Tables 2 and 3) - the inverse dependence of risk on the average elimination time. Most correlation coefficients exceed 0.7, which indicates a strong relationship between the studied parameters.

Table 2. Correlation matrix of the main factors influencing the integral fire risk R_3 for the first cluster.

Variable	Correlations (cluster 1)					
	N_{fire}	$N_{victims}$	$\overline{\tau}_{arrive}$	$\overline{\tau}_{loc}$	$\overline{\tau}_{liq}$	R_3
N_{fire}	1,00	−0,85	−0,34	−0,45	−0,65	−0,85
$N_{victims}$	−0,85	1,00	0,64	0,70	0,82	1,00
$\overline{\tau}_{arrive}$	−0,34	0,64	1,00	0,96	0,94	0,64
$\overline{\tau}_{loc}$	0,45	0,70	0,96	1,00	0,96	0,70
$\overline{\tau}_{liq}$	−0,65	0,82	0,94	0,96	1,00	0,82
R_3	−0,85	1,00	0,64	0,70	0,82	1,00

After conducting a correlation-regression analysis and identifying significant factors and their values for each cluster, we obtain the following regression models to determine the integral fire risk in groups of administrative-territorial units of Ukraine:

$$R_3^1 = \left(5,878 + 0,199\overline{\tau}_{arrive} - 0,87 \cdot 10^{-4}N_{fire} + \varepsilon\right) \cdot 10^{-5}; \tag{12}$$

$$R_3^2 = \left(0,646\overline{\tau}_{arrive} - 0,74 \cdot 10^{-4}N_{fire} + \varepsilon\right) \cdot 10^{-5}; \tag{13}$$

$$R_3^3 = (-5,335 + 0,16\overline{\tau}_{arrire} + 0,212\overline{\tau}_{loc} + 0,166\overline{\tau}_{liq} - \\ -0,9 \cdot 10^{-4}N_{fire} + \varepsilon) \cdot 10^{-5}; \tag{14}$$

$$R_3^4 = (-3,123 + 0,274\overline{\tau}_{arrive} + 0,273\overline{\tau}_{loc} + \varepsilon) \cdot 10^{-5}; \tag{15}$$

Table 3. Correlation matrix of the main factors influencing the integral fire risk R_3 for the second cluster.

Variable	Correlations (cluster 2)					
	N_{fire}	$N_{victims}$	$\overline{\tau}_{arrive}$	$\overline{\tau}_{loc}$	$\overline{\tau}_{liq}$	R_3
N_{fire}	1,00	−0,89	−0,79	−0,63	0,36	−0,89
$N_{victims}$	−0,89	1,00	0,84	0,82	−0,45	1,00
$\overline{\tau}_{arrive}$	−0,79	0,84	1,00	0,81	−0,13	0,84
$\overline{\tau}_{loc}$	−0,63	0,82	0,81	1,00	0,23	0,82
$\overline{\tau}_{liq}$	0,36	−0,45	−0,13	0,23	1,00	−0,04
R_3	−0,89	1,00	0,84	0,82	−0,04	1,00

Table 4. Correlation matrix of the main factors influencing the integral fire risk R_3 for the third cluster.

Variable	Correlations (cluster 3)					
	N_{fire}	$N_{victims}$	$\overline{\tau}_{arrive}$	$\overline{\tau}_{loc}$	$\overline{\tau}_{liq}$	R_3
N_{fire}	1,00	−0,60	−0,69	0,08	0,10	−0,60
$N_{victims}$	−0,60	1,00	0,83	0,22	0,08	1,00
$\overline{\tau}_{arrive}$	−0,69	0,83	1,00	−0,10	0,15	0,83
$\overline{\tau}_{loc}$	0,08	0,22	−0,10	1,00	−0,83	0,22
$\overline{\tau}_{liq}$	0,10	0,08	0,15	−0,83	1,00	0,08
R_3	−0,60	1,00	0,83	0,22	0,08	1,00

Table 5. Correlation matrix of the main factors influencing the integral fire risk R_3 for the fourth cluster.

Variable	Correlations (cluster 4)					
	N_{fire}	$N_{victims}$	$\overline{\tau}_{arrive}$	$\overline{\tau}_{loc}$	$\overline{\tau}_{liq}$	R_3
N_{fire}	1,00	−0,70	−0,51	−0,84	0,46	0,70
$N_{victims}$	−0,70	1,00	0,86	0,88	0,74	1,00
$\overline{\tau}_{arrive}$	−0,51	0,86	1,00	0,75	0,88	0,86
$\overline{\tau}_{loc}$	−0,84	0,88	0,75	1,00	0,88	0,86
$\overline{\tau}_{liq}$	0,46	0,74	0,88	0,78	1,00	0,74
R_3	0,70	1,00	0,86	0,88	0,74	1,00

The standard error of evaluation of the obtained results is less than 5%.

Thus, with the help of correlation-regression analysis, regression models were obtained to determine the integral fire risk in groups of administrative-territorial units of Ukraine. These models allowed to obtain the dependences of these risks on the main factors that characterize the response process of RUs for each cluster, and are also the basis for building models of distribution of RUs by the level of integral risk.

Consider the features of the mathematical model (3) ÷ (11):

1. The objective function of the problem is an expression of the form (12) ÷ (15) depending on which cluster the administrative-territorial unit (coverage area) belongs to.
2. In the case of taking into account the locations of existing RUs, the following restriction must be added to the mathematical modelr:

$$\omega\left(m_i, m_q, v_i, v_q\right) \to \min; \ i = 1, \ldots, N; \ q = 1, \ldots, N_q \qquad (16)$$

where N_q – the number of existing RUs.
3. If the problem of minimizing the consequences of emergencies by dividing the RUs by the level of integral risk of emergencies and dangerous events is solved taking into account the limited resources, then in the mathematical model instead of constraint (11) it is necessary to use the following expression:

$$Q_{res}(N) \leq Q_{res}^* \qquad (17)$$

where $Q_{res}(N)$ – resources needed to create N RUs; Q_{res}^* – resources allocated for the creation of RUs.
4. The objective function of the problem is linear, the constraints are linear, nonlinear and discrete.
5. The type of RUs is determined depending on the objects of protection located in the service area.

Thus, a mathematical model of integral fire risk management is developed and its features are investigated. The target function is the dependence of the integral fire risk on the main factors that characterize the process of response to RUs. The distribution of RUs is carried out taking into account: the normalized response time to emergencies (dangerous events); belonging of high-risk objects and potentially dangerous objects to the areas of departure of units (taking into account other integral risks of emergencies and dangerous events); placement of PDOs in united territorial communities (certain settlements).

3 Conclusions

In this paper the analysis of features of mathematical model of management of integral fire risk is carried out, and also grouping of administrative-territorial units of Ukraine on level of integral fire risk by means of the cluster analysis is carried out. As a result of the analysis, all regions of Ukraine were divided into 4 groups. This will allow to apply an appropriate model of integral fire risk management for each group. Further research will be aimed at developing a method of integral fire risk management, which is expected to be applied to each group of regions.

References

1. Pro skhvalennya Stratehiyi reformuvannya systemy Derzhavnoyi sluzhby Ukrayiny z nadzvychaynykh sytuatsiy. http://zakon5.rada.gov.ua/laws/show/61-2017-p. (in Ukraine)
2. Brushlinskii, N.N., et al.: Osnovy teorii pozharnykh riskov i ee prilozheniia: monografiia. Akademiia GPS MChS Rossii, Moskva, 192 s (2012). (in Russian)
3. Risk Management Practices in the Fire Service. https://apps.usfa.fema.gov/publications/dis play?id=1071
4. Kravtsiv, S.Ya., Sobol, O.M., Maksimov, A.V.: The analysis of integral risks of the territory of Ukraine. In: Problems of Emergency Situations, vol. 23, pp. 53–60. NUCDU, Kharkiv (2016). http://nuczu.edu.ua/sciencearchive/ProblemsOfEmergencies/vol23/Kravtsiv.pdf
5. Kravtsiv, S.Ya., Sobol, O.M.: Hrupuvannya administratyvno-terytorial′nykh odynyts′ Ukrayiny po rivnyu intehral′noho pozhezhnoho ryzyku za dopomohoyu klasternoho analizu. In: Problems of Emergency Situations, vol. 26. pp. 79–86. NUCDU, Kharkiv (2017). http://91.234.43.156/bitstream/123456789/6410/1/kravtsiv.pdf. (in Ukraine)
6. Sobol, O.M., Kravtsiv, S.Ya.: Matematychna model' upravlinnya intehral′nym pozhezhnym ryzykom ta yiyi osoblyvosti. In: Visnyk of Kherson National University, vol. 3, no. 62, part 2, pp. 317–321. KNTU, Kherson (2017). http://91.234.43.156/bitstream/123456789/4172/1/ВІC НИК%20ХНТУ%203%2862%29%20Том%202.pdf. (in Ukraine)
7. Komayk, V.M., Sobol, O.M., Lisnyak, A.A., Sobyna, V.O.: Optymizatsiya pokryttya zadanykh oblastey heometrychnymy ob'yektamy zi zminnymy metrychnymy kharakterystykamy: monohrafiya. NUCDU, Kharkiv, 124 s (2013). (in Ukraine)
8. Kravtsiv, S.Ya., Sobol, O.M., Tyutyunyk, V.V.: Otsinyuvannya parametriv vplyvu na intehral′nyy pozhezhnyy ryzyk za dopomohoyu faktornoho analizu. In: Fire Safety, vol. 30, pp. 99–104. LSULS, Lviv (2017). https://journal.ldubgd.edu.ua/index.php/PB/article/view/18/15. (in Ukraine)
9. Pro zatverdzhennya kryteriyi utvorennya derzhavnykh pozhezhno-ryatuval′nykh pidrozdiliv (chastyn) Operatyvno-ryatuval′noyi sluzhby tsyvil′noho zakhystu v administratyvno-terytorial′nykh odynytsyakh ta pereliku sub″yektiv hospodaryuvannya, de utvoryuyut′sya taki pidrozdily (chastyny). https://zakon.rada.gov.ua/laws/show/874-2013-п. (in Ukraine)
10. Mistobuduvannya planuvannya i zabudova mis′kykh i sil′s′kykh. https://dnaop.com/html/29810/doc-%D0%94%D0%91%D0%9D_360-92__. (in Ukraine)
11. Kravtsiv, S., Sobol, O., Komyak, V., Danilin, O., Al'boschiy, O.: Mathematical model of management of the integral risk of emergency situation on the example of fires. In: Murayama, Y., Velev, D., Zlateva, P. (eds.) Information Technology in Disaster Risk Reduction, vol. 4, pp. 182–195. Springer, Cham (2019). https://doi.org/10.1007/978-3-030-48939-7_16
12. Bureyeva, N.N.: Mnogomernyy statisticheskiy analiz s ispol'zovaniyem PPP «STATISTICA»: uch.-metod. mater. UNN, Nizhniy Novgorod, 112 s (2007). (in Russian)
13. Prohnoz osnovnykh pokaznykiv statystyky pozhezh na 2011 rik. http://undicz.dsns.gov.ua/files/Статистика/2010/prognos_fire_2011.pdf. (in Ukraine)
14. Prohnoz osnovnykh pokaznykiv statystyky pozhezh na 2011 rik. http://undicz.dsns.gov.ua/files/Статистика/2011/Prognoz_2012.pdf. (in Ukraine)
15. Prohnoz osnovnykh pokaznykiv statystyky pozhezh na 2012 rik. http://undicz.dsns.gov.ua/files/Статистика/2012/AD_12_12.pdf. (in Ukraine)
16. Analiz masyvu kartok obliku pozhezh za 12 misyatsiv 2013 roku. http://undicz.dsns.gov.ua/files/Статистика/2013/AD_12_13.pdf. (in Ukraine)

17. Analiz masyvu kartok obliku pozhezh za 12 misyatsiv 2014 roku. http://undicz.dsns.gov.ua/files/Статистика/2014/AD_12_14.pdf. (in Ukraine)
18. Analiz masyvu kartok obliku pozhezh za 12 misyatsiv 2015 roku. http://undicz.dsns.gov.ua/files/Статистика/2015/AD_12_15.pdf. (in Ukraine)
19. Analiz masyvu kartok obliku pozhezh za 12 misyatsiv 2016 roku.http://undicz.dsns.gov.ua/files/2017/2/2/AD_12_2016.pdf . (in Ukraine)

Mathematical and Computer Modeling of Active Movement of People During Evacuation from Buildings

Valentyna Komyak[1]([✉]), Aleksandr Pankratov[2], Vladimer Komyak[1], and Kyazim Kyazimov[3]

[1] National University of Civil Defence of Ukraine, Kharkiv, Ukraine
vkomyak@ukr.net
[2] A.M. Pidgorny Institute for Mechanical Engineering Problems NAS of Ukraine, Kharkiv, Ukraine
[3] Academy of the Ministry of Emergency Situations of the Republic of Azerbaijan, Baku, Azerbaijan

Abstract. One of the forms of protecting the population from emergencies is the controlled evacuation of people from buildings for the required time, calculated on the basis of their design and planning decisions. For this purpose, scientifically sound plans for evacuation of people are developed, the main component of which are the programs of modeling of human flows, which adequately reflect the real processes of movement of people. In this work, it is proposed to take into account the natural deformation of the human body by rotating parts of its body (eg, the shoulder) when modeling flow motion. For this purpose, it is proposed to present the projection of a human body of a set of three ellipses: the main with the possibility of its rotation in the framework of maneuverability with respect to the basic direction of movement, and two ellipses, given by the half-axis's, which are equal to half the length and thickness of the shoulder with the possibility of their rotation. in a given range of angles in the horizontal plane relative to the raised arm of the person. Such a problem arises with the active movement of people in the flow of high density, when the category of movement changes from free to compressed. The paper formalizes the constraints, builds a mathematical model of the active movement of people in the flow, provides examples of computer simulation of the movement of people, which represented by a three-component models.

Keywords: Emergency situation · Mathematical model · Flow simulation of people in the flow · Natural deformations of the human body · Computer simulation

1 Introduction

In the last decade, there has been a tendency for an increase in the number and scale of the consequences of emergencies. Emergencies are accompanied not only by material

© IFIP International Federation for Information Processing 2021
Published by Springer Nature Switzerland AG 2021
Y. Murayama et al. (Eds.): ITDRR 2020, IFIP AICT 622, pp. 246–258, 2021.
https://doi.org/10.1007/978-3-030-81469-4_20

but also by human losses, so in the context of emergencies it is very important to make a quick and correct decision both on the elimination of the consequences of the emergency and on saving people.

1.1 Problem Setting

Possible forms of population protection include the organization of guided evacuation of people from the places of emergency development, in particular from buildings for the necessary time, calculated based on their design-planning decisions. For this purpose, scientifically sound plans for evacuation of people are developed, the main component of which are the programs of modeling of human flows, which adequately reflect the real processes of movement of people. Therefore, an urgent problem is the development of models, methods and software for modeling human flows, which simplify the decision-making process for evacuation of people from.

When modeling the movement of people, the following categories of movement of people on the stream are considered: free, comfortable, active, with high activity. When the movement category becomes active with possible force actions, the flow density increases. Changes in density affect the nature of the movement of people in the stream, changing it from free, in which a person can choose the speed and direction of his movement, to compressed movement, in which he feels the growing force effect of others.

Therefore, an important and unresolved part of the problem is the development of models, methods and software of active movement of people, taking into account the natural deformation of their bodies.

1.2 Paper Objective

The purpose of the article is to analyze the active movement of people with force action and develop models of the human body, taking into account its natural deformities and modeling the active movement of people taking into account their forceful contacts during movement.

To achieve this goal, you need to solve the following tasks:

– to build a model of the human body taking into account its natural deformities;
– to formalize of the constraints of the task;
– to develop a model and algorithm for modeling the active movement of people taking into account their natural deformations;
– to carry out computer simulations of the movement of the flow of people by force action.

1.3 Recent Research and Publications Analysis

An empirical basis for full-scale observations of human flows in buildings of various purposes, which were oriented by theoretical studies [1, 2], although it was the largest in the world in the 1960s, but was only a quarter of that already accumulated by the end of the 70's of the last century. The quantitative diversity of the results of the series of field observations has raised the problem of theoretical substantiation of the observed dependencies between the parameters of human flows. A grapho-analytical method for calculating human flows has emerged [1, 2], although it is laborious for design-planning of practice and does not sufficiently fully reflect the verbal description of the process of human movement.

There was a problem of mathematical description of the dependencies between the parameters of human flows and the description of changes in the states of the flow (its displacements) in space. Difficulties in modeling human flows and ignorance of their patterns led to attempts to replace the processes of motion of real human flows by models of processes of a different physical nature. For example, they model the parameters of human flows using an stream of requests or a hydroanalogy instead [3, 4].

Other analogies and related computer programs are also possible. The western software market provides a large number of such examples [5]. Such approaches are not new to modeling methodology and have long received their appreciation in the scientific literature: "Some are interested in the structure and regularities of the phenomena that lead to the observed result, others - only the results themselves. The first, when modeling, try to reproduce the structure and regularities of the phenomenon, the second - only the results, without resorting to the real mechanisms of their appearance [6].

Currently, "Floutec" software products for simplified analytical and simulation-stochastic models and "Evatec" [7, 8] for the individually-flowing model of humans flow motion are distributed. But the results of the analysis [7] show that there is no model of individually-current movement of people, adequate to the real flow, for people with limited mobile possibilities of mixed composition in a rather wide nomenclature of public buildings of different classes of functional fire danger.

In [9, 10], the problem of modeling the motion of heterogeneous flows of people (people are represented by ellipses) is posed and solved, which boils down to the problem of dense accommodation (displacement) of people with different densities, that is, of their location at each moment of time, taking into account different minimum allowable distances between them according to a number of additional technological restrictions, among which it is possible to distinguish the movement at different speeds, taking into account their maneuverability, comfort of movement, etc.

According to [11] the following categories of motion are observed in the movement of people in the stream: comfortable, calm, active, with high activity. Model [9] can be used for comfortable and free movement of people.

When the traffic category changes and becomes active traffic category with possible force actions, the flow density increases [11]. Density changes have a strong influence on the character of the movement of people in the stream, changing it from free, at which a person can choose the speed and direction of his movement, to compressed movement as a result of a further increase in the density of the flow, in which he feels the increasing force of the surrounding people.

2   Presentation of the Main Research Material

A plurality of people simultaneously walking the common section (area) in one direction forms a human stream [11]. The parameters of the human flow are: the number of people in the stream N, the density D, the velocity $\vec{v}$, the magnitude of the flow P, that is, the number of people passing through the cross-section of the section occupied by set of humans in the unit time. It should be noted that the free space in the flow depends not only on the number of persons, but also on the area occupied by each of them, so the size of people play a role. To account for this factor, it was proposed to enter into the calculation of the density of the flow the area occupied by the person (area of horizontal projection f_i, m^2) [8, 11]:

$$D_i = \frac{N_i f_i}{b_i l_i}.$$

In [9–11], the horizontal projection of a person is taken as an ellipse whose diameters (a_i, c_i) correspond to the width and thickness of the human body. Comfort, which takes into account the natural movements of man, is given by the minimum permissible distances $\Delta\delta$ between people, which takes into account the equidistant lines at a distance $\Delta\delta$ from ellipses, which describe the projection of human bodies on a plane xOy [9].

2.1 Building a Model of the Human Body Taking Into Account Its Natural Deformities

In this work it is proposed to take into account the natural deformation of a human body by rotating parts of his body (eg, the shoulder) when modeling movement. For this purpose it is proposed to represent a human projection by a set of three ellipses: by the main with the possibility of its rotation in the limits of the maneuverability relative to the main direction of movement, and by two auxiliary ellipses according to semi-axes equal to half the length and width of the shoulder with the possibility of their rotation in the range of angles $(-\alpha2; +\alpha1)$ in the horizontal plane relative to the raised arm of the person. Thus, to construct a model of the human body, it is proposed to represent its projection in the form of a non-rigid connection of three ellipses: E_c with the dimensions of the half-axes A and B, and E_l and E_r with the sizes a and b (see Fig. 1). Each object E is associated with placement parameters $u = (v, \theta)$, where $v = (x, y)$ is the object's E translation vector relative to the fixed coordinate system, and θ is the angle of its rotation. In this case, an arbitrary point $p = p(0)$ of the object is mapped to the point $p(u) = v + M(\theta)p^T(0)$, where $M(\theta)$ is the matrix of the operator of rotation of space by an angle $\theta = \varphi$ (see Fig. 2).

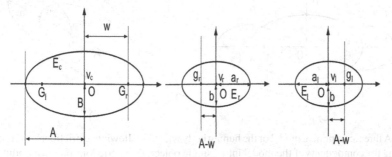

Fig. 1. Three components of the human body model: trunk, right shoulder, left shoulde.

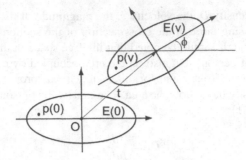

Fig. 2. Illustration to the parametric description of the position of the ellipse on the plane

Let $E(u)$ denote the object $E = E(0)$ rotated by the angle $\theta = \varphi$ and translated onto the vector v. The pairs of points $G(l)$, g_l and G_r, g_r, marked in the first figure (Fig. 3a) are used to "glue" the components of the model into a single object H (see Fig. 3a).

In addition to gluing conditions, a restriction on the ratio of rotation angles is imposed on the relative position of the objects, which follows from physical restrictions on the relative position of parts of the human body (see Fig. 3). Thus, the rotation angle θ_r of an ellipse E_r cannot be greater than the angle $\theta_c + \alpha_1$ and less than $\theta_c - \alpha_2$, where θ_c is the angle of rotation of the object E_c (see Fig. 3b). Accordingly, the rotation angle θ_l of the ellipse E_l cannot be greater than the angle $\theta_c + \alpha_2$ and less than $\theta_c - \alpha_1$.

Thus, it is proposed to use an object $H_i(u_{ci}, u_{li}, u_{ri})$ with the following restrictions on the placement parameters as a model of the projection of the human body:

$$g_l(u_l) = G_l(u_c), \tag{1}$$

$$g_r(u_r) = G_r(u_c), \tag{2}$$

$$\theta_c - \alpha_2 \leq \theta_r \leq \theta_c + \alpha_1, \tag{3}$$

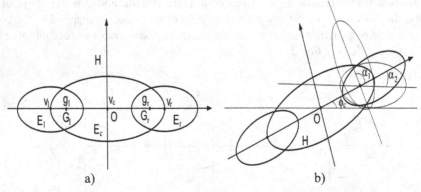

a)   b)

Fig. 3. A three-component model of the human body with the following restrictions: (a) conditions for gluing the components of the model into a single object, (b) restrictions on the mobility of the ellipse modeling the human shoulder

$$\theta_c - \alpha_1 \le \theta_l \le \theta_c + \alpha_2 \tag{4}$$

It should be noted that in conditions of high density of people, the variables a_l and a_r can be included in the number of variable parameters of the model with limitations of the next form

$$\alpha_0' \le \alpha_l \le \alpha_1', \quad \alpha_0' \le \alpha_r \le \alpha_1', \tag{5}$$

allowing to take into account the vertical rotation of the shoulder joint in the model. The values of variables α_0', α_1' is also determined by physical restrictions on the relative position of the parts of the human body and is selected from the anthropological data of the individual.

We will construct a mathematical model of the problem of modeling the movement of people represented by a three-component model, for which we formalize the constraints and the goal function of the task.

2.2 Formalization of the Constraints of the Task

We will describe the conditions for the non-intersection of two objects $H_i(u_{ci}, u_{li}, u_{ri})$ and $H_j(u_{cj}, u_{lj}, u_{rj})$ based on the modification of the quasi-phi function [12] for the case of composite non-rigidly connected objects. It should be noted that when modeling the movement of streams of people at each discrete moment of time, there is a configuration of the placement [13] of objects that approximate the human body.

According to the definition [12], a quasi-phi-function $\Phi'^{E_i E_j}(u_i, u_j, t_{ij})$ for objects $E_i(u_i)$ and $E_j(u_j)$ is defined as a everywhere defined continuous function in all variables, for which the function $\max_{t_{ij} \in U \subset R^m} \Phi'^{E_i E_j}(u_i, u_j, t_{ij})$ is the phi-function of $E_i(u_i)$ and $E_j(u_j)$. Here t_{ij} is the vector of auxiliary variables that belong to a certain subset U of the space R^m (as shown in [12], $m = 1$ and U coincides with R^1).

Further, we use the following important characteristic of a quasi-phi function: if for some t_{ij} it holds $\Phi'^{E_i E_j}(u_i, u_j, t_{ij}) \ge 0$, then $\text{int}E(u_i) \cap \text{int}E(u_j) = \emptyset$ [12].

As is known [14], for two composite objects $T_i(u_i) = \bigcup_{k=1}^{n_i} T_{ik}(u_i)$ and $T_j(u_j) = \bigcup_{k=1}^{n_j} T_{jm}(u_j)$ a quasi-phi-function can be written as

$$\Phi'^{T_i T_j}(u_i, u_j, t_{ij}) = \min\left\{ {}'^{T_{ik} T_{jm}}(u_i, u_j, t_{ij}), k = 1, \dots, n_i, m = 1, \dots, n_j \right\}, \tag{6}$$

where t_{ij} is the vector of auxiliary variables t_{ijkm}, $k = 1, ..., n_i$, $m = 1, ..., n_j$.

We write the condition of non-intersection of two objects $H_i(u_{ci}, u_{li}, u_{ri}) = E_{ci}(u_{ci}) \bigcup E_{li}(u_{li}) \bigcup E_{ri}(u_{ri})$ and $H_j(u_{cj}, u_{lj}, u_{rj}) = E_{cj}(u_{cj}) \bigcup E_{lj}(u_{lj}) \bigcup E_{rj}(u_{rj})$ in the form of a function $\Phi'^{H_i H_j}(u_{ci}, u_{ri}, u_{li}, u_{cj}, u_{rj}, u_{lj}, t_{ij}) \ge 0$. Based on (6), a function $\Phi'^{H_i H_j}(u_{ci}, u_{ri}, u_{li}, u_{cj}, u_{rj}, u_{lj}, t_{ij})$ can be represented as:

$$\begin{aligned}
\Phi'^{H_i H_j}(u_{ci}, u_{ri}, u_{li}, u_{cj}, u_{rj}, u_{lj}, t_{ij}) = \min\{ &\Phi'^{E_{ci} E_{cj}}(u_{ci}, u_{cj}, t_{ij1}), \\
\Phi'^{E_{ci} E_{lj}}(u_{ci}, u_{lj}, t_{ij2}), \ \Phi'^{E_{ci} E_{rj}}(u_{ci} u_{rj}, t_{ij3}), \ &\Phi'^{E_{li} E_{cj}}(u_{li}, u_{cj}, t_{ij4}), \\
\Phi'^{E_{li} E_{lj}}(u_{li}, u_{lj}, t_{ij5}), \ \Phi'^{E_{li} E_{rj}}(u_{li}, u_{rj}, t_{ij6}), \ &\Phi'^{E_{ri} E_{cj}}(u_{ri}, u_{cj}, t_{ij7}), \\
\Phi'^{E_{ri} E_{lj}}(u_{ri}, u_{lj}, t_{ij8}), \ \Phi'^{E_{ri} E_{rj}}(u_{ri}, u_{rj}, t_{ij9}). &
\end{aligned} \tag{7}$$

As can be seen from (7), the conditions for describing the non-intersection of constructed objects are based on the description of the conditions for non-intersection of ellipses.

As follows from [9, 15], the conditions for the mutual non-intersection of ellipses are described by the inequality $\Phi'^{E_iE_j}(u_i, u_j, t_{ij}) \geq 0$, where the quasi-phi-function $\Phi'^{E_iE_j}(u_i, u_j, t_{ij})$ can be written as:

$$\Phi'^{E_iE_j}(u_i, u_j, t_{ij}) = (x_i - x_j)\cos t_{ij} + (y_j - y_i)\sin t_{ij} - R_i - \sqrt{b_i^2 + (a_i^2 - b_i^2)\cos^2(\theta_i - t_{ij})} - \sqrt{b_j^2 + (a_j^2 - b_j^2)\cos^2(\theta_j - t_{ij})}. \tag{8}$$

It should also be noted that the quasi-phi function (6) is normalized, i.e. $\max_{t_{ij} \in U \subset R^m} \Phi'^{E_iE_j}(u_i, u_j, t_{ij})$ there is a normalized phi-function of objects $E_i(u_i)$ and $E_j(u_j)$, and in value coincides with the distance between objects $E_i(u_i)$ and $E_j(u_j)$.

To formalize the conditions of belonging an object $H_i(u_{ci}, u_{li}, u_{ri}) = E_{ci}(u_{ci}) \bigcup E_{li}(u_{li}) \bigcup E_{ri}(u_{ri})$ of area Ω (Ω is a rectangular region with vertices $v_1 = (0,0), v_2 = (L,0), v_3 = (L,W), v_4 = (0,W)$, respectively), we use a normalized phi-function that is built on the basis of an analytical description of the conditions of belonging Ω projections of ellipses $E_{ci}(u_{ci}), E_{li}(u_{li}), E_{ri}(u_{ri})$ on the axis of the global coordinate system in which the domain Ω is defined.

So, an object $H_i(u_{ci}, u_{li}, u_{ri}) = E_{ci}(u_{ci}) \bigcup E_{li}(u_{li}) \bigcup E_{ri}(u_{ri})$ belongs to a rectangular region Ω if the negative phi-function is:

$$\Phi^{H_i\Omega^*}(u_i) = \min_{k=1,\dots,4}(\min(f_{ik_c}(u_{ci}), f_{ikl}(u_{li}), f_{ik_r}(u_{ri}))) \tag{9}$$

where $\Omega^* = R^2 \backslash \Omega \forall i \in \{ci, li, ri\}$ and are performed:

$$f_{i1}(u_i) = x_i - a_i^*, \ f_{i2}(u_i) = y_i - b_i^*, \ f_{i3}(u_i) = L - x_i - a_i^*, \ f_{i4}(u_i) = W - y_i - b_i^*,$$

$$a_i^* = \sqrt{a_i^2\cos^2\theta_i + b_i^2\sin^2\theta_i} = \sqrt{b_i^2 + (a_i^2 - b_i^2)\cos^2\theta_i}$$

$$b_i^* = \sqrt{a_i^2\sin^2\theta_i + b_i^2\cos^2\theta_i} = \sqrt{b_i^2 + (a_i^2 - b_i^2)\sin^2\theta_i}.$$

Conditions (7), (9) are supplemented by the following restrictions:

$$g_{li}(u_{li}) = G_{li}(u_{ci}), g_{ri}(u_{ri}) = G_{ri}(u_{ci}), \theta_{ci} - \alpha_2 \leq \theta_{ri} \leq \theta_{ci} + \alpha_1$$
$$g_{lj}(u_{lj}) = G_{lj}(u_{cj}), g_{rj}(u_{rj}) = G_{rj}(u_{cj}), \theta_{cj} - \alpha_2 \leq \theta_{rj} \leq \theta_{cj} + \alpha_1 \tag{10}$$
$$\theta_{cj} - \alpha_1 \leq \theta_{lj} \leq \theta_{cj} + \alpha_2, \theta_{ci} - \alpha_1 \leq \theta_{li} \leq \theta_{ci} + \alpha_2$$

Thus, work formalized the limitations of the problem of modeling the active movement of people taking into account their natural deformations (functions (7)–(10)).

2.3 Development a Model and Algorithm for Modeling the Active Movement of People Taking Into Account Their Natural Deformations

Let the initial data on the paths of movement of individuals be given in the form shown in Fig. 4

Each area is characterized by the same law of formation of the basic direction of movement. The main direction of movement from a point for a zone with rectilinear movement is specified by a vector connecting points of separators A_m and A_{m+1} (taking into account the homothetic coefficient). The definition of the main direction of movement for this case is clearly illustrated in the figure for the second zone.

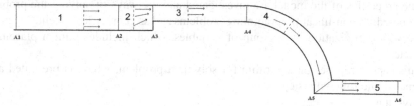

Fig. 4. Presentation of the path of movement

Suppose that at the k-th iteration (with a given time interval Δt, for example, 1 s) in the evacuation area Ω_m there are N_k people with placement parameters $u_{ci} = (x_{ci}, y_{ci}, \theta_{ci})$, $i = 1, 2, ..., N_k$, where (x_{ci}, y_{ci}) are the coordinates of the location of the beginning of the local system of coordinates (current point), and θ_{ci}- the angle of rotation of the i-th ellipse $E_{ci} \subset H_i$ with the size of the half-axes (A_{ci}, B_{ci}).

Since the model of the i-th person is a three-component model $H_i(u_{ci}, u_{li}, u_{ri}) = E_{ci}(u_{ci}) \bigcup E_{li}(u_{li}) \bigcup E_{ri}(u_{ri})$, the values (x_{li}, y_{li}) and (x_{ri}, y_{ri}) are chosen from the anthropological data of the person, and the angles θ_{li} and θ_{ri} determine the spatial shape of the three-component model, so the variable parameters of the model are the parameters $x_{ci}, y_{ci}, \theta_{ci}, \theta_{li}, \theta_{ri}$, that is $H_i(x_{ci}, y_{ci}, \theta_{ci}, \theta_{li}, \theta_{ri})$. Note that the large half-axis of the ellipse E_{ci} is perpendicular to the direction of motion, and the angle of rotation θ_{ci} of the ellipse E_{ci} is determined between the perpendicular to the major half-axis and the vector of the main direction of motion and is determined within the maneuverability m_{ci}, $m_{ci} < 1$ (in meters). The object E_{ci} is also assigned speed characteristics $\vec{v}_{ci}$ (in meters per second).

The mathematical model of the subtask for the k-th iteration in the form of finding the maximum of the total displacement of people N_k in the area of evacuation behind time Δt, i.e.

$$F(u^*) = \max_{u \in W_k \subset R^n} F(u), F(u) = \Delta t \sum_{i=1}^{N_k} \Delta t_i \left| \vec{v}_{ci}(x_{ci}, y_{ci}, \theta_{ci}, \theta_{li}, \theta_{ri}) \right|, \quad (11)$$

$$u = (t_1, z_{c1}, x_{c1}, y_{c1}, \theta_{c1}, \theta_{l1}, \theta_{r1}, t_2, z_{c2}, x_{c2}, y_{c2}, \theta_{c2}, \theta_{l2}, \theta_{r2} \dots,$$
$$t_{Nk}, z_{cNk}, x_{cNk}, y_{cNk}, \theta_{cNk}, \theta_{lNk}, \theta_{rNk}).$$

The domain of permissible solutions W_k is defined by the constraints on the conditions of non-intersection and the conditions of placement of objects

$H_i(x_{ci}, y_{ci}, \theta_{ci}, \theta_{li}, \theta_{ri})$, $i \in I_{N_k}$ (7), (9), restrictions (10) on the boundary of natural deformations of human body, technological limitations on the relative motion time Δt_i of the i-th person and on the angles of their rotation, which are determined within the maneuverability of movement:

$$T_i \geq 0 : \begin{cases} 0 \leq \Delta t_i \leq 1, \\ -m_{ci} \leq z_{ci} \leq m_{ci}, \ i \in I_{N_k} \end{cases}$$

$$n = 7N_k + \frac{N_k(N_k - 1)}{2}.$$

The properties of the model are investigated and the ways of solving the problem are proposed: as non-linear programming problems and as geometric modeling of move people with optimization by a group of variables, which includes human placement parameters.

This paper proposes an algorithm for solving a problem, which is presented as a sequence of the following steps.

Algorithm.

Step 1. The evacuation area is set as a tree (graph). Rebs - segments of corridors, vertices - intersections and points of "gluing" of segments. A segment can have a variable width (which varies linearly). For each segment point, the distance to the exit and the direction of the predominant movement are calculated.

Step 2. A mesh with a small enough step to determine the flow density is superimposed on the evacuation area.

Step 3. The three-component human models are sorted by increasing distance to the exit.

Step 4. In order of sorting, for each of the people in the coordinates of the position of the center and the angle of rotation are determined by the local flux density and the predominant direction of movement.

Step 5. For the selected preferred direction of movement within the maneuverability angle, a finite number of directions is determinedю For each of the directions within the constraints on the angles of rotation of the parts of the human body, the finite number of angles of rotation of the auxiliary ellipses of the three-component human model is analyzed.

Step 6. Among the angles of maneuverability and the corresponding angles of rotation, which simulate the relative position of parts of the human body, rational parameters are found, which allow for a unit of time to make the maximum movement without violations of the boundaries of the segments and without intersection with other ellipses. (The speed of movement is adjusted by the local flux density).

2.4 Computer Simulations of the Movement of the Flow of People by Force Action

The algorithmic support for computer simulation of the optimization of objects' moving was created. The program was developed in the Microsoft Visual Studio 6.0 environment to simulate the process of evacuation of people. As an example and to compare the results, the problem is solved from the manual [11] modeling the movement of people in four corridors 18 m long and 1.65 m wide with a merger into one stream, which moves to the exit on the main corridor. Main corridor has 1.6 m wide and 70 m long and which consists of three sections of 10 m and a section of 40 m to the exit. At the initial time, 28 people are accommodated in each of the four corridors; the initial flow density is set at 1.47 people/m^2. In modeling, people are represented by a three-component model. The velocity is adjusted depending on the local flow density, which is obtained in [11] experimentally. The maneuverability of people is selected from the range $[-0.5; +0.5]$ m. The evacuation process is presented in four fragments in Fig. 5.

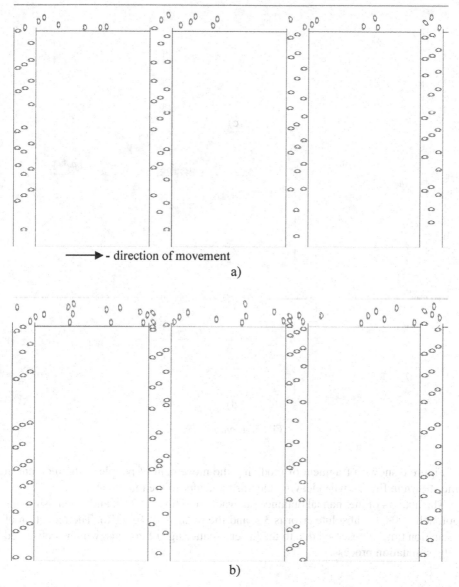

→ - direction of movement

a)

b)

Fig. 5. Computer modeling of active movement of people. The configuration of the placement of people, respectively: a) for 7 s, b) for 10 s, c) for 15 s, d) for 30 s of movements

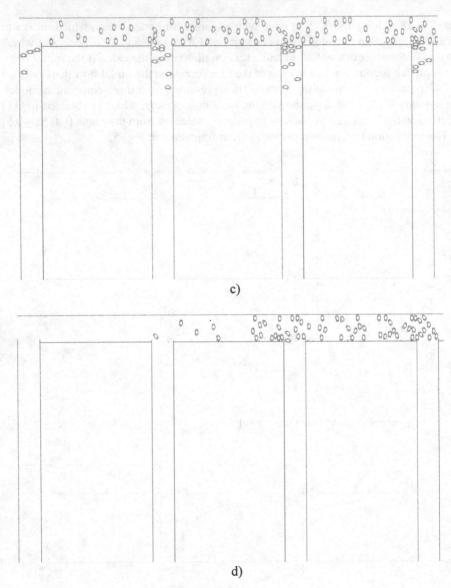

c)

d)

Fig. 5. (*continued*)

Figure 6 shows a fragment of modeling the movement of people at the moment in time shown in Fig. 5c when leaving the third corridor to the main one.

The authors of the manual obtained an evacuation time of 93 s, and when using this approach - 90s, the absolute error is 3 s, and the relative - 0.03 (3%). The reduction of evacuation time is observed due to the faster "scattering" of crowds, which is observed in the simulation process.

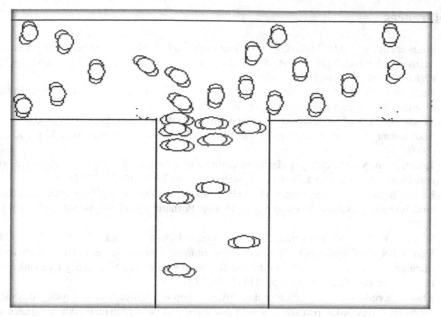

Fig. 6. The position of the people represented at moment in time, which represented by Fig. 5c

3 Conclusions

The anthropological features of a person are analyzed and a three-component model of the human body is proposed, which takes into account the conditions of bonding of the model component into a single complex object and the ratio of rotation angles of the model component arising from physical limitations to the mutual position of body parts. This human model allowed simulating the movement of people along the stream, taking into account their forceful actions that occur with their active movement. The developed mathematical model expands the class of solved tasks of modeling the movement of people. For the constructed three-component model of the human body, analytical expressions of the conditions of their non-intersection and placement in the area, which is the basis of the mathematical model of modeling the movement of people taking into account the force actions between them, were obtained.

The mathematical model is proposed and the algorithm of simulation of active movement of people taking into account natural deformations of bodies is modified. The modification is to take into account the natural deformations of the human body as a three-component's models. The properties of the model in the future will allow you to present the task as a classic task of nonlinean programming and use existing optimization packages. Computer simulation of the movement of people in the stream was carried out taking into account the natural deformations of bodies that occur in their active movement. The results can be used to quickly decide on the choice of evacuation routes in case of emergencies.

References

1. Predtechenskiy, V.M., Milinskiy, A.I.: Proyektirovaniye zdaniy s uchetom organizatsii dvizheniya lyudskikh potokov M.: Stroyizdat (1969). (Pereizdano Berlin, 1971; Koln, 1971; Praha, 1972; U. S., New Delhi, 1978)
2. Predtechenskiy, V.M., Milinskiy, A.I.: Proyektirovaniye zdaniy s uchetom organizatsii dvizheniya lyudskikh potokov M.: Stroyizdat. 375 c. (1979)
3. Tarantsev, A.A.: Modelirovaniye parametrov lyudskikh potokov pri evakuatsii s ispol'zovaniyem teorii massovogo obsluzhivaniya. Pozharovzryvobezopasnost 23(6), 46–55 (2002)
4. Tarantsev, A.A.: Ob odnoy zadache modelirovaniya evakuatsii s ispol'zovaniyem teorii massovogo obsluzhivaniya. Pozharovzryvobezopasnost 23(3), 46–55 (2002)
5. Kholshchevnikov, V.V., Samoshin, D.A., Galushka, N.N.: Obzor komp'yuternykh programm modelirovaniya evakuatsii zdaniy i sooruzheniy. Pozharovzryvobezopasnost 11(5), 40–49 (2002)
6. Shennon, R.: Imitatsionnoye modelirovaniye system. Iskusstvo i Nauka. M.: Mir. 420. (1978)
7. Karkin, I.N., Parfenenko, A.P.: Floiwtech VD – computer-simulation method from evacuation calculation. In: International Scientific and Technical Conference Emergency Evacuation of People from Buildings, Warsaw, pp. 111–118 (2011)
8. Kholshchevnikov, V.V., Parfenenko, A.P.: Sopostavleniye razlichnykh modeley dvizheniya lyudskikh potokov i rezul'tatov programmno-vychislitel'nykh kompleksov. Pozharovzryvobezopasnost 24(5), 68–74 (2015)
9. Va, K., Vl, K., Danilin, A.: A study of ellipse packing in the high-dimensionality problems. Eastern-Eur. J. Enterprise Technol. 1/4(85), 17–23 (2017)
10. Komyak, V., Velev, D., Zlateva, P.: Modelirovaniye dvizheniya potokov lyudey pri evaku-atsii iz vysotnykh zdaniy. Materíali Mízhnarodnoї naukovo-praktichnoї konf. "Problemi tekhnogenno-yekologíchnoї bezpeki: osvíta, nauka, praktika" (Kharkív, 21–22 listopada 2019), pp. 287–289 (2019)
11. Kholshchevnikov, V.V., Samoshin, D.A.: Evakuatsiya i povedeniye lyudey na pozharakh: uchebnoye posobiye. M.: Akademiya GPS MCHS Rossii. 212 s. (2009)
12. Stoyan, Y., Pankratov, A., Romanova, T.: Quasi-phi-functions and optimal packing of ellipses. J. Global Optim. 65(2), 283–307 (2015). https://doi.org/10.1007/s10898-015-0331-2
13. Stoyan, Y.G., Yakovlev, S.V.: Configuration space of geometric objects. Cybern. Syst. Anal. 54(5), 716–726 (2018)
14. Pankratov, A., et al.: Development of models for the rational choice and accommodation of people in mobile technical vehicles when evacuating from buildings. Eastern-Eur. J. Enterprise Technol. 4/4(106), 29–36 (2020)
15. Danilin, A.N., Komyak, V.V., Komyak, V.M., Pankratov, A.V.: Upakovka ellipsov v pryamougol'nik minimal'nykh razmerov. USiM. K. No 5, 5–9 (2016)

Cyber Resilience Strategic Planning and Self-assessment Tool for Operationalization in SMEs

Juan Francisco Carias[1]([⊠]), Saioa Arrizabalaga[1,2], and Josune Hernantes[1]

[1] TECNUN, School of Engineering, University of Navarra, San Sebastian, Spain
jfcarias@tecnun.es
[2] CEIT-BRTA, San Sebastian, Spain

Abstract. With the current high risks of cyber incidents either caused by malicious cyber criminals or by accidents, there is a latent need for cyber resilience. This discipline is a broader than the traditional cybersecurity concept as it aims to give companies an adaptability such that they are "safe-to-fail", i.e. that companies are capable of facing cyber incidents and still continue their operations or recover quickly. Although cyber resilience is a desirable capability in companies it is not easy to operationalize because it requires knowledge, experience, strategic planning and decision-making capabilities. These characteristics are not easily found in companies starting their cyber resilience building process such as SMEs. Moreover, the current literature offers documents to aid in the operationalization of cyber resilience by giving companies several actions or policies that build cyber resilience, but the information on how to strategize an effective cyber resilience building process is often scarce. Therefore, this article proposes a strategic planning and self-assessment tool to aid companies in the strategic planning of cyber resilience building. This tool contains the most important cyber resilience policies for SMEs and natural progressions for them obtained from the experience of 11 experts. With these progressions companies can obtain insights on what is their current state in each policy and what actions they can perform in order to improve that state. Thus, the tool can be helpful to develop effective action plans for cyber resilience building.

Keywords: Cyber resilience · Strategic planning · Self-assessment tool

1 Introduction

Cyber incidents can be very costly for companies. Some studies estimate that the average annual cost per company is around the millions of euros [1]. This large costs are unsustainable for many companies and especially the smaller ones [2]. Although many Small and Medium-sized Enterprises (SMEs) disregard the possibility of being attacked. However, studies suggest that they are the most vulnerable because, as a group, they represent a high payload to the attackers [3]. Cyber incidents can have various causes, malicious or accidental, natural or caused by humans [4, 5]. Regardless, when the performance

© IFIP International Federation for Information Processing 2021
Published by Springer Nature Switzerland AG 2021
Y. Murayama et al. (Eds.): ITDRR 2020, IFIP AICT 622, pp. 259–273, 2021.
https://doi.org/10.1007/978-3-030-81469-4_21

of the company's systems is compromised the company will suffer losses. Therefore, disaster management is undoubtedly necessary in the field of cybersecurity.

Cybersecurity, however, as traditionally defined, does not usually consider the response and recovery after an incident [6]. For this reason, many experts have shifted towards a broader concept of cyber resilience [7–9]. This concept is considered to be the ability of a company to anticipate, detect, withstand, recover and evolve in order to improve their capability of facing adverse situations [10, 11]. Moreover, this concept is also broader in the sense that it requires strategic planning, definition of organizational processes, and more human involvement [8, 9] when traditional cybersecurity usually focused on technical solutions with minimum human interaction [6, 12].

Cyber resilience can be a potential solution to the dangerous cyber scenario in which companies live today. Once operationalized, cyber resilience is meant to make companies safe-to-fail [4]. In other words, cyber resilience intends to make companies flexible, adaptable, ready to face challenges and recover, learn from them and thrive. However, cyber resilience is prudential, not technical, making it difficult to operationalize by requiring strategic-level planning and decision-making which in turn require knowledge and experience in the field.

Although there are several tools meant to aid companies in the operationalization of cyber resilience (e.g. [7, 9, 13]), these tools are often extensive lists of policies, actions and/or metrics with virtually no guidelines on how to prioritize these policies, actions or metrics. Thus, these tools are designed for companies who already have the experience, knowledge, maturity and capacity to manage cyber resilience on their own by prioritizing these policies and strategizing their own cyber resilience building process. However, SMEs usually lack these characteristics due to low access to resources (specialized personnel, investment capability, tools, etc.). Therefore, companies like SMEs with scarce experience and prudential capabilities for decision-making in this field require tools to facilitate their strategic planning to effectively operationalize cyber resilience.

Thus, the purpose of this article is to propose a strategic planning and self-assessment tool in order to aid SMEs in the prioritization and strategy development. The developed tool permits target setting, and action plan development based on the natural progression of 33 policies identified as the most important for cyber resilience management in SMEs, therefore aiding companies in their strategy development process.

This article is structured in the following manner: Sect. 2 contains a brief literature review on current tools for aiding companies in their cyber resilience building. Section 3 describes the methodology used to develop the self-assessment and strategic planning tool. Section 4 explains the results of this study. Section 5 contains a discussion on how the results can aid companies, how to use these results and the limitations of this study. Finally, Sect. 6 contains the conclusions drawn from this study.

2   Literature Review

There is a plethora of tools in the literature that intend to aid companies in their cyber resilience building. Frameworks are one example of these tools that have proliferated and that often include domains and policies to guide companies on what is needed in order to operationalize cyber resilience [7, 9, 13–15]. These frameworks are widely varied, containing from 4 domains [9, 16] into having over 30 of them [13]. There are similarities between some of these frameworks, but often they are not completely equivalent to each other on a policy to policy level or even a domain to domain level.

Similar to frameworks, there are standards that define actions and processes needed to achieve cyber resilience capabilities [17, 18]. These standards can have more strategic insight than frameworks [17], but are also extensive documents without roadmaps on where to start the cyber resilience building process nor how to progress.

On the other hand, there are several documents with cyber resilience Key Performance Indicators (KPIs) [19–22] meant to help companies control and optimize their cyber resilience by using these measurable characteristics of cyber resilience. However, these KPIs often limit to measuring technical capabilities [22] which may not cover all the strategic and human ins and outs in cyber resilience [8].

All of these previously mentioned tools (frameworks, standards and KPIs) often recommend the customization of the tool to adapt it to the company's circumstances and priorities [13, 18, 22]. The indication to customize these tools is reasonable since there is no "one-size-fits-all" solution to the operationalization of a prudential capability such as cyber resilience [13]. However, none of these tools gives insight on how to do this customization or how to prioritize their policies or KPIs. Therefore, these tools require the knowledge and experience to be able to customize them and make decisions in order to build cyber resilience through their usage.

Other tools available for companies to aid in their cyber resilience building process are maturity models [23, 24]. These can be defined as sets of characteristics that define a development in a certain field put sequentially in a limited number of stages or levels [25, 26]. Maturity models are often used to assess the current state of cyber resilience in an entity [10, 27] and due to their nature they are meant to aid companies progress after the initial assessment. However, the current literature only offers capability maturity models, which by nature are meant to describe already implemented processes and more specifically assess how ingrained these processes are in the company's culture [25]. Therefore, these tools can also require experience and an already begun cyber resilience operationalization in order to be fully used by companies since the descriptions of the maturity stages may not be relatable to a company that is at the beginning stages of the operationalization.

Another type of maturity model, the progression models, are descriptions of natural progressions of characteristics, attributes or policies over time from their most basic form into their most complex form sequentially and in a limited number of stages [25]. These type of maturity models are not currently a part of the cyber resilience literature. However, a cyber resilience progression with the natural progression for the different policies would be easier for companies starting their cyber resilience building process to relate to than the evolution of processes and capabilities which they have yet to implement. Therefore, this type of model would be a good tool to better assess the cyber resilience state of the companies and at the same time would give these companies insight on the natural progression that the policies should follow once they implement them. The usage of these advantages of progression models could help address the current scarcity of resources towards aiding in the strategic management of cyber resilience in companies starting their cyber resilience operationalization.

3   Methodology

The methodology for this article can be explained in three main phases:

1. Development of a cyber resilience framework for SMEs.
2. Development of a progression model for each policy in the framework.
3. Development of the strategic planning and self-assessment tool based on the progression model.

These phases will be explained more in depth in the following subsections and a summary is of the methodology and its phases is shown in Fig. 1.

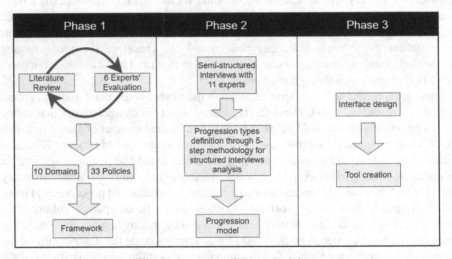

Fig. 1. Summary of the methodology

3.1   Phase 1: Development of the Cyber Resilience Framework

Through a literature review with 65 cyber resilience documents including frameworks, KPIs, maturity models, etc. and the use of the grounded theory paradigm, an initial cyber resilience framework for SMEs was developed. This initial cyber resilience framework was evaluated and iteratively improved through the participation of six experts.

After four iterations of the experts' feedback a cyber resilience framework with 10 domains and 33 policies was developed. More details on the development of the cyber resilience framework can be found in [11].

3.2 Phase 2: Development of a Progression Model

For this phase, 11 experts participated in the semi-structured interviews. These experts were chosen for their vast experience in the operationalization of cyber resilience in their own context. The experts were from 3 possible profiles: organization practitioners (5), cybersecurity providers (3) or cybersecurity researchers (3). These three profiles were selected because practitioners have empirical experience on the implementation of cyber resilience policies in their own companies, cybersecurity providers have insights on how to effectively implement these policies in companies because they do it in a daily basis, and researchers have knowledge on the literature regarding cyber resilience and how it should be implemented. Thus, these profiles should complement each other and enrich the answers obtained in the interviews.

The interviews with these experts were designed in such way that the result of each interview was a progression model for the 33 cyber resilience policies found in previous research [11, 28]. To achieve this, experts were given a script in which the definitions considered for cyber resilience and progression model were explained, the 10 domains and 33 policies were listed and the explanation of the objectives of the interview.

During the interview, the experts had to define their progression model in two steps:

4. Define the starting maturity level from each policy on a 5-level scale where 1 was the least advanced and 5 the most advanced maturity state. This 5-level scale did not assign names to each maturity level besides the number of the level to avoid biasing the answers. Other maturity models in the literature use between 3–6 maturity levels [10, 23, 27] and some also choose not to define the names of each maturity level [10, 27].
5. Describe the progression of the policy from the defined starting maturity until the most advanced maturity state (e.g. if the starting maturity was 2, they had to describe how the policy manifested at that level, then level 3, then 4 and finally level 5).

The experts were asked to do these two steps for each of the 33 policies of the framework defined in the previous phase and were asked to be as realistic as possible while doing so. They were also allowed to skip intermediate maturity level descriptions when they considered the policy stayed the same as in the previous maturity level. All of these interviews were recorded in order to ensure correct transcription of the progressions the experts suggested, and the transcriptions were also sent back to the experts to ensure that their ideas were correctly embodied.

Once the transcriptions were ready, they were analyzed using the 5-step methodology for the analysis of semi-structured interviews as suggested in [29]. In other words, the transcripts from the interviews were carefully read to identify common concepts and characteristics among the progressions described by the experts. These common concepts were grouped in order to define categories or progression types that were later used to code each policy with the most fitting progression type or types. Once the policies and progressions were coded, the mode (most frequent) starting maturity and progression type (or types in case of bimodality) were calculated and this information combined with the experts' input was used to define a progression for each policy with its most common starting maturity level and progression types. A summary of this 5-step methodology is shown in Fig. 2.

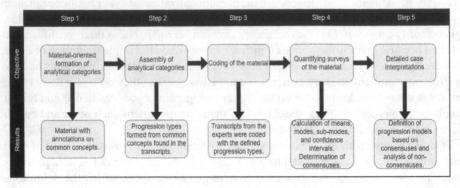

Fig. 2. Transcript analysis methodology summary

3.3 Phase 3: Development of the Strategic Planning and Self-assessment Tool

With the progression model, Microsoft Excel was used to define an interface in which companies could self-assess, then set goals for each policies maturity, and finally define action plans in order to achieve those goals.

The interface was designed to make the tool as user-friendly as possible by using different sheets to self-assess and using a color code to indicate the cells that the user had to modify in each sheet (green background), cells that were defined in previous sheets (blue background), cells from the framework (yellow background) and informative cells (white background).

With the information from the framework, the progression models for each policy and the interface decisions, the self-assessment tool was constructed.

4   Results

Through the use of the methodology described in the previous section, the developed cyber resilience strategic planning and self-assessment tool was based on the 10 domains and 33 policies of the cyber resilience framework for SMEs. With this framework 11 experts were asked to define their own progression model for each if the 33 policies. With the transcripts of the interviews, the common progression types were identified and defined in order to later code the transcriptions with the corresponding progression type for each policy and for each expert. The identified progression types in this step were the ones shown in Table 1.

After the transcripts were analyzed to determine which progression types described each of the expert's progression for each policy better. The most common starting maturity level and progression types for each policy were determined.

Table 1. Identified progression types and their definitions

Progression type	Code	Definition
Investment Increase	II	This code was assigned when the expert's progression description was related to an increase in the resources (mainly economic resources) dedicated to implementing/operationalizing the policy
Continuity	C	This code was assigned when the expert's progression description was based on the increase of frequency in which the policy's actions are performed in the company (i.e. it was done more and more frequently as the level increased)
Specificity	S	This code was assigned when the expert's progression describes an increase in level of detail in which the policy is done as the maturity of the company increases. (i.e. it started in a general way and became more detailed and specific as the level increased)
Expansion	E	This code was assigned when the expert's progression description included the expansion of the policy's action in the company (e.g. the action was performed in some sections of the company and it started being done in more sections as the level increased)
Formalization	F	This code was assigned when the expert's progression description referred to the documentation or systematization of the actions (i.e. when the policy's actions started being intuitive or informal and where standardized and documented as the level increased)
Independence	I	This code was assigned when the expert's progression description mentioned the decrease of dependency of the company from the help of cybersecurity providers or external entities to perform the tasks related to the policy
Optimization	O	This code was assigned when the expert's progression description was based on the measurement and improvement of Key Performance Indicators (KPIs) to optimize the performance of the policy's actions
Proactivity	P	This code was assigned when the expert's progression description represented a change of attitude from the company towards the policy's actions (e.g. from complying to pursuing it for their own perceived benefit). The mention of continuous improvement in actions that could not be quantified was coded under this category as well
No progression	N	This code was assigned when the expert considered that the policy was implemented and had no further progression, or when the starting maturity was considered to be at level 5
Technology	T	This code was assigned when the expert's progression description was related to an increase in technological solutions or required more advanced technologies for the progression of the policy

Table 2. Summary of starting maturity and progression types for each policy

Domain	Policy	1	2	3	4	5
Govern-ance	Develop and communicate a cyber resilience strategy.	Proactivity				
	Comply with cyber resilience-related regulation.	Expansion				
	Assign resources (funds, people, tools, etc.) to develop cyber resilience activities.			Optimization		
Risk Manage-ment	Systematically identify and document the company's cyber risks.			Formalization		
	Classify/prioritize the company's cyber risks.			Formalization		
	Determine a risk tolerance threshold.			Formalization		
	Mitigate the risks that exceed the risk tolerance threshold.			Expansion		
Asset Manage-ment	Make an inventory that lists and classifies the company's assets and identifies the critical assets.	Specificity				
	Create and document a baseline configuration for the company's assets.		Formalization			
			Technology			
	Create a policy to manage the changes in the assets' configurations.		Formalization			
			Technology			
	Create a policy to periodically maintain the company's assets.		Proactivity			
	Identify and document the internal and external dependencies of the company's assets.		Formalization			
			Proactivity			
Threat and Vulnera-bility Manage-ment	Identify and document the company's threats and vulnerabilities.			Formalization		
	Mitigate the company's threats and vulnerabilities.			Optimization		
Incident Analysis	Assess and document the damages suffered after an incident.			Formalization		
	Analyze the suffered incidents to find as much information as possible: causes, methods, objectives, point of entry, etc.			Specificity		
	Evaluate the company's response and response selection to the incident.					N
	Identify lessons learned from the previous incidents and implement measures to improve future responses, response selections, and risk management.			Formalization		
Aware-ness and Training	Define and document training and awareness plans.			Specificity		
	Evaluate the gaps in the personnel skills needed to perform their cyber resilience roles and include these gaps in the training plans.				Continuity	
	Train the personnel with technical skills.			Specificity		
	Raise the personnel's awareness through their training programs.			Formalization		
Infor-mation Security	Implement measures to protect confidentiality (e.g. access control measures, network segmentation, cryptographic techniques for data and communications, etc.)		Technology			

(continued)

Table 2. (*continued*)

Category	Policy			
	Implement integrity checking mechanisms for data, software, hardware and firmware.			Technology
	Ensure availability through backups, redundancy, and maintaining adequate capacity.			Technology
Detection Processes and Continuous Monitoring	Actively monitor the company's assets (e.g. by implementing controls/sensors, IDS, etc.)		Expansion	Technology
	Define a detection process that specifies when to escalate anomalies into incidents and notifies the appropriate parties according to the type of detected incident.			Formalization
Business Continuity Management	Define and document plans to maintain the operations despite different scenarios of adverse situations.		Expansion	Formalization
	Define and document plans to respond to and recover from incidents that include recovery time objectives and recovery point objectives.		Expansion	Formalization
	Periodically test the business continuity plans to evaluate their adequacy and adjust them to achieve the best possible operations under adverse situations.			Continuity
Information Sharing and Communication	Define information sharing and cooperation agreements with external private and public entities to improve the company's cyber resilience capabilities.		Formalization	Proactivity
	Define and document a communication plan for emergencies that takes into account the management of public relations, the reparation of the company's reputation after an event, and the communication of the suffered incident to the authorities and other important third parties.			Specificity
	Establish collaborative relationships with the company's external stakeholders (e.g. suppliers) to implement policies that help each other's cyber resilience goals.			Formalization

Using the starting maturity level and the progression type, a progression model was built for each of the 33 cyber resilience policies. The summary of the starting level of maturity and progression types for each policy is shown in Table 2.

The starting maturity level and progression types shown in Table 2 combined with the responses from experts, whose opinions were coherent with these characteristics, were used to create a progression model for each policy.

Using Microsoft Excel, and the progression model the tool was designed to have 4 sheets. The first sheet contains the self-assessment tool in which the input is the current maturity level of the company for each cyber resilience policy. In a second sheet, the managers can insert the goals for each policy. A third sheet for defining an action plan. And, finally, a fourth sheet for visual representation of the current state of the company and the targets that have been set.

In the self-assessment sheet, the progression models for each policy were inserted so that company managers could select the maturity level according to the description that they considered the company related the most. This sheet by itself already aids companies to examine their current state and therefore can be helpful for them to address their weaknesses and reinforce or maintain their strengths. To select the maturity level, the manager has a cell with a combo box in which the maturity levels are selectable. Once the manager selected the current maturity level for the company, all other descriptions were formatted to have a gray background in order to give a visual cue that the selection had been registered and to highlight the selection to ensure it was aligned with the user's intentions.

Once the company has been self-assessed, the manager can go to the next sheet, the target-setting sheet. In this sheet, the current maturity level selected in the self-assessment is shown as reference for the manager to decide whether the company can progress to further levels or if they wish to maintain the current maturity level. As in the self-assessment, the descriptions for each maturity level are shown in the screen so that the managers can make a decision based on them. Moreover, the interface behaves similarly by formatting with a gray background the non-selected descriptions in order to highlight the selected goal. This sheet is very similar to the previous sheet with the only differences being that it contains the already-filled current maturity level and has a column for the manager to fill the targets. A section of the target setting sheet with the governance domain is shown in Fig. 3.

Once the manager has set the goals, by using the action plan sheet and comparing the descriptions of the current maturity level and the target maturity level, the manager can decide which concrete actions can be used to achieve the goal, set a date to achieve each action and set the resources that will be needed to achieve the action. For instance, looking at the filled information in Fig. 3. In the first governance policy "Develop and communicate a cyber resilience strategy", the action plan sheet would show the manager the descriptions of the maturity level 2 (the selected current state) and level 3 (the selected target maturity. The descriptions are the following:

- Maturity level 2: "Once the cybersecurity basics are met, the strategy centers on protecting the systems according to their risks (implement traditional cybersecurity)."
- Maturity level 3: "The cyber resilience strategy defines resilience requirements based on the risks of the company's assets. The company tries to comply with these resilience requirements to the best of their abilities. This includes having response plans in case of incidents that could harm the compliance with these requirements."

With these descriptions, the manager can get concrete actions needed to progress from level 2 to level 3. For example, "defining resilience requirements" could be the first and most important action needed to progress. Resilience requirements can be defined by

Domain	Policy	Current Maturity Level	Target Maturity Level	1	2	3	4	5
	Develop and communicate a cyber resilience strategy.	2	3	A simple strategy based on intuition and current knowledge is defined with the objective to cover the basic cybersecurity needs. In other words, in this level, companies should prioritize the policies and measures needed to define an effective strategy (asset management, risk management, etc.).	Once the cybersecurity risks of the company's assets are met, the strategy centers on protecting these resilience systems according to their abilities. This includes having response plans in case of incidents that could harm the compliance with these requirements.	The cyber resilience strategy defines resilience requirements based on the company's risks of the company's assets. The company tries to depth on how to make the comply with these resilience systems and processes as requirements to the best of resilient as possible with their abilities. This includes specific plans on how to recover in case the protection methods fail.	The detailed and tries to go in how to make the systems and processes as resilient as possible with the company's previous iterations of the strategy and previous successes or mistakes.	The strategy is continuously improved upon, trying to implement lessons learned from the company's previous iterations of the strategy and previous successes or mistakes.
Governance	Comply with cyber resilience-related regulation.	3	4	The company has identified the cyber resilience related laws and regulations that directly concern their activity.	The company does its best to comply with the most regulations that have been directly related cyber resilience laws regulations.	The company tries to comply with the laws and regulations that have been identified by internally and auditing which are being complied with and which are still in progress.	The company starts exploring laws and regulations that indirectly concern their own cyber activity and sees added value in complying with resilience implementation these laws as a way to and not simply with the improve their cyber intention of complying. resilience.	The company continuously complies with more their demanding regulations driven by their own cyber resilience implementation and not simply with the cyber intention of complying.
	Assign resources (funds, people, tools, etc.) to develop cyber resilience activities.	4	4			Specific, documented budgets and resources are assigned for the fulfillment of the cyber resilience strategy.	The investments in cyber resilience are controlled through KPIs that the company has selected to try to optimize their allocation of resources.	Resources are flexibly moved in order to maximize the benefits of the resources that have been assigned and optimize the values of the company's KPIs.

Fig. 3. Target setting sheet section

classifying assets according to their criticality in the company's core processes. These requirements could also consider the associated risks for each asset. All these ideas can help the manager using the tool to define the actions that in this case would end up improving the company's cyber resilience strategy and cyber resilience capabilities. Therefore, the result of the complete process would be a concrete action plan for cyber resilience operationalization or cyber resilience improvement in the company.

Finally, for visual representation of the self-assessment and the set targets, the tool also generates radar graphs with the information filled in previous sheets. An example of a domain-level radar graph and the governance and asset management domains are shown in Fig. 4.

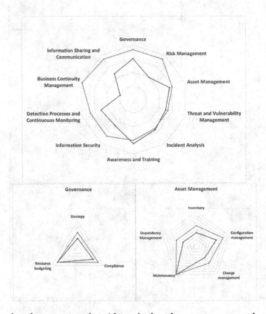

Fig. 4. Example visual representation (domain-level, governance and asset management)

Due to the nature of the tool, it can be used several times by the same company in order to check how the company is improving over time, check whether the actions are working as expected, and reset the goals after each assessment. The self-assessment, especially if it is done repeatedly over time can help the company gain awareness of their current situation and gain experience by trying to improve that situation. Therefore, the tool addresses the necessary profiling or customization required by other aiding documents (frameworks, KPIs, etc.) but in a way in which the manager can simply use the same suggested policies and progressions as a way to define the current company's profile and strategize on how to improve where they consider necessary.

5   Discussion

The main result of this paper is a tool that guides a company manager through a self-assessment and a cyber resilience strategic planning. This tool could contribute by giving some insight on how the natural progression of cyber resilience policies commonly looks and what specific states are common to go through when implementing one of these policies.

As discussed during this article there is usually scarce information on how the policy starts when first implemented by a company and how it progresses until it reaches the most advanced state. Therefore, the descriptions of the initial state and natural progression of companies could be useful in three different scenarios:

1. When a company is starting a cyber resilience operationalization process from the very first steps because it describes in a realistic way the most common first manifestations of the policies.
2. When a manager wants to assess the current state of cyber resilience in a company with limited knowledge and experience in the field because managers can probably relate the current situation to these empirical descriptions.
3. And, when a manager wishes to plan at a strategic level what the next steps of the company should be because once the manager has identified the current maturity, the next levels can be set as goals to aim for, and the descriptions of these next levels should serve as insight on how to achieve them.

Building cyber resilience should also help companies face the current cyber scenario by making them flexible and adaptable towards the possible cyber incidents they may suffer. The adaptability associated with the cyber resilience capability can make companies better at continuing their operations despite adverse events. In other words, the process of building cyber resilience by strategically implementing cyber resilience should in turn increase the ability of a company of being "safe-to-fail".

Moreover, the results of this paper can be combined with previous research on the prioritization of the cyber resilience policies [11, 28]. These studies have attempted to define the priorities of the domains and policies in the presented cyber resilience framework by proposing implementation orders. Although the progression model can help assess the current maturity state of a company and plan future implementations, the implementation order is still necessary to prioritize the policies and decide which policies to start implementing for the most effective results. Having just the progression model while making the strategic plan would be an improvement over having just the list of policies but would still just have partial information on effective ways to prioritize. Where the progression model contributes the most is when defining actions to start the implementation of a policy or to improve upon an existing implementation, but the decision on which policies to implement first should be taken with the aid of an implementation order. Therefore, by combining the implementation order and strategic planning of cyber resilience operationalization, companies should have powerful tools towards an effective cyber resilience operationalization.

As limitation to this study, the experts' vast experience does not overcome their cultural baggage nor the limited sample size. Most of the experts were from the same geographical area, the Basque Country, Spain, an area rich in manufacturing companies. This cultural background could potentially affect their opinions on how the policies progress. For similar reasons, the opinions of a sample of 11 experts may not be generalizable to all companies, and further research should attempt to replicate these results with more experts and from more varied cultural backgrounds to increase the sample size of experts and to statistically validate the results obtained in this study. Furthermore, these results should also be validated and iteratively improved through testing in real situations to enrich the obtained results.

6 Conclusions

This study proposes a strategic planning and self-assessment tool based on a progression model built with data collected from semi-structured interviews to 11 experts. The usage of this tool intends to aid companies by structuring their strategic planning towards realistic goals found in the descriptions of the natural progression of policies that the progression model provides. Correct strategic planning is key to build cyber resilience in a cyber scenario that is noticeably dangerous for all types of companies, but especially for the ones that cannot afford to not be prepared for an unforeseen cyber incident such as SMEs.

Therefore, the tool is meant to help companies build cyber resilience capabilities by facilitating the process of self-assessing their current state while at the same time providing ideas on how to progress. The same tool lets companies set goals and define action plans in order to further assist them in the strategic planning.

Future lines of research should try to mitigate this study's limitations by attempting to replicate the results with more experts and with experts from different cultural backgrounds. Moreover, these results should also be tested in companies to iteratively improve the results by empirical trial and error that often highlights unforeseeable nuances.

Acknowledgement. The authors thank the support from the Basque Government project ELKARTEK 2020 KK-2020/00054.

References

1. Tofan, D., Nikolakopoulos, T., Darra, E.: The cost of incidents affecting CIIS: systematic review of studies concerning the economic impact of cyber-security incidents on critical information infrastructures (CII). ENISA, Athens, Greece (2016)
2. Damiano, M.: VIPRE Announces Launch of VIPRE Endpoint Security - Cloud Edition | Business Wire. In: Bus. Wire. (2017). https://www.businesswire.com/news/home/201710020 05176/en. Accessed 28 Oct 2019
3. Millaire, P., Sathe, A., Thielen, P.: What All Cyber Criminals Know: Small & Midsize Businesses With Little or No Cybersecurity Are Ideal Targets. NJ, USA (2017)
4. Björk, F., Henkel, M., Stirna, J., Zdravkovic, J.: Cyber Resilience – fundamentals for a definition. Adv. Intell. Syst. Comput. **353**, III–IV (2015). https://doi.org/10.1007/978-3-319-164 86-1
5. Luiijf, H.A.M., Nieuwenhuijs, A.H.: Extensible threat taxonomy for critical infrastructures. Int. J. Crit. Infrastructures **4**, 409 (2008). https://doi.org/10.1504/IJCIS.2008.020159
6. Schneier, B.: The future of incident response. IEEE Secur. Priv. **12**, 96–97 (2014)
7. Linkov, I., Eisenberg, D.A., Bates, M.E., et al.: Measurable resilience for actionable policy. Environ. Sci. Technol. **47**, 10108–10110 (2013). https://doi.org/10.1021/es403443n

8. Deutscher, S.A., Bohmayr, W., Asen, A.: Building a Cyberresilient Organization. Boston, MA, USA (2017)
9. World Economic Forum: A framework for assessing cyber resilience. Geneva, Switzerland (2016)
10. INCIBE: Indicadores para Mejora de la Ciberresiliencia (IMC). Madrid, Spain (2019)
11. Carias, J.F., Borges, M.R.S., Labaka, L., et al.: Systematic approach to cyber resilience operationalization in SMEs. IEEE Access **8**, 174200–174221 (2020). https://doi.org/10.1109/ACCESS.2020.3026063
12. Cranor, L.F.: A framework for reasoning about the human in the loop. In: Proceedings of the 1st Conference on Usability, Psychology, and Security, pp. 1:1–1:15. USENIX Association, San Francisco (2008)
13. NIST: Framework for Improving Critical Infrastructure Cybersecurity v 1.1. Gaithersburg, MD, USA (2018)
14. Center for Internet Security (CIS): CIS Controls V 7.1. NY, USA (2019)
15. Hong Kong Monetary Authority: Cyber Resilience Assessment Framework. Hong Kong, China (2016)
16. Linkov, I., Eisenberg, D.A., Plourde, K., et al.: Resilience metrics for cyber systems. Environ. Syst. Decis. **33**, 471–476 (2013). https://doi.org/10.1007/s10669-013-9485-y
17. International Organization for Standarization (ISO): ISO/IEC 27001:2013(en) Information technology — Security techniques — Information security management systems — Requirements. Geneva, Switzerland (2013)
18. International Standards on Auditing (ISA): ANSI/ISA–62443-2-1 (99.02.01) Security for Industrial Automation and Control Systems Part 2-1: Establishing an Industrial Automation and Control Systems Security Program, pp. 1–170 (2009)
19. NIST: Security and Privacy Controls for Federal Information Systems and Organizations (NIST SP 800-53 Rev. 4). Gaithersburg, MD, USA (2013)
20. Tang, C.: Key performance indicators for process control system cybersecurity performance analysis (2017). https://doi.org/10.6028/NIST.IR.8188
21. Nys, J.: How to steer cyber security with only one KPI: the cyber risk resilience. In: RSA Conference, pp. 1–42 (2016)
22. MITRE: Cyber Resiliency Metrics. VA, USA (2012)
23. Department of Energy (DOE): Cybersecurity Capability Maturity Model (C2M2). Washington DC, USA (2014)
24. Pacific Northwest National Laboratory: Buildings Cybersecurity Capability Maturity Model. Washington DC, USA (2019)
25. Caralli, R., Knight, M., Montgomery, A.: Maturity models 101: a primer for applying maturity models to smart grid security, resilience, and interoperability (2012)
26. Carneiro, A.: Maturity and metrics in health organizations information systems. In: Handbook of Research on ICTs and Management Systems for Improving Efficiency in Healthcare and Social Care, Lisbon, Portugal, pp. 937–952. IGI Global (2013)
27. Carnegie Mellon University: Cyber Resilience Review (CRR). In: Dep. Homel. Secur. (2016). https://www.us-cert.gov/ccubedvp/assessments. Accessed 6 Feb 2018
28. Carias, J.F., Borges, M.R.S., Labaka, L., et al.: The Order of the Factors DOES Alter the Product: Cyber Resilience Policies' Implementation Order, pp. 306–315 (2021)
29. Schmidt, C.: The analysis of semi-structured interviews. In: Flick, U., von Kardorff, E., Steinke, I. (eds.) A Companion to Qualitative Research, English, pp. 253–258. SAGE Publications, London (2004)

Monitoring the Health System Saturation Risk During COVID-19 Pandemics

Sofia García, Leire Labaka, Josune Hernantes, and Marcos R. S. Borges[✉]

TECNUN – University of Navarra, Donostia, Guipúzcoa, Spain
{llabaka,jhernantes,mborges}@tecnun.es

Abstract. The pressure on the sanitary system caused by the Covid-19 pandemics put in risk many lives. The unknowns of the pandemic behavior caused problems for a more accurate prediction of the demands for hospitalization and ICU. As a result, two situations were observed: unnecessary expansion of the sanitary system with campaign hospitals and, worse, the saturation of the system with or without expansion. This article proposes the use of a backwards approach to compare the data predicted by a SD model with the real data obtained from the hospitals in the Basque Country. The goal was to calibrate the model to be better prepared for the eventual new wave of infections reducing the risk of collapse or unnecessary response actions to the emergency.

Keywords: Covid-19 · Sanitary saturation risk · SD model

1 Introduction

The crisis generated by the COVID-19 has affected the entire world in a proportion never seen since the 1918 pandemics [1]. To reduce the pressure on the sanitary system, and consequently saving lives, millions of people have been in quarantine, affecting the social living and, according to some scientists, generating severe damage to the economic system [2]. For some economists, the reducing of economic activity can kill more people than the virus and they claim governments should adopt a different model to deal with fear and the deaths of almost a million people since the pandemic begun.

In an attempt to understand the evolution of the virus several predictive models have been developed and applied. [3, 4] The goal was mainly to reduce the number of "don't knows", the most repeated words in the news since the beginning of the covid-19 pandemics [5]. The number of deaths is still high, but it is gradually reducing in many countries. After over 6 months of fight we are gradually reducing the uncertainty, but there are still many questions without answers [6].

The data accumulated during these last months has enabled scientists to learn and understand the evolution of the disease. "Those who cannot remember the past are condemned to repeat it." (George Santayana). Many decisions made in the past would probably be different if we knew what we know now. With that knowledge and information, would we be able to develop more accurate predictive models? We think the

Y. Murayama et al. (Eds.): ITDRR 2020, IFIP AICT 622, pp. 274–286, 2021.
https://doi.org/10.1007/978-3-030-81469-4_22

answer is Yes, and that is the approach of the work reported in this paper as a way to reduce the risk of collapse of the sanitary system.

Now that we have enough data from many communities, we can use real accurate data to apply to a predictive model and tune its parameters by comparing the predictions generated using the model and the real data published by the community. We start from an existent pandemics model, do some changes to make it resemble the covid-19 behavior and run several simulations until we get results close to the reality. The goal is to have at the same time a model tested against the reality and a review of the accuracy of published data, exposing potential incoherencies. With a more accurate model we can run simulations using data from other communities and analyze the differences of behavior through the values of parameters.

Although we tend to think of similar effects of the pandemics in different communities, the numbers do not reflect this similarity. The level of transmission and infection, the mortality and recover rates are examples of these variations. Although we don't have the necessary knowledge to point to why they are different we can at least point how different they were. Having produced a more accurate model we can use it to get prepared for the potential risks, as the covid-19 pandemic continue to produce chaos and stress in most places around the world, as the second wave of infections is demonstrating.

One of the issues that caused enormous concern during the first wave was the risk of saturation of hospitals, in particular the ICU vacancies. After adjusting the predictive model with real data from the first wave, we believe we are now better prepared to estimate the demand and anticipate recommendations to at least reduce the risk of collapse [7]. This, we believe, is the main contribution of this research. Hopefully, we won't need to use the model, but as it happens in many situations in disasters, we rather be safe than sorry (Samuel Lover).

The reminder of this paper is organized as follows. Section 2 that follows this introduction present and explain the SD model adapted to simulate the evolution of covid-19. Section 3 presents the data we obtained for our case study applied for the Basque Country Covid-19 cases. In Sect. 4 we present the methodology and the results of the simulations contrasted against the data from reality. Section 5 we conclude by presenting a discussion on the potential benefits of these results in the form of a set of lessons learned and how this can be used to recommend actions to prevent the sanitary system saturation.

2   The SD Model Developed for the Analysis

A System Dynamics model has been developed to test the real data and analyze the accuracy of the published data. System dynamics is a methodology that allows to model complex systems based on the underlying structure that creates the behavior of the system [8]. This model should be able to reproduce the behavior of the main variables of the pandemics management and in turn, verify the accuracy of the published data.

Figure 1 shows the stock and flow diagram of the SD model.

The stock "Susceptible" represents the population that is susceptible of getting the COVID-19 disease. Based on the transmission rate and the number of active infected cases the number of people that is exposed to the infection is calculated, and with some delay and the infection rate the number of people who finally get infected. This stock

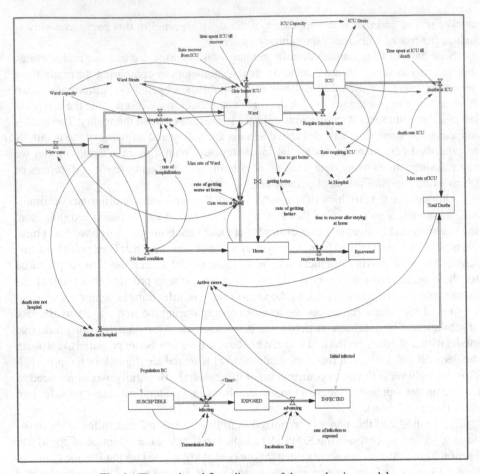

Fig. 1. The stock and flow diagram of the pandemics model

counts the number of total people who has been infected during the whole lifecycle of the pandemic. However, for the analysis of the evolution, the daily cases are represented with the new daily case stock. The current cases are divided into two groups: the ones that are recovered at home and the ones that must go to the hospital because they are more serious. Among those who are in the hospital, those who are very serious are admitted to the ICU. Once they get better they return to the plant and once they are recovered they go home and eventually to the recovered stock. Finally, based on the death rate at ICU, some of the patients who are in the ICU and at home die due to the disease. The total number of people who die is represented in the "Total Death" stock.

3   The Data Used in the Case Study

In order to tune the model to the specific case of the area of the Basque Country in Spain, we gathered data from the daily reports the Basque government published to the public [9]. In these reports, the data about the evolution of the main epidemiological variables are collected. The graphs below represent these data from March 15th to July 12th (120 days), that is, from the moment the total confinement of the population was implemented until the "new normality" was achieved.

As we can see in the graph in Fig. 2, the number of total cases increased abruptly from days 5 to 17 and then the curve continues increasing but with a minor slope. This change in the tendency occurs 3–4 weeks after the first case was detected and 2–3 weeks after the total confinement of the region was implemented. 50 days after the detection of the first case, we can say that the pandemic was under control and the increase of the curve was very low.

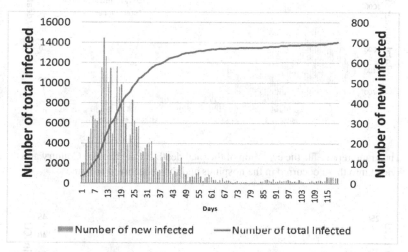

Fig. 2. The graph represents the evolution of the total infected cases and the new daily cases in the Basque Country

Following the same shape of the graph in Fig. 2, the graph in Fig. 3 represents the total number of deaths that occurred in the region of the Basque Country as well as the daily deaths divided into the ones that occurred in the hospitals and the ones at home. The shape of both curves are the same, with different magnitude, and with some delay since as we know the deaths come with some delay. The change in the slope is obtained in day 26 more or less, that is, 10 days after the number of new infected cases started to decrease. The curve stabilized in day 75, 2–3 weeks after the stabilization of the total infected cases.

Very related with the graphs in Fig. 3, we can analyze the total cases and daily cases in hospitals and in ICU, that represents on the one hand the total number of serious cases that can derive in deaths and on the other hand the saturation level of the health system that could also lead to more deaths due to the limited resources to attend to all patients in an appropriate manner. Both graphs (see Fig. 4 and Fig. 5) reaches the maximum level between days 17 and 22, that is, when the curve of the total infected cases changes its tendency. The graph of the total hospitalization reaches the maximum 2–3 days before the graph of number of patients in ICU, since there is a short delay between the moment the people go to the hospital and the moment that the people get in the ICU. From this moment on, the situation was taken under control and the number of new cases start decreasing and the same happened with the number of hospitalizations and the number of cases in ICU.

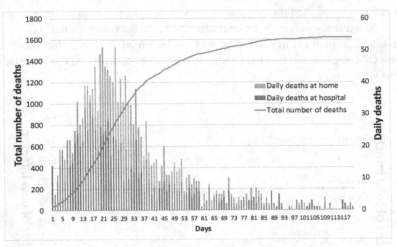

Fig. 3. The graph represents the evolution of the total deaths in the Basque Country and the daily deaths divided into these occurred in the hospitals and those occurred at home

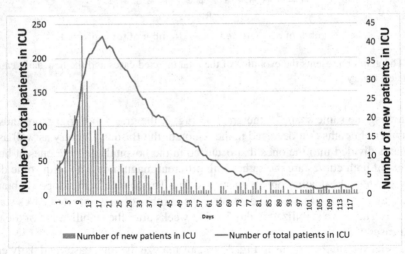

Fig. 4. The graph represents the evolution of the total cases and the daily new cases in ICU in the Basque Country

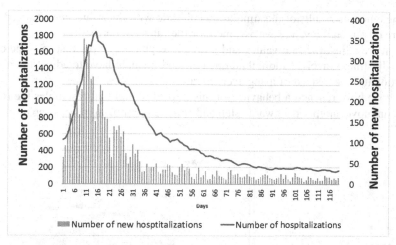

Fig. 5. The graph represents the evolution of the total hospitalization cases and the daily new hospitalization cases in the Basque Country

4   Methodology and the Comparative Results

4.1   The Description of the Methodology

As we mentioned in the previous section, we have four data sets of real data obtained from the evolution of covid-19 in the Basque country, showing the behavior of the following variables: total number of deaths, occupation of ICU beds, number of hospitalizations and the number of infected people. With the exception of the later, which is very dependent on the number of tests, the other three variables are reliable information that we can use for tuning the model, particularly the variables that influence the flow.

A SD predictive model is only useful if it resembles the reality [10]. Our goal then, is to obtain a model that behaves as close as possible to the reality. One way to achieve at least an approximate representation of the reality is to set the model using one or both techniques inspired by the theory of change [11]: "backwards-from-outcome" and "forwards-to outcome". In both approaches, we need reliable information from the reality, a SD model that generates the outcomes for comparison and variables representing the rates that influence the outcome. The "backwards from outcome" approach should be applied when the most reliable is data is at the end of the transformation process, in the case of covid-19 is related to the number of deaths.

Using the elements of the model, we started from this reliable data values and move backwards "one step at a time", i.e., a step required to reach the stock for which we have another set of reliable data. For example, in the model of Fig. 1, we started with the number of deaths to find out the rate of deaths that come from Hospital (ICU stock in our model) and from cases that haven't reached the hospital (Case Stock). The monitoring of the behavior consists of the following phases:

1.   Starting from the most reliable data as input, we assign a set of values to the rates and run the simulation to obtain the output values as prescribed by the model.

2. If the outcome results of the simulation coincide with the values we obtained from the reality, then the values we assumed for the rates are correct.
3. If not, we adjust the rate values and go back to phase 1. Note that in some cases, the adjustment involves more than one rate and we may have to adjust the rates in relation to time instead of using average rates.
4. Once we have reached a behavior for this part of model that resembles the reality, we can move another backwards step and run the monitoring process again.

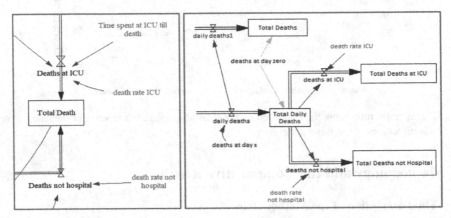

Fig. 6. From the original SD model to the backwards model of Total Deaths

For the monitoring process, we need the part of the full model to monitor, the corresponding backward model to simulate, and the simulation results that will be compared with the data from the reality. To create the backwards model we start from a stock variable, which values are known, create the resulting stocks, which values are also known and assign values to the rates (marked in red) that are the best fit for the resulting stocks. Figure 6 illustrates the first backward step depicting side-by-side part of the full SD model and the corresponding backward model.

The backwards process proceeds until we reach stocks which values from the reality are not available or are not reliable. At this point on there will be uncertainty in the prediction model. In the case of Covid-19 we had to stop at the Case stock, as the real numbers of Infected are very dependent on the number of tests.

4.2 Applying the Backwards Process – 1 – Death Rates from Different Contexts

The total number of deaths is the sum of the three components: home, hospital (not ICU) and ICU). In our model, however, we assumed that all patients who get worse are moved to ICU and therefore the number of deaths in Hospital (not UCI) and its corresponding rate is zero. The sum of rates should total 1 and the sum of deaths at ICU plus deaths elsewhere should be equal the total of deaths. To move backwards in this case is quite simple. We should know either one of the rates or one of the values of deaths besides the total number of deaths.

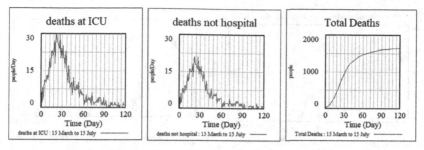

Fig. 7. Results from running the simulation. To be compared with the graphs in Fig. 3

As we mentioned in Sect. 3, we collected the data for the Basque Country to serve at the basis for our backward analysis. The first step aims to find the proportion of deaths that occurred in hospitals in relation to those that occurred elsewhere (Elderly homes, home, work, etc.). The total values for the Basque country were 962 (59.2%) and 663 (40.2%) for hospital and non-hospital deaths, respectively. When we applied these average rates, we get the graphs reproduced at Fig. 7. When we compare to the graphs of the real data presented in Fig. 3, we can notice that they have similar shapes. However, when we compare the daily numbers, we notice some differences, as can be seen in Fig. 8 where we compare the simulation data with the real data.

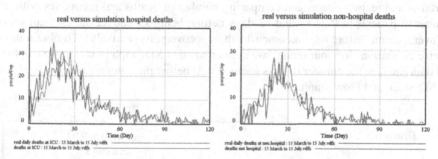

Fig. 8. Comparison with real data and the data obtained by simulation for daily deaths in Hospitals and not-Hospitals

For generating the simulation results in Fig. 8, we assumed for all days a constant rate hospital/non-hospital obtained from the relation between the total deaths. To generate more accurate results, we assumed a different rate for a group of ten days (5 before, five after) obtained by the average proportion of these ten days. In other words, instead of assuming one constant rate for the entire period, we used 12 values corresponding to the average rate of each ten days. The results illustrated by the graphs in Fig. 9 show a better approximation to the reality. This measure is particularly important for long periods (120 days in our case).

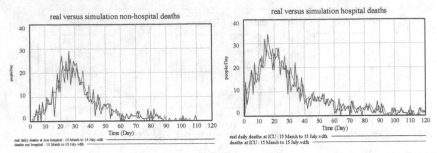

Fig. 9. Comparison with real data and the data obtained by simulation for daily deaths both at Hospitals and at Home, using a lookup table for 10-day rates

4.3 Applying the Backwards Process – 2 – ICU Occupation Rates

Following the ICU path backwards, the process gets more complicated. There is a delay in time between the outcome (death or recover) and the time the patient ingressed in the ICU. To calculate the ICU occupation rate at any time, we should estimate the number of days a patient stays in ICU until the outcome (death or recover). The data exists but it is not available. Thus, we must consider an average estimation to calculate the backward values. The data we have is the daily and accumulated values of all stocks. We can estimate the average time spent at ICU until the outcome by calculating the mortality and recovery rates and comparing number of deaths and recoveries with the number of patients in ICU x1 and x2 days before, being x1 and x2 the estimations of the average time before the outcome (death or recovery, respectively). To obtain more precise estimations for your model, we created another SD graph in which we can feed real data and tune the number of days spent at ICU before the outcome. Figure 10 shows the SD Stock and Flow graph.

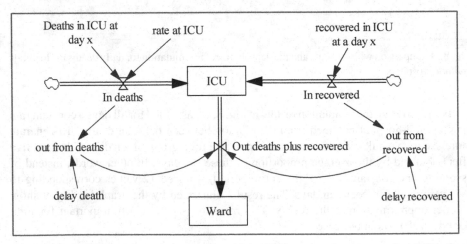

Fig. 10. SD model to explore the occupation of the ICU varying the time spent at ICI before recover or death.

To perform the simulations, we entered the real number of daily deaths occurred in the hospital and the numbers of discharges from the ICU. We could not separate the number of patients that die while in the ICU from those who died at the ward, so we assumed 50% for each origin. The main goal however was to estimate the time spent in ICU before the outcome. An average of 25 days was reported for both, which proved to be inconsistent with the occupation of ICU reported. We only got an approximation of the ICU occupation reported by setting the average rate of stay around 10 days. The results of the simulation in comparison to real data is depicted in Fig. 11.

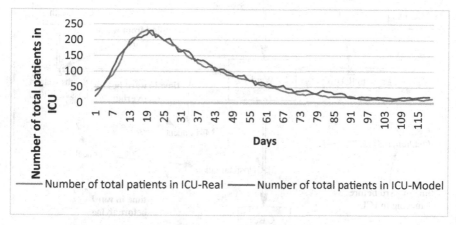

Fig. 11. Real and Simulation data for ICU occupancy

Another possibility for the discrepancy was an overload of the ICU occupancy being solved by the transference of critical patients to other hospital units or an increase of ICU beds. In interviews with sanitary people, we were told the ICU capacity is limited by care takers (doctors, nurses, etc.) available. The ICU capacity can only be increased by transferring personal, suspending other surgeries, or recruiting extra personal.

4.4 Applying the Backwards Process – 2 – Ward Occupation Rates

The next step is to model the ward occupation, working backwards from ICU real data. However, at this point there are many other flows influencing the hospital ward occupation. In addition to those sent to ICU, we will have those people sent home after getting better. There are also the people who died at the ward without passing through the ICU. Besides checking the rates of each of these outcomes (incomes in our backwards model), we will need to work on the variables representing the averages of the number of days a patient occupies a bed in the ward, for each of these outcomes.

There are also different types of cases demanding hospitalization. Most cases are those who get into care after testing positive and showing serious symptoms. A second type are related to those who already tested positive but were sent home because there were not showing serious condition and are returning after getting worse. Finally, those patients returning from a period at ICU that needs a recovery period before sent home.

The Stock and Flow diagram for the backwards analysis of cases is shown in Fig. 12. However, due to the complexity of the model and the lack of real data of each situation, we have not performed simulations to obtain the more precise rates.

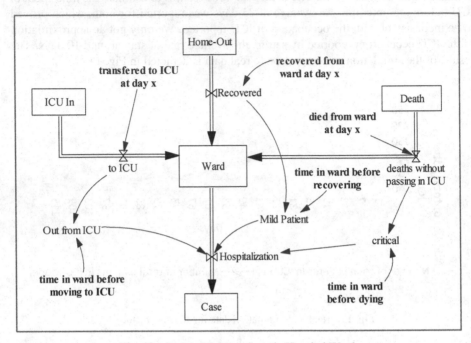

Fig. 12. SD Model for patients in Hospital Wards

5 Discussion and Conclusions

The main goal of this exercise was to reduce the uncertain of the effects of increasing number of covid-19 cases onto the sanitary system. Using the predictive model, we can simulate scenarios and based on the results, recommend actions to reduce the risk of saturation in the sanitary system, which is the main goal of this study. Although we don't need a precise model for planning the sanitary system, we think a prediction closer to the reality brings more confidence to planners.

By making the model to behave as the real data, we increase the accuracy of the rates and therefore, the predictions. The way to use the model in an ongoing situation is as follows:

1. After obtaining the real data for a period of time (the longest, the better) we run the model and make the adjustments in the rates to get results as close as possible of those of reality.
2. With a calibrated model, we run the simulations and generate prediction for the next days (the shortest, the better).

3. The predictions in relation to reality and make the necessary calibrations as described in step 1.

The reduction of the risk of collapsing the sanitary system comes from two alternative directions: we either reduce the income flow of patients or expand the capacity of the sanitary system. Actually, we can do both, but as these measures have consequences, we want to produce results closest to the needs. This way, we mitigate the risks of saturation by adopting only the necessary effort, and consequently, reducing the waste of resources.

We are now in the verge of the second wave of the pandemics, most experts say [12]. We wanted to test our predictions against the real numbers after July 30th, but the number of cases was drastically reduced, and samples were not significant to produce a meaningful comparison. We are in the process of checking the estimations with the real numbers of this second wave. However, before that we need to make some adjustments in the model to resemble the change of conditions. For instance, the death rates were reduced due to advances in the treatment. This reduction also impacted the number of days spent in ICU.

Although we include the number of cases in the main model, we don't use it nor the number of infected people because these numbers are very dependent on the number of tests performed. There is, for instance, a controversial discussion about the seriousness of the second wave in relation to the first. Some scientists considered the underestimation of infections in the first wave makes the second wave not as serious as the first. On the other hand, the number of hospitalizations is higher in this second wave than in the first. This reinforces our claim to make predictions based on real data, not estimations.

Acknowledgements. This research was supported and funded by the Fundación AON under the Cátedra de Catástrofes de la Fundación AON.

References

1. Bedford, J., et al.: COVID-19: towards controlling of a pandemic. The Lancet **395**(10229), 1015–1018 (2020)
2. McKee, M., Stuckler, D.: If the world fails to protect the economy, COVID-19 will damage health not just now but also in the future. Nat. Med. **26**(5), 640–642 (2020)
3. Verity, R., et al.: Estimates of the severity of coronavirus disease 2019: a model-based analysis. Lancet Infectious Diseases **3099**(20), 1–9 (2020)
4. Weissman, G.E., et al.: Locally informed simulation to predict hospital capacity needs during the COVID-19 pandemic. Ann. Intern. Med. **173**(1), 21–28 (2020)
5. What We Don't Know About COVID-19 Can Hurt Us. Time. https://time.com/5874241/dont-know-covid-19-hurt-us/. Accessed 25 Oct 2020
6. DW homepage, COVID-19 half a year later: What have we learned? In-depth reporting on science and technology. https://www.dw.com/en/covid-19-half-a-year-later-what-have-we-lea rned/a-54078531. Accessed 25 Oct 2020
7. IHME COVID-19 health service utilization forecasting team: Forecasting COVID-19 impact on hospital bed-days, ICU-days, ventilator days and deaths by US state in the next 4 months. https://www.medrxiv.org/content/10.1101/2020.03.27.20043752v1. Accessed 25 Oct 2020

8. Forrester, J.W.: Lessons from system dynamics modeling. Syst. Dyn. Rev. **3**(2), 136–149 (1987)
9. Euskadi Homepage, Informes con la actualización de datos sobre la evolución del nuevo coronavirus COVID-19. https://www.euskadi.eus/boletin-de-datos-sobre-la-evolucion-del-corona virus/web01-a2korona/es/. Accessed 24 Mar 2020
10. Wynants, L., et al.: Prediction models for diagnosis and prognosis of covid-19: Systematic review and critical appraisal. BMJ **369**(April), 1–16 (2020)
11. Taplin, D.H., Clark, H.: Theory of Change Basics: A Primer on Theory of Change. ActKnowledge, New York (2012)
12. Coronavirus second wave: Which countries in Europe are experiencing a fresh spike in COVID-19 cases? https://www.euronews.com/2020/10/22/is-europe-having-a-covid-19-sec ond-wave-country-by-country-breakdown. Accessed 25 Oct 2020

Emergency Response Supported by Drones and Experts Perceptions

Henrique Romano Correia[1]([⊠]), Ivison da Costa Rubim[2]([⊠]),
Angélica Fonseca da Silva Dias[2,3]([⊠]), Juliana Baptista dos Santos França[2,4]([⊠]),
and Marcos Roberto da Silva Borges[2,5]([⊠])

[1] DCC/IM (UFRJ), Federal University of Rio de Janeiro, Rio de Janeiro, Brazil
henriquerc@ufrj.br
[2] PPGI (UFRJ), Federal University of Rio de Janeiro, Rio de Janeiro, Brazil
ivisonrubim@ppgi.ufrj.br, juliana_franca@ufrrj.br
[3] Inst. Tércio Pacitti/NCE (UFRJ), Federal University of Rio de Janeiro, Rio de Janeiro, Brazil
angelica@nce.ufrj.br
[4] Federal Rural University of Rio de Janeiro (UFRRJ), Seropédica, Brazil
[5] TECNUN, University of Navarra, Donostia/San Sebastián, Spain
mborges@tecnun.es

Abstract. Emergency situations require quick responses from both experts and those who need support in risk situations. People's perception of emergency situations and its solutions has become an important element of academic and practical research. In this context, the lack of real-time responses can affect sensitive environments and emergency scenarios causing irreparable damage. Thus, this research aims to support specialists involved in emergency response, providing them tools and resources to support their decision-making process. The work proposes a collaborative solution supported by a web application and drones. This solution aims to collect information in a collaborative way of the emergency situation, through the specialists' awareness during a real emergency action. In addition, the results of the research streamline the capture of information, in less time, aiming to minimize the loss of knowledge of specialists. This information made available in an easy way allows the response team to have greater security for actions, generating greater support for decision making, thus speeding up emergency care. This work was evaluated by specialized Firefighters, who already work with drones in actual emergency situations, in Rio de Janeiro, Brazil.

Keywords: Emergency · Information system · Collaborative systems · Decision-making drones · Perception

1 Introduction and Motivation

According to [1], the world market for the use of drones, to support emergency situations, should reach an investment of approximately US $ 14 billion by 2024. This growing investment aims to support emergency response teams, which need to be able to

© IFIP International Federation for Information Processing 2021
Published by Springer Nature Switzerland AG 2021
Y. Murayama et al. (Eds.): ITDRR 2020, IFIP AICT 622, pp. 287–297, 2021.
https://doi.org/10.1007/978-3-030-81469-4_23

respond immediately to these situations when requested [2]. Through an effective emergency response, an incident can be prevented from evolving into a disaster [3]. Even with this promising scenario, emergency responses are not always quick nor captured in a systematic and representative way. As a result, these situations can become confusing, as the lack of information makes the emergency situation seem fragmented, and the available resources may not be properly addressed. In addition, this lack of information generates communication failures between those involved and overloads the command of the operation, causing a lack of establishment of common priorities and objectives [4].

In risky situations, such as emergency situations, the use of information and the collection of expert perceptions can support and help to quickly identify the environmental elements in a given time and space, the understanding of their meaning and the projection of their impact at the moment or in the near future [5–7]. For this, it is necessary to use mechanisms capable of collecting information from the individuals involved in order to support the decision.

Risk factors, in emergency situations, present both to the response team, and to people who need some support in this environment, have a great impact on the emergency response [2]. In this case, the time factor is extremely important, which can mean loss of life, destruction or non-preservation of the environment. Therefore, we consider the importance of assisting decision-making in emergency situations through obtaining, communicating information, and the experts' perception. Perception techniques are used in a system to provide information that supports users' decisions. For group activities, where individuals are expected to have a perception of what is happening, there is a need to provide mechanisms that facilitate the assimilation of perception information so that it is made available to the users [8].

From this perspective, this research aims to investigate how the participants' perception of an emergency situation can support the responses generated. For this, a web solution was designed and developed to support the agents of the emergency response teams, responsible for decision-making, in the action of collecting the experts' perceptions through their observations. This collaborative solution is supported not only by a web application, but also by the use of a drone, with the objective of speeding up the emergency response and exposing fewer human lives during the solution of emergency situations.

For the evaluation of this research, an experiment was conducted with firefighters from the state of Rio de Janeiro (Brazil), and also with an operational team of drone pilots This experiment was organized in two phases: (i) experiment with drone operation specialists and (ii) collect the perception of the experts involved during the experiment. In total, there were the participation of 6 specialists from the High Command of the Firefighters who brought their perceptions about the usability and potential of applying the technological solution experienced in future emergency situations.

This paper is organized into five sections. Section 2 presents concepts of emergency, disaster and related risk and work. Section 3 presents the Communication and Perception approach and its characteristics that underlie the analysis. Following this, Sect. 4 presents the discussion and evaluation of the research. To conclude this paper, Sect. 5 presents our conclusions that highlight the goals achieved and the limitations of this research.

2 Related Works

During an emergency, there is a threat condition that will require urgent action. An effective emergency response can prevent that threat from turning into a disaster. Emergency management includes the creation of plans, arrangements to guide and bring responsibility to all actors involved in responding to the needs of an emergency situation [6, 9]. This situation is characterized as the entire rescue planning and intervention process aimed to reduce the impact of emergencies and responses, helping to mitigate significant social, economic and environmental consequences for the community [10].

There are disasters that can occur without an alert phase, in which the response comes after the action. The response can be supported by preparedness actions taken before disaster strikes. When looking at the elements involved in a disaster, we identified the emergency cycle, which consists of four phases:

1. Prevention - first phase and includes actions aimed at preventing the occurrence of disasters, or reducing the impact of the consequences;
2. Preparation - second phase and includes actions that seek to improve the capacity of individuals and organizations in the face of disasters;
3. Answer - third and more complex phase that encompasses the set of actions taken to help and assist the affected parties, in addition to having characteristics such as: "unpredictability, (high) speed of events, (high) number of people involved, short lead times. decision and action, unavailability of resources, uncertainty about the situation, pressure and stress on those involved" [4]; and,
4. Reconstruction - fourth and last phase, and includes actions for the purpose of recovering the affected parts, such as the reconstruction of an affected community, allowing the return to normality, and always taking into account the minimization of new disasters.

During reconstruction the lessons learned are applied to prevent the effects of new disasters. These lessons support preparation for the response [11]. The authors report that certain types of disasters can be predicted, and we can consider that this alert phase, may or may not exist, and occurs before the disaster, placing itself in the emergency cycle before the response stage. Some examples of disasters that can be predicted are tropical storms and tsunamis, and in scenarios like these, the population can be alerted by the authorities to prepare.

Within the context of an emergency, decision making will vary depending on the complexity of the scenario. There is a discussion about the factors that can affect this decision making, such as the effort made and the chance of it being correct. In addition to these, other factors are relevant, such as the number of sources of information to be considered during the process, and the restriction of processing and memory when a decision maker is under stress, for example. It is also important to note that the information is inserted in the entire process that generates the knowledge required for decision making [7].

According to [12], another factor that requires attention is the communication of risks associated with perception to build a relationship of trust and credibility between the parties involved or exposed to the risks. The author defines that four risk communication paradigms: (a) High risks versus apathy: sometimes individuals are apathetic when facing a serious risk and need to be alerted; (b) Low risks versus high concern: sometimes people are uncomfortable with a small risk and need to be reassured; (c) High risks and high concern: sometimes people are uncomfortable with a serious risk and need to be guided; (d) Low risks versus apathy: sometimes people are apathetic when facing a small risk and do not need attention. For the author, low risks can be related to a clear and immediate communication, which can be established with the use of an artifact such as drones, taking the information immediately, together with the perception of each agent involved.

2.1 UAV

Drones have been used to capture images and support organizations in emergency situations with firefighters, police, humanitarian actions, among others, to provide more efficient aid to the affected regions. Also known as UAVs (unmanned aerial vehicles), they are machines that have been gaining popularity and have seen a dramatic increase in use in recent years [9]. These artifacts are capable of flying without human presence, can be autonomous or remotely controlled, can also be equipped with cameras, allowing the recording of the flight, or even its visualization in real time.

According to [1] over the years, the use of drones has increased, as well as a variety of applications have emerged to meet this growth demand. This artifact has been used as search and rescue operations, which can significantly benefit affected areas (often in large areas) and collect information on the presence of victims and their possible locations [13, 14]. These vehicles are also used in urban searches and rescue to assess damage in areas impacted by natural disasters (dimensioning phase), in which a disaster has hit an urban area with multiple locations, such as buildings or other structures suspected of housing people where survivors can get stuck, demanding rescue, and emergency care.

According to [15], another advantage of using drones is that, by identifying the risk area and the location of the distributed team, it can facilitate rescue work. In this context, experts can, through information capture, a greater number of elements, because different from perceiving means having knowledge and understanding of the events that occur within the group members. For example, knowing who is responsible for a given task, their position and information about the scenario for emergency response situations, having the specialist's knowledge and their perception of the affected area, and possible actions through drone images can mitigate the effort of the emergency response.

2.2 Perception of Support System

The term perception is defined as "knowledge that something exists, or understanding of a situation or subject at the present time based on information or experience" [16]. In aviation, specifically in war, in which the pilot needs to decide quickly and reach the goal, perception leads the individual to better understand the activities he performs and produce more relevant results for the group [5]. In order for individuals involved in an emergency situation to participate effectively in the work, they must be informed about changes in the shared space in the course of group interactions. Perception implies knowledge about what is happening at the moment in the group and also about past activities and future options [17]. The representation known as the 5W + 1H Framework, identifies six basic questions that must be answered when one wants to help an individual to understand something of which he has no prior knowledge. Perception information, therefore, is an answer to these six fundamental questions, as described below:

- Who - information on the presence and availability of individuals in the group, and identification of participants involved in an event or action?
- What - information about the occurrence of an event of interest to the group.
- Where - spatial, location information, the place where the event took place.
- When - temporal information about the event, the moment when the event occurred.
- How - information about how the event occurred.
- Why - subjective information about the intentions and motivations that led to the event.

The following approaches are used to develop a perception mechanism: (i) Interface component - interface components integrated into the system to present perception information to users. (ii) Notification: automatic notifications about events that occurred during group interactions. (iii) Annotation: annotations to enable the user to record ideas, suggestions and comments, especially useful in asynchronous interactions. (iv) Consultation and navigation through the group's memory: search for information about the interactions and activities of each user regarding certain artifacts.

There are two ways to collect the information generated by the expert's Perception. They can be synchronous or asynchronous mode. In synchronous mode, individuals interact at events in the same shared work space at the current time, with immediate notifications, availability for interaction. As for the perception in the asynchronous mode, the participants are informed about the interactions that occurred before the moment when they connect to the system. According to [9], support for perception is derived from a summary interpretation of a complete sequence of events that occurred in a time interval. Information must be at a higher level, such as changes to a given artifact. For [5, 18] there are three main elements of perception, they are:

- Perception of the current situation;
- Understanding of this situation; and
- Projection of the future condition.

In the perception of the current situation the focus is on automated perception of the current situation. To provide the necessary information component, the system must be able to collect, filter, analyze, structure and transmit data. In understanding the situation, perception is not just a view of reality, it is the correct perception of what is relevant to the current reality necessary for a correct, protective, tactical, and strategic response. The last element corresponds to the projection of the future condition, based on the perspectives of different perceptions that individuals infer about their perceptions. This research concentrated efforts on the perception of the current situation, promoting the exchange of knowledge between specialists at the time of the situation in response to the emergency.

3   Research Method and Solution

As we presented in the previous section, information technology through the use of drones can provide decision makers in a geographically distributed environment with the same information as the first stage of situation awareness [5]. The web application "Drones to the Rescue" was developed exactly for this purpose. The original idea was to keep individuals aware of what is happening through the recovery and capture of information in a disaster situation. On the other hand, with the capture of the experts' perception it was possible to review the system to be used in the initial phase of disasters as an emergency response and even in the rescue phase. In this section, we describe the initial idea of the application and its use after expert analysis. The initial version of this application and the previous discussion can be found in [19].

3.1   Perception and Support to Cooperation - Drones to the Rescue Solution

The proposed solution involves three applications: two existing applications, which are responsible for capturing images via drone (DJI Go and Autosync for Google drive), and making them available in the cloud, respectively, and the main application which is the website developed by the authors (Drones to the rescue – developed by the authors) for viewing, editing and collaborating content from the experts' perception. This solution seeks to support the prevention and response stages, within the emergency management cycle, but it can also be useful for the other stages.

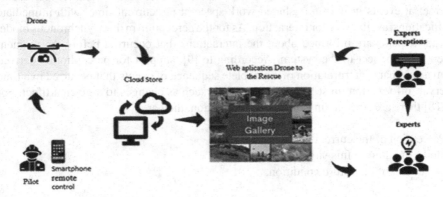

Fig. 1. Drones to the rescue solution and the cooperation among different roles and technology.

In the thought solution, the source of the images, which serve as a central element in the solution, is the camera attached to the drone. The tool "Drones to the Rescue" developed by the authors for collaborative visualization and interaction with the content gives full support to images that were obtained by other means, such as smartphone cameras, photographic cameras, satellite images, drawings, among others, however the authors decided to focus only on the images obtained by drone. The images collected by the drone are stored in the gallery and sent to specialists. Then, each specialist analyzes the image and inserts their observations and analyzes on the location of the incident.

After this action, the images are shared with the team's specialists, returning to the gallery. These detailed images of information from the experts returns to the Gallery to support other emergency response actions. As it is shown in Fig. 1, the imagens captured are presented by the Drones to the Rescue application.

Drones to the Rescue was developed to be a tool for viewing the images obtained by drones. This tool allows the editing of images, the insertion of comments and perceptions of specialists involved, and being collaborative. Figure 2 presents the tool's screen and allows users to interact, supporting the decisions of specialists in emergency situations.

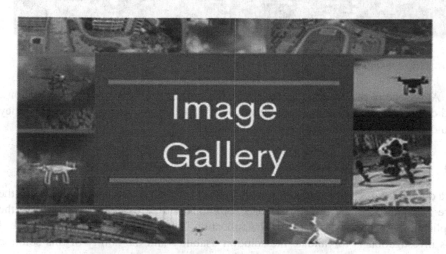

Fig. 2. Screen for image capture in Drones to the Rescue.

The tool presents a gallery with the original images obtained by the drone and stored in the cloud (Google drive) and others that have already been discussed and edited by the roles involved in the emergency. This gallery can be accessed by the featured image on the home screen or by the "Gallery" button on the top menu of the home screen.

4 Experiment Results and Discussion

Firefighters experts were invited to participate in the experiment. The initial phase of the experiment deals with explanations about the drone, the stages of capturing and transferring images to the cloud (remote storage), and the website tool that allows the images editing, comments and visualization. The next phase consisted of presenting the study by simulating a fire in a building that collapses in a university area. During the experiment, all experts had access to the tool in order to observe and collaborate with the domain explored in the experiment. These actions were possible from the images previously captured by the drone (Fig. 3) of a set of buildings under construction. The central idea was to capture the experts' perception by sharing individual knowledge and externalizing it during the experiment. The information input was captured and taken for analysis by other specialists in response to emergencies.

Fig. 3. Image capture.

At the end of the experiment, the specialists portray their experiences, perceptions, and difficulties. In addition, questionnaires were applied to everyone involved so they could evaluate the solution presented and tested.

4.1   Experiment Answers

The questionnaires were carried out with 5 (five) specialists, official firefighters of the Fire Brigade to collect these specialists' opinions and perceptions concerned to the applicability of Drones to the Rescue application in an emergency. The main goal of this investigation is to validate the solution usability and the ability of this solution in capture the specialists' perception inside an emergency. The forms were created in Google Forms. Among the respondents, most had over 20 years of experience in the field of emergency responses, all men and mostly pilots of manned and unmanned aircraft.

The "DJI GO" application, was chosen as part of the solution presented, and analyzed during the experiment. In the evaluations, the respondents reported that the artifact meets the needs of image capture and local download, and the importance of compatibility with DJI drones was highlighted, since all the devices of the specialists are from this manufacturer. The interviewees highlighted that the tool performed a good capture, but that the analysis "depends a lot on the technical knowledge applied by the pilot in the operation of the drone", as well as the presence of adequate cameras for each situation.

Regarding the application "Autosync for Google Drive", which was chosen for the solution with the purpose of sending images automatically to the cloud, the firefighters informed that it would comply with the proposal. Respondents pointed out that the tool would greatly assist firefighters' operations with drones, as today much time is lost in this transmission. In addition, it was informed that the tool would be efficient, as long as there is a well-functioning internet at the place of use.

In general, in terms of ease of use, the tool "Drones to the Recue" was evaluated as intuitive, and "allowed the insertion of the information desired by the specialists", being even interesting for the operation of the firefighters. It was said that the availability of information made through it already "would help operations in the field", so the return was very positive.

Regarding the collaboration theme, they said that the material generated by other specialists through the tool was useful for analyzing the simulated situation, but they did not elaborate in more detail. When asked what tools they apply today in the operation, with a focus on those that allow collaboration, they reported the main use of WhatsApp, as well as the use of Google Drive, Google Maps, YouTube and Facebook (for streaming video), Pix4D (for mapping), SISGRAF and ICad (internal fire brigade platforms). Regarding these tools, they stated that they are "of great use, important for spreading information about the incident", and that they support the operation. A need was also indicated, related to streaming video from the drone's camera, as it would need to be private, and today with the tools they have available it is possible to do it only in public. Another point raised is the delay and the large number of steps until the transfer of photos from the drone to the team working in the emergency, taking today a crucial time in responding to it. In addition, they pointed out that some market tools that exist today, which could support them, have high acquisition and maintenance costs.

Respondents highlighted the importance of transferring images automatically and suggested transferring short videos as well. Regarding the "Rescue Drones" tool, they stated that it concentrates several important functionalities, present in other tools separately, and presents advantages over those used for similar purposes by firefighters, at the present time. They pointed out the "importance of the proposed tool for coordination and registration, for monitoring the emergency event, and for the knowledge and management of the resources available on site". They also said that it can be a facilitator when complemented by other systems in an emergency setting.

The experiment also made it possible to capture experts' perceptions as active participants in emergency response action. For this study, we used two of the elements of perception presented by [18] they are: the perception of the current situation and understanding of this situation. At first, the study focused on gathering information extracted from the expert's perception of the real situation. That is, how this specialist is situated in the context and his actions carried out from the interpretation of the images. In a later moment, the perception of the specialist was sought from the understanding of his role and the tacit knowledge of the specialist. At this stage of the research, perceptions for future impacts were not considered but we believe the images discussed by the emergency professionals using the functions of the application Drones to the rescue can support this kind of perception.

Therefore, the answers collected by experts, support the idea of participants' perception in an emergency. Existing an emergency situation, where it is necessary to have reliable information and a low response time, a solution that will allow data capture, visualization, collaboration and information based on the experts' perception can reverse situations of high degree of complexity.

5   Conclusion

In this paper, we discussed the use of "Drone to the Rescue" application, which was originally designed to capture contributions of different experts in the images took by a drone. We introduced the original definition of perception of the situation and inserted the observations of specialists in the retrieval of information. As presented in Sect. 2, we believe that the perception of emergency responders is based on their own experiences. This information being externalized, it can be retrieved and used in future actions for decision making.

As suggestions brought through the interviews and questionnaire, are: compatibility with systems already used by firefighters, transmission of video feed in real time, access control, support for videos, best reference in photos, organization of content to support at least 3 aircraft in a better way, display of aircraft location in real time on the map.

Also, we need more research on the privacy problem in sharing images. With the study of the domain of emergency management, collaborative decision making, perception of specialists, drones and their uses, the authors was able to propose a collaborative solution to support decision making in an emergency scenario, by obtaining images via drone, and providing information on the scenario in a practical way, and collecting the experts' perception and this were the objectives achieved within the central theme of the work. According to the participants' answers, the goal was successfully achieved by this research. The solution presented the necessary functionalities for the emergency response, provide ways for the capture the specialists' perception and support images viewing, editing and collaboration in an emergency.

For future work, we believe that the evolution of the "Drone to the Rescue" can serve other applications such as: monitoring and support in refugee camps, rescue through monitoring of regions susceptible to terrorist attacks, monitoring of droughts and forest fires, etc. In addition to improving image organization: grouping images captured by source, when there is more than one drone operating, and organizing original and edited images so that they are associated. Also, for future work, we believe the specialists perception should be investigated in more details, exploring how it could support emergency decision and how perception understanding could support technological solutions development.

Acknowledgement. The work of Marcos R.S. Borges has been supported by FAPERJ under grant number E-26/202.876/2018. The work of Juliana Baptista dos Santos França has been supported by FAPERJ under grant number E-26/211.367/2019 (248406).

References

1. Keller, J.: (2015). http://www.militaryaerospace.com/articles/2014/03/uav-spending-2015.html. Accessed 24 Oct 2020
2. Oliveira, M.D.E.: Disaster Management Project Textbook - Operations Command System. Ministério da Integração Nacional, Secretaria Nacional de Defesa Civil, Federal University of Santa Catarina. University Center for Disaster Studies and Research, Florianópolis, Brazil (2010)
3. UNDRR: UN Office for Disaster Risk Reduction (UNDRR): Terminology. https://www.unisdr.org/we/inform/terminology. Accessed 26 Nov 2020
4. Vivacqua, A.S., Borges, M.R.: Taking advantage of collective knowledge in emergency response systems. J. Netw. Comput. Appl. **35**(1), 189–198 (2012)
5. Murayama, Y., Yamamoto, K.: Issues in the use of the recovery watcher for situation awareness in disaster and inclusive communications. In: Murayama, Y., Velev, D., Zlateva, P. (eds.) ITDRR 2019. IAICT, vol. 575, pp. 1–8. Springer, Cham (2020). https://doi.org/10.1007/978-3-030-48939-7_1

6. Reynolds, B., Seeger, M.: Crisis and Emergency Risk Communication 2014 Edition. Centers for Disease Control and Prevention (2014). https://emergency.cdc.gov/cerc/resources/pdf/cerc_2014edition.pdf
7. França, J.B.S., Borges, M.R.S.: Systematizing the impacts projection of complex decisions in work groups. SN Appl. Sci. **2**(7), 1–20 (2020). https://doi.org/10.1007/s42452-020-3086-4
8. Gutwin, C., Greenberg, S.: A descriptive framework of workspace awareness for real-time groupware. Comput. Support. Coop. Work **11**(3–4), 411–446 (2002). https://doi.org/10.1023/A:1021271517844. Special Issue on Awareness in CSCW. Kluwer Academic Press
9. Fontainha, T.C., Leiras, A., de Mello Bandeira, R.A., Scavarda, O.F.: Public-Private-People Relationship Stakeholder Model for disaster and humanitarian operations. Int. J. Disaster Risk Reduct. **22**, 371–386 (2017)
10. Bravo, R.Z.B.; Leiras, A.; Oliveira, F.L.C.: The Use of UAVs in Humanitarian Relief: An Application of POMDP-Based Methodology for Finding Victims. Prod. Oper. Manag. pp. 1–20 (2018). https://doi.org/10.1111/poms.12930
11. Burnham, G.M., Rand, E.C.: The Johns Hopkins and Red Cross Red Crescent Public Health Guide in Emergencies - Second edition (2008). https://reliefweb.int/sites/reliefweb.int/files/resources/Forward.pdf
12. Sandman, P.M.: Trust the public with more of the truth: what I learned in 40 years in risk communication. In: The Peter Sandman Risk Communication Website, 20 October 2009. http://www.psandman.com/articles/berreth.htm. Accessed 23 Oct 2020
13. Murtaza, G., Kanhere, S., Jha, S.: Priority-based coverage path planning for Aerial Wireless Sensor Networks. In: 2013 IEEE Eighth International Conference on Intelligent Sensors, Sensor Networks and Information Processing, pp. 219–224 (2013)
14. Turk, V.: Drones Mapped the Philippines to Improve Typhoon Aid Efforts (2014). http://motherboard.vice.com/read/drones-mapped-the-philippines-to-improve-typhoon-aid-efforts
15. Luis, E., Dolinskaya, I.S., Smilowitz, K.R.: Disaster relief routing: integrating research and practice. Soc. Econ. Plan. Sci. **46**(1), 88–97 (2012)
16. Cambridge.org/dictionary. https://dictionary.cambridge.org/dictionary/english/. Accessed 24 Oct 2020
17. Vieira, V., Tedesco, P., Salgado, A.C.: Models and processes for the development of context-sensitive systems. Update Days in Informatics (JAI 2009), cap8, pp. 381–431. UFRGS, Publishing Company SBC, Porto Alegre (2009)
18. Endsley, M.R.: Toward a theory of situation awareness in dynamic systems. Hum. Factors **37**, 32–64 (1995)
19. Correia, H.R., Rubim, I.C., Dias, A.F.S., França, J.B.S., Borges, M.R.S.: Drones to the rescue: a support solution for emergency response. A support solution for emergency response. In: 17th ISCRAM Conference, Blacksburg, VA, USA, May 2020

Fuzzy Logic Approach to Complex Assessment of Drought Vulnerability

Nina Nikolova[1], Plamena Zlateva[2(✉)], and Leonid Todorov[1]

[1] Faculty of Geology and Geography, Sofia University "St. Kliment Ohridski", Sofia, Bulgaria
[2] Institute of Robotics, Bulgarian Academy of Sciences, Sofia, Bulgaria
plamzlateva@abv.bg

Abstract. Drought is a common climate phenomenon for the territory of Bulgaria, which has a negative impact on agriculture and water resources. Taking into account the undetermined character of drought in regard to drought occurrence, severity and impact the present study proposes a fuzzy logic approach to complex drought vulnerability assessment. The assessment is based on multifactorial analysis integrating climatic (precipitation and air temperature) and non-climatic (distance from the water objects, aspects and soil types) factors for drought occurrence as well as anthropogenic factors (land use types) in order to determine drought susceptibility and vulnerability. In this study, the fuzzy logic model is designed as a three-level hierarchical system with four inputs and one output. Each level of the hierarchical system is consisted of one fuzzy logical subsystem with two inputs. The results of the simulations performed with developed fuzzy logic system using actual data show the importance of climatic factors for drought susceptibility while drought vulnerability depends mainly of anthropogenic factors. The areas with the same susceptibility to drought may have different degrees of vulnerability depending on the type of land use and the number of people affected. The fuzzy logic model is useful for a comprehensive drought assessment, especially for areas for which available data are insufficient.

Keywords: Fuzzy logic approach · Drought susceptibility · Drought vulnerability · Multifactorial analysis

1 Introduction

Drought is a consequence of reduced precipitation over a long period of time. It often occurs in conjunction with several meteorological elements such as high temperatures, strong winds and low relative humidity, which makes this phenomenon very pronounced. In addition, anthropogenic activity, deforestation, urbanization and various types of land use can exacerbate the negative effects of drought. A trend towards a significant increase in the areas in Europe affected by water scarcity has been established. Between 1976 and 2006, the number of regions and people in the EU affected by drought increased by almost 20%. One of the largest droughts was observed in 2003, when more than 100 million people and a third of the EU's territory were affected. The economic losses from

Y. Murayama et al. (Eds.): ITDRR 2020, IFIP AICT 622, pp. 298–314, 2021.
https://doi.org/10.1007/978-3-030-81469-4_24

the drought in Europe in 2003 exceeded $ 13 trillion [1]. The results from the Coupled Model Intercomparison Project Phase 5 (CMIP5) show a decrease of precipitation in Southern Europe, including Bulgaria with about 10–20% during the period 2081–2100 in comparison to 1986–2005 [2]. According to the climate models, an increase in drought and prolonged dry periods combined with high temperatures are expected [3–5]. Considering RCP8.5 emission scenario Spinoni et al. [6] point out that severe and extreme droughts will increase in Europe and over southern Europe the extend of spring and summer drought will be observed.

Drought differs from aridity, low flow, water scarcity and desertification [7]. Aridity is permanent characteristic of the climate in some areas with very low annual rainfall, while drought is a temporary phenomenon. On the other side, water scarcity is a temporary water imbalance that occurs as a result of drought or anthropogenic activities. Due to various causes and consequences, different types of droughts arc analyzed in the scientific publications [8–12].

- Meteorological (atmospheric) drought depends on the amount of rainfall. Defined as the period, generally from months to years, in which the inflow of moisture to an area drops below the normal level under given humid climatic conditions. The atmospheric conditions associated with a deficit of precipitation are different for the individual regions, therefore the meteorological drought have to be defined according to the specifics of the respective region. In addition to the absence or little rainfall meteorological droughts are often characterized by - high temperature and low air humidity. The reason is the high atmospheric pressure and the advection of warm and dry air masses.
- Agricultural drought is associated with the deficit of soil moisture (mostly in the root zone). It is a period when soil moisture is insufficient to meet the water needs of plants and to carry out normal agricultural management.
- Hydrological drought is characterized by a decrease in river flow and usually occurs with a delay compared to meteorological and agricultural drought. Since river basins are interconnected by hydrological systems, a hydrological drought may cover a larger area than that originally covered by a meteorological drought.
- Socioeconomic drought is associated with the effects of water scarcity, which affect socio-economic systems. This type of drought occurs when the demand for an economic commodity exceeds the supply as a result of a shortage of water due to the weather.
- Ecological drought is defined by Crausbay et al. [13] as "an episodic deficit in water availability that drives ecosystems beyond thresholds of vulnerability, impacts ecosystem services, and triggers feedbacks in natural and/or human systems."

Common to all types of drought is the lack of precipitation [14]. From a meteorological point of view, drought is associated with periods of varying lengths with water shortages. The main measure for drought is the insufficient amount of precipitation for a specific activity (i.e. crop growth, irrigation water supply, water level in dams), [15].

Many publication analyze various aspect of drought phenomena in Bulgaria: drought in 90-es and hydrological and economic impact [16]; drought study based on various precipitation indices [11], soil drought [15], theoretical review of methods for drought investigation [17], study drought based on SPI and precipitation anomalies [18], agricultural drought [19–21], wetlands-drought relation [22]. On the other side drought hazard, vulnerability and risk are important topics which are not well investigated in Bulgaria.

The overall objective of the present research is to enlarge the knowledge about drought assessment and to support decision making by presenting a tool for drought assessment in respect to drought susceptibility and vulnerability. In this regard, the specific aim is to propose a fuzzy logic approach to complex drought assessment in selected area regarding to the multiple monitored factors. In order to achieve the aim of study the following tasks are solved: 1) assessment of drought susceptibility based on drought triggering factors, and 2) integration of the results of drought susceptibility analysis with anthropogenic factors and develop a fuzzy logic model for complex drought assessment. The northwest region of Bulgaria (NUTS 2 - Severozapaden) is selected as a case-study area. Considering data availability and fact that the area is mainly agricultural the fuzzy logic model development is directed to the agricultural drought assessment.

2   Factors for Drought Occurrence and Manifestation

Precipitation is the main factor causing droughts, but there are also a number of other climatic factors that increase intensity of dry events (e.g. high temperature or low relative humidity, strong wind, moisture deficit, sunshine, atmospheric pressure, climate peculiarities). In addition to the climatic factors for drought occurrence, the duration of the dry periods, as well as the altitude, the topography, the land use and the extent of the affected areas also influence. The combined action of different climatic factors leads to the manifestation of different types of drought. For example, precipitation in combination with insignificant snow cover and high temperatures is a factor for the manifestation of hydrological drought, while for the agricultural drought occurrence the leading factors are air temperature and wind speed, not precipitation, especially in areas where irrigated agriculture is possible. Due to the fact that soil moisture, sunshine duration and solar radiation are the parameters that are measured in a limited number of stations or are not measured regularly and the data do not cover large areas, most often drought assessment is made based on the precipitation as a source of soil moisture. On the other side extreme high temperature can cause flash drought [23]. Because air temperature and precipitation are the most often measured elements and for which there is a good database the combination of both factors – temperature and precipitation is most often examined in the agricultural drought assessment.

The combined study of air temperature and precipitation makes it possible to assess the dry and rainy periods in terms of conditions for the development of cultivated plants. At above-average rainfall and below-average temperatures, there is the lowest stress for plants. The most stressful conditions are associated with high temperatures and low rainfall. At high temperatures and high precipitation, as well as at temperatures below average, combined with precipitation below average, moderate stress is noted.

The negative effect of drought is determined by its duration, intensity, spatial extent and the number of people affected. Despite of technological development climatic factors, soil types, hydrological peculiarities still have a significant contribution to the negative effects of drought. The risk associated with drought is determined by two factors: 1) the degree of exposure of the area to drought, the possibility of droughts of varying severity and 2) how vulnerable people, infrastructure, economic assets are at risk. Vulnerability to drought is determined by socio-economic factors such as demographic characteristics of the population, technological development, water use, land use, economic and cultural development, and country policy. These factors change over time, and this leads to different consequences of drought events, even when they have the same intensity, duration and spatial extend.

The intensity and consequences of drought depend on the time of occurrence (season, delay of the rainy season, precipitation in connection with the phases of development of major crops). Therefore, each dry year has unique characteristics and consequences. The drought is a complex phenomenon that has a negative effect on various sectors, therefore the assessment of drought risk has to be done on the basis of multi-criteria analysis, including not only meteorological and hydrological parameters but also social and economic aspects.

3 Study Area and Data

The study area is the territory of the northwestern administrative region in Bulgaria – NUTS 2 (Severozapaden) which includes five administrative districts (NUTS 3): Vidin, Montana, Vratsa, Pleven and Lovech. Most of the studied area is a part of the Danube plain located between Balkan Mountains on the south and the Danube River on the north. The relief is flat and hilly, and in the southern and southwestern parts – mountainous (see Fig. 1). The climate is temperate continental and is formed under the influence of predominant air advection from the northwest and north [24].

Agriculture is among the main economic sectors in the northwestern region and in a significant part of the territory the natural vegetation has been replaced by cultivated plants, which increases the vulnerability of the region to drought. Analyzing eight socio-economic indicators as regional GDP, unemployment rate, employment in high-tech sectors, research and development expenditure, motorways network, population density, life expectancy at birth and people at risk of poverty or social exclusion, Dokov and Stamenkov [25] have pointed out that NUTS 2 - Severozapaden is among the least developed Danube-adjacent regions. The low level of socio-economic development is crucial for the lower capacity of the region to adapt to climate change and brings to the greater vulnerability to adverse climatic events, including drought.

In order to achieve the aim of the study the following type of data were used:

- Climatic data – monthly air temperature and precipitation from selected meteorological stations located at the investigated area, and
- Geographic information: some basic data such as Balkan national borders, borders of Bulgaria's NUTS 2 regions, urban areas, hillshade layer (based on STRM elevation data), and some more specific data - rivers, water areas, soils, and Digital Terrain Model (DTM). All basic data layers were used for preparing the maps in addition to the processed specific data used for the assessment of drought susceptibility.

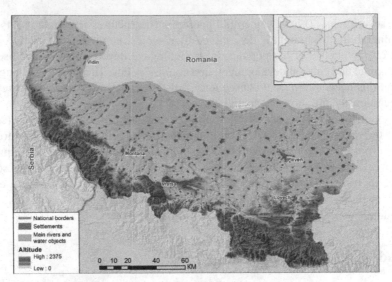

Fig. 1. Study area – NUTS 2 region Severozapad

4 Essence of the Fuzzy Logic Approach

This study proposes a fuzzy logic approach to complex drought assessment that integrates various natural and anthropogenic land factors. Due to the indeterminate nature of drought, the fuzzy logic has been described in several publications as a successful tool to study the drought occurrence, manifestation, impact, hazard, susceptibility and vulnerability [26–29].

The present approach is based on the factor analysis which is recommended for a complex assessment of drought vulnerability [30, 31]. The approach includes two main stages. The purpose of the first stage is to identify the factors influencing drought occurrence and manifestation. Based on the expert knowledge and the peculiarities of the studied area, the factors are grouped into two groups: 1) related to natural forces and 2) indicators of anthropogenic activity. The group of natural factors is divided into two groups: climatic (precipitation and air temperature) and non-climatic factors (distance from rivers, aspect and soil types). In this study, the land use and land cover data from CORINE Land cover are used as indicators of the anthropogenic activity.

The purpose of the second stage is to develop a fuzzy logic model for complex assessment of drought vulnerability based on the identified groups of factors. Here, the fuzzy logic model is designed as a three-level hierarchical system with four inputs and one output. Each level of the hierarchical system is consisted of one fuzzy logical subsystem with two inputs. The fuzzy logic system output gives a drought vulnerability assessment in certain area regarding to the multiple monitored factors.

A scheme of the three-level hierarchical fuzzy system for complex assessment of drought vulnerability is presented on Fig. 2.

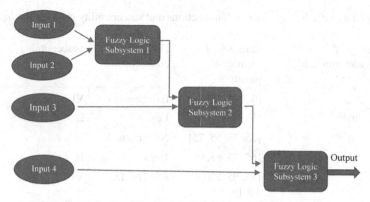

Fig. 2. Three-level hierarchical fuzzy system with four inputs

The following four variables are defined as system inputs on the basis of expert knowledge and the identified factors influencing the drought: Input 1 "Precipitation" (% of climate normal), Input 2 "Air temperature" (according to the percentile distribution), Input 3 "Non-climatic factors for drought" and Input 4 "Anthropogenic factors". In the designed model, two intermediate linguistic variables are defined: Intermediate variable 1 "Climatic factors for drought" and Intermediate variable 2 "Natural factors for drought". The fuzzy logic system output is defined as the linguistic variable "Drought vulnerability degree".

In the proposed fuzzy logic model, the all input linguistic variables, corresponding to the defined four inputs, two intermediate variables and system output are described by five membership functions, as follow: 1) "*Very low (VL)*", 2) "*Low (L)*", 3) "*Moderate (M)*", 4) "*High (H)*", and 5) "*Very high (VH)*". The all linguistic variables are assessed in the given intervals using trapezoidal membership functions as shown in corresponding tables (from Table 1, Table 2, Table 3, Table 4 and Table 5).

Table 1. Numeral values of membership functions and susceptibility levels of the *Input 1*

Precipitation, P (% of climate normal)/determined values/	Trapezoidal membership functions	Drought conditions	Susceptibility level
$95 \leq P$	[93, 97, 100, 100]	Normal	VL
$85 \leq P < 95$	[83, 87, 93, 97]	Mild dry	L
$75 \leq P < 85$	[70, 77, 83, 87]	Moderate dry	M
$50 \leq P < 75$	[45, 55, 70, 77]	Very dry	H
$P < 50$	[0, 0, 45, 55]	Extremely dry	VH

Table 2. Numeral values of membership functions and susceptibility levels of the *Input 2*

Air temperature, T (percentiles)/determined values/	Trapezoidal membership functions	Drought conditions	Susceptibility level
$T \le 10^{-th}$	[0, 0, 5, 15]	Extreme low	VL
$10^{th} \le T < 30^{th}$	[5, 15, 25, 35]	Low	L
$30^{th} \le T < 70^{th}$	[25, 35, 65, 75]	Near normal	M
$70^{th} \le T < 90^{th}$	[65, 75, 85, 95]	High	H
$90^{th} \le T$	[85, 95, 100, 100]	Extreme high	VH

Table 3. Numeral values of membership functions and susceptibility levels of the *Input 3* and *Input 4*

Input 3 Non-climatic factors for drought	Input 4 Anthropogenic factors	Susceptibility level
[0, 0, 0.5, 0.6]	[0, 0, 5.5, 7.5]	VL
[0.5, 0.6, 0.90, 1.0]	[5.5, 7.5, 11, 15]	L
[0.90, 1.0, 1.25, 1.35]	[11, 15, 21. 27]	M
[1.25, 1.35, 1.6, 1.70]	[21, 27, 33, 37]	H
[1.6, 1.70, 2, 2]	[33, 37, 42, 42]	VH

Table 4. Numeral values of membership functions and susceptibility levels of the *Intermediate variable 1* and *Intermediate variable 2*

Intermediate variable 1 Climatic factors for drought	Intermediate variable 2 Natural factors for drought	Susceptibility level
[0, 0, 0.8, 1.1]	[0, 0, 1.3, 1.7,]	VL
[0.8, 1.1, 1.45, 1.75]	[1.3, 1.7, 2.3, 2.7]	L
[1.45, 1.75, 2.1, 2.4]	[2.3, 2.7, 3.3, 3.7]	M
[2.1, 2.4, 2.75, 3.05]	[3.3, 3.7, 4.3, 4.7]	H
[2.75, 3.05, 3.5, 3.5]	[4.3, 4.7, 5, 5]	VH

Table 5. Numeral values of membership functions/susceptibility levels of the *System Output*

Membership functions of *System Output*	*Drought vulnerability degree*
[0, 0, 1.5, 2.5]	*Very low*, VL
[1.5, 2.5, 3.5, 4.5]	*Low*, L
[3.5, 4.5, 5.5, 6.5]	*Moderate*, M
[5.5, 6.5, 7.5, 8.5]	*High*, H
[7.5, 8.5, 10, 10]	*Very high*, VH

The inputs of the first fuzzy logic subsystem are Input 1 "*Precipitation*" and Input 2 "*Air temperature*", and the output variable is the Intermediate variable 1 "*Climatic factors for drought*". The first intermediate variable gives information for drought susceptibility of the territory according to the precipitation and air temperature. The threshold for classifying precipitation data into five levels was determined based on the precipitation anomaly (the deviation of the precipitation totals as a percentage of the multi-year average value – climatic normal). Whereas air temperature data was grouped according to the percentile distribution. Drought susceptibility levels according to the climatic factors is given in corresponding tables (Tables 1, 2, 4).

The inputs of the second fuzzy logic subsystem are Intermediate variable 1 "*Climatic factors for drought*" and Input 3 "*Non-climatic factors for drought*", and the output variable is the Intermediate variable 2 "*Natural factors for drought*" (Tables 3 and 4).

Here, as "*Non-climatic factors for drought*" are considered the distance to the rivers, aspect and soil type. The distance from the rivers (water objects) determines the possibilities and costs for water supply and provision of water for the irrigation. The territory is classified into five susceptibility levels according to the distance from the rivers and taking into account the peculiarities of the investigated area [32]. For this component of complex assessment of drought we used three data layers from the geodatabase developed within the project "Integrated water management in the Republic of Bulgaria" financed by the Japanese government through the Japanese International Cooperation Agency (more known in Bulgaria as JICA geodatabase) – rivers, water objects and Danube riverbed (polygon data layer). All three layers were used to calculate the distance to main water objects (see Fig. 3). After having the distance calculated, the output data layer was reclassified based on the peculiarity of the territory using the following classes according to drought susceptibility: 0–500 m - 1 (very low); 500–1000 m - 2 (low); 1000–2500 m - 3 (moderate); 2500–5000 m - 4 (high); >5000 m - 5 (very high).

The aspect (NW-N-NE, NE-E-SE, SW-W-NW, flat territory, SE-S-SW) affects sunshine duration and quantity of solar radiation. Drought can be observed more often on sunny slopes (with Southern exposure) and most rarely on shady slopes (Northern exposure). For the analysis of the aspect as a component of the drought assessment, a raster data for the elevation were geoprocessed. The input DTM has resolution of 30 m. Based on this layer, we generated the aspect layer. After that, the new layer was reclassified according to drought susceptibility using the following classes: NW, N, NE – 1 (very low); NE, E, SE – 2 (low); SW, W, NW – 3 (moderate); flat territory – 4 (high); SE, S, SW – 5 (very high). (see Fig. 4).

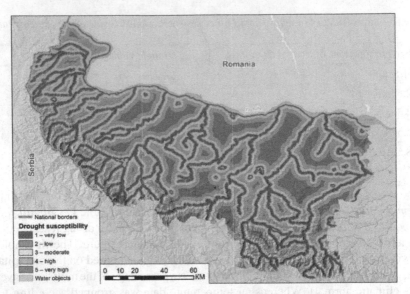

Fig. 3. Drought susceptibility according to the distance from the rivers /water objects

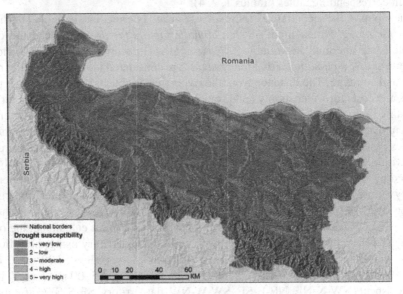

Fig. 4. Drought susceptibility according to the aspect

The soil types are grouped according to mechanical composition - the most susceptible to drought are sandy soils, and the least susceptible - clay, alluvial and boggy soils, (see Fig. 5). For this part of our research, we used another feature class from the geodatabase of JICA – the layer Soils. At the beginning of the data processing the layer had to be converted from vector to raster layer. After that, the different types of soils in this layer were regrouped according to their mechanical composition and reclassified from 1 (least susceptible – clay, alluvial and boggy soils) to 5 (very highly susceptible – sandy soils).

The territorial distribution of each non-climatic indicator was presented on a separate map (from Fig. 3, Fig. 4 and Fig. 5). The composite map of drought susceptibility based on considered non-climatic factors was produced by the combination of the three components in ArcGIS using weighted overlay. The following weights ware used: distance from water objects – 45%; aspect – 35% and soil types – 20%. The output raster data layer has 5 classes of drought susceptibility from 1 (Very low) to 5 (Very high).

In particular, the results from the composite map is used as Input 3 *"Non-climatic factors for drought"* of the second fuzzy logic subsystem.

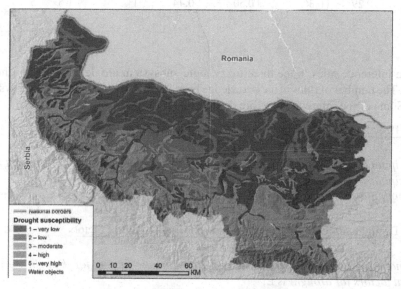

Fig. 5. Drought susceptibility according to the soil types

The inputs of the third fuzzy logic subsystem are Intermediate variable 2 *"Natural factors for drought"* and Input 4 *"Anthropogenic factors"*.

The analysis of the anthropogenic factor gives us a tool to assess vulnerability of the study area to drought. As an indicator for anthropogenic activity different types of land use and land cover was evaluated as well as urban areas which give the information about the people affected by drought. Based on the expert knowledge we grouped selected land use types in five drought vulnerability classes. Each of the selected land use types is assigned a weight according to the Analytic Hierarchy Process method followed by Saaty [33], Nikolova and Zlateva [34], 2018 (Table 6). Most vulnerable are urban areas where the population density is highest.

Table 6. Anthropogenic factors indicators and weights

	Urban areas	Rain-fed agriculture	Irrigated fields	Natural areas	Pastures	Total	Weight %
Urban areas	1.00	2.00	2.50	3.00	3.50	12.0	40
Rain-fed	0.50	1.00	2.25	2.50	2.75	9.0	30
Irrigated fields	0.40	0.44	1.00	1.50	2.00	5.3	18
Natural areas	0.33	0.40	0.67	1.00	2.25	2.4	8
Pastures	0.29	0.36	0.50	0.44	1	1.6	5
Total						30.3	100

The inference rules in the three fuzzy logic subsystem are defined as "If - then" - clause. The number of rules in the knowledge base for each of the fuzzy logic subsystems is 25. Some of the inference rules are defined as follow:

FLS1: Drought susceptibility assessment according to climatic factors

If *Precipitation* is VL and *Air temperature* is H then *Climatic factors for drought* is M;
If *Precipitation* is M and *Air temperature* is VH then *Climatic factors for drought* is H;
If *Precipitation* is H and *Air temperature* is M then *Climatic factors for drought* is H.

FLS2: Drought susceptibility assessment according to natural factors

If *Climatic factors for drought* is VL and *Non-climatic factors for drought* is H then *Natural factors for drought* is L;
If *Climatic factors for drought* is L and *Non-climatic factors for drought* is H then *Natural factors for drought* is M;
If *Climatic factors for drought s* is VH and *Non-climatic factors for drought* is VL then *Natural factors for drought* is H.

FLS3: Drought vulnerability assessment according natural and anthropogenic factors (Complex assessment of drought vulnerability)

If *Natural factors for drought* is H and *Anthropogenic factors* is H then *Drought vulnerability degree* is VH;
If *Natural factors for drought* is L and *Anthropogenic factors* is H then *Drought vulnerability degree* is H;
If *Natural factors for drought* is VH and *Anthropogenic factors* is L then *Drought vulnerability degree* is M.

The fuzzy logic hierarchical system is designed in MATLAB computer environment using Fuzzy Logic Toolbox [35]. The three fuzzy logic are based on Mamdani's inference machines, max/min operations and center of gravity defuzzification [36].

The inference surfaces in 3D for the three fuzzy logic subsystems are shown on Figures 6, 7 and 8, respectively.

5 Results and Discussion

According to the results from the assessment of non-climatic factors for drought occurrence, presented by the composite map (see Fig. 9) most part of the investigated area has low or moderate degree of drought susceptibility. Low drought susceptibility is characteristic for 30.8% of the territory of Northwestern administrative region of Bulgaria (NUTS 2 – Severozapaden) and 42.7% of the territory have moderate drought susceptibility.

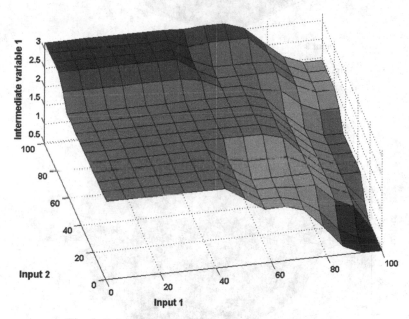

Fig. 6. Inference surfaces of the Fuzzy logic subsystem 1.

On the other side climatic factors are more important natural factor for drought occurrence than non-climatic and due to various values of air temperature and precipitation totals drought susceptibility of the given area can be different. Many simulations with developed fuzzy logic system have been performed using particular values of input variables to calculate the "Drought vulnerability degree" in investigated area. Some simulation results for the regions of two towns located in the investigated area (Vidin – northwestern part and Pleven – eastern part) are shown in Table 7. Vidin is located in the region with moderate drought susceptibility according to the non-climatic factors while for the region of Pleven low to moderate drought susceptibility is characteristic.

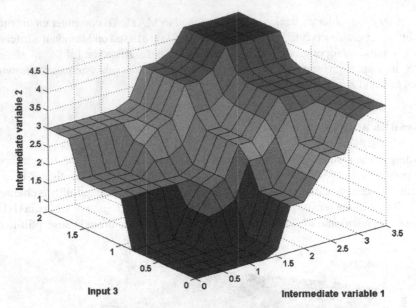

Fig. 7. Inference surfaces of the Fuzzy logic subsystem 2

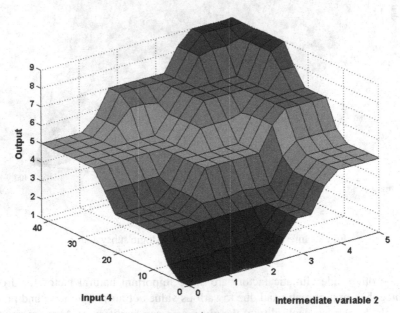

Fig. 8. Inference surfaces of the Fuzzy logic subsystem 3

Depending on the type of land use and how many people are affected, areas with the same susceptibility to drought may have different degrees of vulnerability.

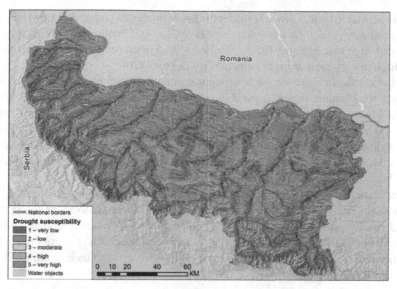

Fig. 9. Composite map – drought susceptibility according to the non-climatic factors for drought in Northwestern administrative district of Bulgaria (NUTS 2 – Severozapaden)

The results of the present analysis show the importance of the climatic and anthropogenic factor for drought susceptibility and vulnerability.

Table 7. Complex drought vulnerability assessment of the investigated area with particular values of the input variables (selected simulation results)

Input 1	Input 2	Intermediate variable 1	Input 3	Intermediate variable 2	Input 4	Output
Vidin						
121.2 VL	74 M - H	1.87 M	1.08 M	3 M	30−40 H - VH	7 H
51.8−52 H - VH	97 VH	3.16 VH	1.08 (M)	4 H	35.5−36.5 H - VH	8.14−8.69 H - VH
Pleven						
108.7 VL	13.1 VL - L	0.47 VL	0.97 L - M	1.54 VL - L	30−33 H 34−42 H - VH	5 M 5.61−6.18 M - H
69 H	13.3 VL - L	1.92 M	0.72−1.08 L - M	3 M	30−40 H - VH	7 H

When climatic factor (*Input 1 - Air temperature* and *Input2 - Precipitation*) determines very high susceptibility to drought (*Intermediate variable 1* = 3.16) and according to the non-climatic factors drought susceptibility is moderate (*Input 3* = 1.08) then overall susceptibility is high (*Intermediate variable 2* = 4). If anthropogenic factor shows high to very high susceptibility (35.5 ≤ *Input 4* ≤ 36.5) then complex drought assessment shows high to very high drought vulnerability degree (8.14 ≤ *Output* ≤ 8.69).

If climatic factor show very low drought susceptibility (*Intermediate variable 1* = 0.47) and non-climatic factor (*Input 3* = 0.97) indicate low to moderate susceptibility then drought susceptibility of the territory is very low to low (*Intermediate variable 2* = 1.54). When anthropogenic factor shows high vulnerability (*Input 4* = 30–33) then complex drought vulnerability is moderate (*Output 4* = 5). If the *Input 4* has a value between 34 and 42 it is shows high to very high vulnerability and the complex drought vulnerability is moderate to high (5.61 ≤ *Output 4* ≤ 6.18).

In the case that climatic factors determine moderate susceptibility to drought (*Intermediate variable 1* = 1.92) and non-climatic factors show low to moderate susceptibility (*Input 3* has values between 0.72 and 1.08) natural factors indicate moderate drought susceptibility (*Intermediate variable 2* = 3). When according to the anthropogenic factor (30 ≤ *Input 4* ≤ 40) drought vulnerability is high to very high then complex drought vulnerability is high (*Output* = 7).

6 Conclusion

The present study shows the importance of complex assessment of various factors (natural and anthropogenic) for drought occurrence and vulnerability. In general, the investigated area is low to moderate susceptible to drought. Nevertheless, the drought susceptibility and vulnerability also depend on peculiarities of air temperature and precipitation regimes as well as on anthropogenic factors as type of land use and concentration of the population. In particular, the most vulnerable to drought are the settlements and urban areas which are located far from the water bodies and especially when the climate parameters show high drought susceptibility.

A fuzzy logic model to complex drought assessment is developed by the comprehensive analysis of natural and anthropogenic factors. The results from the analysis prove the usefulness of the proposed fuzzy logic approach as a good tool for drought vulnerability assessment, especially for areas for which available data are insufficient.

The major beneficiaries of the proposed work will be scientific researchers working on the problems related to natural, economic and social dimensions of drought. Future work will focus on the expanding territorial scope of the presented research work in order to validate the model for different territories. The information about the adaptive capacity of the study areas will be included in further analyses, which will bring to better understanding of drought impact on various human activities.

Acknowledgements. This work has been carried out in the framework of the National Science Program. "Environmental Protection and Reduction of Risks of Adverse Events and Natural Disasters", approved by the Resolution of the Council of Ministers № 577/17.08.2018 and supported by the Ministry of Education and Science (MES) of Bulgaria (Agreement № Д01-363/17.12.2020).

References

1. DG JRC: Climate Change and the European Water Dimension (A report to the European Water Directors) (2005)
2. IPCC: Climate Change 2014: Synthesis Report. Contribution of Working Groups I, II and III to the Fifth Assessment Report of the Intergovernmental Panel on Climate Change. Pachauri, R.K., Meyer, L.A. (eds.). IPCC, Geneva, Switzerland (2014). 151 p.
3. Dai, A.: Increasing drought under global warming in observations and models. Nat. Clim. Change **3**, 52–58 (2013)
4. Trnka, M., et al.: Agroclimatic conditions in Europe under climate change. Glob. Change Biol. **2011**(17), 2298–2318 (2011)
5. Trnka, M., Hlavinka, P., Semenov, M.A.: Adaptation options for wheat in Europe will be limited by increased adverse weather events under climate change. J. R. Soc. Interface **12**, 20150721 (2015)
6. Spinoni, J., Vogt, J.V., Naumann, G., Barbosa, P., Dosio, A.: Will drought events become more frequent and severe in Europe? Int. J. Climatol. **38**, 1718–1736 (2018). https://doi.org/10.1002/joc.5291
7. Van Loon, A.F.: Hydrological drought explained . WIREs Water **2**, 359–392 (2015). https://doi.org/10.1002/wat2.1085
8. Wilhite, D.A., Glantz, M.H.: Understanding the drought phenomenon: the role of definitions. Water Int. **10**(3), 111–120 (1985)
9. Maracchi, G.: Agricultural drought – a practical approach to definition, assessment and mitigation strategies. In: Vogt, J.V., Somma, F. (eds.) Drought and drought mitigation in Europe. Advances in natural and technological hazards research, vol. 14, pp. 63–78. Springer, Dordrecht (2000). https://doi.org/10.1007/978-94-015-9472-1_5
10. Hisdal, H., Tallaksen, L.M.: Estimation of regional meteorological and hydrological drought characteristics: a case study for Denmark. J. Hydrol. **281**, 230–247 (2003). https://doi.org/10.1016/S0022-1694(03)00233-6
11. Koleva, E., Alexandrov, V.: Drought in the Bulgarian low regions during the 20th century. Theoret. Appl. Climatol. **92**, 113–120 (2008)
12. Mishra, A.K., Singh, V.P.: A review of drought concepts. J. Hydrol. **391**(1), 202–216 (2010)
13. Crausbay, S.D., et al.: Defining ecological drought for the twenty-first century. Bull. Am. Meteorol. Soc. **98**(12), 2544–2550 (2017)
14. WMO: World Meteorological Organization. Drought and Desertification. Report on the Eleventh Session of the Commission for Climatology, Havana, WMO/TD-No 605 (1993)
15. Alexandrov, V.: Soil drought monitoring (review). In the project: building capacity for sustainable land management in Bulgaria. UNDPGEF, 2005–2008, C. 42 (2006)
16. Knight, G., Raev, I., Staneva, M.: Drought in Bulgaria: A Contemporary Analog for Climate Change. Ashgate, Aldershot (2004)
17. Alexandrov, V. (ed.): Methods for monitoring and estimation of drought vulnerability in Bulgaria, National Institute of Meteorology and Hydrology, Bulgarian Academy of Science, Sofia (in Bulgarian) (2011)
18. Nikolova, N., Alieva, G., Voislavova, I.: Drought periods in non-mountainous part of south bulgaria on the background of climate change. Geographica Pannonica **16**(1), 18–25 (2012)
19. Popova, Z., et al.: Vulnerability of Bulgarian agriculture to drought and climate variability with focus on rainfed maize systems. Nat. Hazards **74**(2), 865–886 (2014). https://doi.org/10.1007/s11069-014-1215-3
20. Popova, Z., et al.: Droughts and climate change in Bulgaria: assessing maize crop risk and irrigation requirements in relation to soil and climate region. Bul. J. Agric. Sci. **21**(1), 35–53 (2015)

21. Petkova, B., Kuzmova, K., Berova, M.: The main abiotic stress factors limiting crop cultivation and production in Bulgaria. Climate changes, drought, water deficit and heat stress. Agric. Sci./Agrarni Nauki **11**(26) (2019)
22. Radeva, K.: Water-dependent ecosystems and their role for reducing drought risk. In: Scientific conferences. Geography and regional development, Sozopol, September 2020, pp. 198–202 (2020). ISBN 978-619-91670
23. Mo, K.C., Lettenmaier, D.P.: Heat wave flash droughts in decline. Geophys. Res. Lett. **42**, 2823–2829 (2015). https://doi.org/10.1002/2015GL064
24. Rachev, G., Nikolova, N.: The climate of Bulgaria. Sofia University Year Book. Faculty of Geology and Geography, vol. 101, Book 2-Geography (2008). (in Bulgarian)
25. Dokov, S., Stamenkov, I.: Measuring the complex socio-economic development of the Danube-adjacent NUTS2 Regions. Forum geografic. Studii și cercetări de geografie și protecția mediului **XVII**(1), 152–160 (2017). https://doi.org/10.5775/fg.2017.103.d
26. Huang, S., Chang, J., Leng, G., Huang, Q.: Integrated index for drought assessment based on variable fuzzy set theory: a case study in the Yellow River basin China. J. Hydrol. **527**, 608–618 (2015)
27. Papakonstantinou, X., Iliadis, L.S., Pimenidis, E., Maris, F.: Fuzzy modeling of the climate change effect to drought and to wild fires in Cyprus. In: Iliadis, L., Jayne, C. (eds.) AIAI/EANN -2011. IAICT, vol. 363, pp. 516–528. Springer, Heidelberg (2011). https://doi.org/10.1007/978-3-642-23957-1_57
28. Wu, D., Yan, D.H., Yang, G.Y., Wang, X.G., Xiao, W.H., Zhang, H.T.: Assessment on agricultural drought vulnerability in the Yellow River basin based on a fuzzy clustering iterative model. Nat. Hazards **67**, 919–936 (2013). https://doi.org/10.1007/s11069-013-0617-y
29. Safavi, H.R., Esfahani, M.K., Zamani, A.R.: Integrated index for assessment of vulnerability to drought, case study: Zayandehrood river basin Iran. Water Resour. Manag. **28**, 1671–1688 (2014)
30. González-Tánago, I., Urquijo, J., Blauhut, V., Villarroya, F., De Stefano, L.: Learning from experience: a systematic review of assessments of vulnerability to drought. Nat. Hazards **80**(2), 951–973 (2015). https://doi.org/10.1007/s11069-015-2006-1
31. IPCC: Managing the Risks of Extreme Events and Disasters to Advance Climate Change Adaptation. Field, C.B., Barros, V., Stocker, T.F., Dahe, Q. (eds.). Cambridge University Press, Cambridge (2012)
32. Lui, X., Zhang, J., Cai, W., Tong, Z.: Assessing maize drought hazard for agricultural areas based on the fuzzy gamma model. J. Integr. Agric. **12**(3), 532–540 (2013)
33. Saaty, R.: The analytic hierarchy process – what it is and how it is used. Math. Model. **9**(3–5), 161–176 (1987)
34. Nikolova, V., Zlateva, P.: Geoinformation approach for complex analysis of multiple natural hazard. Int. Arch. Photogramm. Remote Sens. Spat. Inf. Sci. ISPRS Arch. **42**(3W4), 375–381 (2018)
35. Mathworks: Matlab. https://www.mathworks.com/products/matlab.html
36. Bede, B.: Mathematics of Fuzzy Sets and Fuzzy Logic . Part of the Studies in Fuzziness and Soft Computing, vol. 295. Springer, Heidelberg (2013). https://doi.org/10.1007/978-3-642-35221-8

Author Index

316   Author Index

Printed in the United States
by Baker & Taylor Publisher Services